T0214490

Lecture Notes in Computer Science 11262

Commenced Publication in 1973
Founding and Former Series Editors:
Gerhard Goos, Juris Hartmanis, and Jan van Leeuwen

More information about this series at http://www.springer.com/series/7408

Cristian Bogdan · Kati Kuusinen
Marta Kristín Lárusdóttir · Philippe Palanque
Marco Winckler (Eds.)

Human-Centered Software Engineering

7th IFIP WG 13.2 International Working Conference, HCSE 2018
Sophia Antipolis, France, September 3–5, 2018
Revised Selected Papers

Springer

Editors
Cristian Bogdan ⓘ
KTH – Royal Institute of Technology
Stockholm, Sweden

Kati Kuusinen ⓘ
University of Southern Denmark
Odense, Denmark

Marta Kristín Lárusdóttir
Reykjavík University
Reykjavik, Iceland

Philippe Palanque
Paul Sabatier University
Toulouse, France

Marco Winckler ⓘ
Nice Sophia Antipolis University
Sophia Antipolis, France

ISSN 0302-9743   ISSN 1611-3349   (electronic)
Lecture Notes in Computer Science
ISBN 978-3-030-05908-8   ISBN 978-3-030-05909-5   (eBook)
https://doi.org/10.1007/978-3-030-05909-5

Library of Congress Control Number: 2018964130

LNCS Sublibrary: SL2 – Programming and Software Engineering

This Springer imprint is published by the registered company Springer Nature Switzerland AG
The registered company address is: Gewerbestrasse 11, 6330 Cham, Switzerland

Foreword

The 7th International Working Conference on Human-Centered Software Engineering, HCSE 2018, was held during September 3–5, 2018, on the SophiaTech Campus of the University of Nice Sophia Antipolis, which is located in the French Riviera. HCSE is a bi-annual, single-track working conference organized by the IFIP Working Group 13.2 on Methodology for User-Centred System Design, which aims at bringing together researchers and practitioners interested in strengthening the scientific foundations of user interface design, examining the relationship between software engineering and human–computer interaction and on how to strengthen human-centered design as an essential part of software engineering processes. Previous events were held in Salamanca, Spain (2007); Pisa, Italy (2008); Reykjavik, Iceland (2010); Toulouse, France (2012); and Paderborn, Germany (2014); and Stockholm, Sweden (2016).

This edition of HCSE was focused on the interdependencies (overlapping and possibly conflicting dependencies that might occur) between user interface properties (such as usability, ux, privacy, trust, security, reliability, among others). We were also concerned by how stakeholders and developers value diverse user interface properties and how they manage conflicts between them (when a property might degrade the value of another). Our aim was to cover a large set of user interface properties and try to reveal their inner dependencies. The ultimate goal was to contribute to the development of theories, methods, tools, and approaches for dealing with multiple properties that should be taken into account when developing interactive system.

The HCSE 2018 program received contributions from Austria, Belgium, Canada, Denmark, Finland, France, Germany, Iceland, Italy, Malaysia, Netherlands, Nigeria, Norway, Portugal, Russia, Spain, Sweden, Tunisia, and the UK. All contributions were peer-reviewed and received at least three reviews in each of the two rounds of reviews including meta-reviewing and shepherding. The Program Committee made use of the possibility to recommend accepting submissions in other categories than they were originally submitted for in some cases. The final decision on acceptance was based on an additional meta-review after the authors had improved their contributions according to the review results. In addition, authors of accepted contributions were invited to improve their work according to the comments and suggestions received during the conference before being included in the present proceedings. In total, HCSE accepted 11 full research papers (acceptance rate of 38%), seven late-breaking results (acceptance rate of 24%), and posters and demos. Our sincere gratitude goes to the members of our Program Committee, who devoted countless hours to providing valuable feedback to authors and ensuring the high quality of the HCSE 2018 technical program.

The program was organized in five technical sessions, a demonstration session, and the inspiring keynote "Functionality, Security, Usability – Pick 2? A Passionate Argument Against False Tradeoffs" delivered by Prof. Angela Sasse, from Ruhr University Bochum, Germany. We thank Prof. Dr. Angela Sasse for the inspiring talk. Similarly to the previous editions of HCSE, we ran an interactive session where the participants worked together in small groups on the identification of the dependencies between properties and proposing solutions to overcome possible conflicts. The results were reported in a plenary session where participants were able to comment and to contribute to the ideas. We thank Prof. Regina Berhnaupt, from Eindhoven University of Technology, The Netherlands, for organizing and chairing the interactive session. The conference program is available at http://www.hcse-conference.org/programme/.

HCSE 2018 was sponsored by the Université Nice Sophia Antipolis, Les Bibliothèques Nationales, Inria, CNRS, tobbi pro, laboratory I3S, Springer, and the IFIP TC13 whose generous support was essential for making HCSE 2018 special and successful! We also would like to thank our devoted members of the Program Committee who were responsible for the quality of the papers selected for presentation at the conference. Finally, our thanks go to all the authors who did the research work and especially to the presenters who sparked inspiring discussions with all the participants at HCSE 2018 in Sophia Antipolis.

For further information about past and future events organized by the IFIP WG 13.2, their members and activities, please visit the website http://ifip-tc13.org/working-groups/working-group-13-2/.

November 2018

Marco Winckler
Kati Kuusinen

IFIP TC13 - http://ifip-tc13.org/

Established in 1989, the International Federation for Information Processing Technical Committee on Human–Computer Interaction (IFIP TC 13) is an international committee of 37 member national societies and 10 Working Groups (WGs), representing specialists of the various disciplines contributing to the field of human–computer interaction (HCI). This includes (among others) human factors, ergonomics, cognitive science, computer science, and design.

IFIP TC 13 aims to develop the science, technology, and societal aspects of HCI by: encouraging empirical research; promoting the use of knowledge and methods from the human sciences in the design and evaluation of computer systems; promoting better understanding of the relation between formal design methods and system usability and acceptability; developing guidelines, models, and methods by which designers may provide better human-oriented computer systems; and, cooperating with other groups, inside and outside IFIP, to promote user-orientation and humanization in system design. Thus, TC 13 seeks to improve interactions between people and computers, to encourage the growth of HCI research and its practice in industry and to disseminate these benefits worldwide.

The main aim is to place the users at the center of the development process. Areas of study include: the problems people face when interacting with computers; the impact of technology deployment on people in individual and organizational contexts; the determinants of utility, usability, acceptability, and user experience; the appropriate allocation of tasks between computers and users especially in the case of automation; modeling the user, their tasks, and the interactive system to aid better system design; and harmonizing the computer to user characteristics and needs.

While the scope is thus set wide, with a tendency toward general principles rather than particular systems, it is recognized that progress will only be achieved through both general studies to advance theoretical understanding and specific studies on practical issues (e.g., interface design standards, software system resilience, documentation, training material, appropriateness of alternative interaction technologies, guidelines, the problems of integrating multimedia systems to match system needs and organizational practices, etc.).

IFIP TC 13 stimulates working events and activities through its WGs. WGs consist of HCI experts from many countries, who seek to expand knowledge and find solutions to HCI issues and concerns within their domains. The list of WGs and their area of interest is given below.

WG13.1 (Education in HCI and HCI Curricula) aims to improve HCI education at all levels of higher education, coordinate and unite efforts to develop HCI curricula, and promote HCI teaching.

WG13.2 (Methodology for User-Centered System Design) aims to foster research, dissemination of information, and good practice in the methodical application of HCI to software engineering.

WG13.3 (HCI and Disability) aims to make HCI designers aware of the needs of people with disabilities and encourage development of information systems and tools permitting adaptation of interfaces to specific users.

WG13.4 (also WG2.7) (User Interface Engineering) investigates the nature, concepts, and construction of user interfaces for software systems, using a framework for reasoning about interactive systems and an engineering model for developing user interfaces.

WG 13.5 (Resilience, Reliability, Safety, and Human Error in System Development) seeks a framework for studying human factors relating to systems failure, develops leading-edge techniques in hazard analysis and safety engineering of computer-based systems, and guides international accreditation activities for safety-critical systems.

WG13.6 (Human–Work Interaction Design) aims at establishing relationships between extensive empirical work-domain studies and HCI design. It promotes the use of knowledge, concepts, methods, and techniques that enable user studies to procure a better apprehension of the complex interplay between individual, social, and organizational contexts and thereby a better understanding of how and why people work in the ways that they do.

WG13.7 (Human–Computer Interaction and Visualization) aims to establish a study and research program that will combine both scientific work and practical applications in the fields of human–computer interaction and visualization. It will integrate several additional aspects of further research areas, such as scientific visualization, data mining, information design, computer graphics, cognition sciences, perception theory, or psychology, into this approach.

WG13.8 (Interaction Design and International Development) is currently working to reformulate its aims and scope.

WG13.9 (Interaction Design and Children) aims to support practitioners, regulators, and researchers to develop the study of interaction design and children across international contexts.

WG13.10 (Human-Centred Technology for Sustainability) aims to promote research, design, development, evaluation, and deployment of human-centered technology to encourage sustainable use of resources in various domains.

New WGs are formed as areas of significance in HCI arise. Further information is available at the IFIP TC13 website: http://ifip-tc13.org/.

IFIP WG 13.2 Members

Officers

Chair

Marco Winckler — Université Nice Sophia (Polytech), Sophia Antipolis, France

Co-chairs

Cristian Bogdan — KTH Royal Institute of Technology, Stockholm, Sweden
Marta Kristin — Reykjavik University, Iceland
    Larusdottir

Secretary

Kati Kuusinen — University of Southern Denmark, Denmark   .

Members

Carmelo Ardito — University of Bari, Italy
Balbir Barn — Middlesex University, London, UK
David Benyon — Edinburgh, UK
Regina Bernhaupt — Technical University Eindhoven, The Netherlands
Birgit Bomsdorf — Fulda University, Germany
Jan Borchers — RWTH Aachen University, Germany
Anders Bruun — Aalborg University, Denmark
John Carroll — Virginia Tech, USA
Bertrand David — Ecole Centrale de Lyon, France
Anke Dittmar — University of Rostock, Germany
Xavier Ferre — University of Madrid, Spain
Holger Fischer — Paderborn University, Germany
Peter Forbrig — University of Rostock, Germany
Tom Gross — University of Bamberg, Germany
Jan Gulliksen — KTH Royal Institute of Technology, Sweden
Anirhuda Joshi — ITT Bombai, India
Rosa Lanzilotti — University of Bari, Italy
Célia Martinie — Paul Sabatier University, France
Philippe Palanque — Paul Sabatier University, France
Fabio Paternò — IST-Pisa, Italy
Michael Pirker — ruwido, Austria

Stefan Sauer	Paderborn University, Germany
Ahmed Seffah	Lappeenranta University of Technology, Finland
Jan Harvard Skjetne	SINTEF, Norway
Alistair Sutcliffe	University of Manchester, UK
Ricardo Tesoriero	University Castilla-La Mancha, Spain
Jan Van Den Bergh	Hasselt University, Belgium
Janet Wesson	Port Elizabeth University, South Africa

Observers

Naqvi Syed Bilal	Lappeenranta University of Technology, Finland
Selem Charfi	HD Technology, France
Shamal Faily	Bournemouth University, UK
Nassim Mahmud	University of Liberal Arts Bangladesh, Bangladesh
Antonio Piccinno	University of Bari, Italy
José Luís Silva	Instituto Universitário de Lisboa, Portugal
Jonathan Tolle	Thales Alenia Space, France
Enes Yigitbas	University of Paderborn, Germany

Organizing Committee

General Conference Chairs

Marco Winckler   Université Nice Sophia Antipolis, France
Kati Kuusinen   University of Southern Denmark, Denmark

Technical Program Committee

Philippe Palanque   Université Paul Sabatier, Toulouse, France
Cristian Bogdan   KTH Royal Institute of Technology, Stockholm, Sweden
Marta Kristin   Reykjavik University, Iceland
     Larusdottir

Program Committee

Balbir Barn   Middlesex University, UK
Anders Bruun   Aalborg University, Denmark
Selem Charfi   LAMIH, France
Bertrand David   Ecole Central de Lyon, France
Anke Dittmar   University of Rostock, Germany
Shamal Faily   Bournemouth University, UK
Xavier Ferre   Universidad Politécnica de Madrid, Spain
Holger Fischer   Paderborn University, Germany
Hermann Kaindl   Vienna University of Technology, Austria
Rosa Lanzilotti   University of Bari, Italy
Célia Martinie   Paul Sabatier University, France
Fabio Paterno   CNR-ISTI, Italy
Alistair Sutcliffe   The University of Manchester, UK
Ricardo Tesoriero   University of Castilla-La Mancha, Spain
Jan Van Den Bergh   Hasselt University, Belgium
Enes Yigitbas   Paderborn University, Germany

Local Organizing Chairs

Alain Giboin   Inria Sophia Antipolis Méditerranée, France
Anne-Marie   Université Nice Sophia Antipolis, France
     Pina-Dery
Philippe Renevier   Université Nice Sophia Antipolis, France
     Gonin

Sponsors and Partners

Sponsors

Partners

International Federation for Information Processing

Laboratoire d'Informatique, Signaux et Systèmes de Sophia Antipolis

Contents

Tools and Tool-Support

Usability Evaluation and UI Testing

Posters and Demos

HCI Education and Training

From Startup to Scaleup: An Interview Study of the Development of User Experience Work in a Data-Intensive Company

Kati Kuusinen[1]([⊠])(iD), Martin Kjølbye Sørensen[2],
Nicklas Mandrup Frederiksen[2], Niclas Kildahl Laugesen[2],
and Søren Holm Juul[2]

[1] MMMI Institute, University of Southern Denmark, 5320 Odense M, Denmark
kaku@mmmi.sdu.dk
[2] University of Southern Denmark, 5320 Odense M, Denmark
{maso13,nifre12,nilau12,sojuu12}@student.sdu.dk

Abstract. Small startups often do not have the resources or the skills for upfront qualitative user studies and user experience design. Instead, they operate in market-driven environment where requirements are often invented and validated through frequent releases. The research on how startups do this in practice is scarce. Even less is known about what kind of engineering and user experience practices would help startups to survive and grow into successful businesses. This paper describes how user experience work emerged and grew in a data-intensive startup company operating in the financial sector in Denmark. The paper is based on the interviews of four persons with different roles in the startup. The emerging issues in user experience were found to be in the lack of skills in user experience and in balancing between the use of quantitative and qualitative user data. To conclude, it seems evident that startups would benefit from user experience practices but more research is needed to develop practices that would suit for this particular context.

Keywords: Agile development · User experience · Startup · Scaleup

1 Introduction

All software development companies balance between process control and flexibility in their ways of working. Small startups tend to remain in the more flexible end of the scale with less defined development processes [21]. Even agile management approaches such as Scrum [20] can be too tedious and limiting for startups to follow with their small resources. However, when they start to scale up, grow, they often face the need for more structured approach for their development work.

© IFIP International Federation for Information Processing 2019
Published by Springer Nature Switzerland AG 2019
C. Bogdan et al. (Eds.): HCSE 2018, LNCS 11262, pp. 3–14, 2019.
https://doi.org/10.1007/978-3-030-05909-5_1

Regarding user experience (UX) [15], startups often start with minimal and restricted product versions and with limited advance information from the potential user segment [9,10]. However, small companies are more sensitive to customer influence than larger ones [21] and they can even fail in validating their business model because of poor UX [9]. Although there have been attempts to guide startups in organizing their UX effort with their often so scarce UX resources and skills [10], the scientific understanding of the meaning of UX and methods for human-centered development in startups and scaleups is still emerging.

This paper presents an interview study conducted in a Danish company on the edge of the "growth chasm" i.e. a startup turning into a scaleup. We interviewed three out of the ten permanent staff members (chief information officer/IT manager, data scientist, and software developer) and a part-time UX consultant trainee. We present their views on UX and the practices they had experimented with in their software development over the years. Furthermore, we discuss those views and practices in relation to the agile UX and startup literature.

The rest of the paper structure is as follows. Section 2 gives an overview to the related work. Section 3 presents the research method. Section 4 describes the interview findings. Section 5 discusses the findings in relation to previous research. Finally, Sect. 6 is the conclusion of the paper.

2 Background

2.1 Agile UX

Agile UX work in established companies is often based on the integration of human-centered development practices with the agile process model (such as Scrum [20] or Kanban [14]) the company uses. Based on a recent systematic review, frequently recommended practices in agile UX include conducting little UX design work before starting implementation, doing iterative design and development, and having a cohesive product design [3]. Commonly used practices include usability testing, creating user stories, having users directly involved in the development, and using scenarios [3]. There, however, is no evidence of the suitability or applicability of these approaches to UX work in startups.

2.2 Startups and Culture of Experimenting

Startups often comprise of small teams that might have lack in skills and experience [8]. They operate with scarce resources in extremely uncertain, high-risk conditions and therefore have a strong time pressure and urge for short time to market [8]. Startups operate in market-driven environment where requirements are often invented and validated through frequent releases [5] instead of continuous customer involvement as in agile. Software startups do not necessarily follow any software development methodology although there are some directed at them. One of them is the lean startup [19]. It describes the business model hypothesis driven build-measure-learn loop where business or design ideas are built into falsifiable hypotheses that are tested in experiments with real users in actual markets. The outcome is then taken as validated learning to the following loop. This approach is especially aimed for highly dynamic environments where both customers and the product under ideation are unknown and thus customer value cannot be guaranteed by creating more or better designs; i.e. for the typical startup environments.

Larger established companies have also been adopting lean startup practices in their internal startups [6,18] and with innovation experiment and continuous experimentation systems [2,7,17,23]. Yaman et al. [23] report that UX team especially was keen on reaching a state where they could make data-informed decisions. Their expectation was that being able to refer to the data would increase both developers and stakeholders buy-in for the design decisions. Another benefit they saw in the approach was being able to focus the improvement effort on the most used features and remove unused features [23]. Being able to remove features will be extremely important in continuous development as otherwise the software will just continue growing.

2.3 Startup Antipatterns

Klotins et al. [12] analyzed 88 startup experience reports revealing three antipatterns Fig. 1, one per each startup phase. The first antipattern can happen during the build of the first version if the introduction to the market fails to happen fast or cheap enough or if the product itself is not competitive enough. The second one can happen if customers are not attracted to the product or the product is not developed further fast enough. Finally, the third one can happen in the phase where the company should grow into new markets if the company fails in keeping the customers happy or the costs down, or because they are not able to get beyond the initial market. Thus, the authors claim that many of the reasons behind startup failures could be mitigated by better engineering practices. Many of the symptoms might also be tackled with better UX practices as they are related to difficulties in attracting people or keeping them satisfied with the product. Thus, it seems clear that startups would benefit from appropriate UX practices and skills.

2.4 UX in Startups

Hokkanen et al. [11] studied UX practices and needs in startups. In their sample of eight Finnish startups, five developed their product having the owners' own personal needs in mind and one developed it for the assumed average user. Feedback was gathered mainly from friends whether or not they belonged to the target user group. Two of the startups had interviewed potential users, three had conducted informal user testing and two had used paper prototypes at some point. All of them used Google Analytics. Most commonly mentioned need towards the scaleup phase was to utilize user data analytics to better understand the user but none of the companies had a clear plan or strategy for the use of analytics or for UX work.

Hokkanen et al. [10] present a UX strategy framework for startups. They suggest that startups concentrate on sellability of their product through its attractiveness, approachability and professionalism.

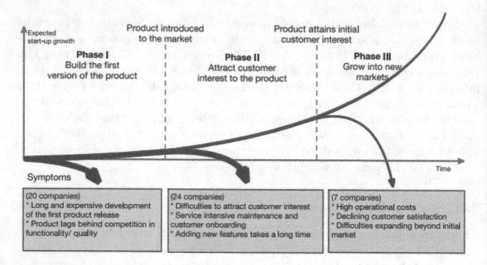

Fig. 1. Startup progression phases and symptoms for anti-patterns [12].

3   Method

The goal of the study presented in this paper was to add to the understanding of how startup companies see UX and working towards improving it in the context of their agile software development. The study was thus explorative in nature and we chose to conduct it as a series of semi-structured interviews in one single startup.

The study was conducted as student work over a 5 ECTS research methodology course aimed at master level software engineering students at the University of Southern Denmark in fall 2017. The first author was in charge over the course and the rest of the authors were students on the course planning, conducting, analyzing and reporting the study in the supervision of the first author. The first author contacted a number of companies with a few topics related to software engineering and the company either picked the topic they were most interested in or refused to participate. The first author then discussed with the company representative to find a relevant research question within the topic to be studied in the company. The companies were selected from a pool of Danish companies that had indicated their interest in working with software engineering students. The first author selected the research approach based on the research question and suitability in the organizational context (interview study in this case) and guided the participating companies by email on how to pick suitable research participants among the staff. The incentive for the participating companies was that companies got the student report of the study they participated in and thus learned more about themselves and perhaps got some suggestions on how to improve from the current state.

The students working in groups of three to four selected a topic they wanted to investigate as their course project. The students created study plans including short literature reviews, interview guides, and informed consent forms in the supervision of the first author and had to have them approved by her before starting the data gathering. The students handled the communication with the companies in the supervision of the first author from there on. They also chose who they want to interview and agreed on the practicalities directly with the companies.

3.1   Study Plan

The students selected to conduct the interviews in a semi-structured format as follows. Interview was introduced as an informal conversation where the conversation was driven by a series of questions that had been established beforehand. The entire interview was structured through an interview guide that served to ensure that all practicalities were handled and the most essential questions were asked. A semi-structured interview type was chosen based on the varying roles of the interviewees. The interviewer improvised further questions based on the response and investigated interesting topics further.

3.2   Procedure

The interviews were conducted at the company office in November 2017. All four interviewees had different tasks and roles at the company which gave a broader insight in the company's ways of working. The duration for the interview was approximately 45 min each and it was recorded. Before the interview took place, the interviewee was asked to sign a consent form which said that they agreed to the recording of the interview and that they had the right to not answer a question and if they felt uncomfortable they where allowed to stop the interview at any time. The recordings were transcribed and deleted when the report was ready, three months after the interviews at the latest.

The purpose of the interview was to establish how the staff work with UX and agile practices. Thus, the main questions were about how user experience is addressed in the company and how to improve UX work in the company. The first participant was the chief information officer (CIO)/IT manager. He organized all the projects the company handles. He was also the person who arranged the weekly Scrum meetings. The second participant was a data scientist who worked with internal systems. He was primarily working with the backend so he extracted all the data from the database that needed to be analyzed. The third participant was a student trainee who studied user experience design at the university and worked with new templates for the company website, where he made some split tests that dealt with new design choices. The fourth participant was a software developer, who was responsible for all the coding on the different platforms that they worked on. See Table 1 for an overview of the interviewees.

Table 1. Interviewed roles.

Code	Role	Age (years)
J1	Chief information officer (CIO)/IT manager	48
J2	Data scientist	25
J3	UX consultant	25
J4	Software developer	26

3.3 Analysis

We analyzed the transcribed interview data using Qualitative Data Analysis as described in [13]. Before coding the interview data, the students excluded irrelevant information by first excluding bits with no information and afterwards removing any data that did not have any significance to the topic. When each piece of information was extracted from the transcripts and coded, the students together used physical affinity diagram [] in which each single piece of information was written down on a post-it note and first grouped by interviewee and then thematically as themes arose from the data. Grouping the information by interviewee gave a clear view of how the different job positions saw the pros and cons and grouping the information by topic gave a quick overview of how much energy the company put into the agile workflow and in user-centered design. Lastly, the affinity wall made it easier to outline the data and to promote discussion.

4 Results

4.1 Studied Company

The studied company had about 10 full-time employees and 15 trainees/student assistants working for them. Maturity-wise the company seemed to be in the so-called scale-up phase [1,4]: it already had validated its product on the marketplace and had a steady and rather sustainable income. It also had existed for more than five years already. The leading brand of the company was an online consumer-finance service. Their business idea was to focus on online banking services instead of traditional retail services and face-to-face contact with the customer. They utilized online advertising services such as Google AdWords and Facebook Ads to attract new customers.

4.2   User Experience Work in the Company

In the early years, the company had not invested much effort into ensuring good UX of their services. The company did not have a UX designer or team and they did not pay much attention in creating UX designs before implementation. From the beginning, the company had leaned on profitability as an indicator of good UX: If the customers clicked on it, they assumed it worked for them.

Later on, they had added randomized experiments (A/B tests, or split tests) where half of the customer population was randomly exposed to one design version whereas the other half was exposed to another design version. This was done to compare between two design versions to pick the most profitable ones to be used in the system. They considered that these experiments ensure good user experience as the design choices were validated on real users in the production environment. However, they acknowledged that this method did not give an explanation on why it worked but they considered it enough for the startup company at that point as it guaranteed acceptable revenue. They were able to use this approach because of the high volume of users accessing the site; the company got enough data for each experiment approximately in less than a week. Had they not had such an extensive user base, they think they would have taken another kind of approach to UX.

Recently, the company had realized that they needed to increase their focus on the user experience in their products and they hired a student assistant in a part-time UX consultant role. The assistant's job was to create and conduct both qualitative and quantitative user surveys and report the results to the development teams. Quantitative surveys often combined online user questionnaires with usage data analysis such as clicks or user interaction patterns. They also surveyed users intention and behavior in qualitative online studies. The company still did not conduct user interviews or utilized other user study methods requiring personal contact with the users.

4.3   Scrum vs Kanban in UX Work

The company had utilized Scrum with one week sprints for years. A new sprint normally started each Monday with a sprint planning meeting where all relevant staff members together groomed the backlog and picked tasks for the sprint to begin. Together they chose the tasks that they would commit to as a team. Interviewees considered this as helpful and the developer (J4) told about the calming effect of being aware of their tasks for the sprint already in the beginning of the week. The data analyst (J2) said he liked dividing his tasks into smaller and more manageable pieces for clarity. This practice also allowed them to rearrange tasks to accommodate possible bugs or changes in the environment each week.

Due to the tools they used for managing the development workflow, the interviewees reported on having to do quite a lot of not directly value-adding administrative work because "everything had to be commented and logged in the system". One of the interviewees mentioned that he kept forgetting to update the backlog after completing a task. Another said that he sometimes felt like an accountant because of all the listing and registering tasks.

As the UX consultant worked only part-time, he did not attend to the sprint planning meetings. Instead, he regularly had meetings with the CIO about his progress and results. This also meant that his tasks got assigned outside of the company's Scrum board. As a consequence, the UX consultant mostly worked alone and managed his own work by himself. He and other team members felt that it was problematic to use Scrum for UX work, especially with one week sprints as the UX surveys could not be finished in a week. This made the company to switch to Kanban. The interviewees described how they prioritized and organized tasks in different columns on a digital Kanban tool. The columns had labels indicating the state of the task. When talking about UX design choices, the programmers explained that they made the design choices by themselves. The developer responsible for the task made UX design decisions alone. The UX consultant was not assigned to the task nor was the CIO interfering in the decisions. The design decisions made in the company were based on general assumptions and/or gut feelings. However, when faced with larger decisions, developers talked to their boss. In this case, they commonly came up with two or more designs and launched them in a split test. The primary goal for the test was to provide information for design choices and the solution that generated more clicks than the other was usually selected for the next version as-is.

The UX consultant was working on a UX design guideline for the company and all the interviewees believed that this guideline would greatly help them in their UX design decisions in the future so that they could base the decisions on something more than general assumptions.

Later on, they decided to abandon Kanban and go back to Scrum. However, all the interviewees agreed that they do not want to use "text-book Scrum". Instead they would taylor Scrum for their needs. They would only take the parts that worked for them, change some of the other things and completely opt not to do some. They believed that going back to the "Scrum inspired" ways of working would provide them more structure and improved collaboration.

The UX consult expressed some concerns in the choice of going back to Scrum fearing of the short sprints and having to deliver finished work within the sprint. This was especially a concern in relation to qualitative user tests. While the Scrum team ran a weekly sprint, it was difficult for the UX consultant to stick to the timeboxed sprint. As he stated, his "work cycle looked more like the rigid waterfall model than fast iterating sprints". His work cycle often consisted of research, analysis, and learning how to improve the UX. As he put it, to study the customer, analyze the data, and then do some design requires more time than a week. In his opinion it is impossible to adapt and come up with results every week. When asked how he believed it should be done he suggested the dual track model with separate UX and development sprints running in parallel, similarly to [22]. In this way, the UX consultant would be able to start on finding UX solutions for a new problem while the programmer is finishing up with the old problem. When the programmer is ready for a new problem, the designer will already have something ready for him to do so that they can stay effective. The UX consultant also believed that he would have an opportunity to do qualitative user tests within a sprint while the programmer would be working on implementing a solution or testing the code. The interviewees all agreed that they liked working in an agile workflow and they could not imagine that anything else would fit the company better. They had some differences as to how well they believed the current Kanban solution worked compared to Scrum. They all apart from the UX consultant agreed that going back to their own version of Scrum is the right choice. They were not concerned about managing qualitative UX tests while working with Scrum although they did not have an exact plan for how to do it.

5 Discussion

The UX practices in the studied company seem comparable to those Hokkanen et al. [11] observed in the eight studied Finnish startups. The company strongly relied on usage data and split tests but they had not acquired qualitative data from the users to explain their choices. They also relied on the thought that the action of clicking indicates liking or a positive reaction. They had not planned their UX activities and they did not have a UX strategy. Instead their UX awareness had grown little by little, encouraged by the pressure to acquire a larger user base and later also by the urge to keep the acquired users satisfied.

The studied company seemed to have already crossed the first two chasms in the Klotins et al.'s [12] antipattern model. They had successfully brought the product into market and attracted users to the product. Currently, they were on the third chasm where they need to grow into new markets, control the costs, and to keep their current and future users happy. They have started to conduct user surveys. Designing good and effective surveys and being able to transfer the learnings into the design is not, however, an easy task. Perhaps adding a few user interviews in the method palette could help them to better empathize with the user.

The company had used Scrum for years but they tried changing to Kanban soon after hiring a UX person. In their study of the fitness of Scrum and Kanban to UX, Law et al. [16] conclude that Kanban is generally better suited with UX work. Our study supported this. The company chose to go back to Scrum after trying out Kanban although they thought Kanban was better for integrating UX work with other development efforts as it did not force UX work into timeboxes. However, based on research evidence, UX can be integrated to either process model.

The company had adopted practices from both lean startup type build-measure-learn loop and Scrum. They did not follow any process model strictly but picked practices that they felt suitable for them. They could slip from these practices when they, for instance, were in hurry which indicates that the selection of the practices was not a strategic choice but maybe convenience reasons played a significant part in it. The company probably would benefit from a strategic planning of their ways of working such as planning of the experiments more carefully to reflect business or design ideas instead of using them to solve difficulties in making individual design choices.

Startups operating in web and cloud environments often have the benefit of getting a large usage data. This data can offer a vast amount of information if collected and analyzed wisely. It seemed that the studied company did not fully utilize the potential of the data which is in line with the finding of [11]. Thus, the startup, and maybe startups in general, would benefit from improved skills in user-oriented data analytics. However, the dilemma that was experienced also with survey data remains: the challenging task of utilizing the data in successfully guiding the design decisions unfortunately requires great skills and experience in UX research and design.

5.1   Research Quality

The study was conducted by inexperienced students as course work and thus the interview might not have captured all relevant issues. For instance, some nuances and reasons behind the choices the company made remained unanswered. The study would have benefited from a validating round of interviews or discussion over the findings with the company representative.

The study was conducted in a single startup company and thus the results reflect only that particular startup. We however utilized several mitigation strategies such as theory triangulation and interviewing a rather large number of roles in the small startup where the total number of permanent staff members was only ten. Our results can be reflected in the light of previous research which supports the credibility of our results.

UX in startups is an understudied topic with only few studies focusing on it. Thus, our study offers a novel contribution to the academic field by confirming the previous results, offering a qualitative, deeper view in a single representative startup, and by explaining the previous research conducted in larger companies in the context of startups.

6   Conclusion

We conducted an interview study on UX practices and agile ways of working in a single Danish startup. We increased the understanding of the ways of working by describing the practices and challenges the startup has encountered during its lifetime. We conclude that more research is needed to create practices and knowledge on UX that can be applied in small startups operating with scarce resources and UX skills. It is becoming clear that better engineering and UX practices can help startups in their volatile first years as they struggle to acquire users and to keep them happy. These practices should take into account not only the characteristics of startups but also the market-driven environment in which they operate. Therefore, the UX practices ought to arise from experimenting with real users and adding qualitative insight into that. Moreover, the current human-centered software engineering literature in general would benefit from more research on how to conduct UX work in data-driven development environments as it is a trend in software engineering beyond the startup scene.

References

1. Aernoudt, R.: Executive forum: the scale-up gap: and how to address it. Ventur. Cap. **19**(4), 361–372 (2017). https://doi.org/10.1080/13691066.2017.1348724
2. Bosch, J.: Building products as innovation experiment systems. In: Cusumano, M.A., Iyer, B., Venkatraman, N. (eds.) ICSOB 2012. LNBIP, vol. 114, pp. 27–39. Springer, Heidelberg (2012). https://doi.org/10.1007/978-3-642-30746-1_3
3. Brhel, M., Meth, H., Maedche, A., Werder, K.: Exploring principles of user-centered agile software development: a literature review. Inf. Softw. Technol. **61**, 163–181 (2015)
4. European Commission: Europe's next leaders: the start-up and scale-up initiative (2016)
5. Dahlstedt, A., Karlsson, L., Persson, A., NattochDag, J., Regnell, B.: Market-driven requirements engineering processes for software products-a report on current practices. In: International Workshop on COTS and Product Software: Why Requirements are So Important (RECOTS) (2003)
6. Edison, H.: Lean internal startups: empowering software product innovation in large companies (2017)
7. Fagerholm, F., Guinea, A.S., Mäenpää, H., Münch, J.: The right model for continuous experimentation. J. Syst. Softw. **123**, 292–305 (2017)
8. Giardino, C., Unterkalmsteiner, M., Paternoster, N., Gorschek, T., Abrahamsson, P.: What do we know about software development in startups? IEEE Softw. **31**(5), 28–32 (2014)
9. Hokkanen, L., Kuusinen, K., Väänänen, K.: Early product design in startups: towards a UX strategy. In: Abrahamsson, P., Corral, L., Oivo, M., Russo, B. (eds.) PROFES 2015. LNCS, vol. 9459, pp. 217–224. Springer, Cham (2015). https://doi.org/10.1007/978-3-319-26844-6_16
10. Hokkanen, L., Kuusinen, K., Väänänen, K.: Minimum viable user EXperience: a framework for supporting product design in startups. In: Sharp, H., Hall, T. (eds.) XP 2016. LNBIP, vol. 251, pp. 66–78. Springer, Cham (2016). https://doi.org/10.1007/978-3-319-33515-5_6
11. Hokkanen, L., Väänänen-Vainio-Mattila, K.: UX work in startups: current practices and future needs. In: Lassenius, C., Dingsøyr, T., Paasivaara, M. (eds.) XP 2015. LNBIP, vol. 212, pp. 81–92. Springer, Cham (2015). https://doi.org/10.1007/978-3-319-18612-2_7
12. Klotins, E., Unterkalmsteiner, M., Gorschek, T.: Software engineering in start-up companies: an analysis of 88 experience reports. Empir. Softw. Eng., 1–35 (2018)
13. Lacey, A., Luff, D.: Qualitative data analysis. Trent Focus Sheffield (2001)
14. Ladas, C.: Scrumban-Essays on Kanban Systems for Lean Software Development. Lulu. com, Seattle (2009)
15. Law, E., Roto, V., Vermeeren, A.P., Kort, J., Hassenzahl, M.: Towards a shared definition of user experience. In: CHI 2008 Extended Abstracts on Human Factors in Computing Systems, pp. 2395–2398. ACM (2008)
16. Law, E.L.C., Lárusdóttir, M.K.: Whose experience do we care about? Analysis of the fitness of scrum and kanban to user experience. Int. J. Hum. Comput. Interact. **31**(9), 584–602 (2015)

17. Olsson, H.H., Bosch, J.: From opinions to data-driven software r&d: a multi-case study on how to close the 'open loop' problem. In: 2014 40th EUROMICRO Conference on Software Engineering and Advanced Applications (SEAA), pp. 9–16. IEEE (2014)
18. Owens, T., Fernandez, O.: The Lean Enterprise: How Corporations Can Innovate Like Startups. Wiley, New York (2014)
19. Ries, E.: The Lean Startup: How Today's Entrepreneurs Use Continuous Innovation to Create Radically Successful Businesses. Crown Books, New York (2011)
20. Schwaber, K., Beedle, M.: Agile Software Development with Scrum, vol. 1. Prentice Hall, Upper Saddle River (2002)
21. Sutton, S.M.: The role of process in software start-up. IEEE Softw. **17**(4), 33–39 (2000)
22. Sy, D.: Adapting usability investigations for agile user-centered design. J. Usability Stud. **2**(3), 112–132 (2007)
23. Yaman, S.G., et al.: Introducing continuous experimentation in large software-intensive product and service organisations. J. Syst. Softw. **133**, 195–211 (2017)

Get Realistic! - UCD Course Design and Evaluation

Marta Larusdottir[1]([⊠]), Virpi Roto[2], Jan Stage[3], and Andres Lucero[2]

[1] Reykjavik University, Menntavegur 1, 101 Reykjavik, Iceland
marta@ru.is
[2] Alto University, P. O. Box 11000, 00076 Aalto, Finland
{virpi.roto, andres.lucero}@aalto.fi
[3] Ålborg University, P. O. Box 159, 9100 Ålborg, Denmark
jans@cs.aau.dk

Abstract. There is an increasing demand for software, suitable for large segments of users with different needs and competences. User-Centred Design (UCD) methods have been used in the software industry and taught to software developers to meet the various needs of users. The field of UCD covers a broad set of topics that can be covered in a range of courses with various content. In this paper we describe the design of a two-week course focusing on teaching UCD methods to students with various backgrounds that are useful for the students in the future. The course schedule included lectures and workshop activities where the lecturers taught UCD topics and coached the students in developing skills for using the selected UCD methods during the course to design and evaluate an interactive system. Additionally, we describe two types of course evaluations that we conducted: qualitative weekly evaluations and a post-course survey.

The results show that students were in general positive about the course content and the combination of lectures and workshop activities. Hi-fi prototyping was the UCD method that the students rated as being most useful for the course and their future. They particularly liked how realistic these were for the users. The least useful method in the course and in the future was "Walking the Wall", where students read an affinity diagram and make design suggestions. Finally, we suggest changes for a prospective course, based on the results of the evaluations.

Keywords: User centred design course · User centred design methods
Computer science curricula · Course design · Course evaluation

1 Introduction

User-Centred Design (UCD) is a rich and varied discipline. The basic aim is to combine design and evaluation in the development of a software system and focus these activities on the prospective users of the system that is being developed. The literature includes extensive research on UCD concepts, principles and methods. One of the classical references provides an overview of the discipline [21]. Other references focus on the principles behind UCD [9], or try to identify how software practitioners define and work with UCD [8].

Teaching UCD is of key importance in order to increase its influence in software development. Software development will not change towards a more user-centred approach unless there are practitioners available with UCD skills. Nevertheless, the literature on teaching of UCD is very limited. An early workshop aimed to produce a list of skills that are necessary and important for UCD practitioners. They see UCD as a process that should yield a high level of utility and usability by developing good task flows and user interfaces. Therefore, UCD practitioners should have the knowledge, skills, and other characteristics needed for considering and involving users [6].

Only a few authors discuss or present the design of courses on UCD. Seffah and Andreevskaia [23] present the approach behind and the content of a course on human-centred design for university students in computer science, who will be future practitioners in software development. They describe a list with 17 different skills on design and evaluation that should be developed in a UCD course, but do not mention UCD methods or report which ones they taught, if any. They neither outline the contents of a specific course nor any experiences from teaching it.

A stronger focus on teaching of UCD has been present in elementary and secondary school level. In England, for example, teaching design and technology was introduced at that level, and there is considerable documentation of content and experiences from this teaching. Nicholl et al. [26] found that contrary to official directives, there was a clear lack of opportunities for pupils to experience user-centred approaches when undertaking tasks in classes on this topic. Thus there are studies that provide insight into the teachers' teaching practices on user-centred design. In relation to this, there is significant literature on teaching of design and creativity in elementary and secondary school, e.g. Hill [10].

The introduction of UCD in software organizations is the focus of some research literature. This literature typically describes how developers in a software organization was introduced to and trained in UCD methods, e.g. [3, 12].

A different stream of research focuses on training of people with mental disabilities to participate in UCD processes. Waller [25] reports from training workshops where users and people who use augmentative and alternative communication were introduced to the UCD process and the related methods. Feedback from participants indicates that they felt more empowered to evaluate systems and to engage in the design of new systems. Prior [22] have adapted UCD methods for a similar purpose.

One of the challenges when teaching a topic like UCD is to assess the quality of the course and its impact on the participants. Some of the aforementioned literature on introducing UCD in software organizations includes such assessment activities. Contrastingly, the limited literature on university level teaching of UCD that is mentioned above, has much less focus on assessment.

This paper reports from an empirical study of a course in UCD for university-level students. We describe and discuss the specific topics within UCD we decided to teach, how we assessed the impact of the course on the participants, and outline a redesign of the course based on the experiences gained. In the following section, we provide a more detailed overview of selected literature on teaching of UCD methods and evaluation of UCD methods used in industry. In Sect. 3, we describe our case which was a two-week university course in UCD. Section 4 presents the method used in our study of the course. In Sect. 5, we provide the results from the study of the course. In Sect. 6 we explain the lessons learned and the reaction to those. In Sect. 7 we discuss the study and provide the conclusion in Sect. 8.

2 Related Work

In this section we will describe some of the literature on how to teach UCD methods, on the evaluation of UCD methods in industry and on the google design sprint process.

2.1 Teaching UCD Methods

In this section we study which UCD methods are seen as important to teach, and focus especially on the methods used for design. Our literature review on UCD course design, reported in the previous chapter, showed that UCD courses for university-level students have not reported the set of methods taught on those classes. Therefore, we broadened our scope to cover publications reporting more general courses on HCI rather than just UCD, since UCD methods are under the HCI methods umbrella. In this section we report two works supported by The Special Interest Group on Computer-Human Interaction by the Association for Computing Machinery (ACM SIGCHI). These works have been influenced by a broad range of international experts in the field and are therefore worth a closer analysis.

First, an annual 'Introduction to HCI' course at the CHI conference[1], ACM SIG-CHI's premium conference provides an overview to HCI for newcomers in the field, including content on theory, cognition, design, evaluation, and user diversity [17]. The design content on this 4-h course focuses on user-centered design methods such as surveys, interviews, focus groups, ethnography, and participatory design. Due to the short duration of the course, only the principles of each method are covered, and the course participants are not supposed to gain skills on using these methods.

Second, ACM SIGCHI has conducted an international project 2011–2014 in order to document HCI educators', practitioners', and students' perspectives on the most important topics in HCI [5]. While the project was not focusing on UCD but the broader field of HCI, the authors see human-centeredness in the core of HCI: "HCI focuses on people and technology to drive human-centered technology innovation" (ibid. p. 70). The outcome of this SIGCHI Education Project is a list of HCI topics that were seen as very important or important by the study respondents, and a recommendation to "offer a flexible, global, and frequently refreshed curriculum" (ibid., p. 72). The living curriculum is important because technological advancements constantly bring new topics to be studied.

Since our focus in this paper is on UCD methods, we investigate the methods that were prioritized by all respondents in surveys across the time frame of the SIGCHI Education Project. The important methods risen from the survey are divided into design

---

[1] https://sigchi.org/conferences/conference-history/chi

methods and empirical methods. The design research methodologies considered important or very important are interaction design, interviews, observation, paper/low-fidelity prototyping, prototyping (general), and usability testing. The empirical methods listed were for academic researchers (e.g., problem formation and research design) and not UCD methods to be taught for practitioners.

Churchill et al. [5] report the results of an English-language survey (n = 616) in more detail. Interaction design was mentioned as the most important subject (discipline) in HCI, and experience design as the most important topic. Agile/iterative design, experience design, interaction design, and participatory design were rated as the most important design paradigms in HCI. In design methods, for example, field study, interviews, prototyping, usability testing, and wire-framing were rated as very important. Churchill et al. [5] suggest that these results provide a valuable starting point for a unified vision of HCI education. However, we have not found scientific publications reporting students' perspectives on the usefulness of different UCD methods as part of an interaction design project.

2.2 Evaluation of UCD Methods Used in Industry

In this section we give an overview of some of the current literature on how usability techniques have been integrated in software development in industry.

Bygstad, Ghinea, and Brevik [4] surveyed professionals working at Norwegian IT companies to investigate the relationship between software development methodologies and usability activities. In their findings, there was a gap between intention and reality. The IT professionals expressed interests and concerns about the usability of their products, but they were less willing to spend resources on it in industrial projects with time and cost constraints. The results of their survey also revealed that the IT professionals perceived usability activities and software development methods to be integrated, which the authors believed is a positive sign.

Bark et al. [1] conducted a survey on the usage and usefulness of HCI methods during different development phases. They examined whether the type of the software projects had any effects on HCI practitioners' perception of the usefulness of the methods. The results show that there was fairly little correlation between the frequency of using a particular technique and how useful it was perceived by the HCI practitioners. One conclusion in the study is that HCI practitioners tend to have a personal and overall evaluation of the different techniques rather than evaluating the actual usefulness of the methods in their daily work when developing particular software.

An international web-based survey by Monahan et al. [19] reported the state of using several field study techniques and how effective they were considered to be by usability practitioners in education and industry. The results show that more than half of the respondents rated observations as an extremely effective method and about 40% of the respondents rated user testing as extremely effective. The most influential factor for choosing a method for participants working in the software industry was time constraints.

Venturi, Troost and Jokela [24] investigated the adoption of user centred design (UCD) in software industry. The results of the study show that the most frequently used method was user interviews. Additionally, hi-fi and low-fi prototyping methods were frequently used. Overall, the most frequently used evaluation methods are qualitative, allowing rapid feedback to the design activities using expert and heuristic evaluation or "quick and dirty" usability test methods. The results also show that UCD methods are typically used during the early phases of the product life cycle.

A survey study on the usage of 25 usability techniques was conducted in Sweden by Gulliksen et al. in 2004 [8]. The results show that the usability techniques that received the highest rating by the usability professionals were those that were informal, involved users and were concerned with design issues. Techniques such as expert-based evaluations and benchmarking that do not involve users, received the lowest ratings by the usability professionals. There was a general agreement among the participants that it is important to integrate usability techniques into the software development process they were using. Some participants mentioned difficulties during the integration, especially those that were using RUP (Rational Unified Process) as their development process.

Another survey study was conducted in Sweden in 2012, where the usage of 13 user centred design methods in agile software projects was studied [13]. The methods used by more than 50% of the participants were: workshops, low-fi prototyping, interviews and meetings with users. The most frequently used methods were: low-fi prototyping, informal evaluation with users and scenarios. These were used at least twice a month. The participants also rated the usefulness of using the methods. More than 90% of the participants rated formal usability methods as "very good" or "fairly good", but that method was typically used twice to six times a year.

2.3 Google Design Sprints

Created as a means to better balance his time on the job and with his family, Jake Knapp optimized the different activities of a design process by improving team processes. Knapp noticed that despite the large piles of sticky notes and the collective excitement generated during team brainstorming workshops, the best ideas were often generated by individuals who had a big challenge and not too much time to work on them. Another key ingredient was to have people involved in a project all working together in a room solving their own part of the problem and ready to answer questions. Combining a focus on individual work, time to prototype, and an inescapable deadline Knapp called these focused design efforts "sprints".

A big important challenge is defined, small teams of about seven people with diverse skills are recruited, and then the right room and materials are found. These teams clear their schedules and move through a focused design process by spending one day at each of its five stages (i.e., map, sketch, decide, prototype, test). On Monday, a map of the problem is made by defining key questions, a long-term goal, and a target, thus building a foundation for the sprint week. On Tuesday, individuals follow a four-ste Created as a means to better balance his time on the job and with his family, Jake Knapp optimized the different activities of a design process by improving team processes. Knapp noticed that despite the large piles of sticky notes and the collective excitement generated during team brainstorming workshops, the best ideas were often generated by individuals who had a big challenge and not too much time to work on them. Another key ingredient was to have people involved in a project all working together in a room solving their own part of the problem and ready to answer questions. Combining a focus on individual work, time to prototype, and an inescapable deadline Knapp called these focused design efforts "sprints".

The Design Sprint [16] is a process to solve problems and test new ideas by building and testing a prototype in five days. The main premise for Google design sprints is seeing how customers react before committing to building a real product. It is a "smarter, more respectful, and more effective way of solving problems", one that brings the best contributions of everyone on the team by helping them spend their time on what really matters. A series of support materials such as checklists, slide decks, and tools can be found on a dedicated website (https://www.thesprintbook.com).

3 The Case – Experimental Design Course

This paper reports an international course that was planned during early 2017 and executed in July-August 2017 as an intensive course. The Experimental Design Course at Tallinn University, Estonia, lasted for two weeks, Monday to Friday. The main learning objective on the course was ability to apply common user-centred design methods and interaction design tools in practice during a two-week interaction design sprint. A total of 18 international students worked on designing and evaluating a software system, and used altogether 15 UCD methods along the way. The students brainstormed ideas for the systems themselves, so they worked on five different systems, but all used the same methods for analysing, designing and evaluating the systems. The students worked in five groups, with three or four members in each group, which were formed by the lecturers. The strategy while forming the groups was to have varying backgrounds, genders, and nationalities in each group. The course schedule is illustrated in Table 1.

Table 1. The schedule of the course for the two weeks.

Week 1	Monday	Tuesday	Wednesday	Thursday	Friday
Morning Hands-on work in italics	Introduction	Contextual interviews, Introduction to UX	Introduction to Interaction design, Affinity diagram	Scenario, LoFi prototyping	UX goals, SUS, Preparing presentations
Afternoon Hands-on work in italics	Visioning workshop	Contextual interviews, Affinity diagram	Personas, Scenarios. Walking the wall	LoFi prototyping, Heuristic evaluation	Interim presentations
Week 2	Monday	Tuesday	Wednesday	Thursday	Friday
Morning lecture	Usability evaluation	HiFi prototyping	HiFi prototyping	UX evaluation, HiFi prototyping	UX evaluation, Preparing presentations
Afternoon workshop	Usability evaluation	Usability evaluation, Redesigning	Usability evaluation, Redesigning	HiFi prototyping	Final presentations

The students generally had lectures and group work sessions from nine in the morning until around four in the afternoon, see Table 1 for the schedule. During the first three days the students were introduced to the following user centred design methods: Visioning, contextual interviews [11], affinity diagram [18] or KJ method [15], walking the wall, personas and scenarios [11]. After an introduction of the method the students used each of the methods with supervision from the lecturer. The next two days the students were introduced to user experience (UX) goals [14], they made low fidelity prototypes on paper of the user interface and evaluated those through heuristic evaluations [20]. They also used the System Usability Scale (SUS) questionnaire for evaluation [2] and additionally evaluated the interface according to their UX goals. During the second week the students were introduced to formal usability evaluations. They prototyped the interface using the Just-in mind prototyping tool (https://www.justinmind.com/) and did an informal think aloud evaluation on that prototype. After redesigning the prototype, the students stated measurable usability and UX goals and made a summative user evaluation to check the measurable goals. At the end of the course all the students presented their work to each other with a 15 min presentation to the class. In Table 1 the course schedule can be seen. We chose the methods introduced to the students partly on results on what methods IT professionals rate as good methods for UCD [13].

The students were asked to develop some software for international students in a foreign country, but otherwise they could choose the domain for their application. Two groups wanted to assist students find courses, one focused on choosing courses at a particular university but the other group focused on courses within a subject of interest between universities. Two groups chose to assist international students in food related issues. One group wanted to assist in buying food in a foreign country and the other in hearing about and learning recipes from local and international students.

Figure 1 shows illustrations of the paper based prototype of the first four screens the users meet from the student group assisting in buying food at the grocery store.

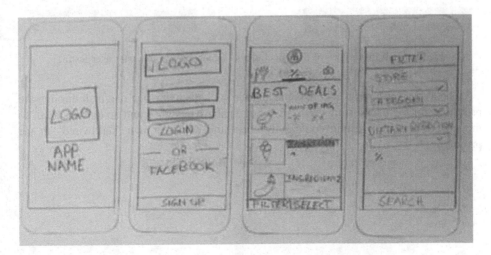

Fig. 1. Illustrations of the low-fi prototypes from one of the groups.

The focus in the student projects was chosen because it was easy for the students to imagine how the user groups are, since they were themselves in the same postion. Additionally, we chose this because they students were asked to collaborate between groups during user testing, acting as users for another group and getting students as users to their user testing. With this approach we ensured that the students would find participants for their user testing that were representative for the user groups.

On Fig. 2, there are illustrations of hi-fi prototypes of the best deals screen before and after the formal user testing session.

Fig. 2. Hi-fi prototypes of the "Best deals" screen before and after user testing.

The hi-fi prototypes were clickable and the students had made one path through the prototype for the user testing. There was not database designed and no data inserted, so the user in the user testing could only chose the data that was "hardwired" in the prototype.

4   Method

This section explains the background of the students and the data gathering methods.

4.1   Background of the Students

The students had various backgrounds, both concerning nationality, gender, age and education. The 18 students were from 11 countries: 8 students from the Nordic countries, 7 from other European countries, 1 from Canada, and 2 from Asia. We had 10 female students and 8 male. The age range was from 22 to 42 years. We had five students with a high school degree, studying for the Bachelor degree, 10 students having a Bachelor degree, out of which seven were studying for their Master degree, and three with a Master degree, where one was studying at a PhD level. The fields of their study was: Computer Science (four students), Collaborative and industrial design (three students), Interaction design (two students), and one student in each of the fields: Informatics, human centred technology, international design business management and software engineering.

Seven students had been working at software companies and the time span was from three months up to more than five years. The jobs roles included: Advisor/mentor, analyst, consultant, lead UI/visual designer, service design intern, test developer, UX designer, UX manager and UX researcher. Some students mentioned more than one job role they had had. We did not ask particularly about, if they had taken similar courses previously, but in the informal discussions with students we found that some of them had quite good knowledge and skills in the subjects of the course, while others had not seen similar material before.

Some examples of the types of software the students had been developing in industry include: Online systems for music learning; survey tool based on a map, a software system to support the diagnosis protocol of children with ADHD (Attention Deficit Hyperactivity Disorder), websites where one can order food from shop with same day delivery, software for supporting weather measurements and software for issuing credit cards and handling money transfer.

4.2   Data Gathering Methods

Two methods were used to gather feedback from students on their opinions on the course: a weekly evaluation form for collecting open-ended feedback, and a questionnaire on the UCD methods taught on the course. Both were distributed on paper at the end of the week. The methods will be described in more detail below.

The Weekly Evaluation. Students were asked to draw their right hand on an empty A4 sheet of paper as the last thing in the afternoon during both Fridays, so data was gathered twice with this method during the course. In the space of the thumb, they were asked to write what they thought was good during the current week, in the space for the index finger, things they wanted to point out, in the third finger space what was not good, in the space for the fourth finger what they will take home with them and the fifth finger what they wanted more of. The students wrote sentences, so this was a qualitative method. The students handed in their evaluation by putting it in a box that was placed at the back of the room, so the lecturers did not watch who was delivering in the evaluation forms, to keep the anonymity. When all the students had handed in their evaluations, we asked if there was something that they wanted to share with the group. There were open discussions for about 15 min of improvements that could be made to the course.

When we had gathered the evaluations after the first week, one of the lecturers inserted all the answers from the students to a Google spreadsheet to be able to share those with the other lecturers. As this was meant to be a formative evaluation method, the results were discussed and some changes were made to the schedule according to the feedback. The results were analyzed with thematic analysis [7].

The Method Questionnaire. The questionnaire was on paper and contained 3 pages. On the first page there were: 4 questions on the student's background, 3 questions on their currently highest achieved degree, one question on whether they were studying currently or not, and 4 on their current education (if applicable). Also, on the first page they were asked if they had worked in the industry. If so, they were asked to fill in 5 more questions about the work role and company.

On the second page of the questionnaire the students were asked to rate their opinion of the UCD methods used on the course. For each method they were asked to rate:

(a) If the method was thought provoking;
(b) if the method was useful for the course; and
(c) if they thought that the method would be useful for their future job/education.

For each item we provided a 7-point scale from 1 = not at all to 7 = extremely so. The 15 methods they evaluated were: Visioning, Contextual interviews, Affinity diagram, Walking the wall, Personas, Scenarios, UX goals, Low fidelity prototypes (paper prototypes), Heuristic evaluation, Evaluation of lo-fi prototypes with user using the SUS questions, Evaluation of lo-fi prototypes with user using the UX goals, Hi-fi prototyping (digital), Think-aloud evaluations of hi-fi prototypes, Measurable usability goals setting and Summative evaluation (usability and user experience).

On the third page, there was just one open question for any other comments that they would like to share with us. They had a full A4 page to freely share their comments.

The questionnaire was filled in right after the retrospective hand evaluation during the last session of the class. The students typically used 20 min to fill in the questionnaire. When all the students had filled in this questionnaire, discussion was facilitated on the overall evaluation on the course.

5   Results

In this section the results both from the weekly evaluations and the Methods questionnaire will be described.

5.1 Results from the Weekly Evaluation

The students wrote one or two sentences of each of the five categories: What was good; what they wanted to point out; what was not as good what they would take home with them and what they wanted more off. When all the students had handed in their evaluations, we asked if there was something that they wanted to share with the group. There were open discussions for about 15 min of improvements that could be made to the course. Some of the comments were quite detailed, e.g., 2 students commenting on one particular lecture by the Chilean guy, and a particular subject (the list of the emotions for setting UX goals) and some comments are more general, e.g., one student saying that the lectures were interesting. Four students commented on the group work projects in some way and four on meeting new people and their openness. Six commented on the teachers in some way and three on the lectures and their subject. We got four comments on having different teachers during the course and one particularly commented that it was good to have both group work and lectures the same day.

5.2 Results from the Methods Questionnaire

Results from the methods questionnaire were calculated and analyzed and are presented in Table 2. We calculated the average grade for the 18 students. The scale used was 1 to 7, where 1 = not at all to 7 = extremely so. We have marked the methods getting the highest grading and the lowest grading with colors.

Table 2. Results from the methods questionnaire

UCD methods	Thought provoking	Useful in the course	Useful in the future
Visioning	4,6	5,4	5,1
Contextual inquiry	5,1	5,7	5,7
Affinity diagram	4,5	4,9	4,8
Walk the Wall	4,0	3,5	4,0
Personas	4,2	4,7	5,1
Scenarios	4,1	4,8	5,1
UX goal setting	5,7	6,2	6,3
Lo-fi prototyping	4,9	5,9	5,5
Heuristic Evaluation	4,4	4,6	5,1
Evaluation of lo-fi prototypes - SUS	4,6	5,3	5,3
Evaluation of lo-fi prototypes - UX	5,0	5,4	5,1
Hi-fi prototyping (digital)	5,8	6,8	6,8
Think-aloud evaluation	5,6	6,2	6,2
Measureable usability goal setting	5,4	6,1	6,2
Summative evaluation	5,7	6,3	6,4

The method getting the highest score in all phases (the immediate, the course period and for the future use) was Hi-fi prototyping, where the students made prototypes using the Just-in mind tool. This is when the ideas really came to life and we could see that they students loved this activity. They even stayed up until after midnight to make the prototypes work and look good. The second highest for the course was Summative evaluation, where the students measured effectiveness, efficiency, satisfaction and UX factors. UX goals setting and Think aloud evaluation had the same score as the third and fourth best method for the course.

The students gave the method: Walking the wall the lowest grading. During walking of the wall, the students got visitors from other groups that should suggest design ideas for the group while reading an affinity diagram showing results from interviews with users. A paired-samples t-test was conducted to compare the difference of the ratings of the walking the wall method and the hi-fi prototyping. There is a statistical difference in the grading of walking the wall (M = 3.53, SD = 1.94) and hi-fi prototyping (M = 6.78, SD = 0.55) with (p = 0.01). One student mentioned that this activity was rather useless since the students did not use the results of this activity in the next one. The second lowest as useful for the course was the heuristic evaluation. This could be because, the students did two evaluations one after the other without redesigning their designs between the evaluations. The third lowest in the grading for usefulness in the course was the method Personas. This could also be because the Personas where not really used again during other activities.

The open comments students gave overall about the course were quite positive. The background of the students varied, from being studying on BS level to a PhD level, and some students had been and were working in industry. The negative comments show clearly that the course was too basic for some students. Most of the comments could be met by giving more clear description about the course, like timings and objectives of the course should be clear in the course description.

6 Lessons Learned and Reactions

In this section we will describe the lessons learned based on the results from the evaluations from students and the evaluations from the lecturers present at the course. We will first give a summary of the lessons learned and then present the changes made to the course schedule as a reaction to the lessons learned.

6.1 Lessons Learned

In summary, we have described above how we successfully taught a course on UCD for university-level students. We have also presented the specific topics within UCD that were included in the course. In addition, we have described how we assessed the impact of the course on the participants and outlined a redesign of the course based on the experiences gained.

Two methods were used to evaluate the course by gathering feedback from students on their opinions about the course and the methods taught: an open-ended evaluation form for collecting qualitative feedback, and a questionnaire. Our results demonstrate the general usefulness of these techniques for course evaluation. It was valuable to get feedback from the students after the first week and discuss with them what adjustments could be made for the second week. Some comments were on the dissemination of the course so some students thought that the course description, so we could explain why this happened. Additionally, we chose sometimes to give the students more time during the workshops, if they did not manage to finish using a method within the timeframe scheduled. We thought they would appreciate not strictly following the plan, but some students commented that we did not follow the announced course schedule in details and found it stressful. Also we had not clearly stated that students should be there until 16, so some students were upset that this was not made clear.

The students were generally positive about the course content, and they particularly liked the combination of lectures and workshop activities every day, and the involvement of several teachers. Altogether, they used 15 UCD methods during the course. The first observation from the results is that four UCD methods were rated highest: hi-fi prototyping, because the prototypes were very realistic for the users; summative evaluation, where they measured effectiveness, efficiency, satisfaction and UX factors; setting UX goals and think-aloud evaluation. It was also obvious observing the students that when they got to do the running prototypes they stayed until late at night. That was the only day during the two weeks that they got so focused in using the method we had introduced to them. The UCD methods that the students rated lowest were "Walking the Wall", where students should read an affinity diagram and suggest design ideas. They commented it took long time to use the method and the output was not that valuable. The students also gave heuristic evaluation and personas low rating. We had indications that the reasons for these low ratings were that the results were either not used in subsequent activities or not used at all.

The students used the UCD method one after the other and the previously used should feed information to the next method. The students found it hard to see the relevance in walking the wall and making personas and found these methods a bit disconnected to the remaining methods. On the other hand, they saw the relevance in conducting user testing and iterating the prototypes accordingly. They did three evaluations and iterated the prototypes afterwards, first an informal evaluation of the paper prototypes, then evaluating the UX goals and the third was user testing. This was mostly scheduled during the second week. Some students commented that they would have liked this to be earlier in the course. These comments inspired us to change the course schedule accordingly for the next round of the course.

The latter observation demonstrates that teaching of a method without relevant application of it is very difficult. Rather than being a problem with the method itself, this is a reminder for us educators of the importance of planning teaching activities in a way that students can hopefully understand their logic and make direct connections with their ongoing learning process. Many students commented that they would have wanted to be in more direct contact with users and not only meet the students taking part in the course. They really stressed that they wanted the user testing to be as realistic as possible.

6.2   Reaction to Lessons Learned

Since the students rated realistic prototypes highly and user evaluations, but commented that these methods could have been introduced earlier in the course, we have decided to teach these methods during the first week of the course during the summer 2018. This schedule fits very well to the Google design sprint schedule, where the fourth day focuses on making realistic prototypes and the fifth day focuses on conducting user evaluations with 5 users. We will base the course schedule on the Google design sprint schedule.

During the first week we will follow the Google design sprint schedule completely, like explained in Sect. 2.3. During the second week we will cover user experience in more detail. The students set UX goals and evaluate against those goals. They redesign the hi-fi prototypes and evaluate once more to gather feedback on the user experience. Overall, the focus during the first week is on designing the right product, and during the second one the focus is on designing the product right.

We will choose methods from the Google design sprint process to get the overall idea about the product, setting the stage, setting a long term goal, mapping, sketching, speed critique and storyboarding. These will be the new methods that we will cover. Some are similar to the once given in the course 2017, like sketching is similar to low-fi prototyping, but is now done in context with other methods that are used in advance in the course. We will not include the contextual interviews, the scenarios, the affinity diagram and the walking the wall methods. Also heuristic evaluation will not be covered. These methods were not highly rated by the students and we believe the methods of Google design sprints will work better for the course.

7   Discussion

In relation to hi-fi prototyping, students seemed to particularly like this method, especially how realistic the resulting prototypes were for the users. This finding is in line with the ideas behind the Google Design Sprint [16] with its main premise of seeing how customers react before committing to building a real product. This finding also seems to suggest that for similar one-to-two week student projects, something like Google Design Sprints can help students focus by providing a big challenge, time restraints, and bringing the best individual contributions of everyone on the team.

While the context, respondents, and the questionnaire used in this study were quite different from those used by Churchill et al. [5], we briefly discuss one difference between the results of these two studies. In our study, hi-fi prototyping was rated highly, while in [5], hi-fi prototyping was not even mentioned, although paper/low fidelity prototyping and prototyping (general) were seen highly important. The reason might be that the students enjoy hi-fi prototyping with the modern prototyping tools and see paper prototyping too cumbersome or old-fashioned. Future work is needed to properly study the usefulness of teaching lo- vs. hi-fi prototyping for students.

In relation to software development practice, it is interesting to compare the UCD method ratings made by the students to the frequency of use of UCD methods reported by practitioners. Venturi et al. [24] found that hi-fi prototyping and heuristic evaluation was used frequently, setting quantitative usability goals less frequently, and quantitative usability evaluation (summative) and Personas least frequently. So except for heuristic evaluation, there is good correspondence. This shows that it is possible to effectively teach several of the methods that are most relevant in practice.

8 Conclusion

This paper reports from an empirical study of a two week intense course in UCD for 18 international university-level students. The schedule was switching between lectures and workshops using 15 UCD methods. We used two methods to evaluate the course content and schedule, a weekly questionnaire and a method questionnaire measuring the usefulness of the methods. Both course evaluation methods gave good insights into how to adjust the course for the next occasion. Since the students rated hi-fi prototypes and formal user evaluations highly and commented that these methods were used quite late in the course schedule, we have decided to follow the Google design sprint process during the next occasion of the course. Then hi-fi prototypes will be conducted during the fourth day of the course and formal user evaluations on the fifth day. This will give the students the possibility to see some realistic output earlier in the course, which seems to be appreciated by the students.

References

1. Bark, I., Følstad, A., Gulliksen, J., McEwan, T., Benyon, D.: Use and usefulness of HCI methods: results from an exploratory study among nordic HCI practitioners. In: McEwan, T., Gulliksen, J., Benyon, D. (eds.) People and Computers XIX - The Bigger Picture, pp. 201–217. Springer, London (2006). https://doi.org/10.1007/1-84628-249-7_13
2. Brooke, J.: SUS: a quick and dirty usability scale. In: Jordan, P.W., Thomas, B., Weerdmeester, B.A., McClelland, I.L. (eds.) Usability Evaluation in Industry, pp. 189–194. Taylor & Francis, London (1996)
3. Bruun, A., Stage, J.: Training software development practitioners in usability testing: an assessment acceptance and prioritization. In: Proceedings of the 24th Australian Computer-Human Interaction Conference (OzCHI 2012), pp. 52–60. ACM, New York (2012)
4. Bygstad, B., Ghinea, G., Brevik, E.: Software development methods and usability: Perspectives from a survey in the software industry in Norway. Interact. Comput. 20(3), 375–385 (2008)
5. Churchill, E.F., Bowser, A., Preece, J.: The future of HCI education: a flexible, global, living curriculum. Interactions 23(2), 70–73 (2016)
6. Dayton, T.: Skills needed by user-centered design practitioners in real software development environments. In: Report on the CHI92 Workshop, SIGCHI Bulletin, vol. 25, no. 3, pp. 16–31 (1993)
7. Ezzy, D.: Qualitative Analysis: Practice and Innovation. Psychology Press, Hore (2002)
8. Gulliksen, J., Boivie, I., Persson, J., Hektor, A., Herulf, L.: Making a difference: a survey of the usability profession in Sweden. In: Proceedings of NordiCHI 2004, Tampere, Finland, pp. 207–215 (2004)
9. Gulliksen, J., Göransson, B., Boivie, I., Blomkvist, S., Persson, J., Cajander, Å.: Key principles for user-centred systems design. Behav. Inf. Technol. 22(6), 397–409 (2003)

10. Hill, A.: Problem solving in real-life contexts: an alternative for design in technology education. Int. J. Technol. Des. Educ. **8**, 203–220 (1998)
11. Holtzblatt, K., Wendell, J.B., Wood, S.: Rapid contextual design: a how-to guide to key techniques for user-centered design. Elsevier, San Francisco (2004)
12. Häkli, A.: Introducing user-centred design in a small-size software development organization. Master thesis, Helsinki University of Technology, Department of Computer Science and Engineering (2005)
13. Jia, Y., Larusdottir, M.K., Cajander, Å.: The usage of usability techniques in scrum projects. In: Winckler, M., Forbrig, P., Bernhaupt, R. (eds.) HCSE 2012. LNCS, vol. 7623, pp. 331–341. Springer, Heidelberg (2012). https://doi.org/10.1007/978-3-642-34347-6_25
14. Kaasinen, E., et al.: Defining user experience goals to guide the design of industrial systems. Behav. Inf. Technol. **34**(10), 976–991 (2015)
15. Kawakita, J.: The Original KJ Method. Kawakita Research Institute, Tokyo (1991)
16. Knapp, J., Zeratsky, J., Kowitz, B.: Sprint: How to Solve Big Problems and Test New Ideas in Just Five Days. Simon and Schuster, New York (2016)
17. Lazar, J.K., Barbosa, S.D.: Introduction to human-computer interaction. In: Extended Abstracts of the 2018 CHI Conference on Human Factors in Computing Systems, p. C03. ACM (2018)
18. Lucero, A.: Using affinity diagrams to evaluate interactive prototypes. In: Abascal, J., Barbosa, S., Fetter, M., Gross, T., Palanque, P., Winckler, M. (eds.) INTERACT 2015. LNCS, vol. 9297, pp. 231–248. Springer, Cham (2015). https://doi.org/10.1007/978-3-319-22668-2_19
19. Monahan, K., Lahteenmaki, M., Mcdonald, S., Cockton, G.: An investigation into the use of field methods in the design and evaluation of interactive systems. In: Proceedings of the 22nd British HCI Group Annual Conference, People and Computers, pp. 99–108 (2008)
20. Nielsen, J., Molich, R.: Heuristic evaluation of user interfaces. In: Proceedings of the SIGCHI Conference on Human Factors in Computing Systems, pp. 249–256. ACM (2016)
21. Norman, D.A., Draper, S.W. (eds.): User Centered System Design: New Perspectives on Human-Computer Interaction. Erlbaum, Hillsdale (1986)
22. Prior, S.: HCI methods for including adults with disabilities in the design of CHAMPION. In: CHI 2010 Extended Abstracts on Human Factors in Computing Systems (CHI EA 2010), pp. 2891–2894. ACM, New York (2010)
23. Schwaber, K.: Scrum development process. In: OOPSLA 1995 Workshop on Business Object Design and Implementation (1995)
24. Venturi, T., Troost, J., Jokela, T.: People, organizations, and processes: an inquiry into the adoption of user-centered design in industry. Int. J. Hum. Comput. Interact. **21**(2), 219–238 (2006)
25. Waller, A., Balandin, S.A., O'Mara, D.A., Judson, A.D.: Training AAC users in user-centred design. In Proceedings of the 2005 International Conference on Accessible Design in the Digital World (Accessible Design 2005). BCS Learning & Development (2005)
26. Nicholl, B., Hosking, I.M., Elton, E.M., Lee, Y., Bell, J., Clarkson, P.J.: Inclusive design in the key stage 3 classroom: an investigation of teachers' understanding and implementation of user-centred design principles in design and technology. Int. J. Technol. Des. Educ. **23**(4), 921–938 (2013)

Helping Teams to Help Themselves: An Industrial Case Study on Interdependencies During Sprints

Jil Klünder[1]([⊠])([iD]), Fabian Kortum[1], Thorsten Ziehm[2], and Kurt Schneider[1]

[1] Leibniz University Hannover, Software Engineering Group, Hannover, Germany
{jil.kluender,fabian.kortum,kurt.schneider}@inf.uni-hannover.de
[2] Arvato SCM Solutions, Hannover, Germany
thorsten.ziehm@arvato.com

Abstract. Software process improvement is a very important topic. Almost all companies and organizations face the necessity for improvement sooner or later. Sometimes, there is obvious potential for improvement (e.g., if the number of developers does not fit the project size). Nonetheless, fixing all obvious issues does not necessarily lead to a "perfect" project. There are a lot of interdependencies between project parameters that are difficult to detect – sometimes due to the influences of social aspects which can be hardly grasped.

We want to support the process of improving daily work by simulating and visualizing how project parameters evolve over time. Our approach is based on building a System Dynamics model that takes into account key performance indicators as well as assumptions about social aspects. In the present case, we chose parameters of capacity, customer satisfaction, and mood. The model uncovers interdependencies between the available parameters. Furthermore, it is able to simulate consequences of different preconditions and incidents during a sprint such as change requests.

In this contribution, we present our approach and apply it in a case study with three agile teams in industry. We build a System Dynamics model and use it for sprint simulations. Our analysis determined, e.g., the teams' productivity during the sprint and their workload each day. The simulation increased the teams' awareness of the negative influences due to interventions during the sprint.

Keywords: Process improvement · Simulation · System dynamics
Agile software development teams · Social aspects

1 Introduction

Companies strive for a good rate of successful projects. To reach this aim, they often face the necessity for software process improvement. There are various existing approaches to improve the development process [14]. However, it does

Published by Springer Nature Switzerland AG 2019
C. Bogdan et al. (Eds.): HCSE 2018, LNCS 11262, pp. 31–50, 2019.
https://doi.org/10.1007/978-3-030-05909-5_3

not necessarily suffice to apply the existing approaches. Implementing an agile environment is a commonly used possibility to overcome many problems. Hence, it is a common way to improve the process [14]. However, becoming agile is not always the key [8]. The same problem may occur when implementing other approaches to improve the development process. We expect that team members lack an understanding for the interdependencies within the entire software development process [13]. This lack can reduce the success when implementing existing approaches.

We assume that a simulation model can increase this understanding by simulating and visualizing the dependencies [13]. In this contribution, we present an objective, data-based approach for visualizing and discovering project dynamics and tendencies which may be too subtle to be found by humans or which are too obvious to recognize the major consequences. To facilitate the application of our technique, we base our approach on already existing or easily collectible data for example from tools like JIRA. Based on this data, we automatically calculate correlations and interdependencies between the variables like productivity (represented by finished story points), mood (represented by scales from psychology [20] or from a mood board with emoticons) or the capacity. These calculations result in a System Dynamics model simulating and visualizing the hypothetic state of a sprint with given preconditions. When a team is modeled with System Dynamics, that team can use the model to recognize factors hindering an optimal sprint or impediments that need to be resolved in order to be more successful.

In this paper, we present our approach and its application in a case study at Arvato SCM Solutions[1]. The company initiated a collaboration with the Leibniz University Hannover considering fundamentals about methods and toolchains. These fundamentals would reveal, e.g., the tendencies of sprint success criteria, customer satisfaction during a sprint, or factors influencing a positive impression by the client. The industry partner had already experienced general impediments such as changing the scope of a sprint which has negative effects to reach the sprint goal. During the kick-off of the collaboration, an interest in social interactions and dependencies in the teams arose. The Software Engineering Group at Leibniz University Hannover has some experiences in analyzing interactions in a team such as the FLOW method[2] for information flow analysis in developer teams or tools for the analysis of interactions in meetings [17]. Developers, manager, Scrum master and product owner[3] of the industry partner wanted to

---

[1] https://scm.arvato.com/en.html.

[2] http://www.se.uni-hannover.de/pages/en:projekte_flow.

[3] At Arvato SCM Solutions, the manager, Scrum master, and product owner build a triumvirate for a team. The manager is responsible for the people management and their personal evolution, the Scrum master is responsible for the processes in the agile environment and the product owner is responsible for the enhancements of the product and the functional stories.

know if these tools can be applied in an agile environment and if they can help to get better results for a sprint if the teams know their social impediments.

Arvato SCM Solutions wanted to get a supportive tool helping a development team to identify its impediments to reach the goal of its sprints. In particular, such a tool would help Scrum master and product owner to realize which influences their behavior can have.

As a further requirement, the team members should be able to understand the outcome of the model, i.e. the result of the simulation needs to be reliable. Otherwise, the team may refuse the model.

Building such a model is not trivial. While some parameters such as productivity (in terms of finished story points) can be easily quantified, others such as mood cannot. Hence, we need to combine both qualitative and quantitative data. We can formulate our research question as follows:

> RQ: *Is it possible to build a System Dynamics model including both qualitative and quantitative data with comprehensible, i.e. traceable, results?*

As a first step towards this aim, the researchers from Leibniz University Hannover analyzed three development teams at Arvato SCM Solutions. The teams had just started their agile transition to Scrum some months before the study began. One team was in sprint number 22, another in sprint number 13 and the third team in sprint number 8 (with a length of two weeks per sprint). The case study took place over a duration of 18 months starting with a data collection and ending with the presentation of the model and its application. The duration of the study was due to the explorative nature. Replications of this study will not take that much time.

The simulation of the sprint and the analysis with the System Dynamics model uncover i.a. the fact that the teams' productivity increases towards the end of a sprint. Some of the found issues can also be found in other teams. Nonetheless, the model does not adequately represent the process and the interdependencies between the variables in a team of another organization. Therefore, we describe our approach to build the model. This procedure can be applied to other teams with a different data set.

The paper is structured as follows: In the following section, we give an introduction to System Dynamics. Previous work related to our research topic is presented in Sect. 3. Section 4 gives an overview of the study we conducted at Arvato SCM Solutions. It also provides information on building the model. We discuss our results in Sect. 5 and conclude in Sect. 6.

2 Background: System Dynamics

System Dynamics was developed to understand the behavior of complex systems [3]. In the 1950s, Forrester [3] presented his approach for modeling different parameters in order to understand industrial processes. System Dynamics enables holistic analyses and simulations of complex and dynamic behaviors. The simulation is based on a model taking into account relationships between various project parameters. Forrester [3] presented a strategy for identifying such relationships and for modeling and simulating the interdependencies. We use this approach to gain more profound insights into the interdependencies and the project's dynamics [4].

2.1 Causal Loop Diagrams

Causal loop diagrams visualize interrelations between different variables in a system [3]. An example is visualized in Fig. 1. *Mood* (1), *Productivity* and *Customer Satisfaction* are considered. A positive marked directed edge (2), a so-called **positive causal link**, denotes a positive relation, i.e. if customer satisfaction increases, mood also increases. It is also possible to visualize negative relationships, i.e. if one parameter increases, the other one decreases and vice versa. Such links are called **negative causal links**. One example for this relationship is the influence of unexpected incidents during the sprint on mood: The more incidents, the more dissatisfied developers, i.e. the lower the amount of positive affect.

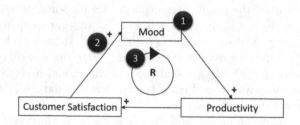

Fig. 1. Exemplary causal loop diagram visualizing a positive reinforcing loop.

A **reinforcing feedback loop** is defined to have an exponential increase or decrease. Mathematically, this is equivalent to having an even number of negative links (where 0 is also even). In Fig. 1, the reinforcing loop is visualized by (3). A **balancing feedback loop** is associated with reaching a plateau. This is equivalent to having an odd number of negative links. A balancing feedback loop is denoted as visualized with a "B" (instead of the "R" in (3)) and an arrow pointing counterclockwise [4].

2.2 Stock and Flow Diagram

Stock and flow diagrams concretize causal diagrams by quantifying the system. They are used to study and analyze systems on a more detailed level. An example is visualized in Fig. 2. These diagrams consist of **stocks** (1) and **flows** (3). A stock represents an entity, i.e. parameter, that changes over time. A flow defines the rate of a change in a stock. So far unknown influences and parameters can be visualized by a **cloud** (2). In the given example, we have an influence of something not specified (2) on *mood* (1). The rate of the influence is defined by the flow (3).

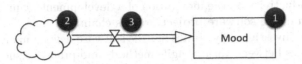

Fig. 2. Exemplary stock flow diagram.

Each flow can be concretized by an equation. These equations and the feedback loops enable a simulation of the process. The better the equations define the influences, the more accurate is the simulation in the end.

3 Related Work

This paper aims at analyzing interdependencies between different parameters during a sprint. Some of these parameters are **social aspects** like communication behavior [9,10]. Since soft factors can be hardly quantified, the commonly used methods to analyze human beings are rather subjective. In this approach, we use already established methods for modeling and simulating the specific context, for instance with **System Dynamics** [3] to combine qualitative and quantitative data.

Klünder et al. [9] quantify communication behavior using the so-called FLOW distance. FLOW distance is a measure for indirections in information flow. Furthermore, the authors measure moods and social conflicts using scales which are established in psychology like the scale for positive and negative affect [20]. This way, the authors are able to find statistically significant relationships between communication behavior, mood, and social conflicts [9].

Herbsleb and Mockus [5] also investigate on communication behavior. They analyze the behavior of co-located and distributed work teams. Their study is based on quantified data from the source code change management and a survey. The authors aim at finding causes for delay in distributed teams. Herbsleb and Mockus [5] are able to uncover relationships between delay, communication, coordination, and geographical distance. They report a decrease in the frequency of communication with an increasing physical separation [5].

These studies base on subjective quantified data which often depends on the perceptions of the team members (cf. [9]). All proposed metrics we are able to measure are integrated into our approach.

To find interdependencies between qualitative and quantitative parameters as well as to integrate assumptions, we modeled the results using System Dynamics.

The idea of simulating human factors and other project parameters is not new. Abdel-Hamid and Madnick [1] investigated dynamic events in Software Engineering. They present different case studies of large software projects.

Furthermore, they propose the use of metrics which help to measure the relevant aspects. Based on the data records and their experiences, the authors build system models with different complexities. Abdel-Hamid and Madnick [1] give a detailed overview of various dynamic models underlining, for example, the influence of productivity on the motivation of a development team. Furthermore, they present an entire software project process chain.

Cao et al. [2] investigate dynamics in agile software development. They model interdependencies between various agile methods and practices such as pair programming, customer involvement or refactoring and organizational parameters such as productivity or cost. The authors also use System Dynamics to generate the simulation model [2].

Madachy [15] models communication behavior and other team parameters. He simulates qualitative models to understand process dynamics. His work is based on formal boundary expressions with a wide range of parameter settings.

Hoegl et al. [6] present a concept about the quality of teamwork. They identify factors influencing the success of software projects. They consider aspects such as team performance and satisfaction. The relevant factors for teamwork are communication, coordination, a balance of contribution, mutual support, effort, and cohesion [6]. The authors base their results on an empirical study providing data from 575 developers and project leaders in 145 German software development laboratories [6].

Shiohama et al. [19] deal with the question of an appropriate iteration length. They present a procedure to calculate the recommended iteration length by simulating the sprint. They integrate parameters such as the development team, the probability of incidents during the sprint and the complexity of the project.

In previous studies, Kortum et al. [11] have already explored team behavior in academic software projects. The first models [7,11] base on machine learning classifier and enable forecasts for key communication metrics. But these models only considered linear dependencies and few quantitative data. We want to extend these approaches by also considering non-linear interdependencies [13] and qualitative data.

In contrast to the already existing approaches, we do not want to answer a specific question using our simulation. Indeed, we want to explore team dynamics to uncover unexpected interdependencies. Nonetheless, we integrate results of already existing models such as measurements, metrics and best practices for setting up the model. Furthermore, we integrate data types which have – to the best of our knowledge – not yet been considered in related approaches. These are results from an interview study uncovering the information flow and results from a workshop representing subjective assumptions about the relationships to use unquantifiable data such as moods[4].

---

[4] There are possibilities to measure moods (e.g. with the PANAS scale [20]). But in our case study, it was not possible to measure moods retrospectively.

4   Study: Setting up the Model

In order to examine the applicability of our approach, we conducted a case study in a company. The whole study based on a collaboration between Arvato SCM Solutions and the Leibniz University Hannover.

4.1   Methodology

Our general approach can be divided into several phases starting with the data collection and ending in the simulation model. An overview of these phases is visualized in Fig. 3.

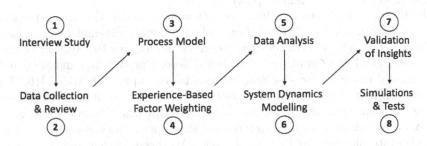

Fig. 3. Overview of the process

(1) Phase one starts with *interview studies* to get to know the culture of the company and the processes from an external viewpoint. We need to gain these insights in order to prepare the causality model. The structure of the interviews bases on the FLOW method [18] which is an already established proceeding in software engineering to get an overview the information flow within an organization and to get to know the process from different viewpoints.

(2) Afterwards, we collect different kinds of easily available *data records*. It is necessary to receive as much data as possible influencing the main issues which should be analyzed with the simulation model. Later, it is possible to integrate assumptions for non-accessible data (see (4)). We recommend using data for example contained in JIRA such as productivity, finished and open story points, sprint interruptions and so on.

(3) In phase three, we create a potential *process model* also visualizing assumed dependencies between the collected data and other variables like mood. This model does not necessarily rely on the data. Calculations are also not necessary. This first instance of the process model only represents possible and intuitive interdependencies between the variables. It will be validated later.

(4) During phase four, we integrate *subjective perceptions* from different team members, Scrum master, and other involved persons. They are asked to rate

the causal effects in the process model (for example the influence of customer satisfaction on team mood) and to specify and concrete the model. The more different persons the more reliable and the more complete the subjective results are. We recommend using a scale between -3 (for a strong negative relation) and +3 (for a strong positive relation). A rating of 0 indicates no relationship between the two variables. This way, the analyst gains an overview and a first idea of relationships and dependencies. This step is very important for the developers' awareness of the final model.

(5) Afterwards, the *analysis* starts with a visual preparation of the data with respect to history, temporal progressions and other effects. The analyst also looks for relationships between variables in the data set that are easy to detect. In the best case, these relationships also fit the interview study and the model resulting from step (4).

(6) Phase six aims at creating the *System Dynamics model*. This step is the most time-consuming one. A description on how to set up the model can be found in [12] and [13]. We transfer the causality model into the System Dynamics model. The relationships between different project parameters can be retrieved using *explorative data analysis* for example with MINE [16]. This analysis helps to detect dependencies between the variables. Furthermore, the explorative analysis can detect relationships which have been unknown so far. Afterwards, we need to formalize the dependencies in order to include them into the System Dynamics model. We need further analyses, logical associations and a clean-up of the data set with respect to missing data. In this step, we can use the ratings from step (4). For example: In the case that all developers state that the presence of the product owner during the sprint is very important for their motivation, this fact needs to be considered in the model even if there exist no underlying data. This way, we conclude the model step by step. It gets more and more concrete and detailed. The whole model might be too large. Hence, irrelevant factors (according to the aim of the model) can be identified and eliminated. The model's behavior in seldom situations is also very interesting. Hence, the model should be analyzed by running the simulation 1000 times.

(7) In the last step, we *validate the insights* from the model by comparing them with the data sources, i.e. the development teams. This can be done best during a workshop with the developers, the managers and the persons who are responsible for the process. Presenting some behavior and structures with the model may or may not lead to a "wow"-effect. The model aims at increasing the awareness of the involved persons with respect to possibly unknown or forgotten interdependencies. Hence, it is very good if the persons agree with the model.

(8) Now, the persons can start *using and testing the model* by changing some parameters like sprint interruptions. The more intuitively the model behaves, the more they will rely on it. But some unexpected issues are also important to show the impact of the model. It does not aim at forecasting exact values, but it aims at visualizing the system's behavior and increasing the transparency of consequences in order to enable some improvements.

4.2   Execution: Case Study in Industry

The whole study at Arvato SCM Solutions was performed as on-site research, where the researchers got to know the common behavior of managers, some Scrum master, and developers. By being involved in meetings with regular team members participating, the researchers could grasp a better understanding compared to an external person about the collaboration structures and company spirits. The collected impression and representative system data formed the fundamentals of the idea of a simulation model about the team's operational behavior in such this exemplary company.

(1) Some weeks later, the interview studies started according to the *FLOW method* [18]. A FLOW interview has a generalized process starting with some general questions like tasks within the team or the years of experiences of the interviewed person. This way, a basic understanding of the internal processes in the Scrum teams and the information exchange with the product owner and the customer emerged. For each task, the interviewee reports about the outcome as well as incoming, controlling and supporting issues like templates, knowledge or checklists [18]. The researchers interviewed three persons: one product owner, one developer and one SQL expert who is part of two teams. Descriptive data can be found in Table 1. The interviewees are members of the teams we considered in the further analysis. The team members were free to decide whether they wanted to give an interview or not.

Table 1. Overview of the interviewees and the duration of the interviews

	Interviewee I	Interviewee II	Interviewee III
Duration of the interview	2 h	1,5 h	2 hours
Team	1	2, 3	3
Team exists since	3 months	6 resp. 3 months	3 months
Team member since	3 months	6 resp. 3 months	3 months
Role	Product owner	SQL expert	Developer

(2) One researcher from Leibniz University Hannover dedicated two weeks on-site at Arvato SCM Solutions to gain deeper insight into communication behavior and social aspects such as mood, productivity and the collaboration between the team and the product owner. The researcher observed three teams who agreed to participate in the study. Data from JIRA have also been collected from all sprints such as burndown charts, i.e. the reduction of unfinished story cards during the sprint. The researchers received data about sprint results, i.e. finished and not-finished story points, and the burndown charts. Furthermore, data about the teams' capacities and the customer satisfaction which have been collected in the company right from

the beginning have also been included in the model. Unfortunately, there was no data representing the mood of a single team, because the "mood board" is used by all teams. Hence, it only represents the overall mood and it was impossible to distinguish between the data from the three observed teams and all the others in the company.

(3) Afterwards, the modeling phase started by drawing a causality diagram mainly resulting from the insights of the work shadowing. It only contains rather obvious dependencies and relationships. It was designed very light-weighted with some keywords like mood, motivation, productivity and capacity connected by directed arrows. The causality diagram is visualized in Fig. 4. The researchers expect an influence of HR-Capacity, i.e., the availability or absence of developers, on the sprint and the commitment constancy, i.e., the proportion of the story points the team wanted to finish during the sprint and the story points which are finished. This parameter influences customer satisfaction which influences the team mood. This, in turn, influences the whole sprint which also influences burndown charts and the customer satisfaction. The burndown chart represents the number of already finished story points and is hence an indicator of commitment constancy.

(4) The model in Fig. 4 was the basis for the next step. Two researchers met some interested persons from the company in a two-hour-workshop. Two Scrum master and four developers attended the workshop. One manager also temporarily attended the workshop. The participants were asked to rate the relevance of the relationships and find other dependencies. In pairs, they completed the diagram, removed arrows, added weightings representing the number of influences of one parameter on another one, and so on. We used a scale as proposed in the previous subsection in step (4). At the end of this workshop, the researchers had an overall causality diagram representing the perceptions of the persons who are involved in the process. This step was important to increase the credibility of the model. The cumulated results of this step are visualized in Fig. 5. Compared to Fig. 4, we have much more parameters after this step. Most of the parameters from step (3) remain, but the developers and the Scrum master stated a strong influence of meetings like refinements, the retrospective and the review on other factors. Furthermore, they rated the availability of the product owner as important.

(5) Afterwards, the data analysis started. The researchers used system records provided by JIRA and subjective responses about each sprints team capacity and the customer satisfaction. They derived metrics such as productivity as a measure defined via finished story points per hour or the customer satisfaction index derived from the customers' ratings. The metrics were combined for example with timely delivery and resource balancing. Additionally, timestamps have been divided into weekdays, holiday breaks and other events that could influence the teams' regular performances. Due to the information on burndown charts, i.e. the relation of finished and remaining story points, unplanned work (e.g. bug fixing) has also been considered.

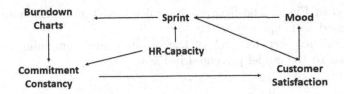

Fig. 4. First causality diagram in the end of step (3)

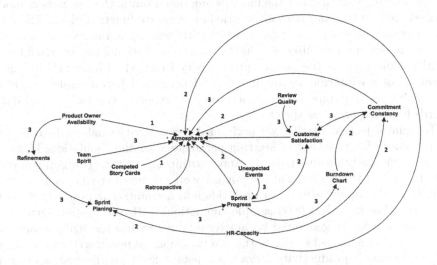

Fig. 5. Causality Model with weighted relationships (+/-: positive/negative relationship (i.e. "the more, the more"/"the more, the less") in the direction of the arrow; 1/2/3: weak/medium/strong relationship)

These incidents could be recognized due to an increasing number of story points in the sprint.

(6) In fact, all this information from the first five steps, especially the outcome presented in Fig. 5, allow to derive a first System Dynamics model based on the standardized stock-flow terminology [4]. In its very first building step, it only gives a system overview of all involved endogenous and exogenous components [4]. For the formalization of functional equations representing the interdependencies between various system components, we applied exploratory factor analysis to describe historical JIRA data in multi-functional equations. The dependencies and influencing factors without available objective data records become distinctively equalized through the rating from step (4).

The System Dynamics module for the productivity is visualized in Fig. 6 (marked with an (x)). This is one part of the whole System Dynamics model. Additionally, a dashboard user interface was built for exploratory simulation without a detailed need for knowing about every single module. A screenshot can be found in Fig. 7. The System Dynamics model and dashboard interface can be accessed and explored online[5].

Performing this step for each of the variables and combining each of the modules leads to the model presented in Fig. 6.

4.3   Verification and Validation

(7) For a better validation of the model's functional units, the researchers modularized each central and relevant metric in a separate function block. The correct functional operating was approached with real input ranges, whereas the outcome passed a plausibility test due to realistic operational ranges. Each functional module such as the one for productivity (marked with an (x)) in Fig. 6 characterizes its internal factor and dependencies and become solely verified in its input and outcome behavior according to experts expectations and data records from the previous sprint.

To gain objective results, we performed a sensitivity analysis to consider the influence of a given set of starting parameters for the simulation. Figure 8 visualizes the daily productivity dynamics within one sprint. The x-axis represents the day of the sprint, and the y-axis covers the productivity on a rational scale. Since the model also takes weekends into account: The productivity is 0 some days. We have run 9000 sample simulations with the System Dynamics model and randomly generated parameter settings within the realistic operating ranges. As visualized in Fig. 8, the 100 variations of parametric inputs show that the common productivity follows a constant level for the first week of a new sprint. The results also sample that most dynamics during a sprint occur during the second half of a two weeks sprint. The course of the curves is comparable. Sensitivity analysis, in particular, involved the parameter inserts for a sprint planning about available human resources (60–150 working hours) and story points (80–120). There is an obvious increase in productivity in the last days of the sprint which seems to keep its proportional distribution regardless of whether teams have to face a high workload or not. In fact, the simulations pointed out that the teams typically finish larger story cards upfront the end of a sprint. Furthermore, they seem to finish story cards even with double speed compared to tasks at the beginning of the sprint. The term "double speed" is relative since the results also can be interpreted as that teams work slower at the beginning of a sprint and increase their regular performance shortly before the due date. In fact, the simulation uncovered some of the real situations that could be also confirmed by the management about their perceived impression on the team's typical workload during a two weeks sprint. When teams faced real pressuring situations due to last minute changes, customer claims, or an inappropriate sprint planning, the resulted team atmosphere became strongly affected, whereas particular situations could be also matched within the system model. This analysis based on a regular sprint with ten days and without extraordinary events decreasing a team's productivity such as holiday breaks. During sprints

---

[5] The System Dynamics model is available via http://www.goo.gl/Bnavhb.

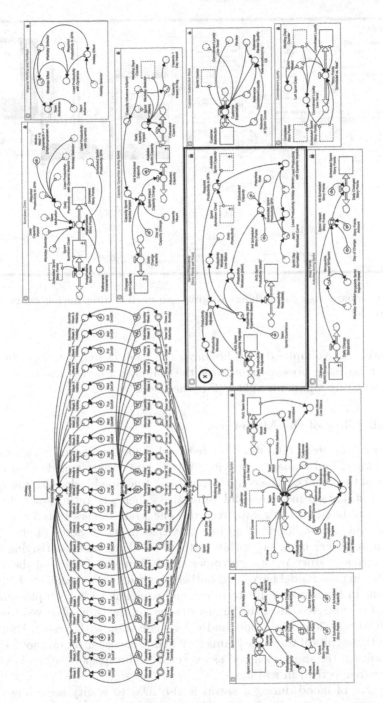

Fig. 6. System dynamics Model. The productivity module is highlighted.

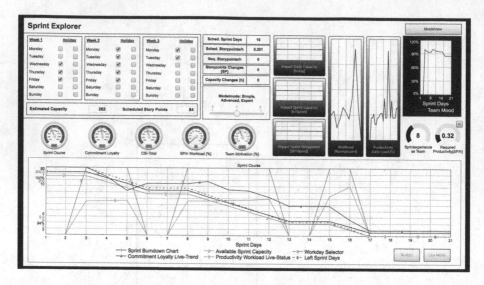

Fig. 7. Dashboard visualizing different sprint parameters after having entered given preconditions

with breaks, for example, due to holidays, the peak of maximum productivity appears to be more present right after the holidays, whereas the productivity tends to reach its minimum right before the break.

4.4 Reliability of the Model

(8) To ensure the credibility of the entire model, some developers, Scrum master, product owner, and manager used it with different inputs and decided on the reliability of the results.[6] The conjunctions of all function blocks with the system resulted in statistical measures and subjective experience ratings as well. They were also validated through data records. The practitioners tested the model using different preconditions of sprints they had in mind. Some of the sprints have been "regular" ones, i.e. sprints without incidents and a satisfying sprint result in terms of story points, customer satisfaction etc. Others of the sprints used for testing the model have been outliers, i.e. with many incidents like bugs, fluctuations in the capacity due to illness and company-wide both pleasant and unpleasant events. According to the practitioners in the three observed teams at Arvato SCM Solutions, the model and the visualization with System Dynamics simulates the sprints of the three teams very well. The visualization shows similar sprint results in the simulation and as expected (in futurespective) and as it has been (in retrospective) in real life.

The curve of mood during a sprint is also near to reality according to the product owner and the developers. This was checked with sprints out of the

---

[6] For validity reasons and to test the generalizability (to some extent) of the model, we also asked team-external persons (but no company-external ones) to test the model.

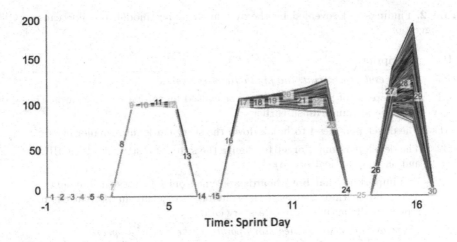

Fig. 8. Productivity variance results from 100 sample simulations

period of data collection, including sprints after this phase and also with sprints in other teams in the company environment at Arvato SCM Solutions.

All in all, the model behaves intuitively in many points. This is very important for the reliability of the model. Nonetheless, there are some relationships which have been perceived to have a lower relevance for the development process.

4.5 Results and Implications

We, i.e. the researcher, manager, Scrum master, and other team members, detected some findings revealed by simulating real and potential sprints with the model. In Table 2, we present some of these weaknesses with suggestions for improvement. The suggestions and the causes for the findings are not complete. The causes need to be identified. This still requires manual effort and background knowledge. Combining the simulation with insights from the researcher's hospitation and the practitioners' experience led to the following result.

5 Discussion

According to our results, we can affirm our research question. It is possible to combine qualitative and quantitative data in a System Dynamics model and maintaining the credibility.

5.1 Threats to Validity

There are some aspects and limitations which may have to threaten the validity of our case study. According to Wohlin et al. [21], we categorize these aspects as *construct, internal, external* and *conclusion validity*.

Table 2. Findings (F) revealed by the system dynamics model, possible causes (C) and suggestions (S)

ID	Description
F1	*In the end of a sprint, the productivity increases*
C1	The increase of productivity may be caused by too large story cards, the developers cannot finish earlier
S1	The developers need to break down the story cards into smaller ones
C2	The developers may forget to change the state of a story card (in JIRA and on the physical board)
S2	It is important that both boards are synchronized (latest in the next daily). Furthermore, at least the state of a story card in JIRA needs to represent the actual state of a story card
F2	*There are often unfinished story points in the end of a sprint*
C3	The goal of the sprint in the number of story points was unachievable
S3	Provide the possibility to learn from former sprints, e.g. how many story points have been finished
C4	There have been too many incidents during the sprint leading to less capacity
S4.1	Try to keep the number of incidents (e.g. helping other teams) small
S4.2	Get to know about planned support in other teams before the sprint starts
C5	There have been undetected dependencies between story cards.
S5	Spend as much time as necessary with planning the next sprint, i.e. backlog refinement, Sprint planning etc
F3	*Incidents influence the motivation, the mood and the productivity*
S6	An incident goes along with adapting the plan. Often, the developers lose focus and realize that they cannot reach their sprint goal. This mostly leads to dissatisfaction
C6	It is often impossible to have no incidents. But avoiding firefighting situations helps the team to keep focused.
F4	*Positive incidents such as story cards that are excluded from the sprint are not always good*
C7	An exclusion of a story card creates the feeling of having much more time for the other story cards. Hence, the productivity decreases
S7	The team should be aware of possible negative impacts of positive incidents. However, with an increasing agile maturity, the team will be satisfied with positive incidents without reducing the productivity

Construct validity. The presented model based on both objective and subjective measures. The causality diagram completely depends on the perceptions of some team members and Scrum master. In the case where we do not have had any objective data for the simulation model, we indicated the dependencies and influences as supposed by the developers. This may have influenced the perceptions of the developers when seeing the overall model and its reliability.

Internal validity. In this contribution, we present the results of a case study with three agile working teams within one organization. We used the data from all teams simultaneously to create one overall diagram. Hence, we cannot make any statements with overall validity. The three teams do not represent the whole width of agile working teams. It is like a case study that generalizations are only limited possible.

Conclusion validity. The data analysis was completely computer-supported. It was based on the MINE [16] algorithm as presented in [12]. Hence, the analysis is objective and the results based on the data, too. But we do not have any objective data for mood. Since we wanted to include this parameter in the model, we used subjective perceptions of experienced team members and Scrum master reporting on the influences of mood on other parameters and vice versa. But this data is only little reliable.

External validity. The results may not be over-generalized. But the proceeding for the creation of the model may be applied to different kinds of teams, even working in different contexts and with other work-organizations like the V-model. Basing the model on the data of other teams or even on different kind of data (i.e., different variables) will surely lead to a different model. At this time, the model is team-specific. But including the data from other teams and extending the model will allow generalizations.

5.2   Limitations for the Use in Industry

The model has restrictions when a team has a high degree of agile maturity. It took more than a year to get the model and the visualization by System Dynamics. In between most of the teams improved their skills. They improved their technical skills, they improved the ability to handle impediments and interventions in the sprint, they improved estimations of the stories, and they improved the skills in team working, communication and other soft skills. In sum, they improved their level of agile maturity. With the new team constellations, the model is difficult to validate, because Arvato SCM Solutions does not collect all the data needed as a database for the model anymore. Because of the agile maturity, these teams do not need all kind of data for their continuous improvement process.

Now the teams can handle interventions and changes in a sprint very well, and they reached the defined goal of the sprint near to 100% defined as committed vs. achieved story points. Also, the product owner has high confidence in the development team and therefore the mood is good – mostly. Because of the combination of missing data and the stable mood, the model and the visualization do not work anymore for our teams – at least in the current version.

Retrospectively, Arvato SCM Solutions could identify the same tasks for improvement for a team through this simulation. For example, most of the stories in a sprint were set to state *"done"* during the last three days in a sprint. This could mean that the team is most productive only at the end of the sprint. But according to the experiences of the managers at Arvato SCM Solutions, in most cases, there are too many stories in a sprint with more than 13 story points for a story, which is the largest possible number of story points for a single story card. They are too big. The teams do not have a chance to finish this story earlier in a sprint. One solution is to increase the ability of the team to split bigger stories into smaller ones which require knowledge in story splitting.

A conclusion: The module and System Dynamics simulation is working very well for teams which are in the transition from an old work environment to an agile framework like Scrum. There is a need to collect a lot of data to use this model and tooling. But using a ticket system like JIRA, facilitates the selection. It is not easy to identify the correct actions for improvement. However, the simulation will support a team to make their challenges more visible. Finding the right solutions will depend on the team, and they have to try out different ways.

5.3   Interpretation

Software process improvement is an important topic for many teams and organizations. However, detecting the potential for improvement is not always easy since most processes are too complex to see the interdependencies "on the fly". Tools can support the detection of issues that may be improved.

Software development teams prefer support by tools and the management tends to use visualizations. Visualizations like burndown charts show the current state and the past progress of a sprint. This System Dynamics model can simulate the next sprint and visualize a sprint result under different circumstances such as added or deleted stories, added resources supporting the team, sick members or members of vacation, etc. Based on the results, the team and the Scrum master can identify the challenges and try different variants and find potential solutions.

This concrete model and the simulation are only helpful for teams when they use Scrum as a work environment and do not have a mixture of a classic work environment such as the waterfall model. The goal of a successful sprint should be nearby 100% of achieving the committed stories and story points. A permanent over- or under-commitment for a sprint does not help to get a stable team result. Two other preconditions for using this model is to have a stable team, and the sprints have to have a fixed length for a long time.

To use this model, it is important to have a good base of data and information. All data about the sprints (stories, story points and the states of the stories) should be in a ticket system like JIRA. The information about team capacity and mood factor should be tracked in parallel. When this data is available for a team, this model can be adopted by another organization.

In summary, this model can be a good addition to the general toolset for Scrum. By simulating future sprints and running sprints from the past with different circumstances, the challenges and impediments in a team can be better analyzed – and supported by a tool. All these information can help a team and the Scrum master to identify the next actions to increase their agile maturity and in the end the productivity and profitability of a team.

A foresight: This model and its simulation is a good base for full-service tooling which can be used by each Scrum team. All needed information for the sprint (stories, story points, length of a sprint, etc.), the number of team members, a capacity planning of the team and other parameters for soft factors should be tracked in one tool. JIRA is a system which handles most of the information when it is used as a ticket system by the development team. It is also possible to develop add-ons in JIRA to put additional data into a sprint. So an add-on for JIRA bringing in all needed parameters to the general sprint data can be used to visualize sprints with a different view.

6 Conclusion

In this contribution, we presented strong synergies between different techniques for analyzing teams. We combined statistical and information flow analysis to build a System Dynamics model simulating interdependencies between various team parameters in agile software development. We extended quantitative data from JIRA by subjective ratings from the teams. This combination of objective and subjective statements on interdependencies helped to form the simulation model with a good prescription of dynamic team behavior during sprints.

The outcome of running the simulation fits the first expectations of both the researchers and the developers as well as Scrum master, product owner, and manager. Despite the model simulates the reality very well and is easy to use, the time for the realization needs to be shortened to replicate this study. Currently, the model is limited in the possibilities for the application. It may be adapted to other teams and organizations, but at the moment, it is only applicable to the development teams at Arvato SCM Solutions or comparable ones. But within the scope of application, the model represents the reality very fine-grained and reveals interdependencies which have not been observed before.

References

1. Abdel-Hamid, T., Madnick, S.E.: Software Project Dynamics: An Integrated Approach. Prentice-Hall Inc., Upper Saddle River (1991)
2. Cao, L., Ramesh, B., Abdel-Hamid, T.: Modeling dynamics in agile software development. ACM Trans. Manag. Inf. Syst. (TMIS) 1(1), 5 (2010)
3. Forrester, J.W.: World Dynamics. Wright-Allen Press, Lawrence (1971)
4. Forrester, J.W.: System dynamics, systems thinking, and soft OR. Syst. Dyn. Rev. 10(2–3), 245–256 (1994)
5. Herbsleb, J.D., Mockus, A.: An empirical study of speed and communication in globally distributed software development. IEEE Trans. Softw. Eng. 29(6), 481–494 (2003)
6. Hoegl, M., Gemuenden, H.G.: Teamwork quality and the success of innovative projects: a theoretical concept and empirical evidence. Organ. Sci. 12(4), 435–449 (2001)

7. Klünder, J., Karras, O., Kortum, F., Schneider, K.: Forecasting communication behavior in student software projects. In: Proceedings of the 12th International Conference on Predictive Models and Data Analytics in Software Engineering. ACM (2016). https://doi.org/10.1145/2972958.2972961

8. Klünder, J., Schmitt, A., Hohl, P., Schneider, K.: Fake news: simply agile. In: Proceedings of the Conference on Projektmanagement und Vorgehensmodelle 2017 (2017)

9. Klünder, J., Schneider, K., Kortum, F., Straube, J., Handke, L., Kauffeld, S.: Communication in teams - an expression of social conflicts. In: Bogdan, C., Gulliksen, J., Sauer, S., Forbrig, P., Winckler, M., Johnson, C., Palanque, P., Bernhaupt, R., Kis, F. (eds.) HCSE/HESSD -2016. LNCS, vol. 9856, pp. 111–129. Springer, Cham (2016). https://doi.org/10.1007/978-3-319-44902-9_8

10. Klünder, J., Unger-Windeler, C., Kortum, F., Schneider, K.: Team meetings and their relevance for the software development process over time. In: Proceedings of Euromicro Conference on Software Engineering and Advanced Applications (2017)

11. Kortum, F., Klünder, J.: Early diagnostics on team communication: Experience-based forecasts on student software projects. In: Proceedings of the 10th International Conference on the Quality of Information and Communications Technology (QUATIC), pp. 166–171. IEEE (2016)

12. Kortum, F., Klünder, J., Schneider, K.: Characterizing relationships for system dynamics models supported by exploratory data analysis. In: Proceedings of the 29th International Conference on Software Engineering and Knowledge Engineering. KSI Research Inc. (2017)

13. Kortum, F., Klünder, J., Schneider, K.: Don't underestimate the human factors! exploring team communication effects. In: Felderer, M., Méndez Fernández, D., Turhan, B., Kalinowski, M., Sarro, F., Winkler, D. (eds.) PROFES 2017. LNCS, vol. 10611, pp. 457–469. Springer, Cham (2017). https://doi.org/10.1007/978-3-319-69926-4_36

14. Kuhrmann, M., Diebold, P., Münch, J.: Software process improvement: a systematic mapping study on the state of the art. PeerJ Comput. Sci. **2**, e62 (2016)

15. Madachy, R.J.: Software Process Dynamics. Wiley, Hoboken (2007)

16. Reshef, D.N., et al.: Detecting novel associations in large data sets. Science **334**(6062), 1518–1524 (2011)

17. Schneider, K., Klünder, J., Kortum, F., Handke, L., Straube, J., Kauffeld, S.: Positive affect through interactions in meetings: the role of proactive and supportive statements. J. Syst. Softw. **143**, 59–70 (2018)

18. Schneider, K., Stapel, K., Knauss, E.: Beyond documents: visualizing informal communication. In: Requirements Engineering Visualization, 2008. REV 2008, pp. 31–40. IEEE (2008)

19. Shiohama, R., Washizaki, H., Kuboaki, S., Sakamoto, K., Fukazawa, Y.: Estimate of the appropriate iteration length in agile development by conducting simulation. In: Agile Conference (AGILE), 2012. pp. 41–50. IEEE (2012)

20. Watson, D., Clark, L.A., Tellegen, A.: Development and validation of brief measures of positive and negative affect: the PANAS scales. J. Pers. Soc. Psychol. **54**(6), 1063 (1988)

21. Wohlin, C., Runeson, P., Höst, M., Ohlsson, M.C., Regnell, B., Wesslén, A.: Experimentation in Software Engineering. Springer, Heidelberg (2012). https://doi.org/10.1007/978-3-642-29044-2

Participatory Ideation for Gamification: Bringing the User at the Heart of the Gamification Design Process

Thomas Vilarinho[1]([✉]), Babak Farshchian[2], Jacqueline Floch[1], and Ole Gunhildsberg Hansen[2]

[1] SINTEF, Trondheim, Norway
{thomas.vilarinho,jacqueline.floch}@sintef.no
[2] Norwegian University of Science and Technology, Trondheim, Norway
Babak.Farshchian@ntnu.no, ole.gunhildsberg.hansen@gmail.com

Abstract. Gamification, i.e. applying game elements in non-game contexts, is been increasingly used for designing systems and application elements to foster user engagement, enjoyment and support behavior change. Experts agree that, to be efficient, gamification strategies should be designed in a user-centric fashion. However, current user-centered design approaches in gamification primarily involve users during user research and iterative testing. In this paper, we describe an ideation approach for involving users in the conceptualization of gamification, making the gamification design process a more participatory activity, a process done with the user rather then for the user. Our results show that our method fostered participation without confining creativity. Participants were able to generate many ideas, several of them being "out of the box".

Keywords: Participatory design · Gamification · Ideation

1 Introduction

Computer supported applications are increasingly using gamification for boosting user-engagement and motivation, and for supporting behavior change. Gamification corresponds to the usage of game elements in non-game contexts [2]. It has been applied in multiple domains such as health [11], education [4] and energy [21]. Empirical studies show positive outcomes [9] of using gamification for supporting behavior change. Gamification aims to evoke enjoyment and support users' inherit goals. Therefore the design of gamification requires a deep understanding of the users' context and needs [3]. As a result, different user-centric approaches for designing gamification are proposed [3,7,14,16,18]. However, the articles above, and others reviewed in [17], involve users chiefly during the user research or the testing of solutions, even if experts consider it important to involve users in the design of the solution as well.

© IFIP International Federation for Information Processing 2019
Published by Springer Nature Switzerland AG 2019
C. Bogdan et al. (Eds.): HCSE 2018, LNCS 11262, pp. 51–61, 2019.
https://doi.org/10.1007/978-3-030-05909-5_4

Taking the Human-Centered Design Process as specified in the ISO 9241-210 [5], and illustrated on Fig. 1, as a baseline, current research in gamification shows that users are involved mainly in the phases of "Understanding and specifying the context of use" and the "Testing" in the current gamification design approaches. The phase of "Producing the design solution", which includes an ideation (the formation of ideas and concepts) step and the development of the prototype itself, often do not involve the users and, in fact, are rarely and little described when it comes to gamification design [17]. Including the users into the "Production of the design solution" elevates the process from *user-centered* design towards a *participatory* design, and, consequently, increases the chances of more deeply understanding the users and reaching their tacit knowledge [20].

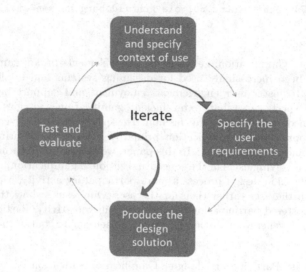

Fig. 1. ISO Human-Centered Design Process, adapted from [5]

Designing a gamification concept is a challenging task as it requires the designers to build strategies that support the behavioral outcomes wished by the users based on the activities that lead to those behavior in accord to the users' context and their motivation. The complexity behind the gamification concept design may be one of the reasons why designers have not involved users in this step of the process. Consequently, the gamification ideation approaches described in the literature, such as [15], are tailored to be used by designers and researchers, and have been tested with those stakeholders, rather then with end-users.

In our research, we try to address the lack of scientifically published approaches for participatory ideation within the gamification design. We propose an approach for conducting the ideation of gamification design in a participatory fashion. Our approach involves getting users to brainstorm gamification concepts, taking into consideration the elements for reaching their behavioral goals. We investigate the suitability of this approach in terms of generating high-quality ideas, whether its structure effectively triggers the users' participation and whether it restricts the creative process:

- Does the approach facilitate participants engagement? Do moderator(s) need to intervene often, stirring the process?
- Do participants restrict themselves to ideas based on the presented gamification mechanics or do they go beyond that? Do they bring ideas linked with theirs inherit motivation?

2   The Ideation Approach

Our approach focuses on ideation. We, therefore, assume that the user research was already done to understand the users' needs and context. It relies on the facilitators having previously uncovered the **behavioral outcomes** wished by the target users, the **activities** that contribute to those outcomes and motivations and barriers linked to those activities.

The proposed ideation approach is rooted in the building blocks of gamification, as defined by [9], where motivational affordances [23] are implemented with the intent to trigger psychological outcomes that lead to behavioral outcomes. Our approach is designed as a workshop structured in 5 steps:

1. Introduction: Mutual introduction and possible ice breaking activities followed by a presentation of the workshop context and purpose.
2. Presentation: The workshop moderator presents the findings from earlier user research, and introduces gamification to participants.
3. Ideation: Participants generate ideas in a brainstorming process.
4. Ideation review: Participants review the ideas, possibly discarding, rating or prioritizing some of them.
5. Closing: The workshop moderator thanks the participants and informs them about the next steps of the overall gamification design process.

The Introduction and Closing steps have no strict format. They should be tailored according to whether the participants already have participated in the user research, and whether they are familiar with the overall process.

The Presentation step summarizes the desirable, but still unreached, **behavioral outcomes** for the target user group, and the **activities** that contribute to those outcomes. By **activities**, we mean application features or real-world user activities supported by the application for reaching the outcomes. For example, registering food intake is an **activity** that can support a desired **behavioral outcome** of losing weight or pursuing a diet.

For being able to build meaningful gamification, the **activities** must fall under a "gamification design fit" as described in [3]:

- Activities must support users to reach their desired behavioral outcomes;
- Users should demonstrate a lack of motivation for performing such activities, for example when the activity is time-consuming or perceived as boring;

– The activity performance can contribute to basic psychological or social motives such as mastering a skill, achieving autonomy, socializing, etc.

Ensuring the "gamification design fit" essentially means that the activities to be gamified are those that the user lacks motivation to perform despite them having a positive effect in contributing to reach his/her goals. It is a crucial step in order to address possible gamification pitfalls described in [12]: such as, encouraging behaviors that do not contribute to the user goals or not supporting the development of an intrinsically motivating underlying psychological or social motive. Therefore, participants should be allowed to feedback and discuss the **behavioral outcomes** and related **activities** presented, especially if they were not part of the user research which uncovered those.

After going through the **behavioral outcomes** and related **activities** with the participants, the workshop moderator introduces gamification to them. For that purpose, we created a set of cards describing different popular gamification mechanics, such as points, badges and progress bars, and mapping these mechanics to motivational aspects fostered by them. Figure 2 illustrates the card used

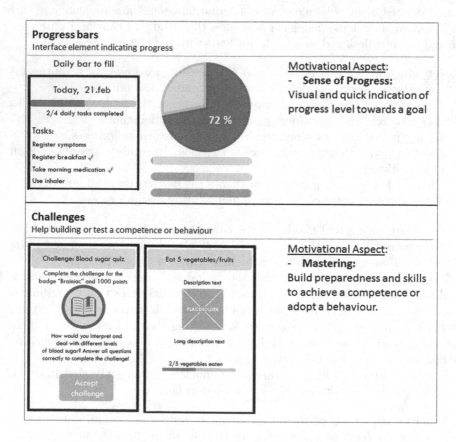

Fig. 2. Progress bar and challenge cards example

for presenting progress bars and the one for challenges. The whole set can be retrieved in [10].

The card format follows recommendations from evaluations of similar cards used for inspiring and guiding brainstorming [15]: each card describe the underlying motivational aspect, and represents this with a concrete example of a gamification mechanic supporting it.

The cards are not part of a game to be played during the workshop, as in [15]. We did not want to introduce game-play rules which could hinder the creative process nor complicate the Ideation step. Instead, the cards rather serve as cues illustrating how concrete mechanics can affect the user motivation needs, more similarly to how cards were used in [8]. Thus, the intention of using the cards is to dismantle some of the complexity behind gamification design.

The motivational aspects illustrated in the mechanics, the **activities** and the **behavioral outcomes** are the core components our approach tries to root the ideation into. They serve as the mechanism to focus the brainstorming and guide the Ideation into coming up with concepts that effectively support the users to achieve their behavioral goals.

During the Ideation step, the workshop moderator should ask the participants to select a **behavioral outcome** of their interest and brainstorm gamification ideas that can motivate them on performing activities that support such outcome. For that, it can be useful to draw a table in a white board or flip-chart in order to easily map the different ideas in relationship to their respective goals and activities (see Fig. 3 for an illustration of such table). The cards should be available for participants to consult and draw inspiration about how to concretely address a motivational aspect connected to an activity.

In case the participants struggle to come up with ideas, moderators should not push participants to go through the cards, but rather ask them questions, similarly to innovation steams as proposed in [3], to help them reflect on support needs related to their activities and goals. For example: "What challenges are inherent in [activity]?", "Why is this [goal]/[activity] challenging?", etc. In that way, the facilitation becomes more value oriented rather then technology driven.

Usually, the first ideas generated during brainstorming are not the best ones. The last ideas generated tend to be of higher quality [19]. Therefore, it is useful to review the ideas with the participants for understanding whether some ideas can be merged, and some should be discarded, and to set priorities on ideas.

3   Evaluation Set-Up

The proposed ideation approach was designed in the context of the European research project MyCyFAPP [1]. The aim of MyCyFAPP is to provide health self-management support to persons affected by Cystic Fibrosis (CF), with focus on nutritional aspects. The user needs were identified [6] and a non-gamified mobile application had been co-designed [22]. The treatment of CF is very demanding. Even if the co-designed CF application helps users managing their health, the application features require users to dedicate some of their scarce

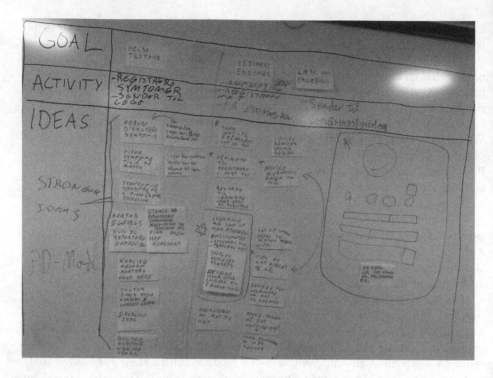

Fig. 3. Ideas resulting from brainstorming session

time to the self-management of the disease. Consequently, the CF application falls under the "gamification fit" scope. Designers in the project therefore decided to investigate whether gamification elements can be added to further motivate the users.

Before evaluating the ideation approach with persons with CF in the context of MyCyFAPP, two workshops were conducted involving healthy persons and using a fictive related scenario: designing gamification for the existing application MyFitnessPal[1], a mobile application that supports nutrition tracking towards weight loss. Each of those workshops involved a single participant interested in nutrition management, akin of the researchers but not familiar with the research. One participant had experience with games and gamified applications, the other did not. The **behavioral goals** "Helping to control caloric intake" and "Learning about food nutrition" were defined as a basis. We selected the relevant **activities** towards these goals, i.e., registering food intake and visualizing nutrients of food intake during the day.

Then, two other workshops, now using the CF application developed in MyCyFAPP as baseline, were conducted. They followed the same format as the earlier workshops but introduced an additional moderator. Given the demanding treatment and the rarity of the disease, accessibility to persons with CF is

---

[1] https://www.myfitnesspal.com.

a major challenge. Consequently, each workshop included only one CF patient. These patients had earlier contributed to the user research and co-design activities of the baseline CF application. Five different **behavioral goals** identified in the user research were presented at the *Presentation* step of the workshop: (1) Learning about nutrition and how it affects health; (2) Learning and becoming proficient in estimating the enzyme dosage; (3) Following and understanding symptoms together with being able to explain them to the doctors; (4) Remembering medicine intake; (5) Learning more about CF and its treatment. The baseline application activities contributing to those goals, such as registering food intake or keeping a health diary, were also presented and linked to theirs related behavioral goals.

Table 1 provides an overview of the participants age and experience besides the number of ideas in relationship to the workshop and goals, while in the next section we discuss the results and dynamics of the workshops.

Table 1. Workshops overview

Baseline	Age	Stated Gaming experience	# ideas	# goals	Ideation time
MyFitnessPal	24	Play games and use gamified apps	12	2	30 min
MyFitnessPal	23	No experience	10	1	20 min
CF app	22	Play games	21	6	90 min
CF app	16	Play games and use gamified apps	20	4	60 min

4 Evaluation Results

In this section we analyze the results of the workshops in terms of the resulting ideas, the user participation and workshop dynamics.

4.1 Ideas Quality and Scope

In all workshops, participants frequently generated ideas building on top of each other's ideas, leading to the generation of sets of elaborated ideas composed of many elementary ideas. Consequently, some of those elaborated ideas linked different gamification mechanics into a larger gamification concept. For example, in one of the CF workshops, a participant first suggested a forum-like question and answers system for discussing symptoms. He kept bringing up more ideas so that his concept evolved to incorporate: (1) levels and avatars for representing the knowledge around symptoms one has built through the Q&A, (2) special avatars for characterizing doctors and distinguishing their contribution on the Q&A, (3) points for quantifying the contribution to the community, etc.

Another aspect we noticed was that the ideas from participants of the same baseline workshop differed, and, in each workshop, one motivational factor recurred most. While one of the CF participants was more interested in gamifi-cation elements that trigger competition, the other was interested in quantifying and measuring competence development. This highlights the importance of run-ning the approach with a representative user sample covering different character-istics of the user group population as in other user-centered studies [13]. In our tests, the experience of the participants with games or gamification applications did not influence the number of ideas suggested, but it influenced the level of details provided and the amount of time the workshop lasted. Those with more experience would elaborate the ideas further without much support from the moderator. They went beyond gamification elements and suggested additional system features or usability related interaction elements. For example, the afore-mentioned participant suggested having hash-tags and a hash-tag based search for facilitating users to find a specific symptom.

We did not formally evaluate the generated ideas of the workshops. Instead, we reviewed the ideas at the end of each workshop with the participants and discussed which ones they preferred. Participants always found one or two elab-orated ideas that they truly liked and were confident that would motivate them. Some of the ideas on the CF case overlapped with gamification ideas thought by the researchers in MyCyFAPP, while others were completely new. The researchers in MyCyFAPP found these new ideas highly relevant and they were further sketched to feed a future version of the App design.

4.2   Workshop Dynamics

The structure of the workshop seems to work well. Participants were interested and attentive during the presentation part. They talked comfortably and sponta-neously brought ideas during the ideation phase. Moderators mainly intervened to ask details and clarification, not to trigger ideas. Participants did not lose track of the workshop focus. The ideas, in most part, were centered on the wished behavior goal or activities that support that goal.

When it comes to the workshop set-up, a single moderator conducted the first two workshops. In that case, the moderator steered the process while the participants were responsible to express their ideas, write them down in post-its and place them on a board next to the support goal (See Fig. 3). We found out that asking participants to write and place the ideas interrupted their flow of thought. Therefore, two moderators were assigned to run the workshops using the CF App as baseline. There, one of the moderators was dedicated to write down the participants ideas on the post-its and place them on the board. We noticed that relieving the participants from writing down the ideas significantly help them to immerse in the process and further develop the ideas.

The moderators did not have to intervene for participants to start eliciting ideas, but they took an active stance in terms of: repeating participants ideas for acknowledgment of understanding and asking further details about those ideas. Such interventions would often result on the participant further developing his idea, bringing up related ideas and combining some of his ideas. For example, a participant started by stating the following idea for helping him to learn about nutrition: "...there could be some challenges in format of questions, competition questions, so that one can check that he has learned." Then moderators repeated the idea and asked which kind of questions and competition he was thinking about. That lead the participant to describe that he thought of receiving a quiz once or twice a week, and that, by answering it correctly, he would gain points to be counted towards a local and a global leaderboard.

The moderators deepening questions also helped so that the result of the workshops not only consisted of a collection of ideas, but the elaboration of whys and how those ideas would take place. Consequently, the recordings of the ideation became valuable data for further understanding the user and their motivations through thematic analysis. Such result is consistent with the participatory design premise that engaging people in creation activities allow us to tap into their tacit knowledge [20].

The cards also served their intended purpose. Participants used mechanics presented in the cards and described elements of their ideas referring to motivation elements supported by the mechanics. At the same time, the cards did not become the center of attention of the workshop. Participants would seldom go through them (once or twice per session), mainly when they were out of ideas. Furthermore, participants were able to think "out-of-the-box" and did not restrict their ideas to the mechanics described in the cards. They would also refer to concepts they have used or seen in life experiences or other applications which were not present in the cards, such as the already described question and answers system.

We did not directly ask participants whether they had problems understanding the cards or the underlying concepts and examples described on them. However, the fact that they used mechanics and motivation elements from the cards and did not asked for clarifications about them indicates that they were well understood.

5   Conclusions, Limitations and Further Work

The results indicate that the workshop format helps participants produce meaningful gamification ideas without constraining creativity. Participants could come up with many ideas supported by motivational factors, focused on the behavior goals and did not restrict themselves by the presented mechanics.

Similarly other card-aided ideation approaches [8], having the cards as inspirational support elements rather then mandatory building blocks for the ideas led to situations where users would combine mechanics from several cards within an idea to situations where the idea was not rooted into a mechanic exemplified by a card. Furthermore, the presentation step and rooting of the design problem into the activities that lead to the desired behavioral outcome proved sufficient to ensure focus and convergence in the process.

Some of the ideas the participants of the CF workshops came up with had not been thought by the MyCyFAPP researchers and were considered highly promising. This confirms that user involvement in the ideation phase can bring value to the design process, even if the design team knows well the user's needs and context.

However, for confirming the value of the approach, the ideation workshop format should be further tested with other user profiles and in relation to other gamification application domains. The participants in our workshops were from similar demographics (university or high-school students from Norway) and both scenarios were around health self-management.

Another confirmation step is to empirically validate the quality of the ideas through user or expert studies, or, by implementing them and observing the effect of the gamification concepts in real life.

Due to the nature of CF, we could not group patients together and therefore run workshops with only one participant at time. There are no constraints in the proposed approach that prevents executing it with a group of participants. In fact, brainstorming sessions benefit from group participation as it enables bringing together people with different backgrounds. It will be interesting to observe how our method will perform in a set-up with multiple participants at a time. Similarly, it will be interesting to investigate more deeply the cards contribution to the process and the effects of possibly extending the number of cards.

Acknowledgments. Authors of this paper, on behalf of MyCyFAPP consortium, acknowledge the European Union and the Horizon 2020 Research and Innovation Framework Programme for funding the project (ref. 643806). Furthermore, we thank the participants to the workshops for their interest and collaboration. Ole Gunhildsberg Hansen was a student at the Norwegian University of Science and Technology when conducting this research, which is also part of his Master Thesis [10].

References

1. Calvo-Lerma, J., et al.: Innovative approach for self-management and social welfare of children with cystic fibrosis in Europe: development, validation and implementation of an mhealth tool (MyCyFAPP). BMJ Open **7**(3), e014931 (2017)
2. Deterding, S.: Gamification: designing for motivation. Interactions **19**(4), 14–17 (2012)
3. Deterding, S.: The lens of intrinsic skill atoms: a method for gameful design. Hum.-Comput. Interact. **30**(3–4), 294–335 (2015)
4. Dicheva, D., Dichev, C., Agre, G., Angelova, G.: Gamification in education: a systematic mapping study. J. Educ. Technol. Soc. **18**(3), 75 (2015)
5. DIS, I.: 9241–210: 2010. Ergonomics of human system interaction-part 210: Human-centred design for interactive systems. International Standardization Organization (ISO). Switzerland (2009)
6. Floch, J., et al.: User needs in the development of a health app ecosystem for self-management of cystic fibrosis: user-centered development approach. JMIR mHealth and uHealth **6**(5), e113 (2018)
7. Francisco-Aparicio, A., Gutiérrez-Vela, F.L., Isla-Montes, J.L., Sanchez, J.L.G.: Gamification: analysis and application. In: Penichet, V., Peñalver, A., Gallud, J. (eds.) New Trends in Interaction, Virtual Reality and Modeling. HCIS, pp. 113–126. Springer, London (2013). https://doi.org/10.1007/978-1-4471-5445-7_9

8. Halskov, K., Dalsgård, P.: Inspiration card workshops. In: Proceedings of the 6th Conference on Designing Interactive Systems, pp. 2–11. ACM (2006)
9. Hamari, J., Koivisto, J., Sarsa, H.: Does gamification work? – A literature review of empirical studies on gamification. In: 2014 47th Hawaii International Conference on System Sciences (HICSS), pp. 3025–3034. IEEE (2014)
10. Hansen, O.G.: What gamification design do users want in a self-management application for chronic diseases? – The case of Cystic Fibrosis. Master's thesis, NTNU (2017)
11. Johnson, D., Deterding, S., Kuhn, K.A., Staneva, A., Stoyanov, S., Hides, L.: Gamification for health and wellbeing: a systematic review of the literature. Internet Interv. **6**, 89–106 (2016)
12. Knaving, K., Björk, S.: Designing for fun and play: exploring possibilities in design for gamification. In: Proceedings of the First International Conference on Gameful Design, Research, and Applications, pp. 131–134. ACM (2013)
13. Kujala, S., Kauppinen, M.: Identifying and selecting users for user-centered design. In: Proceedings of the Third Nordic Conference on Human-Computer Interaction, pp. 297–303. ACM (2004)
14. Kumar, J.: Gamification at work: designing engaging business software. In: Marcus, A. (ed.) DUXU 2013. LNCS, vol. 8013, pp. 528–537. Springer, Heidelberg (2013). https://doi.org/10.1007/978-3-642-39241-2_58
15. Lucero, A., Arrasvuori, J.: PLEX cards: a source of inspiration when designing for playfulness. In: Proceedings of the 3rd International Conference on Fun and Games, pp. 28–37. ACM (2010)
16. Marache-Francisco, C., Brangier, E.: Process of gamification. In: Proceedings of the 6th Centric, pp. 126–131 (2013)
17. Morschheuser, B., Hamari, J., Werder, K., Abe, J.: How to gamify? A method for designing gamification. In: Proceedings of the 50th Hawaii International Conference on System Sciences (2017)
18. Nicholson, S.: A user-centered theoretical framework for meaningful gamification. Games+ Learning+ Society **8**(1), 223–230 (2012)
19. Osborn, A.: Applied Imagination. Charles Scribner's Sons, New York (1953)
20. Sanders, E.B.N.: From user-centered to participatory design approaches. In: Frascara, J. (ed.) Design and the Social Sciences, pp. 18–25. CRC Press, London (2003)
21. Vilarinho, T., Farshchian, B., Wienhofen, L.W., Franang, T., Gulbrandsen, H.: Combining persuasive computing and user centered design into an energy awareness system for smart houses. In: 2016 12th International Conference on Intelligent Environments (IE), pp. 32–39. IEEE (2016)
22. Vilarinho, T., Floch, J., Stav, E.: Co-designing a mHealth application for self-management of cystic fibrosis. In: Bernhaupt, R., Dalvi, G., Joshi, A., K. Balkrishan, D., O'Neill, J., Winckler, M. (eds.) INTERACT 2017. LNCS, vol. 10515, pp. 3–22. Springer, Cham (2017). https://doi.org/10.1007/978-3-319-67687-6_1
23. Zhang, P.: Technical opinion motivational affordances: reasons for ICT design and use. Commun. ACM **51**(11), 145–147 (2008)

Model-Based and Model-Driven Approaches

A Method for Optimizing Complex Graphical Interfaces for Fast and Correct Perception of System States

Marie-Christin Harre[✉], Sebastian Feuerstack, and Bertram Wortelen

OFFIS - Institute for Information Technology, 26121 Oldenburg, Germany
harre@offis.de

Abstract. The amount of information a human has to process continuously increases. In this regard, successful human performance depends on the ability of a human to perceive a system state as quickly and accurately as possible - ideally with a single glance. This becomes even more important in case several tasks have to be performed in parallel. It was shown earlier that monitoring user interfaces with a limited amount of information can be optimized for fast and accurate perception by combining all information into one integrated visual form. But systems that consist of several parallel tasks, each involving a whole bunch of parameters cannot be condensed into one single visual form. We propose an improved method that supports optimizing entire user interfaces consisting of several parallel tasks for fast and accurate perception (Konect). We evaluated the method in 6 workshops for that a total of 12 designers applied the method, which they learned by written instruction cards. Working in teams of two they were all able to design and optimize their designs first on a single task level (i.e. the original method) and thereafter on the global level (i.e. applying the new version). We evaluated their design outcomes thereafter in a laboratory experiment with 18 participants that were asked to distinguish critical and non-critical situations as fast and accurate as possible. Subjects were significantly faster ($p < 0.001$) and also significantly more accurate ($p < 0.001$) for those designs that were gained by the new version of Konect than those for the old one.

Keywords: Information visualization · Graphical interfaces
High amount of information in parallel · Systematic method

1 Introduction

The amount of information humans are expected to process on a day-by-day basis is steadily increasing. The more automation, the more the human is in charge of supervision. The more tasks are required to be handled in parallel, the more the human is required to divide attention between them. A user interface

© IFIP International Federation for Information Processing 2019
Published by Springer Nature Switzerland AG 2019
C. Bogdan et al. (Eds.): HCSE 2018, LNCS 11262, pp. 65–87, 2019.
https://doi.org/10.1007/978-3-030-05909-5_5

that allows a human to perceive and process relevant information *at a single glance* would be the ideal one in such situations. In the area of automation, this relevant information often can be condensed to two basic questions: First, is something going wrong? And second: why? Model-based user interface engineering has implemented rigorous engineering processes for deriving user interfaces based on several models, such as task analysis and design, domain models [2] and derived intermediary models to display information in a structured and consistent way. For large or complex systems, task analysis typically ends up with a huge amount of identified task-relevant information, which often needs to be processed in parallel to record the system status and make appropriate decisions. For example, it is very important for an operator of a nuclear power plant, a power grid or on a ship bridge to capture a large amount of information efficiently and correctly. But even non-safety-critical systems, such as a booking system at a hotel reception or information dashboards, would benefit from being able to be observed efficiently with just a few glances. For example, more valuable time can be spent interacting with a customer than looking up and collecting that information in the user interface.

The research question that arouses in this context is: How does an engineering process that allows systematic derivation of **complex** graphical user interfaces look like that ensures a high amount of information to be perceived in parallel?

We propose a new version of Konect, a method for designing graphical user interfaces. Konect focuses on condensing information into visual forms (a glyph [36]), which are then optimized for fast and accurate perception [27]. Until now, Konect was applied for graphical interfaces with reduced complexity (not more than 11 information elements). In this contribution we applied the method to design **complex, multi-glyph interfaces** for that each glyph condenses all relevant information for processing one task. Konect comes with an instruction card, which is a five pages long written instruction that enables an interface designer with average design knowledge to apply the method without any prior coaching. We extended this card by an operationalization of three basic well known guidelines: Consistency, simplicity in shapes, and simplicity in colors. In an evaluation study, we show that the operationalization is facilitated by the Konect method and can be successfully used by designers. The resulting interface designs significantly reduce the perception time required to identify important information while at the same time improve perception accuracy.

The paper is structured as follows: First, we describe related works on methods for the design of visual monitoring interfaces that we considered for our work. Then we briefly motivate a use case about vessel performance monitoring in Sect. 3 that we use to introduce the method in Sect. 4 and later detail as it is also our use case for the evaluation. For the evaluation of the impact of the proposed optimization guidelines we hosted six design workshops with two designers per workshop, who first collaboratively applied the original method followed by the new parts of the revised method (Sect. 5.2). Thereafter, we performed a laboratory experiment with 18 participants to measure reaction times on the created original designs in comparison to the ones where the new Konect version was applied (Sect. 5.3). Results are reported in Sect. 6 and discussed in Sect. 7. Supplementary material (Instruction card, workshop material, raw data and data processing scripts) for this study can be found online[1].

2 Related Work

In the context of this work, related work relevant for the design and optimization of human machine interfaces (HMIs) for monitoring can be subdivided in three areas. First, *efficient visual form representation and perception* is a topic that is relevant in data visualization. Second, *engineering processes* like e.g. model-based user interface engineering have been proposed that enable traceable links between design objectives, several intermediate models and the visual forms composing an HMI (e.g. by mappings). Finally, *methods and heuristics for interface composition* have been proposed (e.g. by guidelines) to ensure that single visual forms do not interfere with each other and as a negative consequence decrease the time and accuracy needed to detect anomalies.

In the scope of *efficient visual form representation*, Ware [36] provided a collection of key principles on how to create efficient information visualizations for single data elements. Similar to Ware, Meirelles [23] provides best practices for effective information visualizations. Cleveland and McGill [9] conducted experiments on how accurate individual forms (e.g. color, length) visualizing quantitative data are perceived by the human visual system. They offered guidelines for the visualization of quantitative data, which have been later extended by Mackinlay et al. [21] for nominal and ordinal data types. While Mackinlay et al. and Cleveland and McGill are situated in the data chart visualization domain, our work is focusing on user interface design. In this domain, Shneiderman et al. [31] present rules and key principles for user interface design and Tidwell [32] gives an overview about good design patterns applicable in the user interface design domain. Compared to our work these works have the main emphasis in interaction design while we have a focus on the visualization of monitoring information. Tufte [34] describes design strategies for presenting information about motion, process, mechanism, cause and effect. Gruhn et al. [17] provided best practices for visualizing information quite specifically for monitoring HMIs in the safety-critical domain (e.g. usage of trends, reduction of text). These works offer a profound background about best practices and hints for efficient visual forms for data visualization. However, they do not offer a systematic step-by-step approach in which the knowledge can be applied and therefore the systematic consolidation and application of this knowledge can be a challenge.

Regarding *methods and engineering processes*, Card et al. presented the "visualization pipeline", a sequence of steps and characteristics of a mapping functions for mapping information elements to visual forms [7], but do not state specific guidelines or mappings. Combined versions (step-by-step approach and specification of efficient mappings) exist in the domain of model-based user interface engineering [24]. Approaches in this domain involve the systematic derivation

---

[1] https://hcd.offis.de/wordpress/?p=399.

starting from user scenarios, via task analysis to the modeling of abstract, modality independent to concrete and final, executable user interface presentations [6]. This is based on predefined widgets (e.g. via a toolkit) and thus neglect creative visual forms and are mainly applicable for form based interfaces as toolkit widgets are limited. The idea of Post-WIMP widgets [10] addresses this limitation and arguing to open up the design space for new visual forms that consider new modes of interaction going beyond the desktop. [11] picks up on this topic and proposes COMETS, that implement plasticity and can adapt themselves to various contexts-of-use. Beside these general approaches, some methods have been focused on addressing specific challenges. For instance, Zhang et al. [45] presented a theoretical framework for the creation of relational information displays. Their framework describes properties and structures that focus on the expressiveness in designing visualizations. The Konect method is also situated in this context. It implements a step-by-step process to derive visual forms for specific information elements while considering the tasks and perceptual skills of an operator with regard to fast and accurate perception of visual forms. These works either focus on single visual forms or do not consider interference of visual forms, which might lead to an efficiency decrease with regard to the time and accuracy to perceive e.g. critical states.

Related work regarding *combination of visual forms* has been published by Woods [43]. Woods presented the concept of a "visual momentum", in which he presented guidelines to integrate data across successive displays so that the display system design can support an effective distribution of user attention. This has been later reexamined by Bennett and Flach [3]. The core concept is a consistent usage of display techniques. Wickens et al. [40] presented the "Proximity Compatibility Principle", which demands that information relevant for a common task or mental operation should be rendered close together in the perceptual space. Treisman [33] suggests that when perceiving a stimulus, features are "registered early, automatically, and in parallel, while objects are identified separately" and identified a preattentive stage in that different parts of the brain automatically gather information about basic features like e.g. colors, shapes and can be perceived in milliseconds. Wolfe et al. [42] conducted studies about what supports fast detection of single visual forms (called targets) in a range of other visual forms (called distractors). The authors revealed that feature search becomes less efficient as the target-distractor difference declines and as distractor inhomogenity increases.

3   Fuel-Efficient Operation of Maritime Vessels

The use case to which the method was applied for validation purposes is situated in the maritime domain: Economic vessel navigation is an open issue in the maritime domain. According to studies published by the European Federation for Transport and Environment, the fuel consumption of ships actually increased by 10% between 1990 an 2013 [13]. In 2016 the average design efficiency of ships was even worse compared to 2015 [14]. Much of a ship's emissions arise close to the coast line and probably affect air quality negatively [35]. To further identify the causes of fuel consumption of ships, Ando et al. [1] presented a break down analysis: A high amount of the consumption is caused by the ships speed profile, the distances and the trim. In order to optimize the total energy consumption and reduce emissions, some ships offer user interfaces for vessel performance monitoring in order to be able to make right decisions to save fuel (e.g. use optimal speed, trim etc.). Currently such user interfaces are difficult to use in critical situations as docking: In berthing scenarios information about the distance to the quay wall, the current, position of tug boats or state of the thrusters is of higher importance for the task at hand as this directly affects safety of the ship. Information for the secondary task - save fuel and reduce emissions - has lower priority. Hence, as long as it is quite difficult for the operator to monitor these values, it will not be used in situations near land and port. Therefore, the idea was to design a user interface depicting all relevant information for fuel-efficient operation that can be monitored with minor effort while the operator performs the primary task (like e.g. berthing or maneuvering the ship).

4   Konect: Designing Visual Interfaces for Efficient Monitoring

The Konect method has been proposed to design glyphs that condense several information elements into integrated visual forms. The method consists of four basic process steps (Task analysis, Idea Box Creation, Design Creation and Global Design Adjustment with Composing Guidelines) like depicted by Fig. 1. All steps are performed by following a written instruction sheet. The design phase requires pen and paper as it involves free sketching. The steps are described in the upcoming subsections. For this, we describe the concept of the step and its realization in the vessel performance monitoring use case.

The first three steps focus on the visual form generation, while the fourth step focuses on glyph composition and optimization.

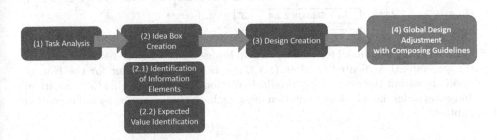

Fig. 1. Model based process for composing graphical interfaces for fast and correct perception.

4.1 Task Analysis

The first step is performing a task analysis to figure out for which tasks an operator has to acquire or monitor information [27]. The result of the task analysis is a task model. Various notations for task models exist like GOMS [8], ConcurTaskTrees (CTT) [29] or the HAMSTERS notation [15], which also considers temporal task relations like introduced by the CTT notation. Figure 2 shows parts of a task model created with HAMSTERS for crew members on ship bridges. The illustration was modified here to highlight the key elements of the task model required for the Konect method. Omitted elements of the task model are indicated by dots (...). The full HAMSTER model is included in the supplementary material (c.f. footnote at the end of the introduction). Optimally, the task model is not created just for the Konect method. Task modeling techniques, like HAMSTERS, can be used for the development and analysis of various aspects of the Human-Machine interaction [12].

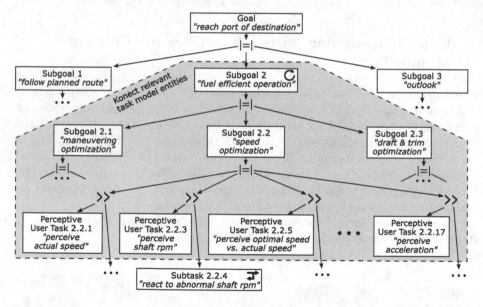

Fig. 2. Part of a task model for officers on ship bridges. Due to space restrictions many parts are omitted, indicated by dots (...). Aspects that are relevant for the Konect method are within the gray box. Graphical notation based on HAMSTERS notation. |=| indicates order independent execution of subtasks. >> indicates sequential execution of subtasks.

The main goal of the crew in our use case is to reach their port of destination. This task is depicted at the top of Fig. 2. To accomplish it several subgoals have to be achieved, like following the planned route, looking out for traffic, performing maneuvers and ensuring fuel-efficient ship operation. We focus on fuel-efficient operation as a use case, because a lot of information needs to be observed in order to assess the ship state with respect to fuel-efficient operation. The task of assessing the state of complex systems can often be decomposed into observing the states of several subsystems. In Fig. 2 the three subsystems associated with maneuvering, speed control and draft& trim control have an influence on fuel-efficient operation and need to be monitored. This is depicted by the three subgoals 2.1–2.3. Typically there is no predefined order in observing the subsystems (indicated by he |=| symbol). To assess the state of a subsystem several information elements must be perceived. In the HAMSTERS notation this is expressed by a set of perceptive user tasks (e.g., Tasks 2.2.1 and 2.2.3 in Fig. 2 for subgoal 2.2). We assume that the order of these tasks is also independent. Perceiving an information element might result in a subsequent reaction, if the value of the information is outside of the desired range. This can also be included in the task model as an optional task (see subtasks 2.2.4). However, the Konect method focuses only on optimizing monitoring tasks, where the user has to observe large amount of information elements. It does not consider interactive aspects. The aspects of the task model relevant for the Konect method are included in the gray area in Fig. 2. Other methods like e.g. dialogue modeling have been proposed to support an interactive navigation between several user interface [22], which is out of scope for this work. An overview on model-based user interface design approaches can be found for example in [24]. The task analysis is important to derive the information that need to be presented by the HMI for the human operator to successfully conduct the tasks. Also the task-based grouping of the information is an outcome since in Konect, each task is represented by one glyph that spatially groups together all relevant information to perform one task.

4.2   Idea Box

The second step is filling the idea box. The idea box aims at fostering creativity of the designer by opening up a design space for one glyph and showing possibilities of visualizing the information at hand with different visual attributes. For each basic task of the task analysis (c.f. subgoals 2.1–2.3) one idea box is setup and filled with all information relevant for performing the respective task. As depicted in Table 1, the idea box consists of five columns:

Importance. The first column rates the importance of the information. The idea box is sorted according to the importance. Listing the important information before less important ones to ensure that the most efficient visual form is used for the most important information. Research on visual attention has identified four main factors influencing visual attention: The Saliency, the Effort, the Expectancy, and the Value of information (SEEV-Model). Whereas the former two factors describe bottom-up effects, the latter two are knowledge-driven (Expected-Value model [39]) and could be understood as the gold standard stating how an operator should optimally distribute her/his visual attention [41]. Konect applies the Expected Value model to derive the importance ranking.

Table 1. Extract of the idea box for the vessel performance use case.

Importance	Information	Insight	Efficiency ranking				Combination
1.6	Actual speed	Perceive quantitative value fast	Length	(1)	Volume	(3)	Symmetry Figure and ground Spatial proxim-
			Slope	(2)	Color hue	(4)	ity
0.8	Actual speed vs. optimal speed	Perceive if value is ok fast	Color hue	(1)	Slope	(4)	Connectedness Continuity Closure
			Shape	(2)	Volume	(5)	Relative size
			Length	(3)			Similarity
0.2	Optimal speed	Perceive quantitative value	Position	(1)	Volume	(6)	
			Length	(2)	Density	(7)	
			Angle	(3)	Saturation	(8)	
			Slope	(4)	Color hue	(9)	
			Area	(5)			
...	...	...	...				

Information. All information relevant for a task and identified by the prior task analysis is listed as a separate row.

Insight. In the third column the insight the human operator should gain when looking at the information is described (e.g. perceive if value is ok fast). Insights are chosen from a predefined set of insights of the Konect method (all possible insights are listed in Table 2). In this regard, one has to keep in mind that one information element can appear twice in the idea box e.g. a speed value with insight to perceive it as quantitative value and speed with insight to perceive if it is ok or not. The insight is obtained and specified within the task analysis of the prior step, e.g. by talking to domain experts as part of interviews.

Efficiency Ranking. Based on the insight, the forth column of the idea box lists the most appropriate visual forms (e.g. color, length) according to an efficiency ranking. The most efficient attribute with regard to time and correctness of the percept is at the top of the list (ranked with (1)). Details about the efficiency ranking can be seen in Table 2.

Combination. Konect aims at generating glyphs – integrated visual forms. For this, all information elements listed in one idea box should be combined in one glyph. The last column lists possibilities to combine visual forms e.g. symmetry or proximity. This is strongly based on the Gestalt laws [38].

Table 2. Table listing predefined insights, the mapping to the visual efficiency ranking and the scientific reason for this mapping.

Insight	Visual efficiency ranking	Discussed by
perceive **quantitative value** perceive **summary (min, max, avg,%)**	position (l), length (2), angle (3), slope (4), area (5), volume (6), density (7), color saturation (8), color hue(9)	[7,18]
perceive **quantitative value (fast)**	length (1), slope (2), volume (3), color hue (4)	[7,16,18,28,31]
perceive if **value is ok**	position (l), color hue (2), texture (3), connection (4), containment (5), density (6), color saturation (7), shape (8), length (9), angle (10), slope (11), area (12)	[7,18]
perceive if **value is ok (fast)** **find** detect **anomaly** perceive **outliers/exceptions**	color hue (1), shape (2), length (3), slope (4), volume (5)	[7,16,18,28,31]
perceive **category/mode** perceive **certainty**	position (1), density (2), color saturation (3), color hue (4), texture (5), connection (6), containment (7), length (8), angle (9), slope (10), area (11), volume (12)	[7,18]
perceive **category/mode (fast)**	color hue (1), length (2), slope (3)	[7,16,18,28,31]
perceive **pattern** perceive **relationships** perceive **trade-offs** **compare** perceive **clusters (groups, similarities)** perceive **paths**	edges/depth/orientation at multiple scales (1), size/location (2), categorical relation (3), coordinate relation (4)	[16,17,32,38]

4.3   Design Creation

The idea boxes created in the previous step for each task are used in the design creation phase. With guidance offered by the box, the designer starts working with the idea box row-wise from top to bottom. For each row of the idea box, the designer chooses the most efficient visual form (e.g. color) for an information. In this step, the designer has to design an exact *instantiation* of this form. Exact instantiation means that for instance an exact color coding is chosen. This can be for instance that a critical or abnormal state is colored in red (e.g. actual speed does not comply with plan speed) while a normal state is colored in green or a neutral color. Another example is the exact instantiation of a *length*. This might be for instance a horizontal or vertical bar.

4.4 Visual Form Composition

Complex interfaces supporting several parallel tasks and therefore consisting of several glyphs need to be carefully designed. Interference between glyphs can have an impact on the overall operator's perception accuracy and reaction time. Looking at related work (e.g. [17–19, 23, 26, 31, 32, 40, 43]) we identified three guidelines as most promising to have an impact on perception performance and accuracy:

Consistency. Use the same visual attribute for the same kind of insight for similar important information elements.
Simplicity in Shapes. Choose simple shapes and visual forms, choose non-accidental visual forms with regard to orientation.
Simplicity in Colors. Reduce colors for elements that do not carry any information besides from structuring the interface.

We are aware that there exist even more guidelines in related work. Based on the basis of human perceptual skills, we decided to use exactly these three guidelines. Details about the reasons are given in the upcoming subsections. Furthermore, the guidelines in related work are presented as abstract hints. We are not aware of a systematic procedure on how to apply these guidelines systematically. But this becomes especially important when dealing with a high amount of information. Thus we operationalized these statements to be used within Konect as follows:

Consistency. All information elements (i.e. rows) of all idea boxes are sorted according to their insights and the chosen visual property for each information is marked (e.g. color or length in the efficiency ranking column). Then these markings are checked to ensure that the same kind of insight (e.g. detect anomaly) is reflected by the same visual property (e.g. color). Furthermore, the same manifestation of the visual attribute needs to be chosen for the same kind of information (e.g. if red is an indicator for a failure, red should be used for this kind of information throughout the entire HMI design). The consistency is necessary for ensuring that pre-attentive perception of critical information is even possible at a global level. Ware et al. [37] stated that pop-out effects depend on the relationship of a visual search target to other targets that surround it. The strongest effect occurs when a single target-object differs from all other objects and where all other objects are identical or very similar to each other [37]. This means they have to be consistent to each other to ensure that an abnormal state directly pops-out and is easily distinguishable form normal state. This aspect is further emphasized based on findings of Wickens et al. [40]. Wickens presented the Proximity Compatibility Principle for display design. This specifies that displays relevant to a common task or mental operation should be rendered close together in perceptual space which means that visual elements representing similar states should be encoded close together e.g. by using similar colors.

Simplicity in Shapes. To ensure simplicity, the metric for estimating the "goodness" of visual shapes [44] must be applied. One indicator for visual form simplicity is it's orientation. If a form is perceived as "non-accidental" with regard to orientation (thus it looks the same regardless of the viewer's perspective) it can be understood as a simple form [4]. For calculating the form simplicity, all visual shapes on the entire glyph designs are rotated and mirrored. Then the number of different appearances of the same form represents an indicator for a shapes goodness. Prior work has shown that the simpler a form is, the easier it can be recognized [36]. More complex shapes lead to higher visual clutter causing a decreased recognition performance due to "occlusion, greater difficulty at both segmenting a scene and performing visual search" [30]. Since this metric figured out to be initially difficult to comprehend, Konect comes with an illustrating example on the instruction card, which is depicted in Fig. 3.

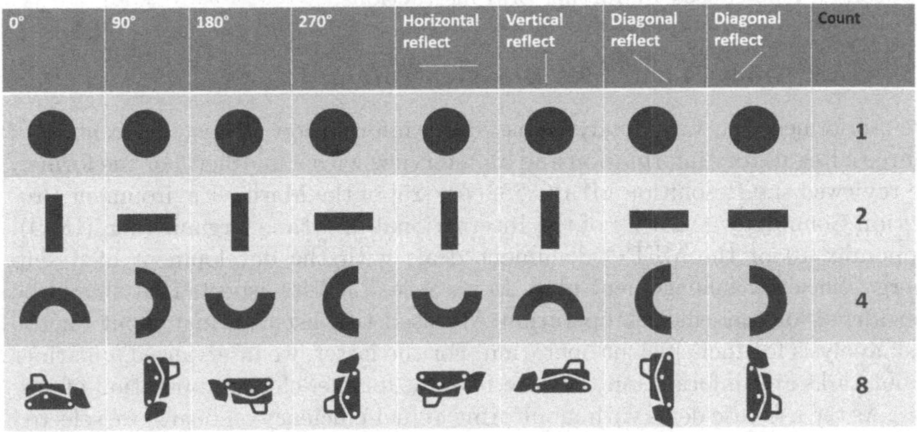

Fig. 3. Instruction card for simplicity in shapes.

Simplicity in Colors. Beside simplicity in shapes also simplicity in colors should be achieved in the user interface design. Therefore, each element on the design is systematically looked at and it is checked against the table whether a color appearing on the design encodes information or if it rather represents *visual sugar*. If the latter is the case, the color should be taken out by being replaced by a neutral color (e.g. grey). This step is especially important to maintain the pop-out effects produced by pre-attentive visible visual forms on a global level. The use of colors should be reduced following the works of Kosslyn et al. that proposed the principle of *Informative changes*. This principle indicates that large changes across properties of a display that do not carry information should be avoided [18, 20].

5   Konect Application for the Vessel Performance Monitoring Use Case

While earlier work applied the method for simple one-glyph user interfaces in the automotive domain [27,28], we applied it in a more complex setting with three parallel tasks in the maritime domain for vessel performance monitoring. For the first steps of the method (the task analysis and idea box generation) we performed domain expert (i.e. ship master) interviews and a literature study. The second part (the design and application of the guidelines) was performed as a workshop with designers. We have chosen this separation to support the evaluation. First, we were interested to start with an identical design space for all designers and second, we were not able to recruit sufficient designers with maritime expertise. Therefore, we provided the designers with the task analysis and initial ordered idea boxes for the three tasks and explained them the role of each task and information at the beginning of the workshop by an instruction sheet. We decided to use a textual description to avoid differences between the information, the different experts got in the workshops and to control the effect a potential bias caused by further oral instructions.

5.1   Task Analysis and Idea Box Generation

We performed the task analysis based on information of two different data sources: Regulatory information and an interview with a mariner. For the former, we reviewed the Resolution MEPC.282(70) [25] of the Marine Environment Protection Committee (MEPC) of the International Maritime Organization (IMO). Appendix 10 of the MEPC document deals with the development of a ship energy efficiency management plan. In its Sect. 5 it lists aspects that should be considered for fuel-efficient operation. We used this list as a first input for the task analysis for fuel-efficient operation. For the latter, we interviewed a mariner about tasks and information that are relevant for fuel-efficient operation of vessels. As the use case deals with monitoring of fuel-efficiency on board, we selected only those tasks that involve ship personnel during voyages. We ended up with a hierarchical task tree of 48 perceptive user tasks for the *fuel-efficient operation* goal, for that each relates to one source of information. At the topmost level, under the goal of a fuel-efficient ship operation, we identified three main subgoals:

Speed Optimization: To save fuel during voyage the speed, acceleration and braking should be minded. Each ship has an optimal speed at which the fuel consumption is minimal. To estimate if the ship is driving at optimal speed the actual speed has to be known and has to be compared to the optimal speed. Furthermore, the ship has to reach the harbor in the right time for unloading cargo to avoid waiting times or problems with the place to berth. This is often called "just in time speed". This speed has also to be minded and compared to the actual speed. Finally, the acceleration is important for saving fuel. A more smooth/constant acceleration reduces fuel consumption. This can be seen with the acceleration trend and the shaft rpm trend – an indicator for the rotation speed of the propeller.

Maneuvering Optimization: Aspects influencing the maneuvering can also lead to higher fuel consumption e.g. headwind or high waves can lead to a higher resistance and thus to higher fuel consumption. Thus the relative wind direction and speed as well as relative wave direction and speed is relevant. Furthermore, the maneuvering should be quite smooth to avoid high fuel consumption (similar to acceleration trend). Thus the rudder angle trend is important and the autopilot state, as the autopilot can ensure smooth adaption of the ships heading according to a set course.

Draft and Trim Optimization: This includes the monitoring of trim (horizontal position of the ship), draft (the part of the ship below water), and the depth under keel (distance of the ship to the ground). For this one has to know that there exists an optimal trim and an optimal draft for each ship for having a minimal possible fuel consumption. This differs from ship to ship. The depth under keel becomes important at a certain value at which the low depth can increase fuel consumption. Thus sometimes the information that the depth under keel is above or below this value is more important than the actual depth under keel.

To generate the idea boxes, we ordered the task relevant information based in the Expected-Value model. Feuerstack et al. [16] showed that the more experts are being ask to determine the Expected-Value model the more the effect of individual errors can be reduced. The authors proposed the HEE software tool to systematically collect the data and to average the data collected. We applied the tool and identified the information gained by the task analysis [25] on current state of the art Vessel Performance Monitoring interface (from Kongsberg and Trelleborg) and asked three experts (a ship master and two Human Factors experts that were aware of the IMO regulations) to determine the relevance of each information for each of the operator tasks and the expectancy of each information with the tool. Expectancy in the context of the Expected Value-Model states how often one expects to perceive new information from a given source (e.g. a presented sensor value).

5.2   Workshop

We organized six workshops with each composed of two Human Factors Engineers or HMI Designers (5 female, 7 male). We captured prior experience of the workshop participants via a questionnaire at the beginning in which the participants estimated their knowledge and competencies according to a Likert-Scale ranging from 1 (never heard of) to 5 (often applied). The participants stated that they have often done an HMI Design (4.6) by applying task analysis techniques (4.08) and information visualization (4.17). They knew the concept of preattentive perception before but did not apply it (3.25). The workshop participants collaboratively applied first the original Konect method ending up with one design of the set depicted by Fig. 4. Afterwards all workshop groups applied the guidelines (4th process step) to end up with one of the optimized designs shown in Fig. 5. We chose groups of two experts to ease our observation of the discussion of the experts in order to get further insights into the reasons for choosing visual forms, the overall HMI Design and their way of working with the method. Each workshop lasted about 3 hours. Within the workshop, we had the following procedure: As starting point, the designers read an instruction card of the Konect method and the use case. The experts received already filled idea boxes and were asked to focus on the third step of the Konect method – the free sketching phase. In this part each pair of experts created a design solution for the maritime use case. No time limit was set for the design creation. Instead, we asked the participants to indicate that they are finished with their design as soon as they are satisfied with their design solution. On average, the designers required around 2 hours to create the design based on the original Konect method. Their design results of the first part of the workshop are shown in Fig. 4.

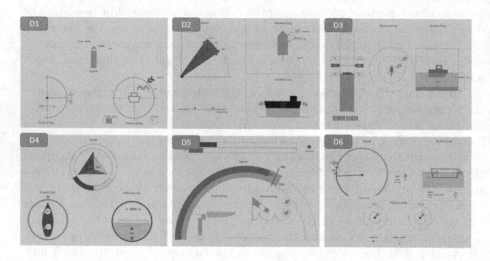

Fig. 4. Designs for the vessel performance use case after step (3) - design creation.

After none of the designers had any additional idea how to further improve the design results, the designers got a second sheet of instructions (they were not aware of a second step beforehand) with the operationalization of the three guidelines as described in the previous section. They were then asked to refine their designs according to these guidelines. The designers needed around one hour to implement the changes to their designs. The results are shown in Fig. 5. We observed the designer teams during their design creations. For applying the guidelines some exemplary changes they implemented were:

Consistency. An example based on the designs in Fig. 4 is for instance the depiction of wind and waves in design D1. In D1 wind and waves are depicted in the right corner at the bottom. The waves are depicted as a wave form which is always red, and the wind with the arrows that are always blue. This has been changed after applying the consistency guideline. Figure 5 shows the designs after application of the composition guidelines. The designers of D1 recognized that green is used as color to indicate an uncritical state throughout the whole HMI and thus applied this color coding also to the wind and wave visualization. Thus a red indicator is used to create a pop-out effect in G-D1 in Fig. 5 while in D1 in Fig. 4 red has been used as indicator for waves, causing the pop-out effect for "red" to be reduced throughout the whole display.

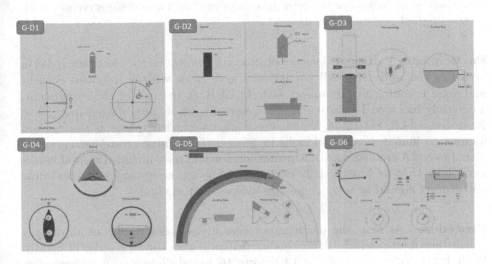

Fig. 5. Designs for the vessel performance use case after step (4) - global design adjustment with composing guidelines.

Simplicity in Shapes. For applying this guideline, the experts rotated and mirrored all shapes of all visual forms used in the HMI design. In case rotation or mirroring of a shape changes its appearance a simpler shape has to be found (e.g. see Fig. 3: a bar is simpler than a half-circle and should therefore be preferred). This can be seen for instance in D2 in Fig. 4: The experts used a circular chart with arrows in the upper left corner to visualize the speed. After applying the guidelines this has been changed to a simple gray bar chart (see G-D2 in Fig. 5).

Simplicity in Colors. For instance in design D4, the experts make extensive use of different colors. All colors that did not carry any information have been reduced, which resulted in the fact that the critical red information in G-D4 in Fig. 5 stands out more saliently.

5.3   Study

With the designs resulted from the workshop, we conducted a laboratory study in front of the computer to estimate the effect of the extended step 4. The participants and the procedure are described in the upcoming subsections. With the experiment, we wanted to investigate in how far step 4 (as shown in Fig. 1 improved the efficiency of the design solution. For this, we had the following hypotheses:

H1. Designs after step 4 are faster to perceive compared to designs created with the original version of the method.
H2. Designs after step 4 have a higher accuracy of the perceived state compared to designs created with the original version of the method.
H0. There is no difference between designs after step 4 and designs created with the original version of the method.

Participants. Participants were recruited via a notice on the electronic bulletin board of the university. All participants gave prior written informed consent and were economically rewarded with 15 EUR at the end of the experiment. The study included 18 participants (14 women), whose ages ranged from 20 to 29 (mean $= 24.5$, SD $= 2.7$). We choose students as participants as the method focuses on human perceptual skills in general (fast and accurate perception of visual cues). A trained maritime professional would have included mental model knowledge that we intentionally excluded as the use case was just one example and Konect should be seen as domain-independent method.

Procedure. At first, the participants were given a description of all designs which they read carefully. After this participants were shown a series of figures. Each figure showed one of the 12 designs (6 initial designs + 6 designs after step 4) in one of five different situations that are either critical or non-critical ($S1$: non-critical; $S2$: critical ship speed; $S3$: critical trim state; $S4$: critical (low) depth under keel; $S5$: critical wind condition). The task of participants was to estimate as fast and accurate as possible, whether the shown situation is critical or not. After pressing a key the image disappeared immediately and participants had to type their response. We measured the correctness of the response and the reaction time between showing the image and hitting the key. The sequence of designs and situations was randomized. However, we wanted to avoid having the initial design and the designs after step 4 of the same design concept (e.g. D1 and G-D1) in one sequence. Therefore we divided the experiment into two blocks (A and B) for each participant. Each A-block contained three initial designs and three composing guidelines designs from different design concepts (e.g., D1, D2, G-D3, G-D4, D5, G-D6). Block B contained the six remaining designs (e.g. G-D1, G-D2, D3, D4, G-D5, D6). To eliminate order effects we randomly assigned designs to the blocks and balanced it across participants. For each design each of the four critical situations (S2-S5) were shown once and the non-critical situation (S1) twice. This was repeated three times resulting in a sequence of $6 \times (4+2) \times 3 = 108$ stimuli shown in each block. To eliminate training effects blocks were iterated two times with pauses between them: A - B - A - B. Only data from the second iteration of block A and B was analyzed. We excluded

5 measurements, considering reaction times >10 s as a failure and < 300 ms as a premature key press, because perception, decision and motor response are unlikely to happen within 300 ms.

6   Results

We expected that the guideline application decreases reaction times and improves accuracy. However, we assumed that other factors also have an influence on the reaction times and accuracy. To take several factors into account, we used a linear mixed model to analyze the data.

We included the usage of the guidelines and the stimulus index as fixed effects in the model, with stimulus index k indicating the k-th situation shown to the participant. When measuring reaction times in laboratory settings a training effect can often be observed, as did [27] when they tested HMIs created with the Konect method. We expected this effect in our experiment and tried to reduce it, by only analyzing data from the second iteration of block A and B. However, a small effect can still be expected. Thus we included the stimulus index as fixed effect. However, we did not expect to observe a significant training effect in the accuracy of responses. Due to individual differences, we expected that reaction times differ for each participants. Thus we added participant as a random factor. Similarly, the six pairs of designers created different design concepts. We expected to record different mean reaction times accuracy values for each design concept, but still expected an improvement for the designs after guidelines were applied. Thus we added the design concept as a random factor. This resulted in the following models (R-typical notation):

$$\text{response time} \sim \text{guideline} + \text{stimulus} + (1|\text{participant}) + (1|\text{design})$$

$$\text{accuracy} \sim \text{guideline} + (1|\text{participant}) + (1|\text{design})$$

Based on likelihood ratio tests we observed a significant effect of the guideline usage both on the reaction times ($\chi^2(1) = 182.17, p < 0.001$), lowering it by about 172 ms ±12.6 ms (standard errors), and on the accuracy ($\chi^2(1) = 43.41, p < 0.001$), improving accuracy by about 4.6 % ±0.7 % (standard errors) from 92.3 % correct responses to 96.9 %. Thus, we were able to accept our hypotheses (H1) and (H2) and reject the null hypotheses (H0).

When exploring the data we realized that adding the designs as a random effect is not sufficient to describe the influence of the design on the reaction times and accuracy. The amount of improvement on accuracy and reaction times when applying the guidelines differs for each design. This sounds plausible. It is likely, that the initial designs of some design teams already adhered to the guidelines to some extent. Therefore the room for improvement after applying the guidelines differs for each design team. Adding random slopes for guidelines to the random effect term of our models (changing (1|design) to (guideline|design)) resulted in a significantly better model fit for reaction times ($\chi^2(2) = 195.19, p < 0.001$) as well as accuracy ($\chi^2(2) = 85.38, p < 0.001$).

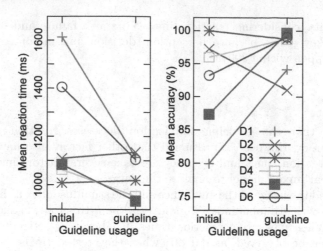

Fig. 6. Effect of guidelines on reaction times and accuracy differs for the different HMI designs.

Figure 6 illustrates this aspect. It shows how reaction times and accuracy changes with guideline usage in step 4 for each design. Those designs, where the initial design version did not perform well, showed the strongest improvement after step 4.

In Fig. 6 it can be seen that the effect size of the guidelines on decreased reaction time and increased accuracy differs between the designs: In case of D1 and D6 a high increase of performance with regard to reaction times and accuracy has been reached while for D4 and D5 a medium effect was visible and for design D2 and D3 nearly no improvement has been made. We assume that this is caused by quality differences in the initial designs: In D2 and D3, which implement a consistent and reduced usage of colors and simple shapes we measured already a fast reaction time and high accuracy. In case of D1 and D6, the designers applied colors inconsistently and used them also for structuring the user interface. In this case, the application of the guidelines strongly improved subjects performance. We assume that the positive effect of the Konect design principles on reaction times and accuracy of individual glyphs is negatively effected by inconsistent usage of colors and shapes across multiple glyphs in case the original method is applied to a higher amount of information. We could show that applying the guidelines improved reaction times and accuracy significantly. When we compare the designs without guideline application and the ones with guidelines application, we could observe that most design teams only changed few aspects of their design. According to our assumption, the reaction times to all visual forms should improve and not only to the ones that were changed. If this is the case we should observe that the reaction times for all situations (S1–S5) for the same design concept should change roughly by the same amount. An indication of this effect can be seen in Fig. 7. It shows the change of reaction times separately for each situation in each design. It can be seen that the range of changes within a design is considerably smaller than the range of changes over all designs. This supports our assumption. However, given our dataset, this is only an indication. To reasonably test this a study design with more than just five situations and even more complex use cases is needed.

In Fig. 7 it can be seen that all reaction times have been improved or almost remained the same – except of design D2 in case of assessing a critical speed. Having a deeper look at the changes done after guidelines application in D2 reveals the reason for this effect: the color coding for assessing a critical speed has been totally removed instead of adapted to a more consistent form. Thus the workshop participants overlooked that they reduced the amount of information shown on the user interface. For future application of the method this problem might be solved by adding an additional review step at the end in which a verification that all information in the idea box are visualized in the design solution is conducted. We are currently working on this step and a tool support to resolve this problem.

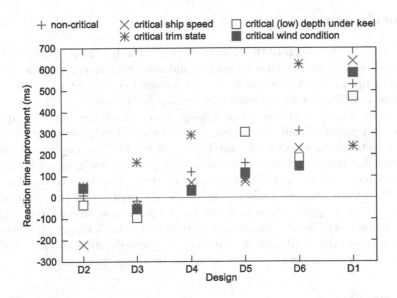

Fig. 7. Change of reaction times for all 5 situations in each design.

7   Discussion

One might argue that the guidelines alone might be good enough to achieve the objective of designing user interfaces that are more efficiently perceived by users without having their operationalization as part of the Konect method: Bornoe et al. [5] tested the improvement process of existing designs with design cards with novice users. The design cards offered hints as they contained principles, an explanation of effect and for what purpose the principle is used. The authors found that the cards diversified the range of system aspects that novices considered and supported ideation. Nevertheless, the cards did not compensate the limited design experience of novices, as the participants had problems implementing them in the design process. With the exact systemization of steps to conduct to implement the guidelines as it is offered by Konect, this problem is addressed and did not appear in the prior described workshops.

The Konect method addresses a very specifc class of user interfaces: Visual user interfaces for monitoring in supervisory control situations with medium to high criticality to timely responses. The method can in principal be used in other contexts, e.g., for designing visualisations for infographics or games. However, fast and accurate perception might not be the optimality criterion in such contexts. Intuitive understanding of visualisations might be more important for infographics, while the joy of use might be a key factor for gaming visualisations. We like to emphasize, that a user of the Konect method should always be aware of the context of use and the criterions that apply to the specific context.

8　Conclusion

We presented an extension to the Konect method, which is used to create glyphs (integrated visual forms) optimized for fast and accurate perception. The method itself opens up a huge design space (since it fosters free sketching), while at the same time is still able to optimize the results for perception. The extension introduces operationalizations of three design principles (consistency, simplicity in shapes and colors). While the original method was not well suited for designing large user interfaces, we showed that the extended method can be applied to design complex user interfaces with multiple glyphs. By workshops with a total of 12 designers working in pairs of two, all of them were able to end up with designs that were created solely by following the written instructions of the method. In a subsequent laboratory study, we could show that 18 participants were on average significantly faster and more accurate in distinguishing between critical and non critical situations visualized by those designs that were created by the revised version than for those designed by the original one.

References

1. Ando, H.: Performance monitoring and analysis for operational improvements. In: International Conference on Ship Efficicency (2011)
2. Balme, L., Demeure, A., Barralon, N., Coutaz, J., Calvary, G.: CAMELEON-RT: a software architecture reference model for distributed, migratable, and plastic user interfaces. In: Markopoulos, P., Eggen, B., Aarts, E., Crowley, J.L. (eds.) EUSAI 2004. LNCS, vol. 3295, pp. 291–302. Springer, Heidelberg (2004). https://doi.org/10.1007/978-3-540-30473-9_28
3. Bennett, K.B., Flach, J.M.: Visual momentum redux. Int. J. Hum. Comput. Stud. **70**(6), 399–414 (2012)
4. Biederman, I.: Recognition-by-components: a theory of human image understanding. Psychol. Rev. **94**(2), 115 (1987)

5. Bornoe, N., Bruun, A., Stage, J.: Facilitating redesign with design cards: experiences with novice designers. In: OZCHI (2016)
6. Calvary, G., Coutaz, J., Thevenin, D., Limbourg, Q., Bouillon, L., Vanderdonckt, J.: A unifying reference framework for multi-target user interfaces. Interact. Comput. **15**(3), 289–308 (2003). https://doi.org/10.1016/S0953-5438(03)00010-9
7. Card, S.K., Mackinlay, J.D., Shneiderman, B.: Readings in Information Visualization: Using Vision to Think. Interactive Technologies Series. Morgan Kaufmann Publishers, Burlington (1999)
8. Card, S.K., Moran, T.P., Newell, A.: The Psychology of Human-Computer Interaction. Erlbaum, Hillsdale (1983)
9. Cleveland, W.S., McGill, R.: Graphical perception: theory, experimentation, and application to the development of graphical methods. J. Am. Stat. Assoc. **79**(387), 531–554 (1984)
10. van Dam, A.: Post-wimp user interfaces. Commun. ACM **40**(2), 63–67 (1997). https://doi.org/10.1145/253671.253708
11. Demeure, A., Calvary, G., Coninx, K.: COMET(s), a software architecture style and an interactors toolkit for plastic user interfaces. In: Graham, T.C.N., Palanque, P. (eds.) DSV-IS 2008. LNCS, vol. 5136, pp. 225–237. Springer, Heidelberg (2008). https://doi.org/10.1007/978-3-540-70569-7_21
12. Diaper, D., Stanton, N. (eds.): The Handbook of Task Analysis for Human-Computer Interaction. CRC Press, Boca Raton (2004)
13. Faber, J., 't Hoen, M.: Historical trends in ship design efficiency. Technical. report (2015). www.transportenvironment.org/sites/te/files/publications/
14. Faber, J., 't Hoen, M.: Estimated index values of ships 2009–2016: analysis of the design efficiency of ships that have entered the fleet since 2009. Technical report 17.7L97.69, CE Delft (2017). https://www.cedelft.eu/en/publications/download/2345
15. Fahssi, R., Martinie, C., Palanque, P.: Embedding explicit representation of cyber-physical elements in task models. In: IEEE International Conference on Systems, Man and Cybernetics (SMC 2016) (2016)
16. Feuerstack, S., Wortelen, B.: The human efficiency evaluator: a tool to predict and explore monitoring behaviour. Kogn. Syst. **2017**(1) (2017)
17. Gruhn, P.: Human machine interface (HMI) design: The good, the bad, and the ugly (and what makes them so) (2011)
18. Hegarty, M.: The cognitive science of visual-spatial displays: implications for design. TopiCS **3**(3), 446–474 (2011)
19. ISO - International Organization for Standardization: ISO 9241: Ergonomics of human system interaction (2006)
20. Kosslyn, S.M.: Graph Design for the Eye and Mind. Oxford University Press, Oxford (2006)
21. Mackinlay, J.: Automating the design of graphical presentations of relational information. ACM Trans. Graph. TOG **5**(2), 110–141 (1986)
22. Mbaki, E., Vanderdonckt, J., Guerrero, J., Winckler, M.: Multi-level dialog modeling in highly interactive web interfaces. In: ICWE 2008 Workshops, 7th International Workshop on Web-Oriented Software Technologies - IWWOST 2008 (2008)
23. Meirelles, I.: Design for Information: An Introduction to the Histories, Theories, and Best Practices Behind Effective Information Visualizations. EBSCO ebook Academic Collection. Rockport Publishers, Beverly (2013)
24. Meixner, G., Paternó, F., Vanderdonckt, J.: Past, present, and future of model-based user interface development. i-com J. Interact. Media **10**(3), 2–11 (2011)

25. Marine Environment Protection Committee: 2016 guidelines for the development of a ship energy efficiency managment plan (SEEMP). Resolution MEPC.282(70), International Maritime Organization (IMO), 28 October 2016. www.imo.org (search: "MEPC.282(70)"), annex 10 to the report of the Marine Environement Protection Committee on its 70th Session

26. Nielsen, J.: Usability Engineering. Interactive technologies. Morgan Kaufmann, Burlington (1994)

27. Ostendorp, M.C., Feuerstack, S., Friedrichs, T., Lüdtke, A.: Engineering automotive HMIs that are optimized for correct and fast perception. In: Proceedings of the 8th ACM SIGCHI Symposium on Engineering Interactive Computing Systems, EICS 2016, pp. 293–298. ACM, New York (2016)

28. Ostendorp, M.C., Friedrichs, T., Lüdtke, A.: Supporting supervisory control of safety-critical systems with psychologically well-founded information visualizations. In: Proceedings of the 9th Nordic Conference on Human-Computer Interaction, NordiCHI 2016, pp. 11:1–11:10. ACM, New York (2016)

29. Paternò, F.: ConcurTaskTrees: an engineered notation for task models. In: Diaper, D., Stanton, N. (eds.) The Handbook of Task Analysis for Human-Computer Interaction. Lawrence Erlbaum Associates, Mahwah (2004)

30. Rosenholtz, R., Li, Y., Nakano, L.: Measuring visual clutter. J. Vis. $7(2)$, 17–17 (2007)

31. Shneiderman, B., Plaisant, C., Cohen, M., Elmqvist, N., Jacobs, S., Diakopoulos, N.: Designing the User Interface: Strategies for Effective Human-Computer Interaction. Pearson Education Limited, London (2016)

32. Tidwell, J.: Designing Interfaces: Patterns for Effective Interaction Design. O'Reilly Media, Sebastopol (2010)

33. Treisman, A.: Preattentive processing in vision. Comput. Vis. Graph. Image Process. $31(2)$, 156–177 (1985)

34. Tufte, E.R.: Envisioning Information. Graphics Press, Cheshire (1990)

35. Viana, M., Hammingh, P., Colette, A., Querol, X., Degraeuwe, B., de Vlieger, I., van Aardenne, J.: Impact of maritime transport emissions on coastal air quality in europe. Atmos. Environ. 90, 96–105 (2014)

36. Ware, C.: Information Visualization: Perception for Design. Interactive Technologies. Elsevier Science, Amsterdam (2004)

37. Ware, C.: Visual Thinking: For Design. Morgan Kaufmann Series in Interactive Technologies. Morgan Kaufmann, Amsterdam (2008)

38. Wertheimer, M.: Laws of organization in perceptual forms. In: Ellis, W. (ed.) A Source Book of Gestalt Psychology. Kegan Paul, Trench, Trubner & Company (1938)

39. Wickens, C.D., Helleberg, J., Goh, J., Xu, X., Horrey, W.J.: Pilot task management: testing an attentional expected value model of visual scanning. Technical report ARL-01-14/NASA-01-7, University of Illinois, Aviation Research Lab, Savoy, IL, November 2001

40. Wickens, C.D., Hollands, J.G., Banbury, S., Parasuraman, R.: Engineering Psychology & Human Performance. Taylor & Francis, Boca Raton (2015)

41. Wickens, C.D., McCarley, J.S.: Applied Attention Theory. CRC Press, Boca Raton (2007)

42. Wolfe, J.M.: Guided search 2.0 a revised model of visual search. Psychon. Bull. Rev. $1(2)$, 202–238 (1994). https://doi.org/10.3758/BF03200774

43. Woods, D.D.: Visual momentum: a concept to improve the cognitive coupling of person and computer. Int. J. Man Mach. Stud. $21(3)$, 229–244 (1984)

44. Garner, W.R., Clement, D.E.: Goodness of pattern and pattern uncertainty. J. Verbal Learn. Verbal Behav. **2**, 446–452 (1963)
45. Zhang, J.: A representational analysis of relational information displays. Int. J. Hum. Comput. Stud. **45**(1), 59–74 (1996)

Data-Driven Usability Test Scenario Creation

Maikel L. van Eck[1][(✉)], Else Markslag[2], Natalia Sidorova[1],
Angelique Brosens-Kessels[2], and Wil M. P. van der Aalst[1,3]

[1] Eindhoven University of Technology, Eindhoven, The Netherlands
{m.l.v.eck,n.sidorova}@tue.nl
[2] Philips, Amsterdam, The Netherlands
{else.markslag,angelique.kessels}@philips.com
[3] RWTH Aachen University, Aachen, Germany
wvdaalst@pads.rwth-aachen.de

Abstract. In this paper, we present a data-driven approach to enable the creation of evidence-based usability test scenarios. By utilising product usage data to create usability test scenarios, we aim to improve the reliability of the test results and to provide better insights into product usability. The approach consists of four elements: the collection of product usage data, the transformation of these data into logs of user activities, the creation of models of user behaviour, and the guided creation of usability test scenarios based on the models. We discuss the challenges that can be encountered when applying this approach based on our experiences with two case studies in product development. We have created a prototype scenario planning tool and performed a preliminary evaluation of the tool with usability engineers working at Philips Healthcare. The evaluation shows that tool-supported evidence-based usability test creation would be valuable in their daily work.

Keywords: User-centered design · Usability testing
Data-driven design · Process mining

1 Introduction

Usability is an important quality that a product needs to posses in order to be successful [19]. If a product is usable, then its users can do what they want to do in the way they expect without hindrance or hesitation. Unfortunately, reports from the industrial practice indicate that it is not straightforward to ensure the usability of a newly developed product [2].

User-Centered Design (UCD) [15] has been devised to cope with this challenge when developing interactive systems [2,19,20]. The central principles of UCD are an early focus on users and their activities, the evaluation and measurement of product usage, and an iterative design process. Through this approach the findings from user testing related to usability and user experience can be used to inform the designer of a product in a relevant manner [2]. By focussing on the user of a product, UCD aims to consciously incorporate usability at every step of the design process of a product.

The purpose of performing a usability test as part of UCD is the collection of empirical data to measure usability aspects in a reliable and objective manner and to identify design problems [2,3,19]. An important element of a usability test is the *test scenario*: the sequence of tasks and activities executed by the test participants. The closer the test scenarios represent reality, the more reliable the test results and the resulting insights into product usability [19].

The creation of usability test scenarios is challenging for several reasons. Test scenarios are usually created manually by usability engineers, covering a limited number of tasks and activities compared to the real behaviour of product users [6], so the creation is affected by the biases of the engineers. These biases can arise because the usability engineers generally know a lot about the product being tested and what the full set of possible product features is, but they may have limited knowledge regarding the way product features are actually used in practice, in which combinations and in what order [17]. This issue can lead to insufficient test coverage, with a focus of testing whether product improvements are effective in very few scenarios, without considering other product functions that may be negatively affected by the change. The challenge of limited test coverage is especially important in safety critical systems, where testing is done to ensure that there are no usability issues that can lead to hazardous situations [10]. Furthermore, finding the right participants to represent the target user group is essential [3], but not trivial if there exist heterogeneous subgroups. For example, test participants should be selected with different levels of training if training levels are found to strongly influence the set of product functions used by a user.

To address these challenges and improve the reliability of product usability testing, we propose a *data-driven approach* to create evidence-based usability test scenarios based on product usage data. An increasing number of products contain functionalities that collect product usage data that is sent back to the manufacturer [9,17]. This type of data can be used to create models that represent the behaviour of the product users, using data science techniques such as process mining [1]. Such models provide insights into existing user behaviour [2,16], which we can use to create usability test scenarios that accurately reflect product usage [4,6]. Additionally, the models can help identify differences in behaviour between user groups to assist test participant selection. The usability engineers will still need their domain knowledge to create good test scenarios, but they can be assisted with observational data to make the right choices when deciding on test tasks and their ordering.

The main contributions of this paper are the following. We present a data-driven approach for the creation of evidence-based usability test scenarios, as shown in Fig. 1. Its four main phases are: (1) the collection of data regarding product use, (2) the transformation of the data into logs of user activities,

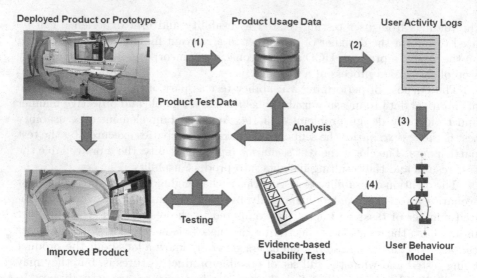

Fig. 1. A data-driven approach for the creation of evidence-based usability test scenarios. Its main phases: (1) product usage data collection, (2) user activity log creation, (3) user behaviour discovery, and (4) usability test scenario creation.

(3) the creation of models of user behaviour using process mining techniques, and (4) the creation of usability test scenarios based on the models. We build upon earlier work related to specific phases of this approach in the context of the development of two different products within Philips [9,11], in order to discuss the challenges that can be expected in practice for each phase of the approach. We have implemented a prototype scenario planning tool to support the approach, guiding usability engineers in the creation of evidence-based usability test scenarios. Finally, we discuss a preliminary evaluation of the developed scenario planner.

The structure of this paper is as follows. First, in Sect. 2 we review related work on usability testing, data and model-driven product development, and test scenario creation. In Sect. 3 we introduce the two cases studies and in Sect. 4 we briefly describe usability testing and the challenges of conducting reliable usability tests. In Sect. 5 we present the approach for the creation of evidence-based usability test scenarios. Then in Sect. 6 we describe the design and implementation of the scenario planning tool. In Sect. 7 we discuss the evaluation of the developed tool. Finally, in Sect. 8 we provide conclusions and discuss future work.

2   Related Work

In [17] a framework is proposed for post-deployment product data usage, describing the necessary development practices and organisational mechanisms to take advantage of the collection of product data in the development of software-intensive embedded systems. This framework can be used for a coarse classification of the level of product data usage within an organisation, but it does not provide details on how to achieve higher levels of product data usage maturity or the challenges encountered when implementing such levels of data usage.

In the areas of Model Driven Development (MDD) and Behaviour Driven Development (BDD) there exist various product development approaches that argue for the need to model user behaviour [2,14,16,20]. Task models for describing interactive systems are used during the early phases of the user-centered development cycle to gather information about user activities. Such models bring additional advantages to task analysis: they structure the gathered information about user activities and enabling the use of software tools to analyse and simulate user behaviour [4]. However, these approaches feature manual modelling of product user tasks and activities by the product developers, which is very time consuming [10,14]. Instead, we propose to leverage product usage data and advances in analytics techniques [1] to mine models of user behaviour.

The main goal of our approach is to improve the reliability of usability testing, which is especially important in safety-critical systems [4,10]. Demonstrating that the design of a medical device is compliant to relevant safety and usability requirements is a serious problem. The use of models of user behaviour can help to show that hazardous situations can be avoided or mitigated. However, as argued by [10], it is not feasible to expect regulators to construct models of products after their development, so ideally manufacturers produce models as part of their design process.

Several product development approaches argue for the creation of usability test scenarios based on models of user behaviour [6,10,14]. However, these models are based on the understanding of the developers of possible user behaviour, without explicit support of actual data regarding e.g. the frequency and ordering of use of specific product features. With these approaches, the test scenario generation is based on state machine models and their simulation with either exhaustive enumeration of all possibilities or scenarios that are randomly generated on the basis of the enabled user tasks in each state. Unfortunately, exhaustive usability testing is not possible in most organisations due to the balance of benefits and costs of testing [19]. Therefore, we propose a combination of domain expertise from usability engineers supported by statistical information based on product usage data to create evidence-based usability test scenarios.

Usability testing can also be seen in the context of requirements engineering and its related testing practices. Requirements engineering is concerned with the identification, modelling and documentation of requirements for a product or system and the context in which the system is used [18]. The aim of requirements engineering is to learn what to develop before the system design is finished. Usability characteristics can be part of the non-functional requirements of a product, however the focus of requirements engineering is usually on the functional requirements of a product. Validation of the implementation of requirements generally involves testing, but handling of non-functional requirements in such tests is often ill defined [18].

3 Case Studies

In the following, we discuss the challenges encountered in practice for each phase of the data-driven approach we propose. This discussion is supported by examples from two different product design case studies within Philips, which we were involved in during earlier work on specific phases of the approach [8,11].

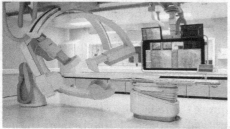 

(a) A medical imaging system used in mini-   (b) A smart baby bottle sleeve with an
mally invasive treatments.   interactive app.

Fig. 2. Two products developed in Philips for which usage data is collected.

The first product is a *medical imaging system* shown in Fig. 2a. This X-ray system is used to perform minimally invasive treatments during medical procedures. During such procedures, it is sufficient to make a small incision through which an introduction element such as a catheter is used e.g. to place a stent in a blocked artery. The collection of product usage data and modelling of the clinical workflow during these procedures is described in more detail in [11].

The second product, shown in Fig. 2b, is a *smart baby bottle* sleeve equipped with various sensors and connected to an interactive app, described in [5,8]. The sleeve sensors included a temperature sensor, a 3D accelerometer, a light intensity sensor, and a sound level sensor. The purpose of this product is to enable parents to collect personal and meaningful insights into the feeding of their baby. The app provides reports, data visualisations and recommendations to the parents based on the collected sensor data.

Although both products are developed by Philips, one at Philips Healthcare and the other at Philips Design, there are some very clear differences between the two case studies. The medical imaging system is an example of a very complex device with many functionalities, different ways in which it can be used and its usage requires extensive training. By contrast, the smart bottle is a simple device, with one main usage scenario that can be executed by any caregiver. The development cycle and the product maturity is also different, with the medical imaging system already deployed in many different hospitals and new improved versions of the system being developed iteratively, while the smart bottle is a new product for which the usage data comes from prototypes tested with a select group of parents. In addition, the type of data collected is different with the smart bottle recording sensor data measurements and the imaging system logging various messages for service and maintenance purposes.

Steps	Task	Instruction
-	Scenario	As a physician, today you will perform a Cerebral Coiling for an aneurysm on a biplane X-ray system. The next patient, Mark Smith, is now on the table in the exam room.
1	Correct identification of patient	Confirm if the correct patient is selected so the procedure can start.
-	Scenario	As we will be working in the exam room, put on the Lead Apron.
2	Correct identification of live image	Where do you expect to see Live Frontal and Lateral X-ray images here in the Exam room?
-	Scenario	In this case, access will be gained via the groin.
3	C-arm motion	Turn the Frontal C-arm to the groin and move the table if necessary so that you can visualize the groin on the screen.
4	Change Source Image Distance	Move the Frontal detector closer to the patient's body.
5	Activate fluoro with footswitch	Now use Frontal fluoro to place the guiding sheath.

Fig. 3. Example of a part of a test scenario for a medical imaging system.

There are also several aspects that the two products from the case studies have in common. Both are internet connected products that have functionalities to send usage data back to the manufacturer, which is essential for the first phase of our approach. Both products also have strong safety requirements. For the imaging system used in a medical environment this is evident, but for the smart bottle it is also important e.g. that the reported food temperature is accurate to prevent burns.

4 Usability Testing

The purpose of performing a usability test is to identify design problems through the collection of empirical data measuring usability aspects in a reliable and objective manner [2,3,19]. The basic elements of a usability test are the following: a set of *goals* the product users aim to achieve, the corresponding *tasks* or *activities* involving the product through which they aim to achieve those goals, and an accurate *representation of the actual working environment* or the context in which the product is used. These elements can be combined into test scenarios that are executed by a representative sample of end users during a usability test. An example of a sequence of tasks in a test scenario is shown in Fig. 3.

The test scenarios executed in a usability test are meant to imitate actual work that the participant would perform using the product and therefore they should be realistic. For example, when testing a medical imaging system, a test scenario is only mirroring realistic operation if the user first moves the scanner to the correct position and then captures an image. During validation of the product functionality, these tasks could also be performed in reverse order, but this would not reflect normal operational behaviour. A test scenario adds context to the tasks that the testers perform and provides them with a motivation to carry out each task. With a realistic scenario, participants will find it easier to stay in their role and overcome hesitation during their use of the product and the closer that the test scenarios represent reality, the more reliable the test results and the resulting insights into product usability [19].

In addition to providing insights on product usability, usability tests can also form an essential part of the testing for product safety [4,10]. In fact, user error has been a significant factor in over 50.000 adverse event reports, including at least 500 deaths, between 2005 and 2009 related to medical infusion pumps in the United States [10]. However, to demonstrate the safety of a product it is not sufficient to only show that each task can be safely executed in isolation because some safety problems may only manifest through a succession of actions. For example, making several x-ray images with a medical imaging system may result in a safety issue if the setting of the radiation dose used per image has been increased beforehand to a level not meant for making many successive images. Therefore, it is important to test the entire context in which the tasks occur with realistic test scenarios that consist of successions of actions that can also be expected to occur in practice [6].

Unfortunately, creating realistic test scenarios can be challenging [2,6,14]. To create a realistic test scenario, the usability engineer needs to have in depth knowledge of the product features, the tasks performed while using the product and the context in which the product is used. The list of tasks has to match those that the product users would perform to achieve the intended goals of the product, both in content and the order in which they have to be performed during the test. However, usability engineers on the product development team may not be familiar with all possible variations of use that occur in practice [17]. For example, the way in which medical imaging systems are used differs per country and sometimes even per hospital. This means that, especially for complex products that require significant training or education to use, it can be challenging to create test scenarios that accurately represents how the intended target audience will use the final product in a real setting.

5   Approach

To address the issues presented above, we propose a data-driven approach that enables evidence-based usability test scenario creation. A graphical overview of the approach is shown in Fig. 1. This approach consists of the collection of data and knowledge regarding product use, the transformation of such data into logs of user activities, the creation of models of user behaviour, and the creation of usability test scenarios based on those models and statistical data.

5.1 Product Usage Data Collection

The first step in the User-Centered Design cycle is to understand the context in which the product is used [15]. This step is essential because you can only improve a product if you know exactly what the problems are that users encounter and what the underlying root cause of each issue is. Without understanding of the context of use, it is difficult to set up an effective usability test [19]. To understand how users behave when using the product in practice it is important to collect sufficient data and combine this with knowledge of the product itself [17].

In the context of the product data usage framework presented in [17], our approach assumes that the data usage maturity of the product is at least at the level of *Diagnostics*. This means that we assume a real-time, or close to it, collection of usage data that is effectively stored and accessible. The usage data is ideally linked to specific product functionalities so that it becomes possible to relate functions to user tasks. Evidence-based usability testing can then help to reach the maturity levels of *Feature Usage* analysis and *Feature Improvement*.

It is easier to collect data for a product that is already deployed and is now being improved or for which a successor is being created than for a completely new product. For truly new products, for which perhaps only prototypes exist, there may not be any usage data available to work with. However, if product prototypes are given to real users for testing purposes, as happened in the development of the smart bottle, then some usage data can already be collected early in the development cycle. Alternatively, if access to end users is really not possible, the developers can create artificial usage data by using product prototypes in a manner similar to end users during a test role-playing session.

There are different types of data that can be collected to help understand the context of use. For example, observational data of activities from field studies, subjective descriptions of users from reviews, sensor data measured by the product itself, or usage logs from an accompanying application or service. For the purpose of this approach, sensor data and product usage logs, like the one shown in Fig. 4, that are linked to product functions are the most useful types of data, as these machine logs provide objective information to quantify product feature usage. However, observational data can be used to relate the machine logs to actual user tasks, if this knowledge is not known to the developers. User reviews can be helpful in determining which tasks are problematic and important to be tested.

EventTimestamp	FrStand_Rlo	FrStand_Ce	FrStand_Dt	FrStand_Pr	FrStand_RD	FrStand_Sa	FrStand_ZM	Table_Ht	Table_Lt	Table_Lo	Table_Tl	Table_Cr	Table_tw	Table_pv	Table_pvg	Table_pva	BrakeEngaged	AbnormalBehaviorLAT	AbnormalBehaviorLNG
01-01-15 10:48:25	2820	-1.7	1190	0	0	PARK	-86.9	821	70	1074	0	0	-1.4	HORIZONTAL	WORK	TRUE	FALSE	FALSE
01-01-15 10:48:25	2820	-1.7	1190	0	0	PARK	-86.9	821	70	1074	0	0	-1.4	HORIZONTAL	WORK	TRUE	FALSE	FALSE
01-01-15 10:48:28	2820	-1.7	1190	0	0	PARK	-86.9	874	70	1074	0	0	-1.4	HORIZONTAL	WORK	TRUE	FALSE	FALSE
01-01-15 10:48:28	2820	-1.7	1190	0	0	PARK	-86.9	886	70	1074	0	0	-1.4	HORIZONTAL	WORK	TRUE	FALSE	FALSE
01-01-15 10:48:28	2820	-1.7	1190	0	0	PARK	-86.9	883	70	1074	0	0	-1.4	HORIZONTAL	WORK	TRUE	FALSE	FALSE
01-01-15 10:48:29	2820	0	1195	0	0	PARK	-86.9	908	70	1074	0	0	-1.4	HORIZONTAL	WORK	TRUE	FALSE	FALSE
01-01-15 10:48:29	2820	0	1195	0	0	PARK	-86.9	908	70	1074	0	0	-1.4	HORIZONTAL	WORK	TRUE	FALSE	FALSE
01-01-15 10:48:29	2820	-0.1	1195	0	0	PARK	-86.9	906	70	1074	0	0	-1.4	HORIZONTAL	WORK	TRUE	FALSE	FALSE

Fig. 4. Example of a machine log describing how the table position of a medical imaging system was changed by a surgeon during a procedure.

5.2   User Activity Log Creation

The different types of data collected above do not guarantee a clear view on the activities of the users. Depending on the type of data, it can be necessary to transform the raw product usage data into actual logs of activities [4].

Usability test scenarios can be seen as sequences of activities that a test participant has to execute. This means that we are also interested in obtaining such sequences of user activities from the field in order to get a better understanding of the user behaviour. Essential information to obtain is therefore which activities the users performed, in what order and how long they took.

Often, product usage data is collected for maintenance and service purposes or as a side-product of debugging functionalities [17]. In these cases, the usage data may not immediately reveal what people are doing exactly and a relation needs to be established between the product functions instrumented with logging and the actual user task during which the function is used. For example, in the medical imaging system different sensors can detect movement in specific directions of the table on which the patient is lying. However, the recorded data contains detailed technical information, as shown in Fig. 4. From this we need to deduce what task is executed by the user, e.g. specific movements positioning the patient under the scanner or adjusting the table to a convenient working position for the surgeon.

There are different techniques to transform low-level sensor data or logged events into higher-level user tasks and activities. There is a large body of work on activity recognition and complex event processing [7,12]. For example, it is possible to group low-level events based on behavioral activity patterns in order to identify high-level activities that make sense to domain experts [13]. In the case of the smart bottle usage data, it was necessary to use techniques from the signal processing domain combined with clustering techniques to detect shifts in the sensor data that corresponded to actual user activities [9]. For the imaging system, the logged machine-generated events and diagnostic messages were related to user tasks through a combination of domain knowledge and user activity logs obtained from observational studies and self-reporting [11].

In some cases, it can also be necessary to modify the logging developed by the product designers in order to get a better view of what the users are doing. For example, one of the medical imaging systems developed by Philips has a sensor that detects whether a patient is currently lying on the operating table. However, the signal detected by the sensor was not logged in the data sent back to Philips. After changing the data logging, it is possible to recognise the moments where the patient is present on the table, which in turn allows for the recognition of the activities in the clinical workflow of a surgical procedure of putting the patient onto the table and removing the patient.

5.3   User Behaviour Discovery

Once there are activity logs then we can create models of user behaviour. This is often done manually based on the understanding of the developers regarding

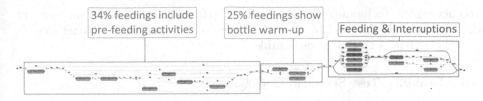

Fig. 5. A discovered end-to-end process model for the use of the smart bottle, showing which activities are performed and in what order. The model is annotated with statistics regarding choices and activity durations.

user goals and product functionalities, but this is very time consuming [10,14]. Therefore, we propose to apply techniques from the field of process mining to automatically discover models of behaviour from activity data [1].

Process mining can be defined as the analysis of processes using the data recorded during their execution. A process in this context is a set of logically related tasks to achieve a certain goal. The data corresponding to the execution of a process can be captured in a log of events, where each event corresponds to the execution of a task at a specific point in time, possibly associated with other data. Hence, user activity logs can be seen as a particular type of event log.

Process discovery works by taking an event log and applying a discovery algorithm to produce a process model that represents the behaviour captured in the log. There are many different algorithms [1] such as the Alpha Miner, the ILP Miner and the Inductive Miner that have been implemented in the open-source process mining framework ProM [21]. Various commercial tools are also available that can discover process models from event logs [1].

The models discovered using a process discovery algorithm are often annotated with statistical data [1,8]. The process model annotations often provide information on the number of occurrences of activities and the likelihood of an activity being followed by another activity. Many process mining tools also show statistics regarding the duration of activities. These annotated models can be used to gain insights into the likely flow of activities of people using a product and how much time is being spent doing what. For example, the model in Fig. 5 was discovered from smart bottle usage data [9] and it showed e.g. that many people filled the bottle before attaching the sleeve, resulting in limited visibility on pre-feeding activities.

There also exist process discovery techniques that aim to provide insights into the relation between different process artifacts [8]. These techniques are suitable for data from environments with multiple products or complex products that consist of multiple objects, sensors or modules that each generate data. The use of such techniques can make the resulting models of each artifact easier to understand than the complex behaviour of the entire system. We used these techniques in the creation of models for the medical imaging system [11] because of the complexity of the system and the difficulty in creating user activity logs. It was not possible to recognise all user activities in the machine data, so we used artifact-centric techniques to discover interacting models for different parts of the system behaviour and to obtain correlations between those artifact models and the activities that were detectable.

5.4   Usability Test Scenario Creation

After obtaining user behaviour models based on activity logs, we can use them to generate evidence-based usability test scenarios. The main challenge we address is in creating the list of tasks that is executed during the scenario. This is achieved by using the models annotated with flow statistics, activity frequencies and durations to provide a usability engineer with the information needed.

Different approaches and strategies exist for the generation of a test scenario from a task or process model [6,10,14], such as the creation of random test scenarios or exhaustive generation. Exhaustively generating all possible sequences of user behaviour from the models is possible in automated test settings, but not for usability testing with real end users. Test participants have limited availability and there is a cost associated to their employment [19]. There are techniques to simplify the behaviour in a model [6], but simplified models can still generate thousands of test cases. When creating random test scenarios, there is no guarantee that they will contain activities that are closely related to the area for which the developers have made product improvements. The risk of this is ineffective usability testing. Therefore, we propose an approach combining domain knowledge from usability engineers with evidence-based user behaviour models.

One combined strategy is to order a set of mandatory tasks in the most likely configuration according to the model. The usability engineer determines the tasks that are essential for the test and those that are most likely to be affected, based on the nature of the product improvement being tested, the features it affects and in what tasks those features are used. For example, if a product improvement has been developed for the medical imaging system that should make it easier to position the patient then usability testing should also focus on activities related to the patient positioning itself and those that are affected by either proper or incorrect patient positioning. The usability test scenario would then be the most likely path through the state-space of the model, given that it contains at least the critical tasks selected by the usability engineer.

Another combined strategy is through tool-supported interactive guidance of the usability engineer while they are creating the test scenario. While selecting tasks to be included in the test scenario, the engineer is presented with information from the model regarding the expected preceding or succeeding tasks and their frequency. This is the approach that we implemented in a scenario planner after discussions with usability engineers, as covered in the next section.

Given a usability test scenario, it is also important to select the appropriate test participants [3]. The discovered models of user behaviour can assist in this if task frequency and ordering statistics are split by user subgroup. If for example certain features in the medical system are used more frequently by specific types or surgeons then product changes affecting those features should be tested with these subgroups. Alternatively, if the models show that a specific group of users

Table 1. An overview of the main requirements of the usability test scenario planning tool.

Requirement	Priority
1. Connection to a static clinical workflow model of user activities with statistical annotations	Must have
2. The current structure and essential elements of the test scenarios are reflected	Must have
3. Possibility to choose the type of imaging system for the usability test	Must have
4. Possibility to choose the type of clinical professional participating in the usability test	Must have
5. Possibility to choose the type of department from the hospital for the usability test	Must have
6. Possibility to choose the type of clinical procedure executed during the usability test	Must have
7. Possibility to create a test scenario for a part of the clinical workflow, not only the whole workflow	Should have
8. Possibility to choose the region where the hospital is located for the usability test	Should have
9. The expected duration of the test scenario is shown	Could have
10. Integration with Philips database systems whose data the static workflow model is based on	Won't have

perform undesirable or incorrect behaviour more frequently than other groups of users for a certain task then product improvements affecting this task should also be tested with these users that potentially benefit most.

6 Scenario Planner

Based on the approach presented in Sect. 5 and discussions we had with usability engineers at Philips Healthcare, we developed a usability test scenario planning tool. The purpose of the scenario planner is to assist usability engineers when creating a usability test scenario by providing them with evidence-based information on the behaviour of product users.

6.1 Requirements Analysis

We performed exploratory research to determine the requirements of the scenario planner. Based on literature regarding usability testing, interviews with usability engineers, and observations in the field (observing both end-users of the medical imaging systems and usability engineers) we established a set of requirements for the scenario planner shown in Table 1.

A central concept of the scenario planner is its use of an internal workflow model to provide information to the usability engineer, based on the product usage data collected by Philips from medical imaging systems in the field. As Philips Healthcare collects data from its imaging systems located all across the world, used in various different hospital departments and for different types of procedures, there is also a need for the selection of the correct model of user behaviour depending on the specific context for which a usability test is being created. However, as the developed tool is only a prototype we did not aim for live integration with the database systems and instead used a static snapshot of the data for the internal model of user activities, i.e. a model of the clinical workflow of using the imaging system.

6.2   Tool Concepts

Based on the requirements analysis several different concepts of the scenario planner were developed. The design process was iterative with feedback from three different usability engineers during the development cycles.

Paper prototypes were developed to discuss the concepts with usability engineers and to get an understanding of their way of working during usability test scenario creation. The first concept, shown in Fig. 6, involved an interactive selection of individual tasks based on observed sequences of activities and possible choices. The user interface was envisioned to show the different phases of a clinical workflow and for each phase a model annotated with transition probabilities would be presented. By clicking on user tasks they would be included in the test scenario. The feedback from the usability engineers for this concept was that showing a complete overview of all possible activities and their relations with corresponding data could result in a very complex model and make it difficult to put together a test scenario.

The second concept in Fig. 7 is a presentation of a number of pre-defined usability test scenarios based on the most likely sequences of user behaviour. The feedback from the usability engineers on the second concept was that, although easy to use, it would not provide much support for the creation of evidence-based usability test scenarios in cases where additional editing is necessary to include essential activities that were not part of the suggested activity flows.

After these design iterations, another paper prototype was built that combines the idea of presenting the user with a likely sequence of user behaviour and the option to interactively modify the scenario based on data. When modifying the scenario, the tool provides the user with suggestions for adding specific activities based on the part of the scenario being changed and data on e.g. the most likely next activity. The prototype was tested with two usability engineers and based on their feedback the implementation of the scenario planner was started.

6.3   Implementation

The scenario planner with limited functionality was implemented as a web application. The application was created using HTML, CSS, JavaScript and PHP.

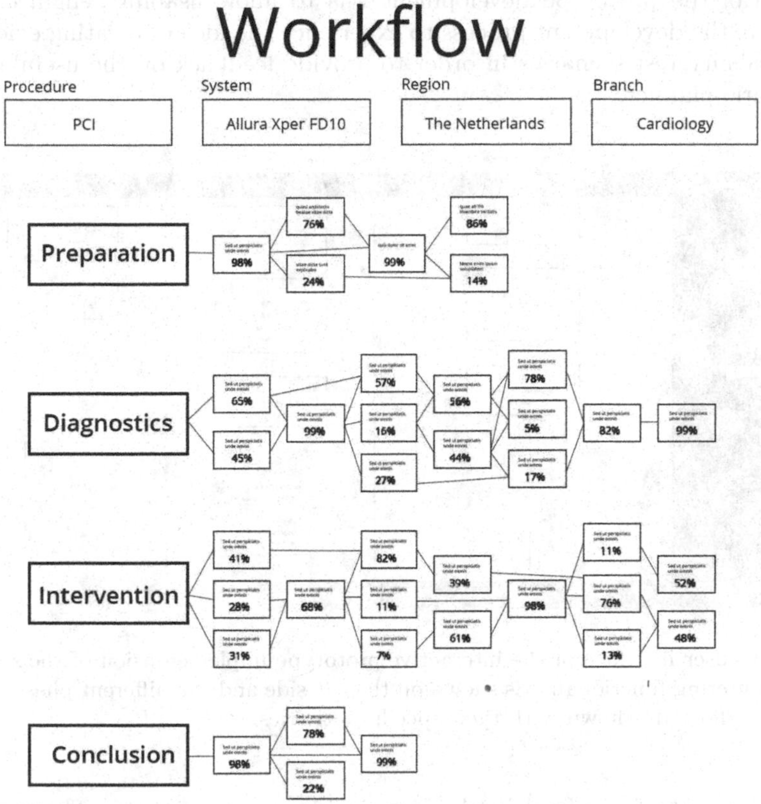

Workflow

Procedure	System	Region	Branch
PCI	Allura Xper FD10	The Netherlands	Cardiology

Preparation

Diagnostics

Intervention

Conclusion

Fig. 6. A design concept of the selection of test activities. The activities are divided over the different clinical workflow phases and their frequency of occurrence is shown. The user selects which activities to include in the test scenario.

Choose your workflow

Procedure	System	Region	Branch
PCI	Allura Xper FD10	The Netherlands	Cardiology

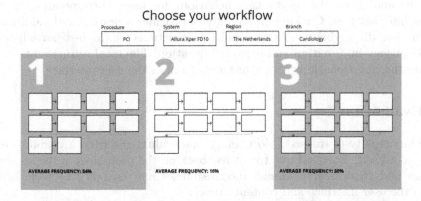

Fig. 7. A design concept based on the selection of a sequence of user activities based on its frequency of occurring in the field.

The goal of the prototype development was to allow usability engineers not involved in the development process to experience the idea of creating evidence-based usability test scenarios in order to provide feedback on the usefulness of the scenario planner.

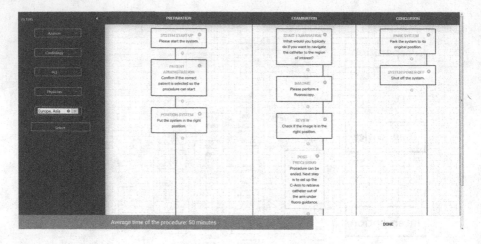

Fig. 8. The user interface of the interactive prototype implementation of the scenario planner. Filtering functionality is shown on the left side and the different phases of the clinical workflow are shown with their specific activities.

A screenshot of the final implementation is shown in Fig. 8. The user can set the filter to restrict the usability test scenario to a specific context and is then presented with a frequent sequence of activities for each phase of the clinical workflow. Activities can be removed or added after existing activities, in which case the tool will suggest appropriate activities to insert at that specific point depending on the most likely behaviour for users corresponding to the chosen filter settings. Clicking on an activity provides a pop-up with additional information, displaying e.g. more detailed instructions for the test participants, task frequency information and expected duration. The total estimated time to execute the test scenario is shown at the bottom of the user interface.

7   Evaluation

The functionality of the scenario planner was evaluated during a usability test of the tool itself. The goal was to get feedback on the usefulness of the scenario planner and to determine design inconsistencies and usability problem areas within the user interface and content areas.

7.1   Test Setup

The usability test was conducted on-site at a Philips location and through Skype. The session captured the participants' navigational choices, task completion scores, comments, questions and feedback. At the end of the test every participant was asked what they like and dislike about the scenario planner, if they miss certain product functions and if they think that the scenario planner fits in their daily work when preparing usability tests.

All participants work as a usability engineer at Philips Healthcare and have experience with usability tests. Nineteen participants were invited and nine participants took part in the test, of which three were already involved in the design process of the scenario planner. The test participants who were not involved in the design process were given a short description how the scenario planner came about and what it can be used for.

Table 2. The usability engineers participating in the evaluation were asked to complete these tasks using the scenario planner.

Step	Task	Instruction	Expected results
1	Start creating scenario	You have a usability test coming up. You are going to test an Azurion system with a physician from the cardiology department	User uses the filters to give specifications to the scenario
2	Add a task	You want to add a task between after review because you want to test a feature that could be used in that phase of the test. How would you do that?	User clicks on a task and gets to see two separate tasks. They will choose one of these
3	Delete a task	You don't want to test reporting. Try to remove this	User clicks on tasks and deletes it while getting the alert that they're deleting a frequent task
4	Access task details	You want to know more about the imaging task. Try to find more info	User clicks twice on the task and sees the overlay with the information
5	Check test duration	What is the duration of the test you want to do?	User notices the time at the bottom of the page and knows how to change it
6	Output results	You are done! Try to get the output of the scenario planner	User clicks at done and notices the alert that they're done

The participants were asked to perform the tasks described in Table 2 using the scenario planner. These tasks form a simple scenario where the test participants are asked to use the scenario planner to create a usability test scenario for the use of a medical imaging system developed at Philips. Participants were scored per task on completion success rate and their time spent.

7.2   Results

The ability of participants to complete a task without critical errors was rated according to the following four point scale:

1. User cannot complete the task and needs help.
2. User completes the task after a hint from the moderator.
3. User completes the task after some tries.
4. User completes the task immediately.

An overview of the completion scores of each participant for each task is shown in Fig. 9. Tasks scored with a 3 or 4 are considered as successfully completed. All participants managed to successfully complete tasks 1, 2, 3 and 6. However, very few participants completed tasks 4 and 5 without assistance.

Participant	Task 1	Task 2	Task 3	Task 4	Task 5	Task 6
1	4	4	4	2	2	4
2	4	4	4	2	4	4
3	4	4	4	4	2	4
4	4	4	4	2	2	4
5	4	4	4	2	2	4
6	3	4	4	2	3	4
7	4	4	4	2	4	4
8	4	3	4	2	2	4
9	4	4	4	3	2	4
Success	9	9	9	2	3	9
Completion Rates	100%	100%	100%	20%	30%	100%

Fig. 9. The task completion scores for each participant on each task. A task scored with a 3 or 4 is considered successfully completed.

Different parts of the user interface were used in completing the different tasks. The participants managed to successfully use the filters in the side menu to specify the type of scenario they wanted to create. The subsequent modification of the scenario generated by the planner based on an internal workflow model was achieved through buttons placed near the tasks where the user wanted to make the change. These parts of the user interface were intuitive to use. However, the option to access additional task details, which required the user to double click on a task, was less intuitive. The reason why participants required assistance

Table 3. An overview of the main recommendations given by the usability engineers after testing the usability test scenario planning tool.

Recommendation	Priority
1. More intuitive method to access the additional information for activities	High
2. Clear specification in the filtering UI regarding optional and required information	High
3. Better integration of the expected duration of the test scenario in the UI	High
4. Undo functionality to revert accidental deletions of activities	Medium
5. Options to add custom activities to the scenario that are not present in the data and to edit the description or instructions belonging to activities, to reduce the need for editing in Excel afterwards	Medium
6. Save and load functionality for test scenarios	Medium
7. Drag and drop functionality to move tasks around in the scenario planner	Medium
8. Provide more information regarding possible safety related issues or risks	Low

with task 5 was that they assumed that the user interface element used in this task was part of the screen recording device used in the evaluation.

The participants provided feedback on the user interface of the scenario planner. Based on this feedback, the a list of recommendations for changes in the scenario planner was established and prioritised, shown in Table 3. The priority was based on a combination of ease of implementation and impact. In general, they liked the option to export the final scenario to Microsoft Excel and the user interface design for the activity flow. However, accessing the additional task information was not intuitive and it was not entirely clear to all participants what elements on the data filtering were optional and which were required. The participants also indicated that they would like to be able to revert editing mistakes and to save and subsequently edit old usability test scenarios.

The participants also commented on the perceived usefulness of the tool. They were happy with the overall functionality and the concept of evidence-based usability test creation. Eight out of nine participants expressed that they would want to use the tool in their daily work. They indicated the value of knowing how often specific activities are performed and what other activities they are related to. However, in this usability test it was not possible to evaluate how effective the activity and flow statistics are in guiding the scenario creation, due to the fixed nature of the test scenario that the participants created. Some participants suggested that it would be even more helpful if detailed reports were available on activity statistics, e.g. the number of times an activity is executed per procedure type, per day and per hospital.

8   Conclusion and Future Work

In this paper, we have presented an approach to enable the creation of evidence-based usability test scenarios. The approach consists of several different parts: the collection of data on product use, the transformation of the data into logs of product user activities, the creation of models of user behaviour, and the guided creation of usability test scenarios. Based on this approach, we have created a prototype usability test scenario planning tool in co-creation with usability engineers working at Philips Healthcare.

The prototype has been evaluated through a usability test of the tool itself. Overall, the participating usability engineers were enthusiastic regarding the evidence-based creation of usability test scenarios and eight out of nine participants expressed that they would want to use the tool during their normal work. They were able to successfully create a usability test scenario using the tool and provided feedback and recommendations for the future development of the scenario planner, its user interface and the information provided by the tool.

One of the main limitations of our approach is that it requires an existing product for which usage data is available, or a prototype that has been deployed for testing. The limitations of the conducted evaluation of our approach are that the usability test scenarios created during the evaluation were based on a simplified model of the clinical workflow activities and that the created usability scenarios were not subsequently used during a real usability test of a medical imaging system. As a result, the quality of the evidence-based usability test scenarios was not directly evaluated. To address these limitations a more mature implementation of the scenario planner and additional user evaluation are needed.

As future work, we propose an integration of evidence-based usability testing into a full data-driven product development approach. By collecting and analysing data throughout the design cycle it can become possible to identify patterns that correspond to incorrect or undesirable user behaviour. This could be the input for suggestions for additional product improvements, which can then be tested in a subsequent product design iteration. Based on the results of usability testing, the impact of product improvements on different usability aspects can then be measured and compared to the data available on the user behaviour with the previous product version.

Acknowledgements. This work has been conducted in the context of the IMPULS collaboration project of Eindhoven University of Technology and Philips: "Mine your own body", and within the ENABLE-S3 project that has received funding from the ECSEL Joint Undertaking under Grant Agreement No 692455. This Joint Undertaking receives support from the European Union's Horizon 2020 research and innovation programme and Austria, Denmark, Germany, Finland, Czech Republic, Italy, Spain, Portugal, Poland, Ireland, Belgium, France, Netherlands, United Kingdom, Slovakia, Norway.

References

1. van der Aalst, W.M.P.: Process Mining - Data Science in Action, 2nd edn. Springer, Berlin (2016). https://doi.org/10.1007/978-3-662-49851-4
2. Bernhaupt, R., Palanque, P., Manciet, F., Martinie, C.: User-test results injection into task-based design process for the assessment and improvement of both usability and user experience. In: Bogdan, C., et al. (eds.) HCSE/HESSD -2016. LNCS, vol. 9856, pp. 56–72. Springer, Cham (2016). https://doi.org/10.1007/978-3-319-44902-9_5
3. Billestrup, J., Bruun, A., Stage, J.: Usability problems experienced by different groups of skilled internet users: gender, age, and background. In: Bogdan, C., et al. (eds.) HCSE/HESSD -2016. LNCS, vol. 9856, pp. 45–55. Springer, Cham (2016). https://doi.org/10.1007/978-3-319-44902-9_4
4. Billman, D., Fayollas, C., Feary, M., Martinie, C., Palanque, P.: Complementary tools and techniques for supporting fitness-for-purpose of interactive critical systems. In: Bogdan, C., et al. (eds.) HCSE/HESSD -2016. LNCS, vol. 9856, pp. 181–202. Springer, Cham (2016). https://doi.org/10.1007/978-3-319-44902-9_12
5. Bogers, S., Frens, J.W., van Kollenburg, J., Deckers, E., Hummels, C.: Connected baby bottle: a design case study towards a framework for data-enabled design. In: Proceedings of the 2016 ACM Conference on Designing Interactive Systems, DIS 2016, Brisbane, QLD, Australia, 4–8 June, pp. 301–311 (2016)
6. Campos, J.C., et al.: A more intelligent test case generation approach through task models manipulation. In: PACMHCI 1(EICS), pp. 9:1–9:20 (2017)
7. Cugola, G., Margara, A.: Processing flows of information: from data stream to complex event processing. ACM Comput. Surv. 44(3), 15:1–15:62 (2012)
8. van Eck, M.L., Sidorova, N., van der Aalst, W.M.P.: Discovering and exploring state-based models for multi-perspective processes. In: La Rosa, M., Loos, P., Pastor, O. (eds.) BPM 2016. LNCS, vol. 9850, pp. 142–157. Springer, Cham (2016). https://doi.org/10.1007/978-3-319-45348-4_9
9. van Eck, M.L., Sidorova, N., van der Aalst, W.M.P.: Enabling process mining on sensor data from smart products. In: Tenth IEEE International Conference on Research Challenges in Information Science, RCIS 2016, Grenoble, France, 1–3 June, pp. 1–12 (2016)
10. Harrison, M.D., Masci, P., Campos, J.C., Curzon, P.: Verification of user interface software: the example of use-related safety requirements and programmable medical devices. IEEE Trans. Hum Mach. Syst. 47(6), 834–846 (2017)
11. Hoornaar, T.J.: Extracting real-life workflow models from relational data and using these to generate field-based usability testing scenarios at Philips Healthcare. Master's thesis, Technische Universiteit Eindhoven (2017)
12. Liu, Y., Nie, L., Liu, L., Rosenblum, D.S.: From action to activity: sensor-based activity recognition. Neurocomputing 181, 108–115 (2016)
13. Mannhardt, F., de Leoni, M., Reijers, H.A., van der Aalst, W.M.P., Toussaint, P.J.: Guided process discovery-a pattern-based approach. Inf. Syst. (2018, submitted)
14. Mori, G., Paternò, F., Santoro, C.: CTTE: support for developing and analyzing task models for interactive system design. IEEE Trans. Software Eng. 28(8), 797–813 (2002)
15. Norman, D.A., Draper, S.W.: User Centered System Design: New Perspectives on Human-Computer Interaction. Lawrence Erlbaum Associates Inc., New Jersey (1986)

16. Ogata, S., Goto, Y., Okano, K.: Framework for relative web usability evaluation on usability features in MDD. In: Bogdan, C., et al. (eds.) HCSE/HESSD -2016. LNCS, vol. 9856, pp. 73–85. Springer, Cham (2016). https://doi.org/10.1007/978-3-319-44902-9_6

17. Holmström Olsson, H., Bosch, J.: Towards data-driven product development: a multiple case study on post-deployment data usage in software-intensive embedded systems. In: Fitzgerald, B., Conboy, K., Power, K., Valerdi, R., Morgan, L., Stol, K.-J. (eds.) LESS 2013. LNBIP, vol. 167, pp. 152–164. Springer, Heidelberg (2013). https://doi.org/10.1007/978-3-642-44930-7_10

18. Paetsch, F., Eberlein, A., Maurer, F.: Requirements engineering and agile software development. In: 12th IEEE International Workshops on Enabling Technologies (WETICE 2003), Infrastructure for Collaborative Enterprises, 9–11 June 2003, Linz, Austria, pp. 308–313 (2003)

19. Rubin, J., Chisnell, D.: Handbook of Usability Testing: How to Plan, Design, and Conduct Effective Tests, 2nd edn. Wiley, New York (2008)

20. Silva, T.R., Hak, J.-L., Winckler, M.: Testing prototypes and final user interfaces through an ontological perspective for behavior-driven development. In: Bogdan, C., et al. (eds.) HCSE/HESSD -2016. LNCS, vol. 9856, pp. 86–107. Springer, Cham (2016). https://doi.org/10.1007/978-3-319-44902-9_7

21. Verbeek, H.M.W., Buijs, J.C.A.M., van Dongen, B.F., van der Aalst, W.M.P.: XES, XESame, and ProM 6. In: Soffer, P., Proper, E. (eds.) CAiSE Forum 2010. LNBIP, vol. 72, pp. 60–75. Springer, Heidelberg (2011). https://doi.org/10.1007/978-3-642-17722-4_5

MIODMIT: A Generic Architecture for Dynamic Multimodal Interactive Systems

Martin Cronel[1], Bruno Dumas[2], Philippe Palanque[1,3(✉)], and Alexandre Canny[1]

[1] ICS-IRIT, Université Paul Sabatier – Toulouse III, Toulouse, France
martin.cronel@gmail.com, {palanque,canny}@irit.fr
[2] University of Namur, Namur, Belgium
bruno.dumans@unamur.be
[3] Department of Industrial Design, Technical University Eindhoven, Eindhoven, Netherlands

Abstract. This paper proposes a generic interactive system architecture describing in a structured way, both hardware and software components of an interactive system. It makes explicit all the components that play a role in the information processing from input devices to the interactive application and back to the output devices. Along with the generic interactive system architecture the paper proposes a process for selecting and connecting those components in order to tune the generic interactive system architecture for a specific interactive application. This select, connect and tune-on-demand approach helps handle complexity of interactive applications featuring innovative interaction techniques by splitting the interactive software into dedicated functional components. It also supports design flexibility by making explicit the components impacted when the interaction design evolves. This interactive system architecture and its related process have been applied to the development of several real-life interactive systems and we illustrate their application on an interactive application offering multi-mice, multi-touch and leap motion interactions in the context of interactive cockpits of large civil aircrafts.

Keywords: Interactive systems engineering · Input/output devices integration Interaction techniques · Software architectures

1 Introduction

The diversification of technological platforms on which interactive systems are designed, developed and deployed significantly increases the complexity of designers' and developers' tasks. At the same time, such an ever-changing context has made it

© IFIP International Federation for Information Processing 2019
Published by Springer Nature Switzerland AG 2019
C. Bogdan et al. (Eds.): HCSE 2018, LNCS 11262, pp. 109–129, 2019.
https://doi.org/10.1007/978-3-030-05909-5_7

very difficult for researchers belonging to the engineering community on interactive systems, to provide generic approaches to support those tasks. Designers need to go beyond the interactive application design by providing new interaction techniques that encompass new input and output devices which can be very cumbersome to design and evaluate (as for instance fingers clustering in multi-touch interactions [29]). Developers of these systems are repetitively facing the same issues of: (i) new devices integration, software redesign (due to device drivers' evolution) and above all poor reliability of the resulting system due to the low level of maturity of the various components to integrate. Such constraints are even stronger in the area of critical systems where a failure may lead to catastrophic consequences.

This paper addresses these issues by proposing MIODMIT (Multiple Input and Output Devices and Multiple Interaction Techniques) generic interactive system architecture for integrating new input and output devices, along with their more and more (potentially multimodal) sophisticated interaction techniques. MIODMIT identifies the building components that have to be developed for integrating new devices as well as the building components for merging information from these devices in order to offer multimodal interaction to users. As such, MIODMIT helps developers with the design of systems exploiting advanced interaction technologies. While this interactive system architecture is generic (and can thus be applied to many types of interactive systems) it also comes with a set of attributes and related trade-offs giving freedom to developers using it, while constraining them when necessary. Due to its generic nature, MIODMIT needs to be tuned to and adapted for the interactive system under development, especially to the input and output devices and interaction techniques considered. Two case studies (including a real world critical system application) and two illustrative examples illustrate how the architecture is applied, as well as the benefits it brings.

The remainder of this paper is structured as follows. Next section describes relevant related work and characterizes input and output devices. Section 3 details MIODMIT making explicit how it decomposes interactive systems into connected components within a generic interactive system architecture. Section 4 presents the Tune-on-Demand process and makes explicit how to go from a tuned MIODMIT diagram to the implementation. Section 5 presents a real world case study in the area of interactive cockpits. As this application is rather complex, we also present a simple example of interactive system to demonstrate along the paper the application and functioning of the tune-on-demand process in its entirety. The last section concludes the paper, highlighting benefits and limitations of the contributions and identifying potential extensions.

2   Related Work

2.1   Software Side of Interactive Systems Architectures

Architectural models for multimodal interactive systems have been presented in research papers [38] and [39] as a way of explaining the various components of a given system. More generic ones have also been presented, but they are usually bound to one type of modality such as touch interaction [37] or speech interaction [21]. Toolkits and frameworks for supporting the development of prototypes and demonstrations have also been developed such as, for instance, PyMT toolkit [17] for interactive applications offering multi-touch interactions. Similarly SensScreen [34] is dedicated to interactive applications exploiting multimodal management of sensors distributed in the user environment and presents a very high level architecture dedicated to public displays. As far as interaction techniques are concerned, dedicated software architectures have been proposed but focusing on a specific problem raised by a specific kind of interaction technique in an interactive application. For instance [26] presents the Accelerated Touch Architecture and [15] the Layered Multi-touch Architecture but both only address specific problems related to touch input.

MUDRA [19] is one recent exception proposing a framework embedding a generic architecture for multimodal interaction. The main limitation of MUDRA architecture (in terms of genericity) lies in its hardware part which is restricted to a defined set of input devices and does not provide a generic approach making explicit how new devices can be instantiated.

Despite such architecture-based contributions for engineering systems, empirical studies have demonstrated that, generally, developers are coding from scratch [24] as the problem they are facing is only superficially addressed by the existing solutions.

2.2 Hardware Side of Interactive Systems Architectures: Input and Output Devices

In order to provide generic means to deal with the extent of future input and output devices, there is a need to characterize them and, in addition, to provide means for integrating input devices types (according to their characteristics) rather than their instances. Indeed, integration based on types provides an adequate mean to increase architecture genericity. The HCI community has been proposing several taxonomies of input devices taking into account both their hardware and software aspects.

In [6], the software side is prominent as the classification is more abstract and goes beyond the description of the physical capabilities of the input devices. They introduced the "virtual" and "logical" device concepts, which can be used to produce more versatile interaction techniques. The concept of virtual devices allows reasoning in terms of interaction methods without having to consider the input devices themselves. For instance, instead of designing the interaction techniques with low level mouse events (for instance using dx, dy relative quantity of movement as for a mouse), it is described using generic pointing events such as x, y screen coordinates. This allows replacing mouse input devices easily with other devices as long as they produce similar (compatible) pointing events. In order to support this, MIODMIT proposes the refinement of the virtual device concept into two distinctive components called Virtual Device and Logical Device as presented in the section dedicated to the architecture (see Fig. 3).

From a hardware perspective, we classify devices as in [30] as according to the discrete versus continuous nature of events provided. At an abstract level, MIODMIT architecture remains independent and thus generic whatever the category (continuous or discrete) the device belongs to. Nevertheless, the device type will be taken into account at the refinement time (i.e. during the development of the architecture components). This way of dealing with these two types of devices has been identified when integrating different devices such as keyboards, mice, speech recognition, touch input, and more recently gesture input, eye-tracking and speech synthesis. The only constraint (to ensure the correct functioning of the final system) is to make sure that data processing is consistent both in terms of input and output for each component throughout the entire pipe-line of information processing (from input to output) as identified in [28].

In the literature, much less work has been done on addressing the output side of interactive systems and while a plethora of input devices taxonomies is available, output device taxonomies are seldom. Noticeable exceptions are [18] which provides characterization of both input and output devices and [32] which is dedicated to multimodal output engineering. MIODMIT encompasses this work using the same decomposition for output devices as the one for input devices presented above.

3 MIODMIT: A Generic Architecture for Interactive Systems

The Multiple Input and Output Devices and Multiple Interaction Techniques (MIODMIT) generic interactive system architecture explicitly depicts the various components (both hardware and software) of an information pipe-line in modern interactive systems. In that sense, MIODMIT is compatible with the principles and objectives of the Model Driven Architecture approach at OMG (http://www.omg.org/mda). Such systems contain multiple input devices each providing an information flow that are usually fused with other ones to offer multiple (and often multimodal) inter-action techniques. This architecture presents input and output flows as well as how they can be integrated altogether. The following sections present an overview of MIODMIT and detail functionalities and responsibilities of each component via an illustrative example.

3.1 Illustrative Example with a Simple JAVA Application

In order to illustrate how MIODMIT is structured, we use a simple example application developed with Java Swing, presented in Fig. 1. This application allows users to add, modify and remove elements in a database. An element is composed of three attributes: a text field (the name), an enumerated field (the number of children) and a Boolean value (married or not). The list of elements in the database are displayed in the listbox (called mother list). Once added to the database, elements can be selected in that listbox to be deleted or modified.

In terms of input and output modalities, this application is standard, offering a mouse and a keyboard for input, and a computer screen for display.

3.2 MIODMIT Overview

MIODMIT is meant as a thinking and design tool for developers working on the development of advanced interactive systems. It seeks to clearly describe which components are to be designed, built or reused when envisioning such systems, and the interplay between these components.

Fig. 1. Simple JAVA application

The overview of MIODMIT is presented in Fig. 2 while the full description of the generic architecture is provided in Fig. 3. Figure 2 is described from top (left to right) and then towards bottom (right to left). The overview of the architecture is composed of several components each of them represented by a rounded rectangle. When developing systems using MIODMIT developers have to describe the precise behavior of each component. Due to space constraints, we cannot present it here but the interest reader can access full details in [10].

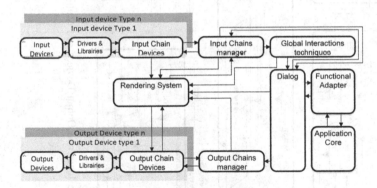

Fig. 2. Overview of MIODMIT

The grayed out boxes labeled "Input Device Type" handle events flow for each type of input device used (according to the classification presented in the related work section). For instance, having two mice and a voice-recognition system would require two separate "Input Device Type" boxes as they do not belong to the same type. The same holds for the output processing. Following the normal flow of events (in which the interactive system is idle waiting for input from users) a given "input device" sends events to the "driver & Library". The "input chain device type 1" transforms the raw data into higher-level information (e.g. transformation of the amount of motion of a mouse (dx, dy) into absolute coordinates for the mouse pointer).

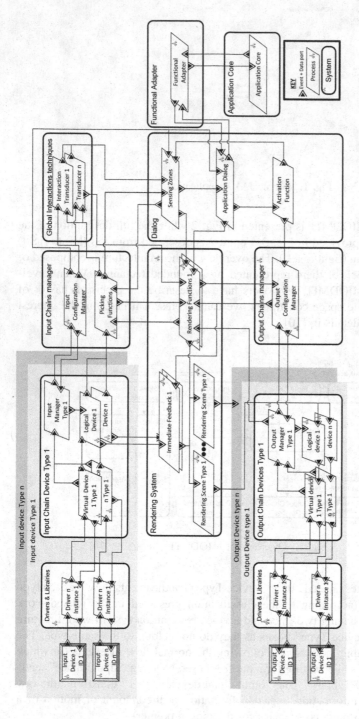

Fig. 3. Multiple Input and Output Devices and Multiple Interaction Techniques expressed in AADL [33]

Such information is then processed by the "input chains manager" (e.g. picking function connecting the input event to user interface objects) that possibly fuses information from the various input devices types. The input chain manager and its output counterpart are also responsible for managing dynamic reconfiguration of interaction when a failure occurs in the flow of events, thus being compliant with [27]. Fused information is then dispatched either directly to the "Dialog" or to "Global Interaction Technique" which behaves as a transducer as defined in [1] and then dispatch information to the "Dialog". Both the "Dialog" and "Application Core" system have a similar responsibility as in standard interactive architecture models such as Seeheim [31] or ARCH [4]. The "Functional Adapter" have a similar responsibility as the "Functional Core Adaptor" in ARCH [4]. The output part processing is a mirror of the input side. The "rendering system" component in the middle of the diagram includes immediate feedback function and more sophisticated state-based rendering functions.

3.3   Inside the Details of MIODMIT

Figure 3 presents the refinement of Fig. 2 making explicit both the content of each component and the information flow between components. Even in its detailed description, MIODMIT remains abstract on purpose which means that each component may be decomposed into several classes. More details about that aspect are given in the case studies section.

The MIODMIT architecture, presented in Fig. 3, uses the AADL notation [33], a standard for describing software architecture which been applied in several domains including automotive and aeronautics. Other notations could have been used but the standard nature of AADL eases its understanding. We do not provide here a description of the elements of AADL but a key is provided at the bottom of Fig. 3.

Input Devices
The first layer of this interactive system architecture is composed of the physical input devices directly handled by the users. In Fig. 3, they are defined with a number corresponding to their type and an ID corresponding to their number within a given type. For instance, two input devices (Input Device 1 ID 1 and Input Device n ID n) represent the fact that both input devices are similar (two mice for instance) but with small functionalities that need to differentiate their drivers. If two identical mice were to be connected, ID will then allow to differentiate them. Figure 3 only details one generic type of device. The addition of a new modality associated with a new input device results in a new set of input devices, new driver(s) and a new input chain, represented within a gray rectangle. In the case of our Java app example, the mouse and keyboard are the input devices.

Drivers
Usually only one device driver is used in an operating system per type of device at a time. This software component is in charge of retrieving (or receiving) raw information from the hardware input device and makes it available for the upper layer.

The driver may also allow some control over the hardware components of the physical input device such as the sampling frequency (e.g. of the touch acquisition in

[25]) or to provide user identification [36]. Drivers are either provided together with the hardware (typically for specific non-standard input devices such as gesture tracking cameras) or by the operating system when the input device is rather standard or has been around for a significant amount of time (typically several years). For instance, mouse and keyboard drivers are handled at the OS level. This component is usually OS dependent and includes the libraries and the API needed for using the device. The API can be a composite object in order to translate information from a low-level language or OS level, to the higher one in the information flow.

Virtual Devices and Logical Devices

Virtual devices are necessary extensions to the logical device concept of Buxton [6] as we take into account explicitly both hardware and software aspects.

For instance, as quickly introduced in the related work section, for a mouse, the virtual device will be a software component mirroring the state of each physical button (pressed or released) and the amount of motion (dx, dy), while the logical device handles the cursor pointer positions (x, y). It is important to note that this is independent of the rendering aspect that is handled in a dedicated set of components ("rendering system" and "output device type" in the architecture). Indeed, these (x, y) values are abstract and how they are presented to the user or fused before rendering is a responsibility not belonging to the input chain.

This distinction allows using a single virtual device, with different logical devices in order to propose different interaction techniques. For instance, with a gesture recognition device such as Leap Motion, with one virtual device (a computerized hand), one logical device could be dedicated to two-dimension interactions, as a pointing device, while another could be used in a 3D environment.

Virtual and logical device components are transducers (as defined in [6]) as they provide processed information to a higher level. Virtual devices can be dynamically instantiated as with plug-and-play devices. Logical devices might also be dynamically instantiated at operations time, as for multi-touch input devices where a "logical input device" component is created each time a finger touches the device [16].

Input Manager

The "Input Manager" component manages the availability and instantiation of devices in order to address configuration and dynamic reconfiguration. This layer is composed of several managers, one per configuration of input devices, each of them being responsible for handling the dynamic aspects of input devices of the same type. At initialization time, these managers are responsible for the instantiation of the input devices and inform "Logical Input Devices" components.

Input Configuration Manager (Input Chains Manager)

One of the specificities of MIODMIT is its intrinsic ability to support dynamic reconfiguration of the interaction techniques. It is a functionality of paramount importance for different systems such as: critical systems, systems with a long exploitation life, systems with long start up procedures (such as civil aircrafts), or systems with a high replacement cost. Indeed, if one or several modalities fail at runtime (also called operation time), it may be critical to offer other modalities for allowing operators to perform their tasks even with degraded or less efficient interactions. To this end, MIODMIT includes an "input configuration manager" which is responsible for handling reconfigurations. It is a unique software component, whatever the amount of input devices is. At runtime, the "input configuration manager" component links the (possibly) dynamically instantiated "logical input devices" components to the relevant "interaction transducers" which are in charge of processing users' input.

Beyond that linking aspect, this manager is in charge of verifying the physical input device configurations to ensure that the current configuration still allows users to trigger all the needed events, and thus to produce all the information that the interactive application is expecting. In the case of input devices failure, the manager would reconfigure the interaction in such a way that the remaining physical input devices could compensate the failing ones (provided that this aspect has been addressed at design time). An example of a behavioral description of such a reconfiguration manager can be found in [27] (and is highlighted in the case study section). It is important to note that in critical systems, the failure must have been expected and so the reconfiguration possibilities are predefined (so that operators can be trained) and not dynamically made.

Input Device Type and Output Device Type
The gray boxes labelled Input Device Type and Output Device Type do not represent component of the architecture. They represent the fact that the components "drivers and libraries" and "input/output chain device type 1" have to handle all the input/output devices of the same type. Mouse and keyboard are examples of different input device type. A screen and a loudspeaker are examples of different output device type.

Picking Functions (Input Chains Manager)
This component channels the input event to the intended sensing zones. These functions are generally handled by the OS for standard devices, but for non-standard interaction, recipients of events must be designed and implement a picking function.

Interaction Transducers (Global Interaction Techniques)
The "interaction transducers" are responsible for generating the high level user events used by the application to trigger the various commands it provides. Usually, one "interaction transducer" is associated with one global interaction technique. These "interaction transducers" perform the recognition of a specific interaction technique which is not linked to a sensing zone such as a button (e.g. an interaction technique such as a double click is a composition of 2 simple clicks performed within a pre-defined temporal window and the click is a succession of a "down" event followed by an "up" event on a button). In the case of multi-touch interaction techniques, the transducer receives fingers' (logical devices) movement and triggers the appropriate high level events based on the gesture recognition or the clustering of fingers. A basic transducer description for two mice can be found in [7], a more detailed one in [1], one for a keyboard in [2] and one for a tactile screen in [16]. A detailed behavioral description of such component can be found in [15]. The global interaction technique component is thus made of multiple interaction transducers, each of them bringing defining one or several interaction technique. The global interaction techniques are not necessarily linked to a special zone. For example, on a Samsung smartphone with

Samsung Experience, a palm swift on the screen will take a snapshot of the screen, whatever the state of the OS is or whatever application is launched.

Sensing Zone (Dialogue and Application Core)

To match the WIMP paradigm, "sensing zone" components include concepts such as interactive widgets (e.g. radio boxes, buttons…). With post-WIMP interaction, those objects are not enough, thus "sensing zones" are to be defined, containing representation parameters (coming from design), their precise behavior as well as how this behavior is triggered (i.e. their local interaction technique). For instance, a "sensing zone" reacts to a specific spoken sentence when highlighted, whereas the rest of the application will not react to the same sentence. The "ok Google" sentence always triggers an event on Android, whichever app is currently active. It is thus a nice example of a global interaction technique whereas a sentence such as "tell me if it's going to rain today" triggers a result only when the Google Now app is active.

Application Dialog

The "Application Dialog" component is a composite component and represents the functional behavior of the application as defined in ARCH [4]. The "Activation Function" component activates or disables the "Sensing Zone" depending on the current state of the application.

Functional Adapter and Application Core

The "Functional Adapter" component adapts the flow of information from the "Dialog" to the "Application Core" as defined in ARCH [4]. The "Application Core" is the component that is responsible of providing the data and services of the application.

Rendering System

The rendering system is composed of several components of two main types: the "rendering functions" and the "rendering scenes". The "rendering function" describes how to present the information of a specific state which might be distributed information in the other components of MIODMIT. The immediate feedback is an example of such a rendering function depending mainly on the information in components "logical devices" and "global interaction techniques". A "Rendering Scene" component composes all rendering function of a given type (e.g. a graphical scene, a sound scene…). These components prepare the final composition of the information before the output processing. They are thus connected to one or several output devices which can effectively present the information to the users.

Output Chain Manager

The "Output Chain Manager" offers the same functionalities as the "Input Chains Manager" presented above. Nonetheless, the main difference is that while the input is event-based, the output is state-based, thus, there is no equivalent to the output, of the "Global Interactions Techniques" component.

Fusion and Fission Engines: A Distributed Function

MIODMIT does not include specific components for fusion and fission as other architecture do [38]. Indeed, in that case, only one device was used (a photo browser) and fusion was located by the device. In MIODMIT, fusion can occur at different levels (e.g. low level with two input devices for a CTRL+Click event or high level where merging speech sentences with mouse event for a "Put that there" multimodal command). Fusion and fission mechanism are thus to be specified within components as for example, fusion engines within the "Global Interaction Technique" component to fuse two (or more) high-level events into a multimodal interaction technique. Engineering issues of multimodal input interactions for a single user have been studied and classified in [6] and a taxonomy based on this classification has been proposed in [23]. Indeed, the various models identified in that survey spread over several components of MIODMIT.

4 Tune-on-Demand Process

According to the type and the number of input and output devices and according to the complexity of the multimodal interaction techniques the generic MIODMIT architecture has to be adapted (tuned) to the specificities of the application under consideration. This section presents a systematic process for tuning MIDOMIT that will be exemplified on case studies in Sect. 5.

4.1 Prototyping

Figure 4 presents a process to tune the generic architecture into a specific one. The top left-hand side (labeled prototyping) represents an abstraction of the user-centered design process of interactive systems. This part is presented in a very abstract way only highlighting the productions that are used as input in the other parts of the process.

4.2 Tuning the Generic Interactive System Architecture

The right-hand side of the diagram (labeled tuning) corresponds to the tuning-on-demand part of the proposed approach while the bottom part focuses on the implementation aspects. These three main phases have been highlighted using gray boxes with dashed lines in Fig. 4. The tuning-on-demand step refines the diagram by concretizing each component of MIODMIT making explicit (in the diagram):

- where software parts (e.g. API; libraries...) provided by the input device's manufacturer are distributed in the architecture,
- if existing code has already been produced where it has to be distributed in the architecture,
- which component have to be coded from scratch.

It is important to note that due to an absence of standards, provided software packages often require to split or merge functionalities in order to fit in the structure of the generic architecture. For instance, the Leap Motion is provided with three software packages: the driver (for a dedicated OS), the library (making it possible to exploit the driver on a dedicated OS and integrating C and C++ API), and a wrapper for high-level programming language (e.g. Java). The driver corresponds to the component "Driver instance" in MIODMIT while the functions in the Leap Motion library cover the "virtual device" component and several interaction transducers (e.g. detection of a

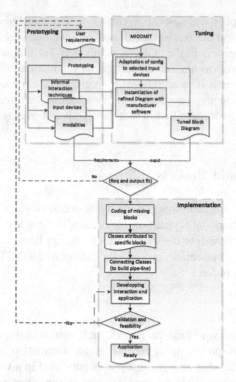

Fig. 4. Process of tuning-on-demand

circle called CircleGesture) located in the "Global Interaction Techniques" component. The wrapper provides functions for all the other components of the input flow but only covers a very limited set of functionalities. The provided set of interaction techniques is basic and has to be extended according to the expected use of the Leap Motion in the application. This is a clever design choice made by Motion manufacturers to allow direct exploitation of the Leap within an application by providing standard interaction techniques but making it also possible to easily extend this set according to the designers' needs.

4.3   Illustration of the Process with the Java Application Example

The result of the application of the tune-on-demand process described above on the Java Application illustrative example is presented in Fig. 5. The Figure can be split in three sections. The left-hand side represent the physical input and output devices used with the Java Application. The center represents the MIODMIT components that are taken care of by the operating system (surrounded by a grey box named "Black Box: OS Windows"). While no access to the Windows source code is given, it remains possible to describe the OS behavior using MIODMIT. Indeed, drivers for a keyboard, mouse and screen as well as part of the rendering system are an integral part of modern OS. The OS merges input and output aspects at hardware level and thus only one component handling both input and output devices drivers is represented. The input and output chains components are merged handling both abstract input abstraction, immediate feedback (position of the mouse cursor on the screen) and graphical rendering (related to the presentation part of the widgets, e.g. display of items in the list box). The window manager of the OS handles picking function (identification of the widgets which are recipients of user input) thus merging input and output chain managers. The right-hand side describe the four components from the MIODMIT architecture that have to be implemented.

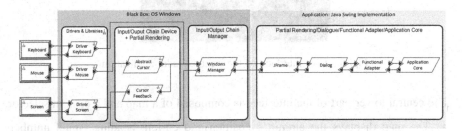

Fig. 5. MIODMIT tuned for Java Application: most of the components of the architecture are integrated within the operating system (especially management input and output devices).

5   A Real World Case Study: A Weather Radar

This case study demonstrates a more complex tuning of the generic interactive system architecture and addresses the issues of integration of input devices as well as the possibility to reconfigure the interaction techniques dynamically. This case study comes from the field of aeronautical critical systems and thus must follow development processes such as the DO178C [12] and certification specifications as defined in CS-25 [11]. In the context of this paper these standards make it impossible to use in critical applications software components for which the code is not available. This prevents using Operating Systems offering integrated handling of devices, drivers... as was the case in the previous example. Indeed, every component of the architecture must be specified and developed from scratch and may be subject to inspection by the certification authorities.

The case study corresponds to a subset of an envisioned weather radar system of civil aircraft providing atmospheric data to the flying crew. This weather radar is controlled by a set of input devices (allowing input from the flying crew) and the processed information is graphically rendered on a computer screen in the cockpit (usually called Navigation Display). This application uses colors and shapes to present information such as dimensions, distance and density of clouds (as visible on the bottom of Fig. 6).

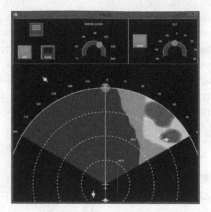

Fig. 6. User interface of the weather radar application

1. The central lower part of the interface is composed of a map and a custom selector:

   - The map displays the aircraft's position and current heading (small numbers from 0 to 360 on the outside circle) as nearby traffic (small blue plane near 40.0 number on the inner circle) and weather information (colored zone on the right-hand side of the image).
   - The custom selector (the small circle at the edge of the biggest circle) controls the heading of the aircraft. When modified, it modifies the information presented in the map display.

2. The upper left part of the interface is composed of three toggle buttons and a custom discrete slider. They provide the following controls:

   - The "HEADING" toggle button (top) controls the heading validation and triggers heading changes,
   - The "ARC" and "ROSE" toggle buttons control the two mutually exclusive display modes of the navigation display,
   - The custom slider (labeled "RANGE SLIDER") defines the zoom level of the navigation display in nautical miles (10 nm, 20 nm...). Current selection is 160 nm.

3. The right upper part of the interface of Fig. 6 called Weather radar control is composed of two widgets:

   - A toggle button "WXR" control the weather visibility on the navigation display,
   - A custom discrete slider controls the weather radar orientation.

5.1   Informal Description (Prototyping Step of the Process)

The informal description provided below is representative of the potential use of several redundant modalities for such application. It is important to note that design aspects of this application is beyond the scope of this paper both in terms of usability and operational validity. In the proposed case study, operators are able to use multiple input devices, modalities and interaction techniques:

- **Input devices:** interaction can take place using a KCCU (Keyboard Cursor Control Unit) which blends a graphical designator (a track-ball) and a keyboard. Two KCCUs are available in the cockpit (one for each pilot) thus enabling parallel interaction with two mice. Such interactions and input devices are available in most recent large civil aircrafts e.g. Airbus A380, A350 and Boeing 787. In the case study, it is also possible to interact in a tactile way using the multi-touch screen presented in Fig. 6.
- **Interaction techniques and modalities:** on top of these input devices, interaction can take place in various ways. Using the multi-touch screen, operators can perform "Flick 2 fingers", "Tap", "Tap long" and "Drag" which are global interaction techniques (i.e. they can be performed everywhere on the screen). Mice are used for triggering events on the WIMP interactors while multimodal events (e.g. "Flick 2 fingers") are assigned (as defined in CARE properties [9]) to the touch screen. In case of a touch screen failure, the mice can be used to trigger high level events previously devoted to the touch screen. In that case the application must be able to switch from one configuration to another. While multi-user interactions with two mice for triggering equivalent multi-touch interactions might be cumbersome, guaranteeing the possibility of events triggering in presence of faulty touch devices was a requirement.

5.2 Overview of the Tuned Generic Interactive System Architecture

According to the process in Fig. 4, the first step, from the prototyping phase, is to refine MIODMIT by specifying all the components. During this refinement, it is important to make explicit where the software provided by the input devices manufacturers is located in the diagram. It is important to note that currently, software packages provided by manufacturers often require splitting or merging in order to fit in the structure of the architecture.

As for the description of MIODMIT in previous sections, Fig. 7 presents an overview of the architecture tuned for the weather radar case study.

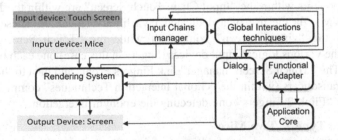

Fig. 7. MIODMIT tuned for the Weather Radar Application

The gray boxes on the left-hand side of the figure correspond to the input and output devices available in the case study. These components will be detailed further in the following sections. The input devices provide input to the "Input chains manager" component. The "input chains manager" component is able to switch between two predetermined input configurations:

- The normal one where touch and mice are available,
- The degraded configuration (resulting from a loss of tactile functionality). This behavior is similar to the one proposed in [27] where reconfiguration was performed at the interaction technique level for keyboards and mice.

As there is only one output device in this case study, there cannot be several output configurations. The "output configuration manager" component is therefore not necessary.

The "Global Interaction Techniques" component contains several transducers that produce high-level events such as "flick-2-fingers", "Combined-Click", "Tap", "Drag", etc. Part of the behavior of those transducers consists of fusing input from multiple input devices thus implementing functionalities of fusion engines. As the weather radar application is a real case study in aeronautics, the behavior of the "Core Application", "Functional Adapter", "Dialog" and a part of the "rendering system" has already been coded. The process of tuning the architecture to include touch and mice interactions does not deeply impact the existing application. Those modifications mainly consist of ensuring that the components connect (plug) and function altogether (play).

The remainder of the "rendering system" concerns mostly the immediate feedback that has to be linked to the two input chains and more particularly, to the "abstract cursor" from the mice input chain and to the "finger" from the touch input chain. These aspects, which are at the center of the contribution, are detailed in the following section.

5.3   Application to the Case Study: Tuning MIODMIT

Input Device Type 1: Touch Screen

Figure 8 presents the tuning of the gray box "Input Device Type 1" from Fig. 3 for a touch-screen device. Adding a touch screen device requires a touch driver (see [13]). All the components within the "Input Chain Touch Screen" are within the Java Virtual Machine (JVM) via the use of a dedicated Java library (JavaFX). These events are retrieved by the "virtual screen" component while the "Touch Screen Manager" instantiates the various logical input devices (fingers in this case) one each time a finger is detected. The "Touch Screen manager" link Fingers events and data to the registered interaction transducers (within the "Global Interaction Techniques" component) as, for instance, the "Flick 2 Fingers" one detecting the eponym interaction.

Input Device Type 2: Two Mice

Even though the mouse is a standard input device, as we use multi-mice interactions, we cannot use drivers provided natively by the operating system. The data from mice is accessed by having a thread polling the JInput library information (e.g. JInput.dll for

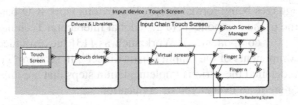

Fig. 8. Tuning MIODMIT for a touch-screen device

windows). The two mice are then handled by the "mice manager" (Fig. 9) that instantiates two virtual mice and two abstraction of cursors. The "mice manager" links these cursors to "interaction transducers" within "Global Interaction Techniques" that recognize high level events such as Click, DoubleClick, etc. and possibly multimodal ones such as combined clicks as defined in [1].

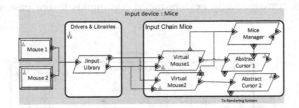

Fig. 9. Tuning MIODMIT for two mice

Output Device: Screen

The management of the screen is straightforward as there is no multiplicity of devices. As there are no redundancies of output modalities in this case study, there is no need for an "output chain manager" component (see Fig. 10).

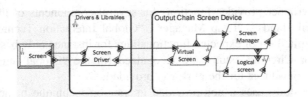

Fig. 10. Tuning MIODMIT for the screen device

5.4 Application to the Case Study: Implementation

Following the process in Fig. 4 after MIODMIT tuning, each remaining component has to be implemented. Implementation concerns the definition of the behavior of each component of the tuned architecture. Such implementation can be done using different programming languages being formal or not. In previous work ICO-based descriptions were used for some of the components (e.g. "Global Interaction Technique" component [21], "Dialogue" [16] component...). Work such as [13] has provided C implementation of all the components of the "Input Chain Kinect". In section "Tune on Demand Process" we have detailed the various implementation steps that are thus not duplicated here as they are generic to every type of application.

5.5 Application to the Case Study: Adding a Device

One of the most important aspects of MIODMIT is its modularity providing flexibility and modifiability to the applications designed. This section highlights the modifications to be made when an additional input device is added, here a Leap Motion (see Fig. 11). Once the device is chosen, two processes can be done in parallel. The first one is to prototype the interaction using the new device (design, evaluation... etc.). The other is to tune MIODMIT for the chosen device and integrate the tuning within the existing application. In the following, we describe how to add a Leap Motion hand gestures tracker as well as corresponding gesture-based commands to our case study.

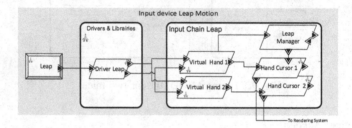

Fig. 11. Tuning MIOMIT for a Leap Motion Device

The Leap Motion is provided with three software packages as explained in Sect. 4.2.

While the wrapper provides functions for several components of the input chain (namely "Virtual Hands", "Leap Manager", "Global Interaction Technique") it only covers a very limited set of expected functionalities for instance only basic interactions (e.g. KeyTap or CircularGesture) are recognized (in the "Global Interaction Technique"), partial transducer for the cursor is provided...

As the case study uses a non-provided interaction technique named Hand-Flick (corresponding to a mid-air "Flick 2 Fingers") the "Global Interaction Technique" component has to be programmed exploiting the functions of the API. Adding this new device as an equivalent modality does not impact the rest of the implementation as long as it provides the same high level events.

6 Conclusion and Perspectives

This paper presented a generic interactive system architecture and its associated tuning process for the engineering of interactive systems. It addresses the issue of the complexity of engineering current interactive systems integrating non-standard input and output devices and offering multimodal interactions. Both hardware and software aspects are described within a single framework.

The generic interactive system architecture makes explicit the relationships between input devices and interaction techniques. It also makes explicit how such elements are related to implementation considerations involving various software entities such as device drivers, transducers, toolkits and APIs. As such, the integration of novel interaction techniques such as gesture interaction is simplified and better structured, and can be tuned depending on the needs of specific applications. The illustrated development process presented helps demonstrating how the MIODMIT generic interactive system architecture can be applied. An example in the field of critical systems, in our case a weather radar panel for civilian aircrafts, shows a real world application of our approach.

The proposed approach brings multiple benefits including the division of complex interactive systems into generic components loosely coupled and highly coherent thus enforcing the locality of modifications. It also brings research work achieved in the area of critical interactive systems (such as self-checking interactors 35 and reconfigurations) to the broader world of mainstream interactive multimodal systems.

Due to its white box principle (each component of the architecture contributes to the processing of input and the production of output) the approach is particularly suitable for interactive critical systems where each component has to be auditable. However, as demonstrated by the classical interactive application example it is also applicable to the engineering of more mainstream interactive systems. The only difference is that some components are directly managed by the programming environment (Java and Java VM) or the operating system on which they are executed.

References

1. Accot, J., Chatty, S., Palanque, P.: A formal description of low level interaction and its application to multimodal interactive systems. In: Bodart, F., Vanderdonckt, J. (eds.) Design, Specification and Verification of Interactive Systems. Eurographics, pp. 92–104. Springer, Heidelberg (1996). https://doi.org/10.1007/978-3-7091-7491-3_5
2. Accot, J., Chatty, S., Maury, S., Palanque, P.: Formal transducers: models of devices and building bricks for the design of highly interactive systems. In: Harrison, M.D., Torres, J.C. (eds.) Design, Specification and Verification of Interactive Systems. Eurographics, pp. 143–159. Springer, Heidelberg (1997). https://doi.org/10.1007/978-3-7091-6878-3_10
3. Bass, L.: Software Architecture in Practice. Pearson Education India, Gurgaon (2007)
4. Bass, L., et al.: The arch model: Seeheim revisited. In: User Interface Developpers' Workshop (1991)

5. Bastide, R., Navarre, D., Palanque, P., Schyn, A., Dragicevic, P.: A model-based approach for real-time embedded multimodal systems in military aircrafts. In: Proceedings of the 6th International Conference on Multimodal Interfaces (ICMI 2004), pp. 243–250. ACM, New York (2004)

6. Buxton, B.: Developing a Taxonomy of Input, chapter 4. http://www.billbuxton.com/input04.Taxonomies.pdf. Accessed 15 January

7. Buxton, B.: A three state model of graphical input. In: Diaper, D., et al. (eds.) Human-Computer Interaction - INTERACT 1990, pp. 449–456. Elsevier Science Publishers (1990)

8. Campos, J.C., Harrison, M.D.: Formally verifying interactive systems: a review. In: Harrison M.D., Torres J.C. (eds.) Design, Specification and Verification of Interactive Systems. Eurographics, pp. 109–124. Springer, Heidelberg (1997). https://doi.org/10.1007/978-3-7091-6878-3_8

9. Coutaz, J., Nigay, L., Salber, D., Blandford, A., May, J., Young, R.M.: Four easy pieces for assessing the usability of multimodal interaction: the care properties. In: Nordby, K., Helmersen, P., Gilmore, D.J., Arnesen, S.A. (eds.) Human—Computer Interaction. IFIP Advances in Information and Communication Technology, pp. 115–120. Springer, Heidelberg (1995). https://doi.org/10.1007/978-1-5041-2896-4_19

10. Cronel, M.: Une approche pour l'ingénierie des systèmes interactifs critiques multimodaux et multi-utilisateurs: Application à la prochaine génération de cockpit d'aéronefs, thèse de doctorat, Université Paul Sabatier, octobre 2017

11. CS-25 - Amendment 17 - Certification Specifications and Acceptable Means of Compliance for Large Aeroplanes. EASA (2015)

12. DO-178C/ED-12C, Software Considerations in Airborne Systems and Equipment Certification, published by RTCA and EUROCAE (2012)

13. Deshayes, R., Palanque, P., Mens, T.: A generic framework for executable gestural interaction models. In: VL/HCC 2013, pp. 35–38 (2013)

14. Feiler, P.H., Gluch, D.P., Hudak, J.J.: The architecture analysis & design language (AADL): An introduction (No. CMU/SEI-2006-TN-011). Carnegie-Mellon Univ Pittsburgh PA Software Engineering Inst (2006)

15. Hamon, A., Palanque, P., André, R., Barboni, E., Cronel, M., Navarre, D.: Multi-touch interactions for control and display in interactive cockpits. In: HCI'Aero 2014. ACM DL (2014)

16. Hamon, A., Palanque, P., Silva, J.L., Deleris, Y., Barboni, E.: Formal description of multi-touch interactions. In: 5th ACM SIGCHI EICS, pp. 207–216. ACM (2013)

17. Hansen, T.E., Hourcade, J.P., Virbel, M., Patali, S., Serra, T.: PyMT: a post-WIMP multi-touch user interface toolkit. In: ACM ICITS, pp. 17–24. ACM (2009)

18. Hinckley, K., Jacob, R.J.K., Ware, C., Wobbrock, J., Wigdor, D.: Input/output devices and interaction techniques. In: Computing Handbook, 3rd edn., Chap. 21, pp. 1–54 (2014)

19. Hoste, L., Dumas, B., Signer, B.: Mudra: a unified multimodal interaction framework. In: ICMI 2011, pp. 97–104. ACM (2011)

20. Kammer, D., Keck, M., Freitag, G., Wacker, M.: Taxonomy and overview of multi-touch frameworks: architecture, scope and features. In: Workshop on EPMI (2010)

21. Kraleva, R., Kralev, V.: On model architecture for a children's speech recognition interactive dialog system. In: Proceedings of International Scientific Conference on Mathematics and Natural Sciences (2009). https://arxiv.org/pdf/1605.07733

22. Ladry, J.-F., Navarre, D., Palanque, P.: Formal description techniques to support the design, construction and evaluation of fusion engines for sure (safe, usable, reliable and evolvable) multimodal interfaces. In: ACM ICMI, pp. 185–192 (2009)

23. Lalanne, D., Nigay, L., Palanque, P., Robinson, P., Vanderdonckt, J., Ladry, J.F.: Fusion engines for multimodal input: a survey. In: ICMI, pp. 153–160. ACM (2009)

24. Latoschik, M.E., Reiners, D., Blach, R., Figueroa, P., Dachselt, R.: SEARIS: software engineering and architectures for realtime interactive systems. In: 24th ACM SIGPLAN OOPSLA, pp. 721–722 (2009)
25. Lee, J.S., et al.: A 0.4 V driving multi-touch capacitive sensor with the driving signal frequency set to (n + 0.5) times the inverse of the LCD VCOM noise period. In: IEEE International Symposium on Circuits and Systems (ISCAS), pp. 682–685 (2014)
26. Ng, A., Lepinski, J., Wigdor, D., Sanders, S., Dietz, P.: Designing for low-latency direct-touch input. In: 25th ACM UIST Conference, pp. 453–464. ACM (2012)
27. Navarre, D., Palanque, P., Basnyat, S.: A formal approach for user interaction reconfiguration of safety critical interactive systems. In: Harrison, Michael D., Sujan, M.-A. (eds.) SAFECOMP 2008. LNCS, vol. 5219, pp. 373–386. Springer, Heidelberg (2008). https://doi.org/10.1007/978-3-540-87698-4_31
28. Nigay, L., Coutaz, J.: Multifeature systems: from HCI properties to software design. In: Proceedings of First International Workshop on Intelligence and Multimodality in Multimedia Interfaces. AAAI Press Publ. (1995)
29. Morris, M., Huang, A., Paepcke, A., Winograd, T.: Cooperative gestures: multi-user gestural interactions for co-located groupware. In: ACM CHI Conference 2006, pp. 1201–1210 (2006)
30. Palanque, P., Bastide, R., Navarre, D., Sy, O.: Computer discretized interaction: from continuous to discrete and back again. In: Workshop on Continuity in Human Computer Interaction, CHI 2000, The Hague (2000)
31. Pfaff, G.E. (ed.): User Interface Management Systems. Springer, Heidelberg (1985). https://doi.org/10.1007/978-3-642-70041-5
32. Rousseau, C., Bellik, Y., Vernier, F.: Multimodal output specification/simulation platform. In: ACM ICMI 2005, pp. 84–91 (2005)
33. SAE-AS5506B: SAE Architecture Analysis and Design Language (AADL), International Society of Automotive Engineers, Warrendale, PA, USA, September 2012
34. Schneegass, S., Alt, F.: SenScreen: a toolkit for supporting sensor-enabled multi-display networks. In: Gehring, S. (ed.) Proceedings of the International Symposium on Pervasive Displays (PerDis 2014). ACM, New York (2014). 6 pages
35. Tankeu-Choitatk, A., Navarrek, D., Palanquek, P., Delerisk, Y., Fabrek, J.-C., Fayollask, C.: Self-checking components for dependable interactive cockpits using formal description techniques. In: PRDC 2011, pp. 164–173 (2011)
36. Vu, T., et al.: Distinguishing users with capacitive touch communication. In: Mobicom 2012, pp. 197–208. ACM (2012)
37. Echtler, F., Klinker, G.: A multitouch software architecture. In: Proceedings of the 5th Nordic Conference on Human-Computer Interaction: Building Bridges (NordiCHI 2008), pp. 463–466. ACM, New York (2008)
38. Vennelakanti, R., Dey, P., Shekhawat, A., Pisupati, P.: The picture says it all!: Multimodal interactions and interaction metadata. In: Proceedings of the 13th International Conference on Multimodal Interfaces (ICMI 2011), pp. 89–96. ACM, New York (2011)
39. Kousidis, S., Kennington, C., Baumann, T., Buschmeier, H., Stefan, K., Schlangen, D.: A multimodal in-car dialogue system that tracks the driver's attention. In: Proceedings of the 16th International Conference on Multimodal Interaction (ICMI 2014), pp. 26–33. ACM, New York (2014)

Task Modelling and Task-Based Approaches

Adding Measures to Task Models for Usability Inspection of the Cloud Access Control Services

Bilal Naqvi[1(✉)], Ahmed Seffah[1], and Christina Braz[2]

[1] Lappeenranta University of Technology, LUT, Lappeenranta, Finland
Syed.naqvi@student.lut.fi
[2] Scotia Bank, Toronto, Canada

Abstract. Access control services in the cloud require defining which users, applications, or functions can have access to which data to perform what kinds of operations. There are thus three dimensions: (1) which users can (2) perform which operations (3) on which data. We speak of: (1) principals (i.e., users or roles), (2) privileges, and (3) objects, corresponding to these three dimensions, respectively. The act of accessing gives rights and privileges such as using or releasing data, modifying the access rights or accomplishing certain tasks. Permission to access also requires identity management. Research studies identify the existence of dependency between usability and security, and that there exists a conflict between the two, for which trade-offs are difficult to evaluate and engineer. This paper proposes a novel methodology for assessing the usability of access control services while ensuring that security requirements are met. The proposed methodology assists in integrating the experience of both security and usability experts by using different Human Computer Interaction methods as a way to identify the usability and security problems in access control security services in the cloud, and capture solutions to resolve such problems.

Keywords: Usable security
Usability in cloud access control and identity management
Usability of security services, security and usability conflict

1 Introduction

In recent years, there has been a significant growth in the adoption and popularity of the cloud-computing segment. However, such growth poses numerous challenges regarding security, usability, environmental sustainability etc. [13]. A wide range of users using different access devices, procedures, and technologies use cloud systems and security services. In cloud computing, authentication is a core requirement and serious concern as access control services protect not only critical IT infrastructures, but also related physical spaces including surveillance rooms, data centers, etc. Access control services in the cloud require defining which users, applications, or functions can have access to which data to perform which kinds of operations. The security challenge concerning user authentication and identity management services includes: (1) authentication, the process of verifying that an individual truly is who s/he claims to be

C. Bogdan et al. (Eds.): HCSE 2018, LNCS 11262, pp. 133–145, 2019.
https://doi.org/10.1007/978-3-030-05909-5_8

and (2) authorization, the process of assigning permissions to users [17]. There are thus three dimensions: (1) which users can (2) perform which operations (3) on which data. Corresponding to these three dimensions, we speak of: (1) principals (i.e., users or roles), (2) privileges, and (3) objects, respectively.

According to Cranor et al. [5], Jøsang et al. [11] and Nielsen [15], security and usability are considered as two opposed quality characteristics related to the user interface and functionality of the security system. One observable belief is that usability advocates support making it easy to use a system, preferably requiring no special access procedures at all, whereas security experts' support making it hard to access a system, at least for unauthorized users. However, there are several cases in which security and usability should be enhanced by modeling their mutual relationships, as an example of such cases, online payment, and e-banking, supervision of critical industrial infrastructures, crisis management and rescue systems. Therefore, more attention should be paid to the front-end of these secure solutions, i.e., how security information is communicated directly and indirectly to users. Usability cannot be treated separately from the security engineering of a system.

This research is a part of a long term project, where the main goal is to propose a framework for assessing the security and usability conflicts in access control services in the cloud while incorporating software measures into HCI task modeling techniques.

2 Measures of Usability in HCI and Security in Software Engineering

Security and usability have been widely recognized as two opposed characteristics [11]. Such opposed relation can be attributed for different reasons. The failure of security experts to measure usability is that usability problems with security systems and services are not just about the UIs usability. Existing literature highlighted that using conventional methods for usability evaluation only assess the usability impact on security effectiveness [12]. Usability and security conflicts and measures should be looked at from different levels. The ISO 27000 series of standards [10] identifies measurable attributes of information security as preservation of confidentiality, authenticity, accountability, non-repudiation, reliability, integrity and availability of information. Such attributes play an important role in measuring that the identified security requirements have been met.

Several researchers have introduced different methods to facilitate the development of usable secure systems. Kainda et al. [12] introduced a security usability threat model. They identified different usability and security factors based on previous studies and categorized them into six different groups of security topics. Authentication is one of these groups. However, the authors have not provided an example to clarify how the proposed model can be applied to measure the usability of security systems. Hausawi and Allen [7] proposed a summative usable security evaluation matrix that aims to help in determining the levels of usability and security quality attributes during the software development lifecycle; their matrix includes three usability factors (efficiency, effectiveness, and satisfaction) and three security factors (confidentiality, integrity, and availability). Zhao and Yue [20] introduced a Cloud-based Storage to manage browser-based passwords, their approach aimed to achieve a high level of security and usability with the desired confidentiality, integrity, and availability properties.

Hayashi et al. [9] introduced a usable security framework, called context-aware scalable authentication, which aims to use multiple implicit factors, such as a user's location, in order to select an appropriate active authentication form to authenticate the user. Nayak et al. [14] sought to enhance the security of the cloud services by introducing mutual authentication scheme using symmetric keys. During the authentication process, the proposed scheme requires the users to login into two accounts, indeed, that may make users feel uncomfortable. Beckerle and Martucci [2] introduced six guidelines for designing usable access control rule sets; they clarified that implementing those guidelines will help in understanding and managing access policies. Hausawi et al. [8] proposed an authentication system, called Choice-Based Authentication Approach (CBAA) which aims to provide better usability by allowing end users to select their authentication method based on their preferences. The authors pointed out that their approach improves security by increasing the difficulty for adversaries by displaying all of the possible authentication methods during the login process. Similar to the CBAA approach, Forget et al. [6] proposed an authentication architecture, called Choose Your Own Authentication (CYOA) which allows users to select a scheme amongst several available options. CYOA enables users to select whichever scheme best suits their preferences, abilities, and usage context.

Faily and Flechais [21], suggest using scenarios to describe how design decisions can lead to an unintentional security compromise caused by the end-user. They further present that these misusability cases can be used to impact design decisions of the developers and to bridge gaps between usability and security.

In the literature, various definitions concerning different attributes (facets, aspects, factors) of usability have been proposed. While security has been interpreted as a purely technical aspect in software development methodologies, some authors think it is more than that, taking instead a strategic dimension, resulting in one of the most important criteria in the governance of Information Communication Technology (ICT). For example, the executive management in companies still think that security technology is all that is required, and therefore 'delegates or downgrades' the issue to the technical departments, and conveniently neglects about the human and organizational concerns [19].

3   Proposal for Usable Security Measurement

The usability security measurement methodology (see Fig. 1) proposed in this paper was developed based on the original concept presented in Braz et al. [3], it aims to achieve this goal specifically while: (1) defining the possible conflicts between usability and security in terms of measures and (2) incorporating these measures into task models and a task-based inspection method. Task models are used to identify and model qualitatively the problematic aspects of the conflicts between usability and security. In comparison with Braz et al. work [5], we have used the ISO 25000 standard series and different measures as a way to quantify, assess and estimate quantitatively how security and usability are connected and how much severe the problem.

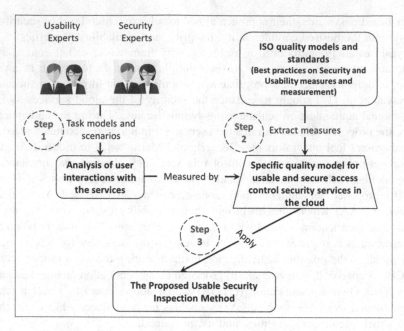

Fig. 1. The proposed usable security measurement methodology

The proposed usable security inspection method was developed using the design science research framework [16]. Following are the three steps of usable security measurement methodology that we propose.

- Step 1 describes how the task models and scenarios can be used by the usability specialists and security experts to analyze the users' interaction with the security services and then identifying and describing both the usability and security problems.
- Step 2 measures the usability and security interdependencies for each task model and the related security and usability problems using a set of measurable usability factors and criteria, correlated with security.
- Step 3 describes how the usable security inspection method is used to assist both the usability and security evaluators in identifying and evaluating the usability of security services. As detailed later, the method will help in the identification of the security and usability users' problems and their severity rate, with respect to the usability criteria and security measures defined in Step 2.

Figure 2 portrays a subset of these measures. For example, the authenticity factor can be measured using the authentication protocols.

$$UAP = X/Y$$

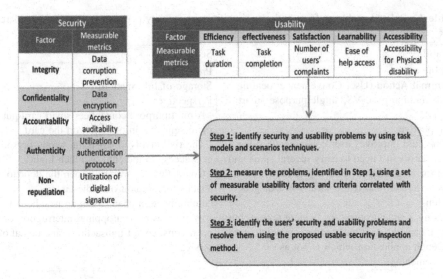

Fig. 2. A possible conflict between authenticity and satisfaction measures

Where UAP stands for utilization of authentication protocols, X is the number of provided authentication protocols, and Y is the number of required authentication protocols that are stated in the requirement specifications. In the same way, usability can be assessed using the satisfaction factor that can be measured using the number of user complaints

$$NUC = A/B$$

Where NUC stands for number of user complaints, A is the number of users' complaints and B is the total number of users. These two ratios help in determining to which extent the usability and security separately can be quantified [1]. Figure 2 shows a possible conflict between authenticity and satisfaction measures. Based on the first step of the proposed methodology, the users' interaction should be analyzed to identify the security and usability problems qualitatively.

For example, a multipurpose contactless smart card token-based authentication (i.e., PIN) is selected to authenticate a user to access to a Multifunction Teller Machine (Table 1). This protocol may affect the users' satisfaction negatively. Security and usability experts can use the task models and scenarios techniques to identify both security and usability problems that lead to the user non-satisfaction for example, consider the task and scenario below.

Task: *Authenticate user to a Multifunction Teller Machine (MTM)*
Scenario: User must authenticate her/himself through a multipurpose contactless smart card token-based authentication (i.e., PIN) in order to have access to different systems.

Table 1. Related problems from both the usability and security perspectives for the considered task

Usability	Security
Problem: Minimal Action (User Convenience: dealing with multipurpose VS. single purpose smart cards). Perspective: - The card improves user convenience since the user doesn't need to carry several cards and memorizing different PIN codes. However, it raises the risk that if the card is lost or gets stolen. - Using a one purpose card is more secure, but this means the user will need to carry one card for each application which is not as convenient.	Problem: Storage of Information. Perspective: - A multipurpose contactless smart card puts more sensitive information on the card - The risk involved when the wrong person gets access to the card, is much higher. - Contactless smart cards open the door to attacks that exploit over-the-air communication channels in an unsolicited way such as eavesdropping, interruption of operations, covert transactions, and denial of service.

Step 1: Identifying the Task Modeling and Scenarios

We used scenarios and tasks models, two well-known HCI techniques for analyzing users and usability problems as well as for understanding and modeling users' characteristics and the context in which the security and usability conflicts occurs.

We introduced a novel definition for a security and usability scenario as follows: a security scenario can be tangible or intangible. A Tangible Security Scenario (TSS) includes physical infrastructure such as control of user's access to buildings and facilities using: for example, biometrics, sending a silent alarm in response to a threat at a Multi-function Teller Machine (MTM), a type of an advanced ATM which provides additional services alongside cash withdrawal, such as video surveillance. An Intangible Security Scenario (ISS) includes data or other digital information: for example, a user who enters sensitive information at registration in order to purchase a concert ticket at an MTM. Both security and usability scenarios aim to detect the security and usability problems that may result when performing a task in a specific context.

To model the tasks and related scenarios, the GOMS (Goals, Operators, Methods, and Selection rules), a family of HCI techniques [4] has been used. GOMS helps the HCI analyst and security designer in making design decisions regarding the required tradeoff between usability and security when they come into conflict. For example, instead of determining and describing the recall password process within an existing Risk-based authentication method, the analyst-designer describes and decides how this user will use such process. Our choice of GOMS was mainly due to our knowledge and previous practical experience of using GOMS method for modelling task and scenarios.

Step 2: Connecting the Tasks' Scenarios with the Related Usability Criteria and Factors

Here, we model security as a usability sub-characteristic: both usability and security are defined in terms of sub-factors that are measures. Seffah et al. [18] introduced a Quality in Use Integrated Measurement (QUIM) model as a consolidated model for measuring usability. As part of our proposed methodology, we selected nine usability sub-factors from the QUIM model, where the selected factors are related with security. The selected usability factors namely efficiency, satisfaction, productivity etc. are presented in Fig. 3.

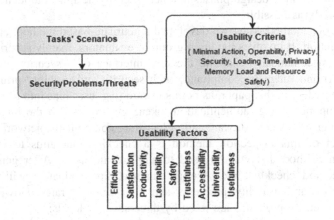

Fig. 3. Connecting the tasks' scenarios and their security problems with the corresponding usability criteria and factors

Each of these factors is broken down into one of the following measurable criteria:

- *Minimal Action* (capability of the application to help users achieve their tasks in a minimum number of steps);
- *Minimal Memory Load* (whether a user is required to keep minimal amount of information in mind in order to achieve a specified task);
- *Operability* (amount of effort necessary to operate and control an application);
- *Privacy* (whether users' personal information is appropriately protected);
- *Security* (capability of the application to protect information and data so that unauthorized persons or systems cannot read or modify them and authorized persons or systems are not denied access);
- *Load Time* (time required for the application to load (i.e., how fast it responds to the user);
- *Resource Safety* (whether resources including people are handled properly without any hazard).

Therefore, after identifying the tasks' scenarios, security experts should analyze them and identify the security problems or threats that may result from each scenario. Thereafter, both usability and security experts should analyze these problems, in order to identify the corresponding usability criteria. Finally, the usability criteria should be mapped to one or more measurable usability factors. In fact, the relation between usability criteria, factors, and security problems can be used to guide a design decision or to assess a design that has already been created.

Step 3: Applying Usability Security Inspection Method
In HCI, inspection is a set of techniques which consist of evaluators to examine, for example, computer security software without involving end users. The method can be used in conjunction with task modeling and with modeling of security as usability sub-factor. Inspection can be conducted during the early phases, mainly requirements analysis and preliminary design phases that help security designers to identify possible problems as early as possible.

As part of our methodology, we developed a heuristic-based method, called usable security inspection. It involves having a group of evaluators, mainly security and HCI designers, to systematically examine the user interface of a security protocol (e.g. authentication) and judge its compliance with security and usability principles. The interface is regarded, in this paper, as both software (e.g. user logs into a Website) and hardware components (e.g. authentication token) towards which the interaction and information transit between software and/or hardware components, network, and users.

The output of this inspection method is a checklist that aims to evaluate the authentication method that will be used to authenticate users. After generating the inspection method checklist, the security and usability evaluators will be able to identify security and usability problems and their severity rates. However, users' usability and security problems are rated by three severity levels:

- *Major*: refers to catastrophic problems that should be given a high fixing priority level, they must be fixed before releasing the software.
- *Intermediate:* it is important to fix this type of problem as soon as possible.
- *Minor*: refers to problems with a low fixing priority level, which means that these problems should be fixed only if there is extra time available.

4   Case Study

This section aims to clarify how to use the proposed usable security measurement methodology for developing usable and secure authentication method to access Multifunction Teller Machine (MTM) account through the user phone.

Step 1: Identifying the MTM's Task Models and Scenarios
The users' tasks to use MTM may include: authenticate user to a system, transfer funds to an international bank account, buy a ticket concert, access a MTM through a mobile phone, deposit a check using checking image and send a silent alarm. For example Table 2 clarifies the related scenario and the required features for the task below.

Task: *Access and authenticate to MTM with your mobile phone*
Based on this scenario, we have identified the usability and security problems and their related perspectives (see Table 3).

Table 2. An example task to access MTM with mobile phone, its related scenario and sub-tasks

Scenario	Sub-Tasks
Customer accesses a MTM via mobile phone in order to make his/her mortgage monthly payment. The phone is equipped with a special chip that enables to communicate with the MTM	Sub-tasks performed using a mobile phone: 1. Select "Access my MTM" from the cell phone main menu; 2. Enter your 4 digit PIN (the PIN is entered on the customer's phone keypad then transmitted to a central server and checked against file saved there); 3. Select "Make a Payment" from the MTM's menu; 4. Select the type of payment which is "Mortgage"; 5. Tap the exact amount; 6. Select "Submit".

Table 3. Usability and security problems associated with the considered task

Usability	Security
Problem: Overwhelm Customers with complexity when dealing with different communication channels.	**Problem:** Credentials across several channels
Perspective - Customers have to manage complexity when dealing with different services offered through different types of communication channels such as MTM, Web, and WAP. - Customers will still be required to authenticate to the system by entering a PIN. Unlike passwords, PINs have no meaning to the customer, and then it might be even harder to remember than a password (i.e., passwords can be created to be pronounceable). PINs become harder to remember for customers who have many different ones to keep track of.	**Perspective** - Using the same authentication credentials for both WAP and MTM channel, can provide convenience for the customers. However, PIN code is the only acceptable alternative for the WAP channel, and is not considered to provide good enough security (i.e., longer PINs (6 or 8 digit PINs) would be more secure than 4-digit PINs). - Additionally, when PIN is used for authentication over the phone, the risk of eavesdropping the telephone line is a supplementary threat, especially since it cannot be encrypted.

Step 2: Connecting the Tasks' Scenarios with the Related Usability Criteria and Factors

Let us consider the task scenario detailed in the previous step to illustrate the applicability of the usability factors and their corresponding criteria using MTM tasks. Table 4 illustrates the procedure to adopt for connecting the tasks scenarios to the related usability criteria and factors.

In addition, for measurement purpose QUIM suggested 127 measures for usability factors [18]. However, other measures can be used for measuring such factors, such as

Table 4. Mapping the tasks' scenarios to the nine usability factors and eight usability criteria

Task Scenario	Security Problem/Threat	Measurable Usability Criterion	USABILITY FACTORS								
			Efficiency	Satisfaction	Productivity	Learnability	Safety	Trustfulness	Accessibility	Universality	Usefulness
Authenticate user to a system	— Storage of Information — Replay attacks — Eavesdropping — Session hijacking — Man-in-the-middle — Verifier impersonation.	**Minimal Action**	●	●		●			●		

those proposed in ISO 25022 [10]. For example, the efficiency can be measured, by measuring how cost-effective is the user, using the following formula:

$$X = TE/C$$

Where TE is the task effectiveness, which refers to whether the task is executed correctly or not, and C is the total cost of the task, where costs could, for example, include the user's time, the time of others giving assistance, and the cost of computing resources.

Step 3: Applying the Usability Security Inspection Method

Based on discussion in Sect. 3 (step 3), we have identified examples of the security and usability review questions in order to generate the usability security inspection method checklist (see Table 5).

From the generated checklist, we have identified security problems, their severity rates and recommendations to resolve them (see Table 6).

Table 5. An example of the usable security inspection method checklist

Usable Security Inspection Method								
Usability Criteria: Security								
Description: Capability of the application to protect information and data so that unauthorized persons or systems cannot read or modify them and authorized persons or systems are not denied access								
#	Usability Review	Occurrence		Comments	Security Review	Occurrence		Comments
1.1	When using different communication channels, is PIN authentication used (i.e., when accessing MTM, Web, and WAP: PINs are easier to remember)?	Y	N	Y / N	Is 6-digits PIN used (i.e. PINs have lower level of security since the number of possible combinations is lower[1])?	Y	N	Y / N	It needs system review to be able to implement it.

[1] Long PINs give stronger security, but bad usability because the PIN is harder to remember and takes longer to type.
[2] With enough memory and/or a crypto processor
[3] This would provide a higher level of security but lower system response time and thereby usability. The risk of eavesdropping the telephone network is a real threat, especially since it cannot be encrypted.

Table 6. An example of security problems related to the security usability criteria

Problem description	Usability criteria	Severity rate	Security Issue	Interdependencies	Recommendations
Unsafe PIN length (Security review1.1)	Security	Major	A MTM machine relies on short, low-entropy PINs for authentication. A four-digit PIN can be broken in less than a second, and a 6-digit PIN in about 10 s, while a 10-digit PIN would likely take weeks to crack.	Performance, efficiency.	(ISO 9564-1 :2002) allows for PINs from 4 up to 12 digits, but also notes that for usability reasons, an assigned numeric PIN should not exceed six digits in length. So ideally, use PINs with a large number of digits for instance a 6-digit PIN.

5 Conclusion

This paper presents a methodological approach for measuring usable security conflicts while featuring how to supplement tasks models with measures for access control services in the cloud. A practical contribution is the use of such approach for the evaluation of access control security services in the context of cloud. The enhanced task models with measures aimed at detailing the interrelationships and conflicts between security and usability. In comparison with the existing models for designing usable security authentication mechanisms (such as [15]), the approach introduces clear steps to improve the usability of user authentication and access control services in the cloud. An important aspect is that the methodology does not only point out general security and usability recommendations, but specifies explicitly how a compromise can be established when these two key factors come into conflict.

References

1. Azuma, M.: Software products evaluation system: quality models, metrics and processes— International Standards and Japanese practice. Inf. Softw. Technol. **38**(3), 145–154 (1996)
2. Beckerle, M., Martucci, L.A.: Formal definitions for usable access control rule sets from goals to metrics. In: Proceedings of the Ninth Symposium on Usable Privacy and Security. ACM (2013)
3. Braz, C., Seffah, A., Naqvi, B.: Integrating a Usable Security Protocol into User Authentication Services Design Process. CRC Press, Boca Raton (2018)
4. Card, S.K., Newell, A., Moran, T.P.: The psychology of human-computer interaction (1983)
5. Cranor, L.F., Garfinkel, S.: Security and Usability: Designing Secure Systems that People Can Use. O'Reilly Media Inc., Farnham (2005)
6. Forget, A., Chiasson, S., Biddle, R.: Choose your own authentication. In: Proceedings of the 2015 New Security Paradigms Workshop, pp. 1–15. ACM (2015)
7. Hausawi, Y.M., Allen, W.H.: Usable-security evaluation. In: Tryfonas, T., Askoxylakis, I. (eds.) HAS 2015. LNCS, vol. 9190, pp. 335–346. Springer, Cham (2015). https://doi.org/10. 1007/978-3-319-20376-8_30
8. Hausawi, Y.M., Allen, W.H., Bahr, G.S.: Choice-based authentication: a usable-security approach. In: Stephanidis, C., Antona, M. (eds.) UAHCI 2014. LNCS, vol. 8513, pp. 114– 124. Springer, Cham (2014). https://doi.org/10.1007/978-3-319-07437-5_12
9. Hayashi, E., Das, S., Amini, S., Hong, J., Oakley, I.: CASA: context-aware scalable authentication. In: Proceedings of the Ninth Symposium on Usable Privacy and Security. ACM (2013)
10. ISO/IEC: ISO/IEC 27000: Information technology – Security techniques – Information security management systems – Overview and vocabulary. International Organization for Standardization (2014)
11. Jøsang, A., Zomai, M.A., Suriadi, S.: Usability and privacy in identity management architectures. In: Proceedings of the Fifth Australasian Symposium on ACSW Frontiers, vol. 68, pp. 143–152. Australian Computer Society, Inc. (2007)
12. Kainda, R., Flechais, I., Roscoe, A.: Security and usability: analysis and evaluation. In: International Conference on Availability, Reliability, and Security, ARES 2010, pp. 275–282. IEEE (2010)

13. Marinos, A., Briscoe, G.: Community cloud computing. In: Jaatun, M.G., Zhao, G., Rong, C. (eds.) CloudCom 2009. LNCS, vol. 5931, pp. 472–484. Springer, Heidelberg (2009). https://doi.org/10.1007/978-3-642-10665-1_43
14. Nayak, S.K., Mohapatra, S., Majhi, B.: An improved mutual authentication framework for cloud computing. Int. J. Comput. Appl. **52**, 5 (2012)
15. Nielsen, J.: Security & Human Factors (2000). https://www.nngroup.com/articles/security-and-human-factors/
16. Peffers, K., Tuunanen, T., Rothenberger, M.A., Chatterjee, S.: A design science research methodology for information systems research. J. Manag. Inf. Syst. **24**(3), 45–77 (2007)
17. Salini, P., Kanmani, S.: Survey and analysis on security requirements engineering. Comput. Electr. Eng. **38**(6), 1785–1797 (2012)
18. Seffah, A., Donyaee, M., Kline, R.B., Padda, H.K.: Usability measurement and metrics: a consolidated model. Softw. Qual. J. **14**(2), 159–178 (2006)
19. Von Solms, B., Von Solms, R.: The 10 deadly sins of information security management. Comput. Secur. **23**(5), 371–376 (2004)
20. Zhao, R., Yue, C.: Toward a secure and usable cloud-based password manager for web browsers. Comput. Secur. **46**(10), 32–47 (2014)
21. Faily, S., Fléchais, I.: Finding and resolving security mis-usability with mis-usability cases. Requirement Eng. **21**(2), 209–223 (2016)

Enriching Task Models with Usability and User Experience Evaluation Data

Regina Bernhaupt[1,3]([⊠]), Philippe Palanque[1,2], Dimitri Drouet[3],
and Celia Martinie[2]

[1] Department of Industrial Design, Eindhoven University of Technology,
Eindhoven, the Netherlands
r.bernhaupt@tue.nl
[2] IRIT, ICS, Toulouse, France
{philippe.palanque, celia.martinie}@irit.fr
[3] ruwido, Neumarkt, Austria
Dimitri.Drouet@ruwido.com

Abstract. Evaluation results focusing on usability and user experience are often difficult to be taken into account during an iterative design process. This is due to the fact that evaluation exploits concrete artefacts (prototype or system) while design and development are based on more abstract descriptions such as task models or software models. As concrete data cannot be represented, evaluation results are just discarded. This paper addresses the problem of discrepancy between abstract view of task models and concrete data produced in evaluations by first, describing the requirements for a task modelling notation: (a) representation of data for each individual participant, (b) representation of aggregated data for one evaluation as well as (c) several evaluations and (d) the need to visualize multi-dimensional data from the evaluation as well as the interactive system gathered during runtime. Second: by showing how the requirements were integrated in a task modelling tool. Using an example from an experimental evaluation possible usages of the tool are demonstrated.

Keywords: Task models · User study · Usability · User experience
Evaluation · Formal description

1 Introduction

There is a fundamental belief in human-computer interaction that an iterative design and development process leads to interactive systems with a higher usability and a better user experience compared to other forms of a more sequential design and development process [3]. In user centered processes by nature iterative [34], key to success is first, to focus on the user and try to understand what users want and need to do with a system and second, to evaluate the system from early on in the design and development process [3, 33].

Evaluation results focusing on usability and user experience are often difficult to be taken into account as evaluation exploits concrete artefacts (prototype or system) while design and development are based on more abstract descriptions such as task models or software models. The connection between what users are doing (their tasks) and how

© IFIP International Federation for Information Processing 2019
Published by Springer Nature Switzerland AG 2019
C. Bogdan et al. (Eds.): HCSE 2018, LNCS 11262, pp. 146–163, 2019.
https://doi.org/10.1007/978-3-030-05909-5_9

changes in the user interface or choices in the user interface affect the overall usability and user experience of the system are difficult to understand and describe. Main drawback is the missing support to connect results and findings from user evaluation studies to the description of what users are doing and errors users make [14].

To solve this problem task models and their associated tools can be used, to store and describe the data from the evaluation study, and combine the results from the real time evaluation study with the real time visualizations of the system. Task models bring several benefits when applied in the development process: they support the assessment of effectiveness (as sub-dimension of usability [20]) [10, 37], they can support the assessment of task complexity [15, 34, 41], help in the construction of training material [27] and they support the redesign of the system [8]. Task models that are enhanced with data from user studies can be used as shared artefacts by all the stakeholders of design, development, and evaluation to enable such a connection.

To cover all possible results from an evaluation study a notation language and the related tool must support the following aspects:

(1) Represent data from the actual use of the system during evaluation: Representing data from user studies can enhance task models, for example the task model can show frequencies of choice from the user for a certain option or activity.
(2) Support analysis on scenario-basis as well as on task model level: User study results on the other side are most often not connected to the overall user goals and how scenarios are representing the real work of the users: Supporting the analysis of result based on a tasks model can provide insights beyond standard (statistical) analysis formats and usability problem reports.
(3) Represent data from each individual user in the evaluation as well as from several studies at different iterative development stages: Results from one or several user studies with the same system are often not analyzed as data is stored independently, storing all results in relation to a task model can provide means to gain insights about how changes in the user interface affect usability and especially how iterations of a system affect the overall user experience over time.

To complete such an approach of extending a notation to describe user evaluation study results, a notation is presented, a tool enabling such functionality is described and using as example an experimental evaluation of a television user interface the possible usages of the tool are demonstrated.

2 Related Work: Task Models and Data from User Studies

Introduced by [35, 36], task models for describing interactive systems are used during early phases of the user-centered development cycle to gather, understand and analyze the behavior of users when interacting with the system. A task model can be as simple as a sentence in a word document (e.g. the user is withdrawing money from the ATM) or more specific using notations like ConcurTaskTrees [36] to describe users' activities.

2.1   A Brief Overview on Notations and Their Tools

There is a broad range of notations supporting the notation of users' tasks. Table 1 gives a summary opposing two example task notations and their related tools. Concur-Task Trees [32, 41] for example enable to describe tasks in detail, providing notations to describe low-level task elements (LTL) as well as sub-task levels (STL). Recent extensions include the ability to include even errors in this notation []. CTT offers a set of operators allowing to represent temporal relationships between tasks and do have the expressive power to represent collaboration. Compared to CTT, task notations like a hierarchical task analysis (HTA) do have less expressive power. HTA needs an additional algorithm (plan) to describe temporal relationships and does not support collaborative activity. The main goal of TKS was to describe knowledge and information needed to perform a task. The notation HAMSTERS allows precise description of the task model integrating the concepts of CTT, HTA and TKS. It provides refinements to these concepts like a user task can be more refined in HAMSTERS making explicit if a user task is cognitive (analysis/decision), perceptive or motoric. CTT has only a generic user task in its notation.

Table 1. Overview on notations and their expressive power x indicating full support (x) indicating partial support

Notations	LTL	STL	ERR	OP	COOP
CTT [32], [41]	x	x	(x)		
HTA	x	(x)	(x)		
TKS		x		x	
HAMSTERS	x	x	x	x	x

Notations for task models are typically supported by tools. For CTT the corresponding tool is called CTTe, for HTA normally paper-based approaches are used. For the HAMSTERS notation the tool is having the same name. For later stages, especially when performing evaluations that ask the user to perform a task, there are evaluation tools available. For example Morae [30] allows to represent each button-press a user was performing during the study. Table 2 details the abilities of such systems, especially the ability to incorporate data from the system model (SYS), data from the user study including system, evaluator, scenario, conditions (STUD) and the ability to represent properties beyond usability like dimensions or factors of user experience (UX) and the ability to enable different types of visualization that include data visualization of more than one user study (VIZ+).

The inclusion of evaluation data including continuous data like video (but no live evaluation data) has been proposed by Mori et al. [31]. This early work did not detail how such data can be analyzed related to the different scenarios that users can perform, nor how evaluation results from different users as well as different studies would be aggregated and visualized.

Table 2. Overview on tools and their expressive power X indicating full support (X) indicating partial support

	SYS	STUD	UX	VIS
HTA	No	No	No	No
Hamsters	X	X	X	X
Morae [30]			(X)	X

2.2 Data Produced During User Evaluations

The term user evaluations in this article is used to describe a broad set of methods, or combinations of methods, that can be used at all stages in the design and development cycle of an interactive system to understand or evaluate usability and/or user experience as software quality to inform, improve and enhance the next iteration of the system design and development [23]. They necessarily involve the end-user of the interactive system. User studies can be classified using the following dimensions [21]:

(a) The stage or *phase in the software design and development process* the user study is conducted in: user studies can be used at all stages in the development process to understand end-users motivations and goals when only having a paper prototype or to evaluate an existing full-fledged system to understand how to improve for example the effectiveness with the system. At early stages user studies will more likely focus on the identification of usability problems or understanding a user experience dimension like the type of emotion the user interface design shall support.

(b) Focus on behavioral or attitudinal data: Behavioral data describes what users are doing (most often recorded with a set of video cameras to identify users body position or how the user is interacting with the product), while attitudinal data refers to users thoughts, feelings or insights.

(c) Quantitative vs. Qualitative data: When focusing on quantitative data user studies can be performed with the scientific rigor of an experiment, while qualitative data, for example textual descriptions of usability problems, can be generated with a quick and simple usability test with only five users. Following conventions from statistics data is further categorized as nominal, ordinal, interval and ratio data [16].

(d) The majority of user studies asks the user to perform a predefined set of activities (scripted), but studies can also simply ask the user to interact with the product without any detailed instructions (natural) or observe current usages and non-usages of the system (non-usage or alternative system usage). Combinations of the three forms are common in studies, e.g. asking the user to freely discover how to interact with the system (e.g. the discovery of the product), followed by a set of fixed instructions on what activities to perform.

(e) User studies can be performed in the lab or in the field, both with the option of remote participation.

(f) In terms of time, user studies are limited to few hours or less, and thus provide only a snap-shot of an experience [22]. To cover long-term user experience user studies can be repeated over time, providing data that is showing how experiences change over days, weeks or months of usage [1].

3   User Studies and Task Modelling: Problem Description

The *focus* of this work is on usability and user experience studies that can be performed at all stages of the development cycle but at least *use a functional interactive prototype and have reached a stage where the task of the user can be analyzed and described.* They involve end-users and produce behavioral and attitudinal data that can be qualitative or quantitative. The focus is on studies that are prepared with an *explicit methodological design (scripted)* that involves the *usage of the product* or service, and can be conducted in the lab or the field. Usability studies typically are performed as one session of about an hour with the product, thus deliver a snapshot of an experience. Methods that do not involve the end-user like expert methods [7] or automatically performed evaluation methods are currently not considered.

3.1   Performing a User Evaluation

A user evaluation begins with the identification of the study goals, user groups and a script how the study is performed. It can include aspects like checklists on demographics for selecting participants in the study, planning and set-up procedures for the study (e.g. balancing of conditions/participant groups). Most common for the script of the user evaluation is to give the user a description of a specific situations e.g. "Assume you are just coming home from work and you are planning what you might watch on TV together with some friends in the evening" and a task e.g. "you are browsing your electronic program guide on TV to see what is airing at 20:30". A script consists of a number of such tasks to be performed by each of the participants of the study. A set of *n* participants is conducting the study. Each individual user performing the set of prescripted tasks is called a "run" or study run.

Once all the *n* runs are performed, data is classified, analyzed and aggregated. The presentation of the results of such studies can vary from simple reports with lists of usability problems, to sophisticated statistical analysis of the data gathered during the study. It is thus important to understand what types of data are acquired with such studies, and how the data from studying a product can be used to inform the (re-) design of a system for the next iteration of the product.

3.2   Data Produced by User Evaluation and Analysis of Results

Evaluation studies produce additional information and data including *demographic data* or users *pre-knowledge.* To understand user experience dimensions questionnaire items or interview questions can include users preferences (e.g. questions like favorite brands bought and used), but also dimensions like users' needs or values, or descriptions of users' behavior.

While the user is interacting with the system behavioral and attitudinal data (data can be both qualitative and quantitative) is gathered. Data can be observed directly by the evaluator during the user evaluation or data can be analyzed after the study, most common is the usage of audio recording or video.

For *user experience,* data includes answers of the study participant to interview questions or remarks from the participant, ratings e.g. naturalness of interaction, stimulation, perceived challenge and necessary skills, personal involvement the user estimates (this can be a user describing involvement in the task, answers to an open or closed interview questions or simply a value to indicate a rating on a rating scale) [11]. Data for user experience dimensions like emotion or involvement can be measured by recording heart rate or skin conductance. Emotions can be detected in facial expressions analysis recorded video data (objective) or using simple ratings from the user indicating their emotional state (e.g. using EmoCards [12]).

To summarize: data from user studies can be classified in (a) qualitative vs quantitative data with data types including nominal, ordinal, interval and ratio, (b) continuous vs. discrete data (e.g. bio-physiological measurements during the whole study vs. naturalness rating on a discrete scale) (c) data associated to the overall system (e.g. the SUS questionnaire evaluating the whole system) vs. data associated to an atomic element (like a motoric movement of the user than cannot be further disaggregated) and (d) data associated to a single event or time stamp (t) or data associated to events over periods of time. For the visualization of these data types [40] it is important to state that obviously data can have various dimensions like one-dimensional data (the overall SUS value from the questionnaire ranging from 0 to 100), two-dimensional data (eye-tracking data represented as heat maps), three-dimensional data (manipulation of 3D objects in a user interface) and multi-dimensional (when representing changed precision of the user over a learning period in a 3D user interface).

For the analysis of gathered data in the user evaluation data a variety of approaches and methods from statistics is available. Most common is the representation of data using standard descriptive statistics including mean, standard deviation and/or variance and median and modus, frequency tables or correlations. Results from questionnaires like the SUS [9] or AttrakDiff [2] are values that are based on aggregated means which are normalized. Given the study had experimental conditions all types of inferential statistics for parametric and non-parametric data can be applied indicating significant differences between the conditions of the experiment or A/B testing.

3.3   How Task Models Relate to and Complement User Studies

In a classic iterative design and development process four phases are performed iteratively: analysis, design, implementation and evaluation [3]. Goal of such an iterative process is that findings and insights from the evaluation phase inform the analysis and design phase in a relevant way, which especially in Industry is very often not the case [5]. A detailed description on how to relate and complement task models with user studies (called PRENTAM) can be found in [3].

PRENTAM starts with a task analysis producing data that can be used for task modelling. Representation of the task models can be used to extract scenarios (or select tasks) that should be used during the evaluation study. This allows to check for completeness in terms of tasks for the user evaluation study or studies performed. Due to the task model it is also possible to forecast what type of data has to be collected: e.g. when the task models shows a user input it implies that the system (or system model) receives a value that should be registered during the study or when the task model describes a motor task variables like reaction time or video data on how the user was moving/behaving have to be recorded.

Once the study was performed the data produced is analyzed and data is prepared (e.g. preparing values like mean, minimum or maximum) to be ready for injection in the task model. Inserting the data collected during the study overcomes one of the main limitations of task models not to represent real usage data. With real usage data, task models can be used to reason about possible choices and how to enhance the usability of the system e.g. if it is discovered that the majority of users is performing a certain kind of error.

For the analysis aspect of data the storage of data related to the task model can help understand and investigate the relationship of user experience and tasks performed. Especially for such types of analysis it is important to be able to represent not only one but several user studies that are performed with the system and how associated software qualities like UX change of time. Once analysis of the data in the task models completed the final step in PRENTAM is to mend task and system models if necessary.

3.4   Need for Extensions in Task Models

To enable such injection of data into task models, any task modelling tool needs to be able to:

(1) represent the variety of user evaluation data described above for each participant of the user evaluation (each "run" of the study) including (a) qualitative/quantitative; (b) continuous vs. discrete; (c) from high level data related to tasks to atomic elements of a task model (not only for high level condensed information as proposed by [31]) and (d) represent changes over time.
(2) Enable storage of all aspects of a user evaluation study (participants, system(s) used in the study, scripted scenario the participant performs, conditions (if study is performed as an experiment).
(3) Allow storage of several user studies showing changes over time.
(4) Enable visualization of key aspects for all types of data. Examples for such a visualization can be the real usage of the system with frequencies of choice for options or the visualization of changes in the user experience over time (for example by highlighting these changes with color).

4   Representing Evaluation Data in HAMSTERS

This section presents the HAMSTERS notation and its eponym tool as well as the set of extensions that have been added to them in order to support usability evaluation. According to the sections above, these extensions are centered on the notion of scenarios that is the artefact connecting concrete elements such as prototypes to abstract representations such as user tasks and goals. While Sect. 4.1 presents an overview of HAMSTERS, Sect. 4.2 details the multiple extensions related to scenarios management that were added to HAMSTERS in order to better support usability evaluation activities. In a nutshell, these extensions concern both the interactive scenario browser and the set of tools to connect multiple data sources gathered during evaluation to those scenarios.

4.1   The HAMSTERS Tool and Its Notation

HAMSTERS [29] is a tool-supported graphical task modeling notation for representing human activities in a hierarchical and ordered manner. At the higher abstraction level, goals can be decomposed into sub-goals, which can in turn be decomposed into activities. The output of this decomposition is a graphical tree of nodes. Nodes can be tasks or temporal operators. Tasks can be of several types (see Fig. 1) and contain information such as a name, information details, and criticality level. Only the single user high-level task types are presented here but HAMSTERS has a variety of further task types available.

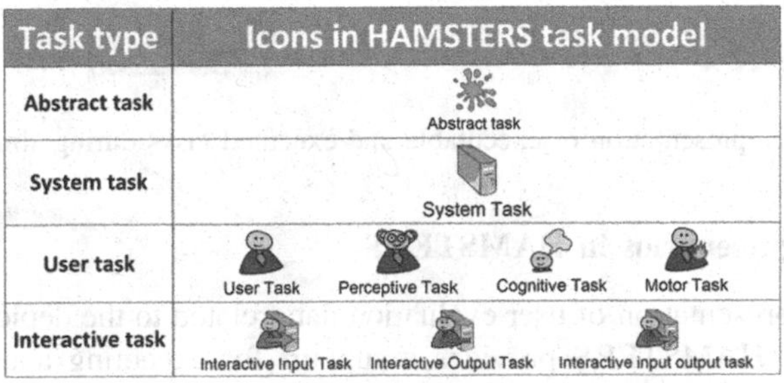

Task type	Icons in HAMSTERS task model			
Abstract task	Abstract task			
System task	System Task			
User task	User Task	Perceptive Task	Cognitive Task	Motor Task
Interactive task	Interactive Input Task	Interactive Output Task	Interactive input output task	

Fig. 1.   High-level task types in HAMSTERS

Temporal operators are used to represent temporal ordered relationships between sub-goals and activities. Tasks can also be tagged by temporal properties to indicate whether or not they are iterative, optional or both. An illustrative example of this notation and the tool can be found in [27].

The HAMSTERS notation and tool provide support for describing and structuring a large number and complex set of tasks, introducing the mechanism of subroutines and generic components [17], and describing data that is required and manipulated in order to accomplish tasks [28]. Furthermore, as task models can be large, it is important to provide the analyst with computer-based tools for editing task models and for analyzing them. To this end, the HAMSTERS task modeling tool provides support for creating, editing, and simulating the execution of task models and can be connected to system models [24].

HAMSTERS provides support to record the steps of task models execution in **scenarios**. New scenarios can be added in HAMSTERS via the simulation panel, indicating the creation of a new scenario as a visual element that appears in the project explorer panel, on the left hand side of the HAMSTERS software environment. Figure 2 shows HAMSTERS with an active scenario representing the currently executed element highlighted (in green) and providing information about: (a) the current tasks that are available for execution (list in the upper part of the simulation panel in Fig. 2); (b) the scenario, i.e. the tasks that have been executed (list in the lower part of the simulation panel in Fig. 2) and (c) the tasks that are available for execution are highlighted in green in the task model (in the central part in Fig. 2).

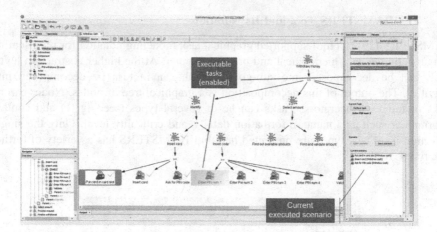

Fig. 2. Representation of executable and executed tasks during simulation

4.2 Extending Scenarios in HAMSTERS

To enable the representation of user evaluation data related to the depicted activities in the task models, HAMSTERS provides a support for executing and recording scenarios. The scenario part of the simulation panel (lower part in Fig. 2) allows browsing a scenario under construction and displays scenarios that have already been produced. However, only one scenario can be browsed at a time (in this task-model view) and the information presented are task sequence, type of task and object values that have been used during the execution of the scenario.

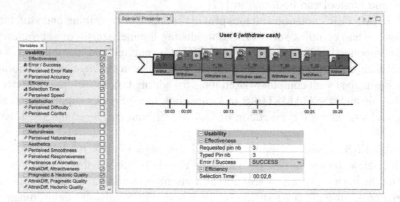

Fig. 3. The selection of variables to be displayed in the Scenario View (left) and the panel "Scenario Presenter" in HAMSTERS (right)

To display data from user studies, a dedicated panel provides support for visualization of a scenario under construction as well as of already existing scenarios. This panel is called the "Scenario Presenter" and is depicted in Fig. 3. Contrary to the model-oriented view in Fig. 2, several scenario can be visualized in this panel and for each presented scenario, two types of interactive visualizations are available a bar chart and a timeline.

The Bar Chart
The bar chart (illustrated in Fig. 3) presents the sequence of tasks that have been executed, from left to right. Each task is represented with a rectangle, displaying the following properties:

- Type of task, visually indicated by the color of the rectangle and by the icon in the top left part of the rectangle,
- task order in the scenario, visually indicated by the number displayed in the middle of the top part of the rectangle,
- task identifier, visually indicated by a code displayed in the middle of the rectangle,
- task short name, visually indicated by a text string, displayed in the lower part of the rectangle,
- data that has been eventually used by the user to accomplish the task, visually indicated by a yellow square in which a "D" is displayed (in the top right part of the rectangle).

The *Scenario Presenter* representation provides support for browsing a scenario and its sequence of tasks, as well as for interacting with them. Clicking on a task displays more information about its characteristics thanks to a dedicated pop-up window that contains details about the accomplished tasks (as well as data used or produced during the task if a "D" square is displayed in the task). As the scenario may contain a great number of tasks, this bar chart implements the fisheye interaction technique [18], enabling an overview of the whole scenario along with detail on demand. When the cursor is moved on a task, the area is centered around the cursor and then the targeted task as well as previous and next tasks are zoomed in.

The timeline (illustrated in Fig. 3) can present the start time, end time and duration of each task in the scenario. It also presents the duration of the scenario itself. Each scenario has an associated timeline that is located under the bar chart of the scenario.

The bar chart and the timeline representations are both interactive and are associated to each other for each scenario (see also Fig. 6, case study). For example, selecting a start time in the timeline will automatically position the center of the fisheye in the bar chart in the corresponding task. The panel *Scenario Presenter* provides support for comparing several scenarios, as several scenarios can be displayed one on top of each other.

4.3 Extensions to Scenarios and to Enrich Task Models

Filtering and Selection of Variables for the Scenario View
To enable the display of data gathered during user studies an interactive panel is available that allows selection of variables that shall be presented in the scenario view.

Figure 10 on the right hand side shows a sample view on such variables, currently displaying all variables for typical usability and user experience dimensions (Variables). A second panel called *Section Filtering* (not depicted) allows to select the type of tasks is displayed thus for exampling enabling the analysis of only cognitive tasks or only motor-tasks.

Representing System, Users, Scenarios/Conditions and Information

To represent information that is stemming from the user studies a set of additional information can be represented in the system (not depicted due to space constraints). A user evaluation is composed of a set of user evaluation runs that are performed in order to assess or evaluate the system. A run is made up of a set of information gathered while one user is performing a set of **planned actions (following the script)** on a given **system**. This set of planned actions is called a **scenario.** In case the user evaluation is based on an experimental set-up or is conducted as A/B testing each condition is represented as a different scenario (with a different system associated). A user evaluation is typically supervised by an evaluator. Activity of the evaluator like giving hints during a study can be represented in the task model and described as co-operative tasks if necessary.

For each condition/scenario HAMSTERS provides a set of most commonly used variables for usability and user experience (see Fig. 10, left, variable panel). In case additional variables currently not represented in HAMSTERS are necessary, the system allows to declare them by simply providing a name and scale (nominal, ordinal, interval, ratio, time, text or external data source). Currently as external data sources the integration of video is possible, the video is displayed below the time line. Furthermore, it is possible to connect HAMSTERS task models to an interactive application [26] and/or to systems' behavioral models [4]. These capability and the capability provided by the Circus environment (including HAMSTERS and Petshop) enables to co-execute all of the models and to monitor user actions and tasks in conjunction with events in the system (like waiting times due to system computation, keyboard presses or mouse clicks). The Circus environment provides support to record this data and to store it in HAMSTERS task models.

5   Demonstration of the Extensions

The tool and its extensions were for the user-centered design and development of an interactive television system. This section shows a small part of the overall project: goal is to demonstrate the usage of HAMSTERS extensions to represent data from the user evaluation.

The user interface prototype consists of a page with 12 tiles (4 columns, 3 rows), see Fig. 4 (left). During the experimentation dots appear pseudo randomized on the tiles. Users have to click on the corresponding area of the remote control to select the indicated tile. Correct selections are confirmed by displaying a green checkmark, incorrect selections with a red cross displayed on the item.

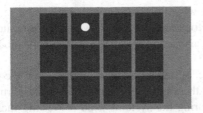

Fig. 4. The user interface and the remote controls with the touch interaction element with haptic landmarks integrated (middle) and without haptic landmarks (right)

Table 3. Dependent variables for usability and user experience dimensions shown to be not correlated in the domain of interactive TV [38]

Usability: Effectiveness	Number of errors; Accuracy [1..5]: very accurate to not accurate at all
Usability: Efficiency	Time to select a target
Usability: Satisfaction	Perceived difficulty [1..5]: very easy to very difficult; user comments on satisfaction [qualitative, text]; Comfort scale [1..5]: very accurate to not accurate at all
UX: Naturalness	Naturalness [1..5]: very natural, not natural at all
UX: Aesthetics	Smoothness [1..5]: very smooth to not smooth at all Responsiveness [1 to 5: very to not responsive Pertinence of animations [1..5]: very pertinent to not pertinent at all
UX: hedonic and pragmatic quality	Attrak Diff questionnaire sub-scales

The user study followed an experimental procedure with two independent variables: type of remote control and visual feedback or no visual feedback. Goal was to investigate if the haptic landmark would improve usability and user experience. Table 3 shows the type of data that was recorded and measured. In terms of UX the dimensions were derived from the domain specific IPTV-UX questionnaire [6].

5.1   Preparing and Performing the User Study: A Process Overview

Following the PRENTAM process [8] a task analysis was performed to identify task performed with the interactive TV system. Tasks were modelled using HAMSTERS including typical TV related tasks like selecting and changing a channel, changing volume or browsing the electronic program guide (EPG).

The process of setting up a user evaluation study based on task models, running the study and feeding back data into HAMSTERS is described in the following section in detail. The following step-by-step process demonstrates the general activities:

(1) **Task Analysis** identifying users task when interacting with TV
(2) **Task modelling** of major tasks performed with an iTV system with iterative refinements to represent even motor and cognitive tasks in the task models in HAMSTERS
(3) Setting up the user evaluation study: formulating the hypothesis for the study, preparing the **script (guidelines)** for the study on what activity each participant has to perform, developing and preparing the systems used for testing including the variations on the remote control.
(4) **Entering all study details**: Once the study details are finalized, information about system used (system with visual feedback, system without visual feedback, conditions (flat remote or remote with haptic landmarks), scenarios, participants and evaluator are entered into the HAMSTERS study set-up forms.
(5) **Declaring all dimensions and variables**: All dimensions and sub-dimensions evaluated (usability: efficiency, effectiveness, satisfaction; UX: aesthetics, naturalness, hedonic and pragmatic quality) are declared in HAMSTER. As the case study was the initial usage of HAMSTERS for such a study, all dimensions as well as variables were registered, in later stages the variables just have to be modified.
(6) **Preparing the scenarios**: Given the two independent variables, we had four conditions in the user study, thus four different scenarios were prepared.
(7) **Running the study:** The study was performed, with all participants in the study performing all four of the scenarios to have comparative measures.
(8) **Preparing and Inserting Data into Hamsters:** Based on all data recorded during the study, the data was checked for outliers, structured and inserted into the HAMSTERS tool, using the simple data entry form for scenarios and forms with varying attributes/variables for the different task types.

5.2   Associating User Study Results into HAMSTERS Scenarios

While performing the case study a variety of possible ways to enhance the integration of data was identified including automatic computation of frequencies and statistic tests or enabling users to freely add, manipulate and arrange data in data cells. But the goal of integrating user study results into HAMSTERS is not to provide functionalities of SPSS or Excel, but to support the analysis of user study results in combination with task models. The final mechanism thus simply supports manual entry and a simple import function.

To integrate user study results in HAMSTERS there are three levels of data:

- Low-level task elements: HAMSTERS provides only a basic data insertion form (see Fig. 5) that lists all currently defined variables in the system and associated task types (if applicable) for each run of a scenario. Data can be imported if strictly following the identified order of variables or is inserted manually.
- Level of activity (or sub-task): Ratings, judgements, feedback from the user, that is related to a certain activity is associated based on when in the scripted study the data was produced. Depending on the level in the task model (from abstract to concrete)

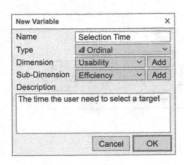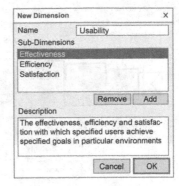

Fig. 5. Data declaration form (left) and dimension declaration form (right)

different forms are available to enter the data either as an additional variable or a standard attribute (see also Fig. 5).

- Data that is associated to abstract sub-tasks or on task or system level: the task model view can show high level data that is inserted in the overall view. This can be information from questionnaires like the SUS or AttrakDiff questionnaire that are typically used to evaluate the whole system.

5.3   Integrating and Representing User Study Results in HAMSTERS

Runs of the user study are represented using the Scenario Presenter View in Hamsters. Figure 6 shows a representation of results for user 6 performing a series of selection tasks with visual feedback given by the system (SelectTargetsFE). It shows averages for success rate, mean selection time, minimum and maximum selection time and average for the rates user experience (attractiveness) and results from the AttrakDiff [2] questionnaire.

Levels of data and their visualization:

(a) directly associated with low-level task element: Scenario Presenter, all values, time-line and video;

(b) Higher level tasks (e.g. for User 6 repeating 24 times the "selection an element task", showing mean, min/max, timeline for these summarized tasks) in the Scenario Presenter.

(c) Representing dimensions or factors like aesthetics, emotion, meaning and value, identification, stimulation, social connectedness in a task model using graphical representations like colors (see Fig. 6); representing choices, error frequencies, etc. using edges and adding information in the graph (see Fig. 6 for choice of an option).

The tool has been extended with a variety of visualization possibilities. There is a dedicated form that enables the user of the HAMSTERS tool to associate values to visualization formats accessible via the visible variables form (see Fig. 7 left). This way the user of HAMSTERS can select variables and the association of values for this variable to certain characteristics (e.g. color range for the Attractiveness Scale that was rated from [1 to 5] is represented in shades from green [1] to red [5]).

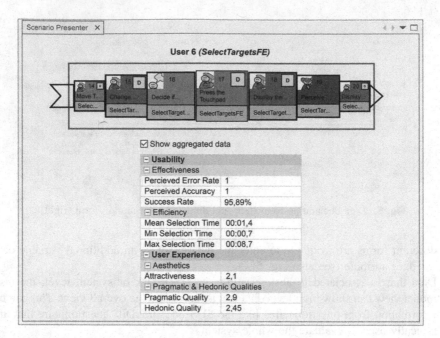

Fig. 6. Representation of user study results in the Scenario Presenter for a motor activity (Color figure online)

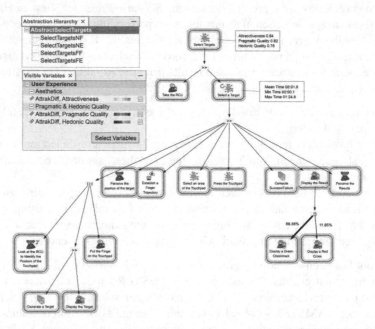

Fig. 7. Representation of user study result related to user experience in the task model indicating variations in the UX dimensions using color panels and representing frequencies of choice (%) on the connecting arrows to support usability analysis (Color figure online)

6 Discussion and Future Work

We proposed different ways to connect task models to interactive applications in the past such as the co-execution with annotated java code [26] or the connection with system models [35]. The connection of the task model with the real system is useful for designers to identify user interface objects and interactions that have to be amended (improved) but also the ones that should be used (or kept as templates) for other/similar designs as they work well. Identifying tasks and parts of the system that show a good usability and a clear contribution to an overall better user experience can help to inform not only the current system, but might also be used for similar systems or applications.

7 Future Work

For the near future the main goal is to investigate the representation of human errors in the task model thus we could make explicit where errors are expected (based on abstract knowledge of human errors) and assess whether they really occur or not. Designs could indeed overcome the presence of error precursors and prevent such errors from occurring. However, in order for designers to work on such aspects, they have to be made explicit and the task model is the only place to do so. HAMSTERS has already been extended [13] in order to represent in an explicit way errors following Hollnagel [19] and Reason [39] classifications. Future work will leverage on such descriptions to introduce results from user studies in the human error elements of task models. This would only require fine tuning of the process presented in [8] and the one on human error identification in [25].

References

1. Roto, V., et al.: All About UX: All UX Evaluation Methods, 17 October 2018. http://www.allaboutux.org/all-methods
2. Hassenzahl, M.: AttrakDiff – Fragebogen, 17 October 2018. www.attrakdiff.de
3. Baecker, R.M. (ed.): Readings in Human-computer Interaction: Toward the Year 2000. Morgan Kaufmann, San Francisco (1995)
4. Barboni, E., Ladry, J.-F., Navarre, D., Palanque, P., Winckler, M.: Beyond modelling: an integrated environment supporting co-execution of tasks and systems models. In: EICS 2010, pp. 165–174 (2010)
5. Bernhaupt, R., Manciet, F., Pirker, M.: User experience as a parameter to enhance automation acceptance: lessons from automating articulatory tasks. In: Proceedings of the 5th International Conference on Application and Theory of Automation in Command and Control Systems, pp. 140–150. ACM, New York (2015)
6. Bernhaupt, R., Pirker, M.: Evaluating user experience for interactive television: towards the development of a domain-specific user experience questionnaire. In: Kotzé, P., Marsden, G., Lindgaard, G., Wesson, J., Winckler, M. (eds.) INTERACT 2013, Part II. LNCS, vol. 8118, pp. 642–659. Springer, Heidelberg (2013). https://doi.org/10.1007/978-3-642-40480-1_45

7. Bernhaupt, R., Navarre, D., Palanque, P., Winckler, M.: Model-based evaluation: a new way to support usability evaluation of multimodal interactive applications. In: Law, E.L.-C., Hvannberg, E.T., Cockton, G. (eds.) Maturing Usability. HIS, pp. 96–119. Springer, London (2008). https://doi.org/10.1007/978-1-84628-941-5_5

8. Bernhaupt, R., Palanque, P., Manciet, F., Martinie, C.: User-test results injection into task-based design process for the assessment and improvement of both usability and user experience. In: Bogdan, C., et al. (eds.) HCSE/HESSD 2016. LNCS, vol. 9856, pp. 56–72. Springer, Cham (2016). https://doi.org/10.1007/978-3-319-44902-9_5

9. Brooke, J.: SUS-A quick and dirty usability scale. In: Usability Evaluation in Industry, pp. 189–194 (1996)

10. Cockton, G., Woolrych, A.: Understanding inspection methods: lessons from an assessment of heuristic evaluation. In: Blandford, A., Vanderdonckt, J., Gray, P. (eds.) People and Computers XV—Interaction without Frontiers, pp. 171–191. Springer, London (2001). https://doi.org/10.1007/978-1-4471-0353-0_11

11. Desmet, P., Overbeeke, K., Tax, S.: Designing products with added emotional value: development and application of an approach for research through design. Des. J. **4**, 32–47 (2001)

12. Roto, V., et al.: Emo Cards, 17 October 2018. http://www.allaboutux.org/emocards

13. Fahssi, R., Martinie, C., Palanque, P.: Enhanced task modelling for systematic identification and explicit representation of human errors. In: Abascal, J., Barbosa, S., Fetter, M., Gross, T., Palanque, P., Winckler, M. (eds.) INTERACT 2015, Part IV. LNCS, vol. 9299, pp. 192–212. Springer, Cham (2015). https://doi.org/10.1007/978-3-319-22723-8_16

14. Farenc, C., Palanque, P., Vanderdonckt, J.: User Interface evaluation: is it ever usable? In: Yuichiro, A., Katsuhiko, O., Hirohiko, M. (eds.) Advances in Human Factors/Ergonomics, vol. 20, pp. 329–334. Elsevier (1995)

15. Fayollas, C., et al.: An approach for assessing the impact of dependability on usability: application to interactive cockpits. In: Proceedings of the 2014 Tenth European Dependable Computing Conference, Washington, DC, USA, pp. 198–209. IEEE Computer Society (2014)

16. Field, A.: Discovering Statistics Using IBM SPSS Statistics. Sage Publication Ltd., London (2013)

17. Forbrig, P., Martinie, C., Palanque, P., Winckler, M., Fahssi, R.: Rapid task-models development using sub-models, sub-routines and generic components. In: Sauer, S., Bogdan, C., Forbrig, P., Bernhaupt, R., Winckler, M. (eds.) HCSE 2014. LNCS, vol. 8742, pp. 144–163. Springer, Heidelberg (2014). https://doi.org/10.1007/978-3-662-44811-3_9

18. Furnas, G.W.: Generalized fisheye views. In: Mantei, M., Orbeton, P. (eds.) Proceedings of the SIGCHI Conference on Human Factors in Computing Systems, pp. 16–23. ACM, New York (1986)

19. Hollnagel, E.: Cognitive Reliability and Error Analysis Method. Elsevier Science, Oxford (1998)

20. ISO 9241-210 Ergonomics of Human-System Interaction Ergonomics of human-system interaction – Part 210: Human-centred design for interactive systems (2010)

21. Jones, M., Marsden, G.: Mobile Interaction Design. John Wiley & Sons, Chichester (2006)

22. Karapanos, E., Zimmerman, J., Forlizzi, J., Martens, J.-B.: Measuring the dynamics of remembered experience over time. Interact. Comput. **22**, 328–335 (2010)

23. Lazar, D.J., Feng, D.J.H., Hochheiser, D.H.: Research Methods in Human-Computer Interaction. John Wiley & Sons, New York (2010)

24. Martinie, C., et al.: Formal tasks and systems models as a tool for specifying and assessing automation designs. In: Proceedings of the 1st International Conference on Application and Theory of Automation in Command and Control Systems, pp. 50–59. IRIT Press, Toulouse (2011)

25. Martinie, C., Palanque, P., Fahssi, R., Blanquart, J.P., Fayollas, C.: Seguin: task model-based systematic analysis of both system failures and human errors. IEEE Trans. Hum. Mach. Syst. **46**, 243–254 (2016)
26. Martinie, C., Navarre, D., Palanque, P., Fayollas, C.: A generic tool-supported framework for coupling task models and interactive applications. In: Proceedings of the 7th ACM SIGCHI Symposium on Engineering Interactive Computing Systems, pp. 244–253. ACM, New York (2015)
27. Martinie, C., Palanque, P., Navarre, D., Winckler, M., Poupart, E.: Model-based training: an approach supporting operability of critical interactive systems. In: Proceedings of the 3rd ACM SIGCHI Symposium on Engineering Interactive Computing Systems, pp. 53–62. ACM, New York (2011)
28. Martinie, C., Palanque, P., Ragosta, M., Fahssi, R.: Extending procedural task models by systematic explicit integration of objects, knowledge and information. In: Proceedings of the 31st European Conference on Cognitive Ergonomics, pp. 23:1–23:10. ACM, New York (2013)
29. Martinie, C., Palanque, P., Winckler, M.: Structuring and composition mechanisms to address scalability issues in task models. In: Campos, P., Graham, N., Jorge, J., Nunes, N., Palanque, P., Winckler, M. (eds.) INTERACT 2011, Part III. LNCS, vol. 6948, pp. 589–609. Springer, Heidelberg (2011). https://doi.org/10.1007/978-3-642-23765-2_40
30. Morae: Software, 17 October 2018. https://www.techsmith.com/morae.html
31. Mori, G., Paterno, F., Santoro, C.: CTTE: support for developing and analyzing task models for interactive system design. IEEE Trans. Softw. Eng. **28**, 797–813 (2002)
32. Nasa: Task Load Index, 17 October 2018. https://humansystems.arc.nasa.gov/groups/TLX/
33. Nielsen, J., Mack, R.L. (eds.): Usability Inspection Methods. John Wiley & Sons, Inc., New York (1994)
34. Norman, D.A., Draper, S.W.: User Centered System Design; New Perspectives on Human-Computer Interaction. L. Erlbaum Associates Inc., Hillsdale (1986)
35. Palanque, P., Bastide, R., Sengès, V.: Validating interactive system design through the verification of formal task and system models. In: Bass, L.J., Unger, C. (eds.) Engineering for Human-Computer Interaction, pp. 189–212. Springer, US (1996). https://doi.org/10.1007/978-0-387-34907-7_11
36. Paterno, F., Mancini, C., Meniconi, S.: ConcurTaskTrees: a diagrammatic notation for specifying task models. In: Howard, S., Hammond, J., Lindgaard, G. (eds.) Human-Computer Interaction, INTERACT '97. IFIP AICT, pp. 362–369. Springer, Boston (1997). https://doi.org/10.1007/978-0-387-35175-9_58
37. Pinelle, D., Gutwin, C., Greenberg, S.: Task analysis for groupware usability evaluation: modeling shared-workspace tasks with the mechanics of collaboration. ACM Trans. Comput. Hum. Interact. **10**, 281–311 (2003)
38. Pirker, M., Bernhaupt, R., Mirlacher, T.: Investigating usability and user experience as possible entry barriers for touch interaction in the living room. In: Proceedings of the 8th International Interactive Conference on Interactive TV&Video, pp. 145–154. ACM, New York (2010)
39. Reason, J.: Human Error. Cambridge University Press, Cambridge (1990)
40. Shneiderman, B.: The eyes have it: a task by data type taxonomy for information visualizations. In: Proceedings of the 1996 IEEE Symposium on Visual Languages, Washington, DC, USA, pp. 336–343. IEEE Computer Society (1996)
41. Swearngin, A., Cohen, M.B., John, B.E., Bellamy, R.K.E.: Human performance regression testing. In: Proceedings of the 2013 International Conference on Software Engineering, Piscataway, NJ, USA, pp. 152–161. IEEE Press (2013)

Rationalizing the Need of Architecture-Driven Testing of Interactive Systems

Alexandre Canny[1(✉)], Elodie Bouzekri[1], Célia Martinie[1],
and Philippe Palanque[1,2]

[1] ICS-IRIT, Université Paul Sabatier – Toulouse III, Toulouse, France
{alexandre.canny, elodie.bouzekri, celia.martinie,
philippe.palanque}@irit.fr
[2] Department of Industrial Design, Technical University Eindhoven,
Eindhoven, Netherlands

Abstract. Testing interactive systems is known to be a complex task that cannot be exhaustive. Indeed, the infinite number of combination of user input and the complexity of information presentation exceed the practical limits of exhaustive and analytical approach to testing [31]. Most interactive software testing techniques are produced by applying and tuning techniques from the field of software testing to try to address the specificities of interactive applications. When some elements cannot be taken into account by the software testing technique, they are usually ignored. In this paper we propose to follow an opposite approach, starting from a generic architecture for interactive systems (including both software and hardware elements) for identifying in a systematic way, testing problems and testing needs. This architecture-driven approach makes it possible to identify how software testing knowledge and techniques can support interactive systems testing but also where the interactive systems engineering community should invest in order to test their idiosyncrasies too.

Keywords: Architecture-driven testing · Interactive system testing

1 Introduction

Interactive systems testing involves different methods and techniques depending on the objectives of these tests. The field of Human-Computer Interaction (HCI) has been focusing on finding defects that affect user-related properties (such as usability, user experience, accessibility, learnability…) developing methods, techniques and tools to perform user studies involving directly the end-users. The field of software engineering has been focusing on finding defects that affect software quality and software-related properties (such as reliability, performance, availability, security…). This field has been developing methods, techniques and tools to perform software studies involving the Application Under Test (AUT) and a list of input to be provided to reveal defects.

Detecting defects in interactive systems requires bringing these two research fields together in order to ensure that, on one side the interactive systems fit with the human capabilities and the work of the users and, on the other side that the interactive systems are correct and behave as expected at any time. Unfortunately, the software engineering

© IFIP International Federation for Information Processing 2019
Published by Springer Nature Switzerland AG 2019
C. Bogdan et al. (Eds.): HCSE 2018, LNCS 11262, pp. 164–186, 2019.
https://doi.org/10.1007/978-3-030-05909-5_10

field has mainly been addressing interactive systems as a standard computing system (for instance abstracting away input and output devices, interaction techniques etc.) and only seminal work from Memon in his PhD [29] was dealing with specific aspects of interactive application testing. More precisely that work was performing testing using events on interactors of WIMP applications (called Graphical User Interface (GUI) testing). However, that work (and what was done later on) remained focused on WIMP interfaces [39] while the field of HCI has been proposing much more efficient and complex interaction techniques (e.g. the survey on menu techniques in [5]). More recently, research work on software programming of interactive applications [25] proposed methods and tools to automatically reveal bad programming practices but this covers only a very small part of the interactive software (the event-handlers and their structuring). What is tested and what is not, is a critical point as, if testing only some parts of the interactive system might reveal defects, the non-tested parts might still jeopardize the actual use of the system. Some recent work has been trying to extend the part of the AUT beyond the GUI by considering the execution platform (e.g. Android [38]). However, even in that work, testing only involves testing via event-handlers, thus remaining close to GUI testing aspects.

In this paper we propose to follow an approach starting from a generic architecture dedicated to interactive systems (including both software and hardware elements) for identifying, in a systematic way, testing problems and testing needs. This architecture-driven approach makes it possible to identify how software testing knowledge and techniques can support interactive systems testing. It also allows identifying where the interactive systems engineering community should invest to design and develop testing techniques complementary to the software engineering ones.

Section 2 introduces informally some of the testing problems that are specific to interactive systems. It demonstrates that those problems span from hardware (input and output devices) to the functional core (non-interactive) of the application. It thus demonstrates the need for testing techniques dedicated to interactive systems. This section also identifies testing principles that could (and should) be applied to support testing activities to address these problems of interactive systems. Section 3 presents in detail the MIODMIT generic architecture for interactive systems and positions the testing problems presented in Sect. 2 on that architecture. Section 4 presents two case studies and the testing problems they raise to make concrete the abstract problems presented in Sect. 2. These case studies exhibit different interaction techniques and different input devices highlighting the variability of interactive systems and how this affects the testing needs. The generic architecture MIODMIT is tuned for each case study and is used to systematically identify those testing needs. Section 5 connects MIODMIT to human aspects thus positioning user testing together with interactive system testing presented in previous sections. Section 6 structures the related work presented in the paper and makes explicit the testing problems that are covered by the literature and the remaining open ones. Section 7 concludes the paper and highlights paths for future work.

2 Informal Description of Problems for Testing Interactive Systems

Since interactive systems relies on a growing set of I/O devices to enable interaction, it is important to look at the testing of both their hardware and their software components. In this section, we present the main principles of software, hardware and usability testing and then use these principles to exemplify some of the problems tester must take into account when testing interactive systems.

2.1 Main Principles of Testing

Main Principles of Software Testing

Software testing is an activity every application should go through, no matter it is interactive or not. The Software Engineering Body of Knowledge (SWEBOK) [11] defines software testing as the dynamic verification that a program provides expected behaviors on a finite set of test cases, suitably selected from the usually infinite execution domain.

A key point in the software testing activity is the definition of the test levels. The test level of an application is defined thanks to two variables: the target of the test and the objective of the test. The targets of testing can be a single module (unit testing), a group of module (integration testing) or the entire software application (system testing). The SWEBOK [11] references 12 objectives of testing such as performance testing or regression testing which are respectively non-functional and functional testing techniques. The non-functional tests refer to the way the software operates (e.g. is it to slow?) whereas the functional tests refer to the extent to which the software behaves properly (e.g. is it producing the correct output for a given set of input?).

Once the testing level is defined, the testing of software application requires three activities: the test case construction, the test suite construction and the test execution. During the testing activity, the tested software is usually referred as the Application Under Test (AUT). In [31], Nguyen et al. details these steps considering the testing of applications with a graphical user interface (GUI) using "standard" widgets (e.g. buttons, label, radio button).

Main Principles of Hardware Testing

The testing of the hardware of interactive systems remains, to the best of our knowledge, a relatively unexplored area. While patents such as [20] proposes testing techniques for testing touch screen at hardware level, no systematic classification of testing requirements for hardware has been issued to specifically address interactive systems. However, hardware testing is a concern in the field of Cyber-Physical System (CPS) engineering that shares some specificities with interactive system engineering.

CPS integrate both physical and computational elements so their engineering requires bridging the continuous analog real world and the discrete digital world. The behavior of CPS is thus similar to the one of modern interactive with multiple I/O devices (e.g. compass, camera, speaker, haptic devices). According to Asadollah et al. [3], hardware testing consists in testing hardware components of CPS, including tests of each component's functionality, which descriptions are based on the system requirements. Amongst the most common and important variable in testing CPS hardware, Asadollah et al. [3] lists memory size, speed, storage capacity, I/O interfaces (ports), synchronization capabilities, etc. They also point out that testing the hardware under specific conditions (e.g. local environment) is required. For interactive systems, this is equivalent to the testing of the interactive system in its context of operation.

It is important to note that as for software testing, test levels may be defined. Hardware tests levels can be described using targets and objectives. For example, testing a touchscreen on its own is comparable to performing unit testing while testing an entire smartphone packing this touchscreen is comparable to performing system testing.

The tested hardware may be referred as the System Under Test (SUT) even though this expression is also used in software engineering. In this paper, we consider that:

- the **AUT** is the application running on the interactive system at testing time. For example, on a Personal Computer where VLC Media Player is running for a video playback, the AUT is the VLC Media Player;
- the **SUT** is the entire interactive system, including its Input/Output devices, drivers, etc. During a video playback with VLC Media Player, the SUT thus includes the screen, the speakers, the soundcard, the remote control (if any), the operating system, the VLC Media Player application, etc.

2.2   Testing Interactive System

To highlight how interactive system testing is difficult, we present in this section some informal examples of the diversity of requirements and constraints that have to be taken into account while testing (Table 1). These examples find their origins in the definitions of elements of interactive systems (e.g. modal window), in the specifications of interactive systems (e.g. hardware capability) or in authors' experiences with interactive systems (e.g. text disappearing or mouse cursor not moving in Windows).

On interactive systems, it must for instance be tested that if multi-touch interactions involve five fingers, the touchscreen must accommodate at least five fingers. This requirement appears in Table 1 (H3) as "The I/O devices must comply with the requirements for the I/O devices of the SUT". Second column of Table 1 assigns a name to each example that will be used later. The third column assigns to each example a component of interactive systems that is involved in this requirement/constraint. This column shows that our examples of requirements and constraints (to be tested on interactive systems) requires testing both software (e.g. Non-Interactive Code, Interactive Code) and hardware (e.g. device) components of an interactive system. However, to the best of our knowledge, no integrated testing techniques offer support for the entire interactive system. A review of the literature regarding "interactive system testing" shows that these keywords link mostly to papers related to GUI Testing. Banerjee et al. [6] define GUI testing to mean that a GUI-based application, i.e. one that has a graphical user interface (GUI) front-end, is tested solely by performing sequences of events (e.g. "click on button", "enter text", "open menu") on GUI widgets (e.g. "button", "text-field", "pull-down-menu"). Thus, hardware is not took into account in

Table 1. Examples of the diversity of requirements and constraints to be tested

Description	Name	Component
Unit testing of the software components that are responsible of providing data and services for the AUT should not reveal defects	N1	Non Interactive Code
Integration of the software components that are responsible of providing data and services of the AUT with the interactive elements of the interactive system should not reveal defects	N2	
A modal window reduces the interaction space only until it is closed	I1	Interactive Code
The position of the manipulator of an input device (e.g. pointer) should evolve in accordance with user action on that device (e.g. mouse pointer going left if the mouse is moved to the left)	I2	
The user can only trigger authorized events (e.g. whenever a file is open the user can trigger the event close file)	D1	
The user can trigger none of the unauthorized events (e.g. a user cannot trigger the event close file if the file is not open)	D2	
The text within a button must always remain visible when the button is visible	P1	Presentation
The grayed-out widgets should not produce event even though the user act on them	P2	
Every available widgets should be reachable (e.g. if the widget is not visible, manipulation of its window should allow the user to make it visible)	P3	
The I/O loop should have performance compatible with human perception (e.g. the movement of the manipulator of the mouse should occur within 50 ms after the mouse has been moved)	H1	Device
The color displayed on the screen should correspond to the one that has been required to be displayed	H2	
The I/O devices must comply with the requirements for the I/O devices of the SUT (e.g. the touchscreen device should handle at least as many fingers as what is needed by the SUT)	H3	
The I/O devices must behave so they prevent undesired repetition of events and produce expected repetition of events (e.g. keeping a key pressed on the keyboard will repeat production of the event associated to that key)	H4	
The behavior of the firmware of the input device should be compatible (e.g. type of data, rate) with the one of the input device driver	D3	Driver
The SUT should prevent removal of needed I/O devices by an application if another application requires access to it (e.g. if a microphone is required all the time by an application (noise detection), another one will not be allowed to access it)	C1	Input/Output Manager
The SUT must be capable of producing high-level events from low-level events that are produced by one input device (e.g. each time the user presses and releases a mouse button, a mouse clicked event is produced in addition to mouse up and mouse down events)	C2	
The SUT must be capable of exploiting multiple output modalities synchronously if the AUT needs it (e.g. sound+video during video playback)	C3	
The SUT must be capable of producing high-level events from low-level events that are produced by multiple input devices (e.g. moving two fingers concurrently in the opposite direction should be interpretable as a pinch event)	C4	

GUI testing. Moreover, as mentioned by [26], GUI testing do not scale properly with advanced GUI (e.g. supporting multi-touch or multimodal interaction). We claim that a better understanding of the role of interactive systems components may help to provide better testing techniques for interactive and so we propose to work on architecture-driven testing techniques.

3 Architecture of Interactive Systems and Its Use for Testing

Interactive systems testing is a complex activity that is only partly addressed by existing testing approaches. Indeed, a review of the literature regarding interactive system testing shows that most of the problems presented in the Sect. 2.2 are not addressed. Most of existing testing techniques [27, 28] focus on GUI (Graphical User Interface) involving standard UI widgets (e.g. Buttons, ComboBox). As GUI heavily exploits the functionalities, the interactive objects and the input devices offered by the underlying execution platform, testing approaches rely on the "good" functioning of the platform and thus testing only addresses behavioral and functional aspects of the application and not the interactive system as a whole. In order to perform a systematic approach to testing we propose an architecture-driven testing for interactive systems. In order to avoid the pitfalls of GUI testing we propose to include hardware and hardware drivers in addition to the more standard software elements. In this section, we first present some architectures for interactive systems and highlight their relevance for identifying components to test. Then, we detail the MIODMIT architecture, a fine-grained architecture covering in a comprehensive way all the elements of "modern" interactive systems. Finally, we highlight the components of the architecture impacted by the problems presented in Sect. 2.2 and describe the testing needs to prevent these problems.

3.1 Interactive Systems Architectures

Since the early 80's, a software architecture (known as the Seeheim model [34]) has been proposed to decompose interactive applications in smaller components. To reflect the evolution of interactive applications and the fact that a large share of application code was devoted to the User Interface, Len Bass et al. [7] proposed the Arch model that was decomposing Seeheim's Presentation component into two, the Logical Interaction component and the Physical Interaction one.

With that modification, 3 out of 5 components are dedicated to the UI and the Physical Interaction component connects to input and output devices (even though not explicitly mentioned in the paper). Beyond that, it does not cope explicitly with multimodal UIs that are nowadays mainstream means of interaction.

The architecture associated to ICon [16] refines carefully the input flow from physical input devices to the application core (see. Fig. 5.1. in [17], p. 148), however, no description of the output management is provided. As interactions frequently involve both perception and action dimensions of user behavior, refining only input does not make it possible to describe real systems.

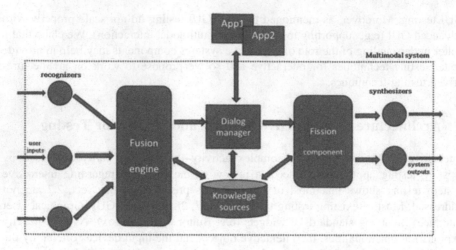

Fig. 1. Architecture for multimodal interactive systems from [15]

As stated above, current interactive applications exploit multiple input and output devices, and interaction with those systems may be multimodal. Some contributions such as [15] (see Fig. 1) present connected components forming an architecture of multimodal interactive applications. This architecture makes explicit a fission component (for output) and a fusion component for input. Such representation is misleading as fusion and fission may be associated with both input and output. For instance, a sentence produced by a speech recognition system might be broken down into words (fission of the input information) to identify commands and parameters [23]. Similarly, a presentation of information might require the combination of multiple information (e.g. the level of danger and a warning message) in order to present fused information to the user (e.g. the warning message in orange color). This demonstrates the importance of having a very detailed and generic architecture for describing and designing interactive systems.

3.2 MIODMIT Generic Architecture for Interactive Systems

MIODMIT [13] is a detailed architecture that makes the interactive systems components explicit including hardware ones (both for input and output). It is thus more representative about interactive systems that the other architectures presented in the related work section. This architecture does not exhibit dedicated fusion or fission engines components, as fusion and fission are functions are distributed over the architecture in several components (explained more in detail in the case study section). Figure 2 presents an overview of the MIODMIT architecture. Each rounded rectangle represents a component of the MIODMIT architecture and arcs represent the communication between component. When an arc between two components is not present, the component cannot communicate (information flow, function call, …) with the other one.

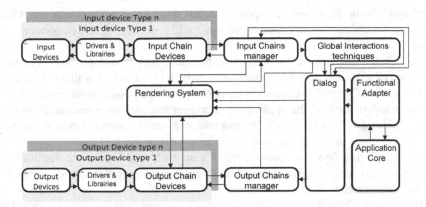

Fig. 2. The MIODMIT architecture (adapted from [14])

The "Input Device Type" greyed-out box describes the information flow for a given type of input device. Each new type of input device requires a separate "Input Device Type". An "Input Device Type" is composed of three components. First, "Input Devices" component is the physical (hardware) input device manipulated by the user (e.g. a mouse or a finger on a touchscreen). The "Input Devices" component sends information to or receives requests of information from the "Drivers & Libraries" software component, which, in turn, makes this information available to the other components of MIODMIT. Less commonly, "Drivers and Libraries" can manage "Input Devices" behaviour such as sampling frequency [24] or providing user identification [40]. "Drivers and Libraries" can be provided either by the "Input Devices" manufacturer or by the operating system if the hardware is standard or has been around for a significant amount of time. Lastly, the "Input Chain Device" component is a software component that mirrors the state of the "Input Devices" hardware (called "Virtual Device"), the "Logical device" of the "Input Devices" hardware (e.g. cursor pointer position for a mouse) and a manager. These components are transducers [2] that transform raw data into low-level information. Virtual device can be dynamically instantiated with plug-and-play devices. Whereas, logical devices can be dynamically instantiated at operation time. For example, each time a finger touches a multi-touch input device, a new logical device associated with the new finger is created. The manager addresses configuration and dynamic configuration of devices.

The "Input Chain Manager" component is an event-based component that processes low-level information and connects such information to user interface objects (e.g. a button) and their location on the screen. This component may fuse information from different input devices to create high-level information (e.g. clicking simultaneously on two mice will produce one click on each and the "Input Chain Manager" might produce higher-level event called "combined click" [1]). In addition, this component manages dynamic reconfiguration of interaction in case of failure[1].

---

[1] As terminology for failures, faults and errors we use the definitions from [4].

The "Input Chain Manager" component sends high-level information to "Global Interaction Technique" component (a transducer [2]) or "Dialogue" component or to the both.

The "Global Interaction Technique" component is a transducer that performs a recognition of a specific interaction technique, which is not linked with a user interface object (e.g. "OK Google" vocal interaction). Moreover, this component generates high-level information used by the application to trigger the various command it provides.

The "Dialogue" and "Core" components are similar components to standard interactive systems architecture such as Seeheim [34] or Arch [7].

The "Rendering System" component is responsible of immediate feedback and other state-based rendering functions. A state-based rendering function describes how to present information of a specific state.

The "Output Chain Manager" component offers same functionalities as the "Input Chain Manager" component. Nevertheless, the "Output Chain Manager" is state-based whereas the "Input Chain Manager" is event-based.

The "Output Device Type" describes the information flow for output device in the same way.

3.3   Locating Testing Problems and Testing Needs Using MIODMIT

In this section, we position the problem listed in Table 1 according to the MIODMIT architecture. This systematic analysis highlights the fact that testing problems may be related to various components of the interactive systems and that a precise description of the interactive system is required to be able to manage all these problems. It is important to note that while some problems affect only one component of the architecture, some of them are distributed over several.

Problems Related to a Single Component of MIODMIT
N1 - Unit testing of the software components that are responsible of providing data and services for the AUT should not reveal defects and N2 - Integration of the software components that are responsible of providing data and services of the AUT with the interactive elements of the interactive system should not reveal defects

In interactive system architecture in general, as well as in MIODMIT, the "software components that are responsible of providing data and services" are part of the **application core**. The testing of these components is well-documented by the software testing community and the techniques for testing the application core of an interactive application are not different from those allowing the testing of non-interactive applications.

I1 - A modal window reduces the interaction space only until it is closed
Modal windows are designed so they force the user to interact with them before they can resume interaction with their parent applications. Thus, *I1* means that developers must verify that any way of closing the modal window will allow user to resume interaction according to their choice within the modal window. This implies testing at the **rendering system** level.

P2 - The grayed-out widgets should not produce events even though the user acts on them

This means that even though the **input chain manager** produces a mouse clicked event over a grayed out button, testing should prove that this event should not be forwarded as a higher-level event produced by the button itself towards other components of the application (such as the dialogue).

H3 - The I/O devices must comply with the requirements for the I/O devices of the SUT

This means that the compliance of every **Input/Output device** with their specifications must be verified before their integration in the interactive system.

C1 - The SUT should prevent removal of needed I/O devices by an application if another application requires access to it

This means that testing the component responsible of dynamic reconfiguration of the I/O in the **input/output chain manager** must be performed in order to ensure that this component will not cause a loss of resource for an application.

C2 and C4 - The SUT must be capable of producing high-level events from low-level events that are produced by one input device/The SUT must be capable of producing high-level events from low-level events that are produced by multiple input devices

This means that the capability of the **input chain device** to produce high-level events specific to a device (e.g. click) must be tested (C2). Moreover, the capability of the **input chain manager** to produce high-level events from the events produced by **input chain devices** must be tested (C4).

C3 - The SUT must be capable of exploiting multiple output modalities synchronously if the AUT needs it

This means that the priority management of the **output chain manager** must be tested.

Problems Distributed Over Several Components of MIODMIT

I2 - The position of the manipulator of an input device (mouse cursor) should evolve in accordance with user action on that device

This problem concerns the entire left part of the architecture, or short loop (input device types, rendering system and output device types). To take it into account, a proper transcription of the user input on the output device is required. For a mouse, this means that:

- Its motion sensor is calibrated properly (**input device**);
- Its **drivers and libraries** are getting data consistently and are computing the mouse acceleration properly;
- The **input chain device** produces high level event notifying the **rendering system** of the new cursor location;
- The **rendering system** makes the proper rendering request to the **output chain device** (including coordinates, shape of the mouse cursor, etc.);
- The **output chain device** combines rendering request from the **rendering system** and the **output chains manager** so the cursor is always drawn of top;
- The **output drivers and libraries** are dispatching the rendering requests to the graphic card properly (correct screen, resolution, etc.)

- The screen (**output device**) is set in the proper input (e.g. HDMI) and is capable of displaying the cursor.

P1 - The text within a button must always remain visible when the button is visible
This means that the **output chain manager** must request the display of the button with the text in it and that the output chain device behave as expected. We do not detail the testing needs for the **output device type** (presented in problem *I2*).

D1 and D2 - The user can only trigger authorized events/The user can trigger none of the unauthorized event
This means that the rendering of the application produced by the **output chains manager** and the **output device type** should reveal which actions are authorized or not (e.g. disabling widgets) and that the problem *P2* has been taken into account.

H1 – The I/O loop should have performance compatible with human perception
This problem is a refinement of problem *I2* that takes human performance into account. The I/O device type and the computing system responsible for the rendering system must be performant enough so they accomplish the whole behavior described in *I2* in an acceptable time regarding human perception.

H2 - The color displayed on the screen should correspond to the one that has been required to be displayed
This means that the **output chains manager** and **output chain type** must only request the display of colors the **output device** is capable to render. Moreover, the screen (**output device**) must be calibrated for its targeted color space (e.g. RGB) and the **drivers and libraries** must be configured properly so they use the screen's color space.

H4 - The I/O devices must behave so they prevent undesired repetition of events and produce expected repetition of events
This means that, at the hardware level (**input/output device**), proper implementation of feature such as de-bouncing must be verified (e.g. for a keyboard **input device**). This also mean, at the **input device type** level, the implementation of character repeat is done properly.

D3 - The behavior of the firmware of the input device should be with the one of the input device driver
This means that the **input device** should always produce information that can be used properly by the **drivers and libraries**. Thus, if the **drivers and libraries** and/or the firmware of the **input device** is/are updated, both elements must still be compatible.

4 Testing Interactive Systems: Two Cases Studies

In this section, we present how to use MIODMIT to identify the testing needs for two different MS Windows interactive systems

- a version of the application designed to be used with a mouse, a keyboard and a trackpad as input devices and a screen as output device;

- a multimodal version of the application with the same input/output devices and adding multi-touch input and speech-recognition. Besides, this application uses a loudspeaker and speech synthesis.

4.1   A Common Application Core for Both Cases Studies

Both case studies are drawing applications that allow manipulating drawings (i.e. creation of colored shapes selected from a finite set of possible shapes and colors). This allows the two applications to share the same Application Core, i.e. the component that is responsible for maintaining a list of created shapes, their color and their position. Since the applications are coded in JAVA, unit testing of the application core is possible using tools such as JUnit. Such testing allow verifying that:

- The services provided by the Shape class (e.g. getColor(), setColor(Color c), getPosition()) behave as expected;
- The class responsible for handling the current drawing behaves as expected (e.g. addShape(Shape s), getNbShape());
- The class responsible of serializing and de-serializing drawings behave as expected (e.g. open(File f), save(), saveAs(File f)).

It is important to note that the testing of all this services independently is however insufficient. Indeed, the internal behavior of the class must also be assessed with respect to user action e.g. the user cannot open a file already open, save an empty file, etc.

4.2   Case Study 1: Mouse, Keyboard and Screen

Informal Description of the Interactive System and Its Architecture
In this first case study, the interactive system specifications are the following: HP Zbook, Operating System: Windows 10; Output device: 14 in. display 1920 * 1080; Input devices: Pointing devices (Integrated trackpad and HID-compliant USB Mouse) and Integrated Keyboard.

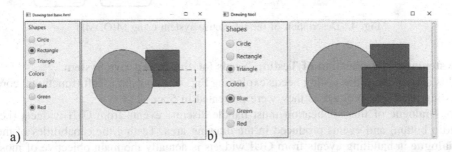

Fig. 3. Screenshots of the interactive application (a) after drawing two shapes and while drawing a third one (b) after drawing four shapes (including one not visible, please notice the scrollbar) (Color figure online)

The user can select the shape and the color by clicking on the associated radio buttons (see Fig. 3). To position the shape in the drawing area, the user has to press the left button of the mouse at the desired location of the first point of a rectangle containing the shape. Maintaining the mouse left button down (dragging) until the desired shape size creates a ghost (Fig. 3a). Releasing the left button adds the shape to the drawing.

Following the «tune-on-demand» process presented in [14], we can produce from MIODMIT a specific architecture (see Fig. 4). The two "pointing device type" are the mouse and the trackpad. The "Mouse Device" and "Keyboard device" represent the hardware part of these input devices. The "Mouse Driver" and "Trackpad Driver" represent the drivers of these input devices. Similarly, the "keyboard device type" is described by the "keyboard device" and "keyboard driver". The "output device type" corresponds to the computer screen composed of a "screen device" and a "screen driver". As computer runs Windows 10, the "Windows Manager" of this Operating System covers entirely the functions of input and output chain components as well as a subset of the functions of the rendering component. The "Windows Manager" contains the "Abstract Cursor" (input chain functions and rendering functions) and the "Feedback Cursor" (output chain functions and the rendering of the cursor). The "Dialogue" component describes the behavior of the interactive application. The "Functional Core" supports the functions presented in Sect. 4.1.

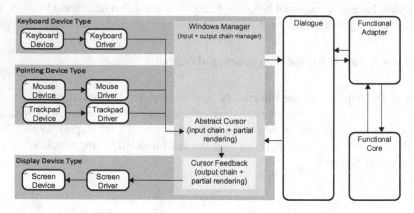

Fig. 4. Description of the interactive system using MIODMIT

Systematic Identification of Testing Needs for the Interactive System

This section identifies testing needs exploiting Fig. 4 from right to left (functional core testing needs are omitted as they were presented in Sect. 4.1.

Dialogue of this application must handle discrete events from GUI widgets (i.e. radio button) and events produced in the drawing area. Testing the capabilities of the **dialogue** in handling events from GUI widgets is actually the main objective of most GUI testing techniques. Indeed, in [29], techniques are designed to test GUI driven by mono-event interactions (e.g. button clicks) which are not suitable for multi-event interaction (e.g. on the drawing area of a graphical editor). While [10, 26] discuss the testing of interactive systems with continuous interaction, these papers mainly addresses multimodality itself and thus do not contribute to dialogue testing. Testing the **dialogue** requires:

- Verifying that it is capable of consuming all the events produced by all the input device types that it must support;
- Verifying that its user-driven state changes only occur in response to authorized events;
- Its transition between states occur as expected.

While developing in JAVA, the operating system and the JAVA Virtual Machine share responsibility over the **Windows Manager**. This component encapsulates the **Input/Output Type/Chain Device/Chain Manager** as well as the **Rendering System** according to MIODMIT terminology. For this reason, testing of the **Window Manager** thus cannot be placed under the responsibility of the developer of the application. However, the actual behavior of the **Windows Manager** raises problems that testers must take into account. Indeed, in the presentation of this case study, we state "the user can select the shape and the color by clicking on the associated radio buttons". However, the radio button is a component from the JAVA Swing library and its standard behavior does not comply with this statement. Indeed, pressing "Space" or "Enter" on a focused radio button would trigger the same "ActionEvent" as the one produced when clicking on it, adding unspecified behaviors to the application. During development, decisions regarding these unspecified behaviors must be made (should they be prevented or not?) so the test cases and suites are prepared accordingly:

- Actions described in the application specifications trigger ActionEvents as required;
- ActionEvents can (or cannot) be triggered by shortcut/hotkeys whether is was (or was not) decided to allow them in the application.

By default, the **Windows Manager** allows users to resize and move the application window. This makes it possible to hide some of the GUI widgets (e.g. Fig. 5c) or some area of the drawing (e.g. Fig. 5a and b: absence of a scrollbar does not give a proper idea of the drawing zone size). Moreover, the **Windows Manager** controls windows arrangement and focus. Testing is thus required to verify that:

- The resizing of the window is constrained enough so none of the six radio buttons are hidden;
- Resizing the window below the size of the drawing area triggers the appearance of scrollbars (e.g. Fig. 3b);
- The application window can receive focus and may or may not be visible.

The **Pointing Device Type** of this interactive system is specific as it contains two input devices: a mouse and a trackpad. The tester must verify that the abstract cursor (and its associated feedback) of the **Rendering System** encapsulated in the **Windows Manager** is capable of handling input from multiple pointing devices and is configured to do so. Indeed, on some interactive systems, each pointing device can be attached to a specific cursor[2] or can be merged in a single cursor (e.g. MS Windows).

---

[2] https://wiki.archlinux.org/index.php/Multi-pointer_X.

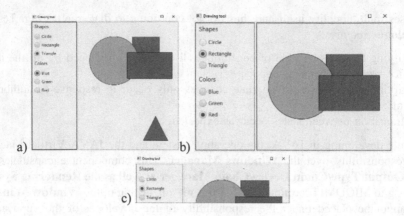

Fig. 5. The application window is (a) extended in height, (b) reduced in height after drawing the blue triangle and (c) reduced in height so radio buttons disappear (Color figure online)

The testing needs regarding the **drivers** and the **Input/Output Devices** of this interactive system were already discussed in Sect. 3.3 (see problems D3 for **drivers** and H2, H3, H4 for **I/O Devices**) and are not repeated here.

4.3 Case Study 2: The Multimodal Drawing Application

Informal Description of the Interactive System and Its Architecture
In this case study, the user can perform the same interaction as in the case study 1, in addition to multimodal ones. Since a touchscreen is available, the user can select radio buttons by touching them and can also draw a shape by sliding a finger in the drawing area. Shapes can be resized using a "pinch" interaction. The user can use a combination of voice and touch to select shape and color from existing shapes in the drawing area:

- Saying "Select this color" and then touching a shape selects the color of the touched shape and a speech synthesis announce "color selected" as in [8];
- Saying "Select this shape" and then touching a shape selects the shape of the touched shape and a speech synthesis announce "shape selected";

In both case, the touch must occur less than 2 s after speaking, otherwise the interaction is discarded.

As for case study 1, we tuned (see Fig. 6) MIODMIT generic architecture using the tune-on-demand process presented in [14]. Input/Output device types have been added as required and the multimodal aspect of the application is handled by the "Input Chains Manager" component (top right of Fig. 6). Part of the behavior of this component is implemented by MS Windows 10, while part has to be programed specifically.

Testing Needs Specific to This Multimodal Interactive System
In this section, we only present the testing needs raised by the multimodal interaction. Testing needs from case study 1 (related to mouse and keyboard interactions) remain.

The **Input Chains Manager** component introduced in this case study is a new source of event for the **Dialogue** as well as a new consumer of events from the **Windows Manager**. A key aspect in testing the **Input Chains Manager** is to support temporal aspects are required. For instance, the fusion mechanism [23] produces the selection event only if the succession of events (speech + touch) occurs within a given temporal window. It is important to note that this interaction technique has to be tested as part of the **Input Chains Manager** as it describes how some events from different input chains are produced and then transferred to the dialogue.

These case studies show that the instantiation of the MIODMIT architecture for a SUT (System Under Test) provides support for a precise identification of testing needs. It provides support in identifying:

- The common components from an application to another (in order to communalize some tests and avoid duplicated testing)
- The impact of a change in the interaction technique on the testing needs

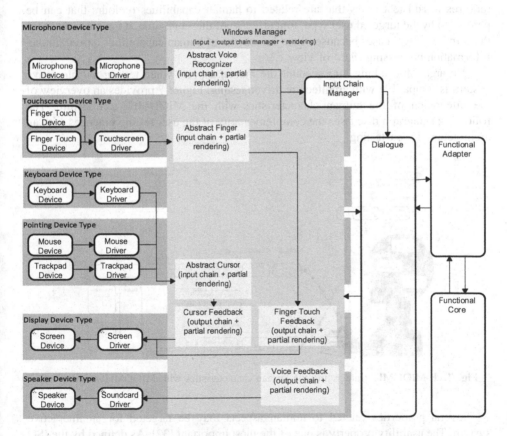

Fig. 6. Architecture of the second case study using MIODMIT

5 Human Aspects in Architecture-Driven Interactive System Testing

MIODMIT provides support for systematically testing all the parts of an interactive system. The focus of the presented work is on the interactive system side. However, while focusing on system, the human cannot be ignored. Testing some or all of the parts of the architecture of an interactive system by function and without taking into account how the future user of the system will use it, belongs to the category of system centric testing or system/software testing. For this category of testing, system/software functions are tested one by one, without caring about how they will be manipulated by the user. But, this category of testing does not take into account human aspects. An interactive system is used by a human in order to perform her/his work. The interactive system has to be at least usable by the users that are targeted for the developed system. User testing aims at taking into account human aspects for the interactive system being developed. Nevertheless, user testing increases the number of testing activities as it requires to add test cases that are related to human capabilities (colours that can be perceived by the targeted user type, font size...). At the same time, it may also decrease the number of test cases because of the limitations of human capabilities (speed human information processing, field of view...).

We argue that taking into account the human aspects when testing an interactive system is compatible with architecture driven testing. Figure 7 provides an overview of the integration of the human characteristics with the MIODMIT architecture. The following paragraph discusses the complementarity of the user testing practices with an architecture driven testing.

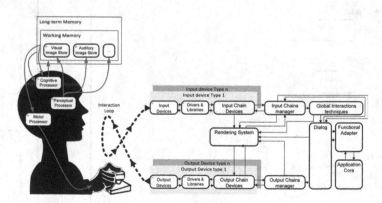

Fig. 7. H-MIODMIT (integrating the human characteristics with MIODMIT architecture)

Several properties related to human aspects may be targeted for an interactive system. The usability property is one of the most important [32]. As defined by the ISO 9241-11 [21], usability is *"the extent to which a system, product or service can be used by specified users to achieve specified goals with effectiveness, efficiency and satisfaction in a specified context of use"*. Another important property that may be assessed for an interactive system, is the learnability property, that can be evaluated by measuring how the interactive system allows the user to reach a reasonable level of usage proficiency in a short period of time [32]. Then, depending on the application domain (entertainment, games, critical systems...), other properties may also be targeted (user experience, dependability...). For example, evaluating user experience with an interactive system aims at measuring properties such as emotion, aesthetics, social connectedness [35]... that may be highly subjective and require specific evaluation processes and techniques. Several aspects of user testing for interactive systems have to be taken into account for the integration of human characteristics with architecture driven testing:

- Iterative evaluation processes are applied to ensure that the user needs are taken into account. Such processes are part of the User Centered Design paradigm which usually encompass several prototyping and evaluation phases [18]. User involvement is a pillar of such processes. User tests are performed for the most possible stages of design of an interactive system (from early design phases with low-fidelity prototypes to the deployment of the interactive system).
- For some properties, user testing can be achieved through predictive measurement (analytical techniques) and does not require direct user involvement. For example, heuristic evaluation technique [32] is based on usability principles that can be examined systematically by a usability expert, in order to detect usability issues for an interactive system. Other example is techniques based on user tasks analysis. Some of these techniques are based on user task descriptions [13, 19], and some of them are based on task models [12]. These techniques provide support to detect usability problems related to the effectiveness criterion.
- For some other properties, user testing requires user involvement (empirical techniques). For example, the wizard of Oz technique [22] is an experimental simulation performed with users. It aims at testing the interactive system by giving the impression to the user that s/he is interacting with the real interactive system. This technique can be used in the early phases of the design process, when the interactive system is partly implemented, in order to refine user needs. Another examples of testing techniques that mandatory requires user involvement are the fine tuning of an interaction technique [33] and the field user testing [36]. For that purpose, several users of the targeted user type are required to perform a limited set of task with a specific setup (part of the final interactive system, specific input device...). These techniques aim at collecting data and at analyzing performance issues (efficiency criterion) and/or subjective metrics (satisfaction, emotion, aesthetics...).

These aspects of user testing have an impact on the required level of fidelity of the interactive system under test, and thus on the precision of the description of the behavior and of the architecture of the interactive system under test:

- For some evaluation techniques, mock ups or low fidelity prototypes are sufficient to perform user testing (example of such technique is the Wizard of Oz [22]). The problem is then to ensure that the results and recommendations for the next iteration of the interactive system are feasible according to the technical constraints. The architecture can here be of great help in providing support to filter and adapt the modifications and adding that are proposed for the future versions of the prototypes.

- For other evaluation techniques, a high-fidelity prototype or even the functional and fully or partly deployed interactive system is required (example of such technique is field user testing [36]). These kind of user testing techniques are expensive as they require to develop and setup an experimentation protocol, and to select and recruit a large number of users. In order to avoid loss of time for the users and/or loss of data for the evaluation experts, the interactive system has to function as specified and should be exempt of defects. In that case, the architecture can also be of great help by providing support to ensure that each part of the interactive system is functioning as specified before user testing. Furthermore, if the analysis of the evaluation highlights that changes are required, the architecture provides support for identifying in which parts the changes have to be performed (locality of the modifications) and thus enables to decrease the impact of these modifications and associated non-regression testing on the whole interactive system (e.g. to modify an input device driver to adapt the sensed speed of movement).

In summary, architecture-driven testing exploiting MIODMIT provides support for user testing whatever evaluation technique is used. More precisely, it supports assessing properties related to human aspects such as usability and user experience. Lastly, we highlighted the fact that even though architecture-based interactive system testing is emphasizing the technology aspect of testing, it is compliant with user centered approaches focusing on user activities and behavior.

6 Related Work

This paper presented how an architecture-driven approach can help identifying the testing needs for interactive systems. We emphasized that some of these needs are partially covered by existing testing techniques while some other are, to the best of our knowledge, not considered. In this section, we present why most of the existing techniques fail in addressing testing components of interactive systems.

First of all, we remind that the testing of the **Application Core** is similar to the testing of non-interactive applications. Due to space constraints, we do not present here the wide-range of techniques for testing non interactive-application.

GUI testing is, at the software level, the closest field to interactive systems testing. Banerjee et al. [6] systematic mapping classified 136 articles on this topic 7 years ago. Despite its age, the findings of this mapping are still relevant; especially regarding the research question "What test data generation approaches have been proposed?". This mapping reveals that models are the most popular test generation methods in the field. While models used for test generation are, from HCI point of view, descriptions of the **dialogue** (see Fig. 3 from [30]: this figure describes the dialogue without naming it), they are not used to test the dialogue as a single component. Indeed, model-based testing tools mostly rely on the state of GUI widgets during testing. Thus, what is tested is that the presentation matches the expected state derived from the dialogue description, not that the dialogue itself is in a correct state (so it might not take into account events from some correctly enabled GUI widgets). [6] distinguishes two other popular test generation techniques: random and capture/replay. Since the random approach is designed for "crash-testing" technique (i.e. events are played randomly on the GUI widgets to verify that the application does not crashes), they cover very partially the dialogue and functional core of the application by revealing they present defects that causes crashes. These techniques do not however reveal the source of the defect. Capture/replay is a technique in which testers records actions on the GUI that are stored to be replayed on the SUT. This is particularly useful for regression testing. However, these techniques addresses only a fraction of the output chain manager and rendering systems. Indeed, recording all the possible actions on both SUT and AUT is an impossible task as soon as one action can be performed several times on the GUI. Due to space constraints, we do not go exhaustively over all the papers presented in [6] and uses acronyms to refer to these techniques. Table 2 presents the components of the architecture covered by existing testing techniques. MBT stands for Model-Based Techniques, C/RT for Capture/Replay Techniques and rand for Random techniques.

Table 2. Components of the architecture covered by testing techniques [P = Partial coverage, NC = No Coverage].

Techniques	Input devices type	Input chain manager	Global interaction technique	Dialogue	Rendering system	Output chain manager	Output devices type
MBT e.g. [6]	NC	NC	NC	P	NC	P	NC
C/RT e.g. [6]	NC	NC	NC	P	NC	P	NC
Rand e.g. [6]	NC	NC	NC	P	NC	P	NC
[10, 26]	NC	P	NC	P	NC	P	NC
[38]	NC	P	NC	P	NC	P	NC

MBT approaches are mainly used to test the behavior of the **Dialogue** component of the AUT. However, [26] proposes, in addition, to use model-based descriptions of multimodal interaction techniques for testing. In MIODMIT terms it means that [26] supports testing of part of the **Input Chains Manager** component. [10] discusses the testing of multimodal interactive system, taking into account the **Input Chains Manager**.

On modern operating systems (e.g. Android), the permission mechanism allows the user to restrict application access to input and output devices, affecting the **Input/Output Chain Manager**. By developing Permission-Aware GUI Testing on Android, [37] supports partial testing of this function handled by the **Input/Output Chain Manager**.

Three columns in Table 2 are not covered by any previous work. Another concern is that existing techniques only support partially the testing of the covered components. Indeed, the **Dialogue** is mostly tested through the state of GUI widgets. The **Output Chain Manager** is mainly tested by checking properties of the GUI widgets via their public accessors, so their rendering is not assessed. On this aspect, we note that the emergence of techniques based on computer vision (in order to assess what the users will be seeing), such as [18] will be of great help to support automated testing.

Overall, we note that there is a need for new dedicated testing techniques to cover all the elements of the architecture of interactive systems.

7 Conclusion

This paper has presented an architecture-driven approach to support testing of interactive systems. This Approach exploits MIODMIT architecture that has been used in multiple domains such as interactive cockpits of large civil aircrafts of multimodal interfaces for new cockpits of helicopters as well as desktop interactive applications [9]. This paper has presented numerous specificities of testing of interactive systems with respect to "standard" software testing. We have shown that known problems in testing interactive systems can be positioned on one or multiple elements of MIODMIT providing details on unit and integration tests problems for interactive systems.

One of the key elements of MIODMIT is its genericity and its capability of handling multiple input and output devices. This is critical for interactive systems engineering as new devices and new interaction techniques are frequently proposed to increase the bandwidth between operators and computing systems. For instance, MIODMIT handles devices such as Kinect, Leap (Motion), speech recognition systems, multiple parallel graphical input devices, just to name a few [14] but was not presented due to space constraints.

In this paper we have also presented how user testing (or more generally user studies) connects to the interactive systems testing which is the focus of this paper. The H-MIODMIT architecture highlights the fact that interactive systems are meant to be used by users and that this specific component (the user as a human) may add (but also relax) constraints on interactive systems testing. Beyond, if user studies needs are known and described while developing interactive systems, software specifications and software testing techniques can support those activities as demonstrated in [33].

Future work will be dedicated to the definition of techniques to support unit testing of each component of MIODMIT but also integration tests (e.g. the immediate feedback loop presented in the paper). The objective is to provide interactive systems developers with adequate solutions in order to test their application beyond the classical "test coverage" and "non regression testing" measures that are unfortunately meaningless when interactive systems are considered.

References

1. Accot, J., Chatty, S., Palanque, P.: A formal description of low level interaction and its application to multimodal interactive systems. In: Bodart, F., Vanderdonckt, J. (eds.) DSV-IS 1996. Eurographics, pp. 92–104. Springer, Vienna (1996). https://doi.org/10.1007/978-3-7091-7491-3_5
2. Accot, J., Chatty, S., Maury, S., Palanque, P.: Formal transducers: models of devices and building bricks for the design of highly interactive systems. In: Harrison, M.D., Torres, J.C. (eds.) DSV-IS 1997. Eurographics, pp. 143–159. Springer, Vienna (1997). https://doi.org/10.1007/978-3-7091-6878-3_10

3. Abbaspour Asadollah, S., Inam, R., Hansson, H.: A survey on testing for cyber physical system. In: El-Fakih, K., Barlas, G., Yevtushenko, N. (eds.) ICTSS 2015. LNCS, vol. 9447, pp. 194–207. Springer, Cham (2015). https://doi.org/10.1007/978-3-319-25945-1_12
4. Avizienis, A., Laprie, J.C., Randell, B., Landwehr, C.: Basic concepts and taxonomy of dependable and secure computing. IEEE Trans. Dependable Secur. Comput. 1, 11–33 (2004)
5. Bailly, G., Lecolinet, E., Nigay, L.: Visual menu techniques. ACM Comput. Surv. 49(4), 60:1–60:41 (2017)
6. Banerjee, I., Nguyen, B., Garousi, V., Memon, A.M.: Graphical user interface (GUI) testing: systematic mapping and repository. Inf. Softw. Technol. 55, 1679–1694 (2013)
7. Bass, L., et al.: The arch model: Seeheim revisited. In: User Interface Developpers' Workshop (1991)
8. Bellik, Y.: Multimodal interfaces: concepts, models and architecture, Ph.D. thesis, University Paris-South 11, Orsay (1995). (in French)
9. Bernhaupt, R., Cronel, M., Manciet, F., Martinie, C., Palanque, P.: Transparent automation for assessing and designing better interactions between operators and partly-autonomous interactive systems. In: ATACCS 2015, pp. 129–139 (2015)
10. Bouchet, J., Madani, L., Nigay, L., Oriat, C., Parissis, I.: Formal testing of multimodal interactive systems. In: Gulliksen, J., Harning, M.B., Palanque, P., van der Veer, G.C., Wesson, J. (eds.) EIS 2007. LNCS, vol. 4940, pp. 36–52. Springer, Heidelberg (2008). https://doi.org/10.1007/978-3-540-92698-6_3
11. Bourque, P., Fairley, R.E., IEEE Computer Society: Guide to the Software Engineering Body of Knowledge (SWEBOK(R)): Version 3.0. IEEE Computer Society Press, Los Alamitos (2014)
12. Campos, J.C., et al.: A more intelligent test case generation approach through task models manipulation. In: Proceedings of the ACM HCI. EICS, vol. 1, pp. 9:1–9:20 (2017)
13. Cockton, G., Woolrych, A.: Understanding inspection methods: lessons from an assessment of heuristic evaluation. In: Blandford, A., Vanderdonckt, J., Gray, P. (eds.) People and Computers XV—Interaction without Frontiers, pp. 171–191. Springer, London (2001). https://doi.org/10.1007/978-1-4471-0353-0_11
14. Cronel, M., Dumas, B., Palanque, P., Canny, A.: MIODMIT: a generic architecture for dynamic multimodal interactive systems. In: Bogdan, C., et al. (eds.) Human-Centered and Error-Resilient Systems Development, HCSE 2018. LNCS, vol. 11262, pp. 109–129. Springer, Cham (2018)
15. Cuenca, F., Coninx, K., Vanacken, D., Luyten, K.: Graphical toolkits for rapid prototyping of multimodal systems: a survey. Interact. Comput. 27, 470–488 (2015)
16. Dragicevic, P., Fekete, J.D.: Input device selection and interaction configuration with ICON. In: Blandford, A., Vanderdonckt, J., Gray, P. (eds.) People and Computers XV—Interaction without Frontiers, pp. 543–558. Springer, London (2001). https://doi.org/10.1007/978-1-4471-0353-0_34
17. Dragicevic, P.: Un modèle d'interaction en entrée pour des systèmes interactifs multi-dispositifs hautement configurables. Ph.D. Université de Nantes (2004). (in French)
18. Göransson, B., Gulliksen, J., Boivie, I.: The usability design process - integrating user-centered systems design in the software development process. Softw. Process Improv. Pract. 8(2), 111–131 (2003)
19. Greenberg, S.: Working through task-centered system design. In: Diaper, D., Stanton, N. (eds.) The Handbook of Task Analysis for Human-Computer Interaction. Lawrence Erlbaum Associates (2002)
20. Ha, T.T., Ghaffari, R.: Simulating Single and Multi-Touch Events for Testing a Touch Panel (2012). https://patents.google.com/patent/US20120280934A1/en

21. ISO 9241-11. Ergonomics of human system interaction - Part 11. Usability: Definitions and concepts (2018)
22. Kelley, J.F.: An iterative design methodology for user-friendly natural language office information applications. ACM Trans. Inf. Syst. 2(1), 26–41 (1984)
23. Lalanne, D., Nigay, L., Palanque, P., Robinson, P., Vanderdonckt, J., Ladry, J.F.: Fusion engines for multimodal input: a survey. In: ICMI, pp. 153–160. ACM (2009)
24. Lee, J.S., et al.: A 0.4 V driving multi-touch capacitive sensor with the driving signal frequency set to (n + 0.5) times the inverse of the LCD VCOM noise period. In: IEEE International Symposium on Circuits and Systems (ISCAS), pp. 682–685 (2014)
25. Lelli, V., Blouin, A., Baudry, B.: Classifying and qualifying GUI defects. Presented at the 8th IEEE International Conference on Software Testing, Verification and Validation, 13 April 2015
26. Lelli, V., Blouin, A., Baudry, B., Coulon, F.: On model-based testing advanced GUIs. In: 2015 IEEE Eighth International Conference on Software Testing, Verification and Validation Workshops (ICSTW), pp. 1–10 (2015)
27. Memon, A.M., Soffa, M.L., Pollack, M.E.: Coverage criteria for GUI testing. In: Proceedings of the 8th European Software Engineering Conference Held Jointly with 9th ACM SIGSOFT International Symposium on Foundations of Software Engineering, pp. 256–267. ACM, New York (2001)
28. Memon, A.M.: GUI testing: pitfalls and process. Computer 35(8), 87–88 (2002)
29. Memon, A.M.: A comprehensive framework for testing graphical user interfaces. Ph.D. thesis, University of Pittsburgh, Pittsburgh (2001)
30. Memon, A.M., Nguyen, B.N.: Advances in automated model-based system testing of software applications with a GUI front-end. In: Zelkowitz, M.V. (ed.) Advances in Computers, pp. 121–162. Elsevier (2010)
31. Nguyen, B.N., Robbins, B., Banerjee, I., Memon, A.: GUITAR: an innovative tool for automated testing of GUI-driven software. Autom. Softw. Eng. 21, 65–105 (2014)
32. Nielsen, J.: Usability Engineering. Morgan Kaufmann, San Francisco (1994)
33. Palanque, P., Barboni, E., Martinie, C., Navarre, D., Winckler, M.: A model-based approach for supporting engineering usability evaluation of interaction techniques. In: Proceedings of EICS 2011, pp. 21–30. ACM (2011)
34. Pfaff, G.E. (ed.): Proceedings of IFIP/EG Workshop on User Interface Management Systems (November 1983, Seeheim, FRG). Springer, Berlin (1985)
35. Pirker, M., Bernhaupt, R.: Measuring user experience in the living room: results from an ethnographically oriented field study indicating major evaluation factors. In: Proceedings of the 9th European Conference on Interactive TV and Video (EuroITV 2011), pp. 79–82. ACM, New York (2011)
36. Rowley, D.E.: Usability testing in the field: bringing the laboratory to the user. In: Proceedings of the SIGCHI Conference on Human Factors in Computing Systems (CHI 1994), pp. 252–257. ACM, New York (1994)
37. Sadeghi, A., Jabbarvand, R., Malek, S.: PATDroid: permission-aware GUI testing of android. In: Proceedings of the 2017 11th Joint Meeting on Foundations of Software Engineering, pp. 220–232. ACM, New York (2017)
38. Song, W., Qian, X., Huang, J.: EHBDroid: beyond GUI testing for android applications. In: Proceedings of the 32nd IEEE/ACM International Conference on Automated Software Engineering, pp. 27–37. IEEE Press, Piscataway (2017)
39. Thimbleby, H.: Reasons to question seven segment displays. In: Proceedings of the SIGCHI Conference on Human Factors in Computing Systems, pp. 1431–1440. ACM, New York (2013)
40. Vu, T., et al.: Distinguishing users with capacitive touch communication. In: Mobicom 2012, pp. 197–208 (2012)

Tools and Tool-Support

A Visual Tool for Analysing IoT Trigger/Action Programming

Luca Corcella, Marco Manca, Fabio Paternò[(⊠)], and Carmen Santoro

CNR-ISTI, HIIS Laboratory, Via Moruzzi 1, 56124 Pisa, Italy
{l.corcella,m.manca,f.paterno,c.santoro}@isti.cnr.it

Abstract. The Trigger-Action programming paradigm has been widely adopted in the last few years, especially in the Internet of Things (IoT) domain because it allows end users without programming experience to describe how their applications should react to the many events that can occur in such very dynamic contexts. Several end user development tools exist, in both the research and industrial fields, which aim to support the increasing need to specify such rules. Thus, it becomes important for application developers and domain experts to enrich such environments with functionalities able to monitor how users actually interact with such rule editors, and show useful information to analyse the end user activity. In this paper, we present a visual tool for monitoring and analysing how users interact with a trigger-action rule editor. The goal is to provide a tool useful to better understand what end users' personalization needs are, how they are expressed, how users actually specify rules, and whether users encounter any issues in interacting with the personalization features offered by the editors. The proposed solution supports the analysis through a dashboard and a set of timelines describing the actual use of the personalization tool, with the possibility to select specific events of interest. It moreover provides data useful for understanding the types of triggers, actions and rules actually composed by users, and whether they effectively exploit the personalization features offered.

Keywords: Trigger action programming · Visual analytics
Log user interaction · Internet of Things applications

1 Introduction

A consequence of the rapid spread of the Internet of Things (IoT) is that the environments where we live and act are increasingly characterized by the presence of a multitude of interactive devices and smart objects interconnected with each other. Since we interact with our applications in such very dynamic and unpredictable environments, it is not possible to foresee at design time how an application should react to all the possible contextual changes that can occur during its use. Only end users can know the most appropriate ways their applications should react to dynamic contextual events. For such reasons, in order to obtain applications able to adapt to the context of use in an effective way it becomes important to allow end users themselves to 'program' the behaviour of their applications.

© IFIP International Federation for Information Processing 2019
Published by Springer Nature Switzerland AG 2019
C. Bogdan et al. (Eds.): HCSE 2018, LNCS 11262, pp. 189–206, 2019.
https://doi.org/10.1007/978-3-030-05909-5_11

In this trend, trigger-action programming has emerged as a useful and intuitive approach. Users can personalise the application behaviour through sets of rules indicating triggers and consequent effects. Triggers can be instantaneous events (corresponding to context changes) and/or conditions that, if satisfied, activate the execution of specific actions. This type of approach has stimulated several contributions both from the research [e.g. 2–5, 9] and industrial viewpoints (IFTTT, Tasker, Zapier, Resonance AI, …). This approach can be adopted in many domains that share the need for supporting tailoring of applications that would benefit from considering the occurrence of dynamic events (smart retail, remote elderly assistance, smart home, industry 4.0, …). Although seemingly intuitive overall, because it mainly asks users to indicate the relevant events and desired actions, sometimes identifying the relevant concepts and understanding how to specify them using the tool is not always clear to people without a programming background. For example, Huang and Cakmak [8] found that users may encounter difficulties interpreting the differences between events and conditions or between action types, and such misunderstandings can cause undesired behaviours.

In this area, IFTTT[1] (If This Then That) has been particularly successful. It has more than 320,000 automation scripts (called "applets") offered by more than 400 service providers. The applets have been installed more than 20 million times, and more than half of IFTTT services are IoT device-related [10]. One large repository of IFTTT rules is even publicly available [18]. Thus, we can foresee in the near future an increasing interest in environments allowing people to provide many rules to personalize their context-dependent applications.

In this perspective, the availability of tools able to analyse how users actually try to personalise their context-dependent applications with such approaches can become very useful, not only for developers of trigger-action authoring environments, but also for IoT application developers and domain experts. We have thus considered previous work in the area of analytic tools for Web site usability, which often log user interactions in order to support identification of potential usability problems. However, the application of such tools to analyse the use of trigger-action programming would not provide the most relevant information. Indeed, differently from existing tools that exploit log analysis for usability evaluation purposes, in this case the goal is not strictly to understand whether there is some bad user interface design, but rather to see how the personalization needs are expressed by users, and whether they have some conceptual problems in expressing them in terms of trigger-action rules.

In this paper, after discussion of related work, we introduce the trigger-action programming environment considered in this study. Then, we discuss the design requirements for the novel analytic system for IoT programming platforms, describe the functionalities supported by the current version, and report on a first user test. Lastly, we discuss the user test on this tool, draw some conclusions, and provide suggestions for future work.

---

[1] https://ifttt.com.

2   Related Work

Our work draws from research on trigger-action programming for IoT applications and tools for visualizing logs of Web interactions.

2.1   Trigger-Action Programming

Both in research and industrial fields there has been interest in the trigger-action programming to allow users to define their own adaptation rules. From the commercial point of view IFTTT is one of the most used application. It provides mechanisms to create rules composed of one trigger and one action. Triggers are events occurring in some connected applications, and cause the execution of associated actions in other applications. The possible applications are grouped according to their intended goal, i.e. environment control & monitoring, calendars & scheduling, news & information. Ur et al. [17] reported on a 226-participant usability test of trigger-action programming, finding that inexperienced users can quickly learn multiple triggers or actions obtained by extending the IFTTT language. Resonance AI^2 is a tool for developers that aims to automate and personalize applications. It provides contextual awareness services to enhance products and services with real-time understanding and reactions based on the current user's environment. Such data become actionable triggers that developers can use to automate or suggest actions in order to personalize apps and devices behaviour.

From the research perspective, we started our study from the TARE [5] trigger-action rule editor that provides the possibility to create rules more flexibly than IFTTT since they can be created as compositions of multiple triggers and actions. In this area, Desolda et al. [3] developed EFESTO, a visual environment that allows users to express rules for controlling smart objects. The followed paradigm is based on the 5W model, which defines some specification constructs (Which, What, When, Where, Why) to build rules coupling multiple events and conditions exposed by smart objects, and for defining temporal and spatial constraints on rule activation and actions execution. Coutaz et al. presented AppsGate [2], an EUD (End-User Development) environment designed to empower people with tools to augment and control their home. AppsGate aims to support different activities such as monitoring the home state and programming its behaviour in a context-dependent manner. Another similar approach is ImAtHome [4], an iOS application built over Apple HomeKit allowing home inhabitants without programming skills to control home automation by means of creating scenes and rules for defining the complex behaviour of a smart home. The approach proposed by [11] aims to address some specific issues of users when writing trigger-action programming rules by a tool, called TriGen, aimed at preventing errors due to too few triggers in the rules by statically analysing a rule's actions to determine which triggers are necessary. Another approach to address some of the issues that users encounter when they specify ECA (Event, Condition, Action) rules is reported in [16]. Still in this area Metaxas and Markopoulos [9] propose a context-range editor supporting end users formulate logical expressions regarding the context, define the

---

^{2} https://www.resonance-ai.com.

concept of affinity regrouping heuristics, and present the mechanisms to apply it throughout the contextual ranges of the involved services. The semantic information that the services disclose lets the editor recognize this affinity and allows it to group terms in logical expressions when they refer to the same aspect (e.g. user's activity).

The monitoring and visualization method proposed in this paper can be useful to analyse the user interactions with these tools as well, since they still support trigger-action rules for IoT applications, and thus their use is characterised by similar user-generated events such as trigger selection, action selection, rule saved.

2.2 Web Analytics Tools

One typical use of the information contained in logs of user interactions is for usability studies [7]. Palmer [12] presents different metrics for measuring usability, and lists different types of methods to evaluate a user interface. UsaProxy [1] exploits a proxy-based solution to access remote Web pages: the proxy adds some JavaScript code to specify the listeners which log the user interaction with the concerned page(s). The output produced by the proxy is a simple list representing the IP address of the connected device, the visited pages, and some events' description, without any particular visualization able to support their analyses. MUSE [13] also exploits a proxy server in order to insert in the target Web pages some code to log user interactions. The logged events are shown in a timeline representation in which it is possible to compare a timeline representing the 'optimal' interaction with the one expressing the 'real' user interactions in order to help designers to discover some usability issues in the user interaction. WELFIT [14] is a tool to identify usage patterns based on client-side event logs and by presenting event stream composition characteristics. The system records usage data during real use, identifies usage patterns, and indicates potential user interface design problems. Harms and Grabowsky [6] proposed to transform the recorded user interaction in task trees that are then checked to identify usability issues. The goal of such contributions is to identify a method to record user interactions and then further analyse the logs in order to highlight usability problems. HistoryViewer [15] is a system that aims to support exploration of log data obtained from user interactions. In this case the goal is to support final users for communication purposes, and not usability evaluators, by describing the interactions that took place in a way they can recall and communicate their own discoveries about the data, not focused on the interaction mechanisms or on difficulties they may have encountered.

Differently from such proposals, in this work we focus on providing designers of trigger-action rule editors and IoT application developers with interactive visualisations supporting exploration and filtering of the logged relevant interaction data, so as to derive higher-level information such as the types of rules that users were interested in creating with the tool, the most popular trigger and action types used, and the types of usage patterns followed by users while interacting with the tool. The visualizations offered also allow them to rapidly identify whether the personalisation rules composition was straightforward or the users had to go through various possibilities before completing their tasks. Moreover, by analysing user logs it is possible to understand what the personalization needs are, how they are expressed by the users, whether their rules actually support the desired results, if the personalization features offered by the editors are sufficient.

3 The Proposed Approach

In this section we first introduce the trigger-action programming environment that has been considered in this study, and then we report on the initial set of requirements that have been identified for the visualizations to provide. Lastly, we describe how it has been instrumented in order to obtain relevant and meaningful log file for further analysis.

3.1 The Trigger-Action Rule Editor

In this study we considered the TARE platform (Trigger Action Rule Environment) [5], which allows users to define their trigger action rules in an intuitive way. The tool is flexible in the order in which users can specify the rules (they can start either from triggers or from actions), they can also re-use a previously defined rule in order to create a new one. Moreover, they can combine multiple triggers by using the Boolean operators AND and OR. The Not operator is also supported to check whether some event has not occurred in a specific period of time.

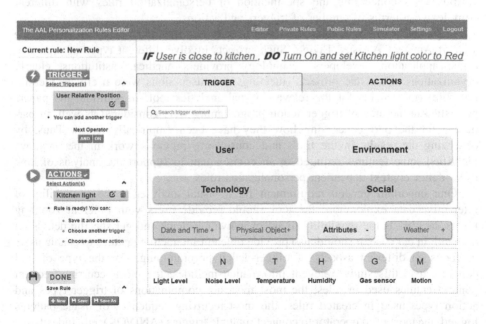

Fig. 1. The TARE editor user interface.

Figure 1 shows the context hierarchy of the Rule Editor: users navigate by first selecting the context dimension to which the considered trigger belongs, and then they go through the associated context categories (and sub-categories), which group together logically related context elements. The leaves of the context hierarchy refer to context entities, and are used to specify triggers and their parameters. For instance, in Fig. 1 the trigger is "IF the user is close to the kitchen", and it involves the context entity "user". Also the possible actions are indicated through a classification based on the type of effects they allow users to achieve (changes to the user interface, changes to the state of some appliances, sending reminders or alarms, …). In addition, TARE provides users with the possibility to search for a specific trigger, by specifying a concept to search for in the hierarchy of the possible triggers. On the left side there is also an interactive panel that indicates the main steps in the workflow associated with rule editing, and continuously provides feedback on what has been done, indications of what can be done from the current state, and thus it can be used to control and activate the various parts of the rule editing.

3.2   The Requirements for IoT Trigger-Action Programming Visual Analytics

TARE has been validated in three different trials, which involved 58 users in total. During the tests, users, who had no prior programming experience, had to perform various tasks concerning the specification of personalization rules with different complexity in terms of number of triggers and actions.

In particular, the rule editor has been used in two interdisciplinary projects in the area of Ambient Assisted Living. Such projects involve different types of organizations: application developers, technology providers, medical institutions, elderly organizations. Thus, the projects' meetings and discussions were useful to identify possible requirements for the relevant visual analytics tool. In addition, the papers published in the area of trigger-action programming were considered as well, in particular for the part concerning how they have been empirically tested. Thus, by observing the results in the trials and considering previous work in the area, we identified some features required in an environment to support the analysis of how users define context-dependent personalization rules.

One important general requirement for a visual analyser is the availability of interactive data exploration: the tool should provide users with different zooming levels, as well as the possibility to select individual items and get specific details on demand. In our case, it should also provide different interactive features to enable users to focus on different aspects of trigger-action programming. For the type of tool considered in this study, relevant information includes: the most recurring/frequent context entities used in rules; the most recurring combinations of trigger types and action types used in created rules; the most recurring sequences of usage patterns logged, the most used operator to connect multiple triggers (AND/OR), etc. Indeed, this type of information can be useful to better understand also the aspects that users prefer to consider in the specification of their personalization rules.

Other useful information that the tool should provide, for each user and also across users, is:

- The rule part users prefer to start editing the rules from (triggers and then actions or vice versa), in order to provide more flexibility in the rule editing;
- The sequence of trigger/action dimensions and entities that users have passed through to reach the trigger/action leaf of interest, in order to assess whether the proposed logical organization of the contextual aspects is intuitive for end users;
- The time spent to create a rule (max, min, average);
- The time spent to modify a rule (max, min, average);
- The number of rules created in each session and in all sessions;
- The number of triggers/actions created in each session and in all sessions;
- The number of rules/triggers/actions that users started to edit without saving them;
- The number of simple/complex rules created by the users (simple rules are rules involving only one trigger, while complex rules are rules which involve a combination of multiple triggers).

We also judged it useful to provide designers with the possibility to filter the results to allow users to configure the list of events they want to focus on, as well as to provide further quantitative information, such as the context dimension and the trigger entity that have been most used in the defined triggers. Such summarized representations of the users' sessions are particularly useful when the number of events becomes very high and difficult to manage.

3.3 The Logs

To support the identified requirements, we had to identify the events that were meaningful to log. We decided to exclude some low-level events to log (such as mouse over, mouse out, blur) that were judged not particularly relevant for the type of planned analysis. We have focused only on the interactions with the trigger and the action hierarchy, and on the editor parts which manage the rules. The logging implementation was done by a JavaScript file which appends handlers to the relevant events supported in TARE and related to rule creation, editing, saving. In particular, we found it useful to log user's selections of:

- "New Rule", "Save Rule", "Save Rule as", "Edit Rule" and "Delete Rule" buttons (used to manage rules);
- "Triggers" and "Actions" buttons (used to go to the part of the tool dedicated respectively to trigger and action specification);
- "AND" and "OR" buttons (used to compose two triggers);
- Trigger/Context Dimension elements, to select one specific trigger dimension (User, Environment, Technology, Social);
- Action Dimension elements (Update/Distribute UI, Change Appliance State, Activate Functionalities, Alarm, Reminder), to select one specific action dimension;
- Trigger type, to select a specific type of trigger within the hierarchy of triggers;
- Action type, to select a specific type of actions within the hierarchy of actions;

- Trigger Operator (to select the operator involved in a trigger specification, e.g. equal, different, more, less);
- Action Operator (to select a specific type of action, e.g. turn on-off, open, close);
- Event/Condition (to specify whether the trigger specification refers to an event or to a condition);
- Entering specific Trigger parameters values (to specify the values associated involved in the specification of a trigger);
- Save/Update/Cancel Trigger or Save/Update/Cancel Action commands;
- Search Trigger Element (to search for a specific trigger in the hierarchy).

4 The Tool Visualizations

In this section we show and discuss the two types of visual information provided.

4.1 The Dashboard

When the tool is accessed, it shows a dashboard (see Fig. 2). On the left hand side, it is possible to select a specific user who interacted with the rule editor, then the dashboard shows an overview of the activities carried out by the considered user: the total rules, triggers and actions created in all interaction sessions, the number of rules which had been modified; the rules that have been specified (described in natural language), the context dimensions involved in the rule editing (see the pie chart on the right showing the percentage of triggers for each contextual dimension), the most used triggers and actions grouped by dimensions and the time of each working session. By "session" we mean the interval of time between a user's login and a user's logout from the system (or the system automatically does a logout after two hours of idle time).

In addition, the tool shows information about the number of rules that have been saved and not (see the bar charts visualised in the bottom part and clustered by session). The unsaved rules are those that the user started to edit and never saved. Such bars are interactive and the user can select each bar to get the details of the concerned rules (e.g. the names of the rules saved). For each trigger/action dimension there is a section which shows the name of the context entities and the number of times they have been used in all defined rules. The dashboard also provides indication of how long each session lasted overall and also how long it took to create and save a specific rule.

4.2 The Timelines

In order to visualize the sequence of relevant events logged during users' activities in a simple manner, we decided to use a dynamic timeline visualization (see Fig. 4), which provides a time-dependent overview of the relevant events that occurred. In particular, when the Timelines tab is selected, it is possible to see for the currently selected user a set of timelines, each one presenting the list of events recorded in an interactive session. In the timelines, each event is identified by a label describing it and including the name of the associated event and the corresponding value: such a value is shown only when this is applicable, e.g. for the leaves of the hierarchy. The timeline is thus a mono-dimensional

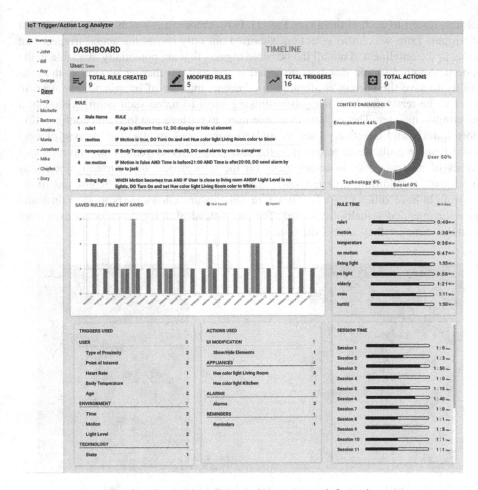

Fig. 2. The dashboard presenting summary information.

visualisation, in which the X axis represents time, according to which the events are ordered, thereby making it easy to see when they occurred. Each timeline corresponds to a user's session. It is worth noting that the events are automatically rearranged in a vertical manner by the library used[3] according to the current level of zoom and the number of labels to visualise, in order to avoid overlapping between labels.

However, due to the large number of events that can be recorded, the timeline could be difficult to interpret (see for example Fig. 4). For this reason, in addition to the possibility to zoom the timeline in and out, the tool provides users with a functionality that allows them to select only the events of interest, so that only specific types of events will be shown in the final visualization (e.g. the events that involve selecting a specific type of context dimension): In addition, in order to allow users to better perceive the differences between the various types of events, they can select a specific

---

[3] http://visjs.org/.

color to assign to each of them (see Fig. 3). Furthermore, it is worth noting that the list of triggers from which this selection is carried out only shows the actual triggers that occur in the timeline and not all the possible triggers that are potentially available in the system. Another option that was provided in the tool as filtering support is the possibility to save the current configuration of events that are of interest for the user, in order to be ready for later use, also allowing users to name such configuration in a meaningful manner. This is done to enable users to retrieve and load this configuration more quickly and effectively later on. Indeed, sometimes an effective filtering process could involve multiple iterations (e.g. the user progressively refines the current set of events of interest so as to better focus on the information s/he currently judges as important). In addition, different visualisations (obtained through different sets of filters) might have different goals. Therefore, this feature allows users to save time and have the intended visualisations ready for use, instead of doing this process over from scratch whenever they access the tool.

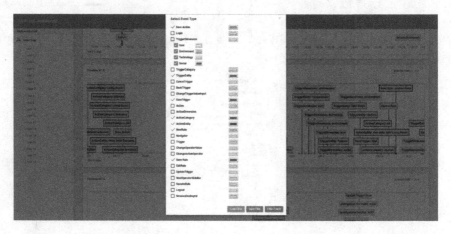

Fig. 3. The Log Filter: only the events of interest have been selected by the user.

Figure 4 focuses on a portion of a timeline obtained when the user created two simple rules: a first rule called "motion-lamp", whose specification is "when there is motion, do turn on the light in the living room", a second rule called "spd-temperature-alarm" whose specification is the following: "when body temperature is more than 30 °C, do send an alarm by sms to caregiver". As you can see from Fig. 4, the associated timeline becomes very crowded without any filtering: this makes interpretation of the succession of events occurring in the timeline problematic. Nonetheless, in spite of this, the timeline shown in Fig. 4 is still able to provide some information that could be relevant for the analyzer. For instance, the timeline highlights the time interval in which the sequence of events associated with a specific rule composition occurred, by displaying an additional red line under the X axis of the timeline. This red line represents a useful cue because it can be used as a reference when performing zooming and filtering operations, and thereby allow users to better focus on how the creation of that rule was actually carried out. Other information that the timeline shown in Fig. 4

provides –although at a coarse grain– is the parts of the timeline in which the interactions were more (or less) close to each other, which could be relevant information for the analyzer. In the example shown in Fig. 4, closer interactions occur in the first part of rule building, whereas more distanced interactions occur in the vicinity of critical actions such as saving actions or saving rules (the user takes more time to think about the rule before actually saving it).

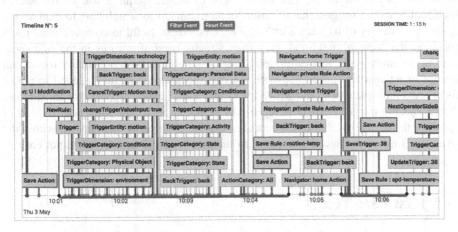

Fig. 4. The timeline associated with the considered example, as initially visualized.

However, in some cases the user may want to further investigate the succession of events occurred in a specific time interval, and observe them at a finer level of detail. Figure 5 shows a visualization obtained from the timeline shown in Fig. 4, by applying some filtering in order to hide events that were judged uninteresting for the user. In particular, the filtering done for obtaining the visualization shown in Fig. 5 only displays events associated with *TriggerDimension*, *TriggerEntity*, *SaveTrigger*, *ActionCategory*, *ActionEntity*, *SaveAction* and *SaveRule* events (which are also visualized in Fig. 3). This is to better understand the interactions occurring in the timeline visualized in Fig. 4 (in particular, for building the first saved rule named "motion lamp"). From Fig. 5 it is possible to see that after exploring several context dimensions without saving any trigger, the user focused on the "environment" dimension, and then

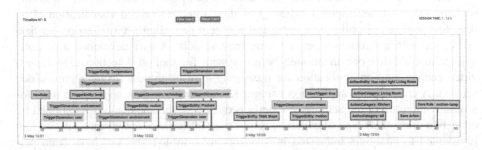

Fig. 5. Timeline obtained by applying filtering to the timeline shown in Fig. 4.

selected "motion". Then the user, after considering on various action categories ("All", "Kitchen"), focused on the action category "Living room". Within that category the user finally selected the action entity "Hue color light living room". This latter event was followed by a "Save action" event, and then a "SaveRule" event, meaning that the rule was actually saved.

Another interesting type of analysis that can be done concerns the use of the search functionality included in the rule editor. For example, frequent use of the search functionality would suggest that the user found it quicker to search than to explore the top-down hierarchy of triggers. Furthermore, it could be useful to compare what users specify in the "search" field and what they actually used afterwards in the rule specification; or analyse whether, after searching for an element, users actually found that element of interest and proceeded with the rule specification or they needed to repeat this process multiple times (and which terms they used in such repetitions). In addition, when a specific trigger element is repeatedly searched for by the same user instead of exploring the hierarchy, this could be a sign that the position of that concept within the hierarchy is not very logical according to the user's model and therefore not easy to locate.

5 A First User Test

In order to assess the usability of the tool a first user test was organized. In particular, we wanted to investigate whether the tool was able to provide usable representations of the interactions carried out by end users with the TARE rule editor, in order to derive useful information about its usability and usefulness.

5.1 Participants

A set of 10 participants fully gender-balanced (5 females) with age ranging between 24 and 49 (mean = 30.4, median = 26, std. dev. = 7.6) were involved in the study. They were volunteers recruited through mailing lists. As for the education of participants, 1 user held a High School degree, 5 a Master Degree, 1 a PhD and 3 a Bachelor. Half users (50%) had already used a visual analytics tool before the test. They mentioned RescueTime, Google Fit, Strava, Elevate, WUP, Wireshark, Matlab (visual toolbox), Apache log viewer, Kibana, Google Fusion Tables, Google Analytics, TensorBoard.

Half of users (50%) had some familiarity with developing applications exploiting sensors. One user developed a system providing a geo-referenced visualization of on fine dust particles of polluting nature, and a system providing a visualization for data associated with a remotely operated submarine vehicle. A user developed a domotic application, another one mentioned both a system for motion detection exploiting a video camera, and an application for measuring light brightness (using a photodiode sensor). A cross-device application using a Kinect sensor and an application used for remotely monitoring the activity of elderly people were the applications mentioned by other two users. This type of expertise seems relevant because the visual analytics tool is oriented to analysers interested in investigating how IoT services have been personalized through trigger action rules by end users.

5.2 Test Organisation

The test was done in a laboratory. During the test, a moderator observed the participants interacting with the tool, annotating whether and how they carried out tasks and also any further relevant issue and remark. The test was organised in four phases: introduction and motivations, familiarisation, test execution, questionnaire. In the test the users were first introduced to the motivations and main functionalities of this work and of the trigger-action rule editor through a PowerPoint presentation, which also contained a video showing an example of use and application of the TARE tool, which was done to better support people unfamiliar with that tool. Next, users had to create a trigger-action rule of their choice (using the TARE tool) and then, through the log visualizer they had the possibility to get familiar with the corresponding timeline visualization.

Then, they had to access the visualizations related to a given user in a particular session. This was selected beforehand for the test and was the same for all users. Users had to accomplish a list of tasks involving the dashboard and the timelines associated with that particular user in that specific session. In particular, the selected session provided data of a user who initially explored the hierarchy of triggers and action without saving any rules and then the user was able to save two rules: the first one involved a time interval longer than the second one, which was characterised by interactions carried out in shorter time range. We judged it more relevant to provide users with relevant log data created by others, which would better reflect more realistic situations of designers/developers analysing the data generated by other users.

Tasks. The tasks to accomplish covered both the information provided by the dashboard (mainly, information about the most used triggers and actions, the most used context dimensions, the number of rules that was successfully saved by users, the time associated with the various user sessions, etc.). In particular, for the dashboard they had to:

- Task1: Provide the name of the session with the highest number of rules created
- Task2: Provide the name of the most used context dimension
- Task3: Provide the name of the most used action dimension
- Task4: Provide the name of the longest session

As for the *timelines*, users had to analyze the time-dependent visualization of the occurred interactions, even using some filtering to better focus only on the most meaningful information. In particular, regarding the *timelines* users had to:

- Task5: Set a filter to visualise only *newRule* and *saveRule* and then describe what they could derive from the visualised information
- Task6: Add further filters (also using different colours) involving *TriggerDimension, CancelTrigger, SaveTrigger*. Then users had to indicate whether and where in the session the user had problems and why.

The test moderator provided users with a PowerPoint slide in which all the tasks were visualised. Users were instructed to solve the tasks by answering the associated questions, by verbally communicating them to the moderator who wrote them down for future analysis. At the end they had to fill in a questionnaire aiming to assess various aspects. They had to provide first some personal information, whether they had previous experiences with visual analytics tools and with applications using sensors. Then, on a 1 (worst) to 7 (best) Likert scale they had to assess usability and utility of the dashboard, the timelines, and the filtering feature. They also had the possibility to provide comments and suggestions, and indicate three positive and three negative aspects in the tool proposed.

The tasks submitted to users were identified in such a way to cover some typical information that could be useful for analysing user interactions with the personalisation editor. In particular, the first four tasks (Task1–Task4) involved the identification of very specific information which was available in the visualisations shown to users: in order to carry out such tasks users had to provide the moderator with an answer to the questions associated with the tasks (e.g. provide the name of the longest session). The last two tasks were more open-ended, and implied analysing and reasoning on the provided data in order to derive more general conclusions. Since Task 6 was mainly a refining of Task5, it was needed to be presented after Task5. For this reason, we decided to follow the same order for all users in presenting all the tasks to them.

5.3 Results

Tasks. All the participants were able to successfully provide the correct answer to the first four tasks associated with the information provided by the dashboard. Nonetheless, they provided further suggestions for improving the dashboard. For example, more than one user suggested to exploit a more consistent use of colours in the dashboard, another user suggested including a scrollbar in the panel showing the sessions associated with a specific user in order to avoid bringing about a too long page in case of a user having many sessions associated. Regarding Task5, all users except two were able to identify that there were some rules that were not saved at the beginning of the considered sessions. This was probably due to the fact that the visualisation showed a red line in correspondence with rules that were actually saved and therefore the two users just focused on this highlighted information. Regarding Task6, as a consequence of the further refining asked in this task, all the users were able to identify that the concerned user at the beginning of the session did not save any rule, while at the end of the session the user was able to save two rules. The most interesting part of this task was the different motivations users gave to that behaviour. On the one hand some of them interpreted this behaviour as an actual issue (e.g. *"the user did not find what she was looking for and therefore was not able to save any rule"*). On the other hand, other users interpreted this behaviour as just the user's need of first exploring the hierarchy for better familiarisation (even saving just some triggers), without necessarily saving any rule. One user also focused on the saved rules (instead of the unsaved ones, as most users did), especially noticing the different time slots needed for saving the two rules and the closer interactions occurring for creating the second rule, deriving that the second rule involved a quicker and more straightforward interaction.

Questionnaire. In the post-task feedback, participants provided positive feedback regarding the tool, and found it easy to perform the tasks. Across all questions, the median ratings were at or above 5.5 on a 7-point Likert-scale (7 = best), as it is possible to see from the following rated aspects:

- Usability of the dashboard (median: 6)
- Usability of the timelines (median: 5.5)
- Usefulness of information provided in dashboards (median: 7)
- Usefulness of information provided in the timelines (median: 6)
- Usability of the feature for setting filters (median: 7)
- Usefulness of the approach for understanding how users exploited the personalisation tool (median: 7)

An overview is presented in the following stacked bar chart (Fig. 6).

Moreover, participants also answered a series of open-ended questions, whose answers have been detailed in the following.

Do you have suggestion to improve the dashboard usability?
One user suggested grouping rules not by session but per day, in order to have more meaningful information for the user. In addition, another user suggested adding the possibility to hide/show some parts of the dashboard in order to allow users to better focus only on the most relevant information. The same user also suggested adding further information for better identifying the sessions (e.g. day, hour), which are currently just subsequently named (e.g. session1, session2).

Do you have suggestion to improve the timeline usability?
One user suggested putting the most recent timeline in the top part of the user interface (whereas now the timelines are visualized following a chronological order, with the most recent ones in the bottom part of the window). Three users complained about the way the labels were vertically visualized. Since the lines going from the labels to the X axis of the timeline are positioned in the center of the label, a user suggested moving such lines in the left-most side of the label (in a sort of a flag-based shape) as a way to better visualize the order of the events while reading the labels. Another user asked for more space dedicated to each single timeline (currently more than one timeline is visualized in the same window). This is to have a better overview of the timeline, while at the same time avoiding scrolling up the visualization vertically, with the risk of losing the overall context of the occurred interactions.

Do you have any suggestion to improve the dashboard utility?
Only a few users provided suggestions for improving this aspect. For instance, one user suggested that the information associated with triggers used should be put under the pie chart showing the percentages of used triggers, since it represents a more detailed refinement of the pie-chart-based visualization.

Do you have suggestion to improve the timeline utility?
Several users did not have any particular suggestions for improving this aspect. A couple of users questioned about the utility of showing some information in the labels, for instance the value that was set for a particular trigger (e.g. "Save Trigger 26").

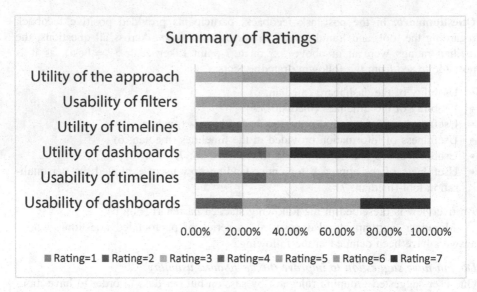

Fig. 6. Stacked bar chart showing ratings assigned to various aspects of the tool.

Do you have suggestion to improve the usability of the filtering features?
Most users appreciated this functionality. Just one user noted that it was not possible to move the window supporting the selection of filters, thus this window could cover the underneath timelines.

Is there any information that you did not find in the tool and you would have had?
One user suggested having further information about users (e.g. a picture) in order to better identify them. Another user said that it could be better adding the option to have the whole window dedicated to the visualization of a specific timeline of interest, so as to have more space for a more convenient visualization. Another user suggested adding in the dashboard a pie chart for visualizing the used actions, along the same line of the one dedicated to triggers used.

Please indicate three positive aspects you found while using the tool
Among the aspects that users mentioned as most appreciated there was the dashboard. It provides the users with an overall view of the interactions done by users, understand where the user found potential difficulties (e.g. in terms of longer time, higher number of interactions). Many users appreciated the possibility of filtering the timelines to better focus on a subset of events of interest.

Please indicate three negative aspects you found while using the tool
Some users complained about the clarity of some labels and how some data were presented. Another aspect regarded the limited space devoted to the visualization of the timeline of interest. Another aspect that was mentioned was the need of vertically scrolling the timelines to get all the relevant information. A user complained about a non-perfectly consistent use of colors (for instance the same color was used in different parts of the dashboard although no specific relationship was held between the associated information).

Do you have further suggestion to improve the tool?
Auser suggested adding further interactivity in the information visualized in the dashboard, so that it is possible for the user to refine and interactively explore the information at various levels of detail. Another user suggested improving the timeline visualization, even grouping together some data for the goal of obtaining lighter and clearer representations. Another user mentioned providing users with the possibility to order some information according to various criteria. For instance, each session could be ordered in terms of duration but also in terms of number of rules saved, etc.

Discussion. The results of the user test were overall encouraging and promising. Users appreciated the type of information provided by the tool and the supported features, and gave us useful and relevant feedback for further improving them.

In general, the users were able to successfully carry out the submitted tasks, showing that the tool is easy to learn since they used it for the first time and the learning phase was minimal. In addition, it was interesting to note how different users explained in slightly different manners the same information represented in the timelines, especially when carrying out Task6, which was the most open-ended task. Some users did not interpret the unsaved rules as a usability issue but just as a sign of users' need to get familiar with the tool and the hierarchies elements, or that some users preferred to restart from scratch instead of editing the elements appearing in the current rule state. Others, instead, interpret such data as a sign of users not finding what they were looking for in the hierarchies. In this regard, the filtering features seem very useful in effectively supporting further exploration and investigation of the information of interest.

6 Conclusions

In this paper we present a method and the features of a supporting tool for analysing the users' behaviour when interacting with a trigger-action rule editor for personalising their IoT context-dependent applications. We discuss the most relevant features for this analysis, provide example visualizations that can be supported, and report on an initial user test.

While in this work we applied the approach to a specific tool (TARE), the type of analysis of the users' behaviour presented can be easily extended and applied to other tools supporting trigger-action programming of IoT context-dependent applications. Indeed, all such tools share a number of key logical concepts on which the visualisations are centred (triggers, actions, rules, trigger operators). Regarding the timelines, by logging the relevant user actions it is possible to derive the usage patterns exploited by users while interacting with the tool.

Future work will be dedicated to extending the functionalities of the visual analytics tool taking into account the feedback from its use, and carrying out further, more longitudinal, empirical validations.

References

1. Atterer, R., Wnuk, M., Schmidt, A.: Knowing the user's every move: user activity tracking for website usability evaluation and implicit interaction. In: Proceedings of the 15th International Conference on World Wide Web, pp. 203–212 (2006)
2. Coutaz, J., Crowley, J.L.: A first-person experience with end-user development for smart homes. IEEE Pervasive Comput. **15**(2), 26–39 (2016)
3. Desolda, G., Ardito, C., Matera, M.: End-user development for the internet of things: EFESTO and the 5W composition paradigm. In: Daniel, F., Gaedke, M. (eds.) RMC 2016. CCIS, vol. 696, pp. 74–93. Springer, Cham (2017). https://doi.org/10.1007/978-3-319-53174-8_5
4. Fogli, D., Peroni, M., Stefini, C.: ImAtHome: making trigger-action programming easy and fun. J. Vis. Lang. Comput. **42**, 60–75 (2017)
5. Ghiani, G., Manca, M., Paternò, F., Santoro, C.: Personalization of context-dependent applications through trigger-action rules. ACM Trans. Comput. Hum. Interact. **24**(2), 3 (2017). https://doi.org/10.1145/3057861. Article 14
6. Harms, P., Grabowski, J.: Usage-based automatic detection of usability smells. In: Sauer, S., Bogdan, C., Forbrig, P., Bernhaupt, R., Winckler, M. (eds.) HCSE 2014. LNCS, vol. 8742, pp. 217–234. Springer, Heidelberg (2014). https://doi.org/10.1007/978-3-662-44811-3_13
7. Hilbert, D.M., Redmiles, D.F.: Extracting usability information from user interface events. ACM Comput. Surv. **32**(4), 384–421 (2000)
8. Huang, J., Cakmak, M.: Supporting mental model accuracy in trigger-action programming. In Proceedings of UbiComp 2015, pp. 215–225. ACM, New York (2015). https://doi.org/10.1145/2750858.2805830
9. Metaxas, G., Markopoulos, P.: Natural contextual reasoning for end users. ACM Trans. Comput. Hum. Interact. **24**(2), 36 (2017). https://doi.org/10.1145/3057860. Article 13
10. Mi, X., Qian, F., Zhang, Y., Wang, X.: An empirical characterization of IFTTT: ecosystem, usage, and performance. In: IMC 2017, pp. 398–404 (2017)
11. Nandi, C., Ernst, M.D.: Automatic trigger generation for rule-based smart homes. In: Proceedings of the 2016 ACM Workshop on Programming Languages and Analysis for Security (PLAS 2016), pp. 97–102. ACM, New York. https://doi.org/10.1145/2993600.2993601
12. Palmer, J.W.: Web site usability, design, and performance metrics. Inf. Syst. Res. **13**(2), 151–167 (2002)
13. Paternò, F., Schiavone, A.G., Conte, A.: Customizable automatic detection of bad usability smells in mobile accessed web applications. In: Proceedings Mobile HCI 2017, Article No. 42, Vienna. ACM Press, September 2017
14. Santana, V.F., Calani Baranauskas, M.C.: WELFIT: a remote evaluation tool for identifying web usage patterns through client-side logging. Int. J. Hum Comput Stud. **76**(C), 40–49 (2015)
15. Segura, V.C.V.B., Barbosa, S.D.J.: HistoryViewer: Instrumenting a Visual Analytics Application to Support Revisiting a Session of Interactive Data Analysis. In: PACMHCI. EICS, vol. 1, pp. 11:1–11:18 (2017)
16. Terrier, L., Demeure, A., Caffiau, S.: CCBL: a language for better supporting context centered programming in the smart home. In: Proceedings of ACM Human-Computer Interaction, vol. 1, EICS 2017, Article 14, 18 p., June 2017. https://doi.org/10.1145/3099584
17. Ur, B., McManus, E., Ho, M.P.Y., Littman, M.L.: Practical trigger-action programming in the smart home. In: Proceedings of CHI 2014, pp. 803–812. ACM, New York https://doi.org/10.1145/2556288.2557420
18. Ur, B., et al.: Trigger-action programming in the wild: an analysis of 200,000 IFTTT recipes. In: Proceedings of the 2016 CHI Conference on Human Factors in Computing Systems (CHI 2016), pp. 3227–3231. ACM, New York (2016). https://doi.org/10.1145/2858036.2858556

Software Support for Coherent Prototyping of 3D Gesture Interactions

Dominik Rupprecht[(⊠)], Rainer Blum, and Birgit Bomsdorf

Fulda University of Applied Sciences, Leipziger Straße 123,
36037 Fulda, Germany
{dominik.rupprecht,rainer.blum,
birgit.bomsdorf}@cs.hs-fulda.de

Abstract. When prototyping applications that include touchless 3D gesture interaction three design matters must be taken into consideration: the gestures the user must execute, the visual representation and the dialog flow. Ideally, these aspects should be considered in parallel, to achieve a coherent design process, and avoid ineffective extra effort stemming from coordination between them. A flexible changeover of perspectives among the separate matters is needed. This paper proposes a software environment that enables the desired coherent rapid prototyping of applications with 3D gesture interactions. Its core consists of two types of mapping and a so-called co-simulation functionality. The environment facilitates combining existing software tools from industry and literature to cover the three design matters, i.e. specification and simulation of UI prototypes, gestures, and dialog models. It assists developers at design time in the specification of gestures and in binding them to UI prototypes as well as to statecharts used for defining dialog models. Relevant coherency information is used to offer the option to evaluate gestures at runtime in the context of UI prototype and dialog model. The co-simulator manages the synchronized simulation of all relevant artefacts once a gesture event occurs. Therefore, it enables quickly building prototypes that go beyond the capabilities of the individual tools. This paper describes the usage of the proposed environment in form of a case study with several software tools, each covering one of the three design aspects. It also shows its general applicability, meaning that it can be used with other tools too.

Keywords: Gesture development · Interaction design · User interface design
Model-based development · Development support

1 Introduction

When developing applications with touchless 3D gestures, three design matters and their mutual dependencies are important [2]:

- The gestures: The movements and/or static poses of the human body or parts of it required to execute an intended interaction with a system must be defined.
- The presentation: The user interface must be designed and developed that informs the user about the required gestures and presents the system feedback.

© IFIP International Federation for Information Processing 2019
Published by Springer Nature Switzerland AG 2019
C. Bogdan et al. (Eds.): HCSE 2018, LNCS 11262, pp. 207–218, 2019.
https://doi.org/10.1007/978-3-030-05909-5_12

- The dialog: The dialog flow specifies the interactions and their sequences, e.g. the conditions and point in time a specific gesture invokes a system functionality.

Bomsdorf and Blum [2] state that the design of gestures, presentation and dialog span a coherent design space, with different involved stakeholders (different project participants like user interaction designers, end users or software developers). Each of them needs specific tool support for one up to all the design matters. Gestures appropriate to interact with the system must be identified and specified in detail as part of this process. They can be bound to the presentation (e.g. starting with simple UI prototypes) and to dialog models. After that connection, the prototype of an application can be evaluated iteratively. The three design aspects must be kept synchronized. Furthermore, an easy switching between the different axes of the design space is needed. For instance, if a designer alters gestures, this could also imply modifications of the presentation, to present suitable affordances to the user.

Software support of this coherent, three axes design space may be pursued by two kinds of approaches for enabling an easy switching between the axes of the design space. A single integrated tool can be a reasonable option if it combines functionalities to create UI prototypes and dialog models and bind gestures to them [2]. It has the advantage that users benefit from a consistent terminology and user interface typically present in a single software tool. However, the downside is that prospective users first need to familiarize with such a new design tool and put their usual tools aside. This may impede the acceptance of the new tool. Also, due to the fact, that gesture sensors are not yet usable via plug and play, such single integrated tools must be altered for every new gesture sensor to be added. In addition, as industrial practice and the literature show, state of the art tools for these different design spaces exist and are widespread and established. Therefore, this work proposes a solution that integrates these existing software tools with the aim to support a coherent rapid prototyping of 3D gesture interaction and a flexible change of perspective between the three axes of the design space.

The next section presents related work focusing on the dialog axis and its combination with 3D gestures, as well as on the presentation axis and its combination with 3D gestures. This is followed by related work concerning the concept of co-simulation. Section 3 gives a broad overview of the software environment proposed in this paper and demonstrates the integration of the above-mentioned tools in form of a case study. Section 4 shows how the proposed environment is applicable to other tools or other interaction techniques. The paper concludes in Sect. 5 with a summary and discussion of possible future developments.

2   Related Work

2.1   Model Based Approaches for Dialog Modeling

In model-based approaches the focus is on the systematic development of an interactive systems. According to Meixner et al. [7] the "interface model" consists of all used models, divided into task, dialog, and presentation, while the dialog constitutes the central point. The latter describes the interaction of a user with the user interface and the resulting invocation of system functionality - largely independent of a specific technical implementation and look and feel. The concrete presentation is developed later. Often, Harel statecharts are used to specify dialog models (e.g. Feuerstack et al. [4]). Their central concepts are dialog states, transitions between these states, triggers set off by user actions that cause these transitions, and conditions to control them. Different modeling tools that implement this kind of statecharts are the Scade Suite[1], the Nutaq Model-Based Design Kit[2], or Yakindu[3], which is utilized in the work described in this paper. These modeling tools help designers to produce valid diagrams via automatic checks and auto-complete functions (cf. Kistner and Nuernberger [5]).

To prove the quality of the workflow of an application, user inputs can be simulated by triggering them in the UI of the modeling tool, while the reactions of the system are visualized with animated diagrams (cf. Pintér et al. [8]).

A connection of gestures with dialog models (working in the dialog-gesture design space) can be found in the work of Feuerstack et al. [4] and Bomsdorf et al. [3]. Both allow executable models to be controlled by gestures. But, dialog model and gestures are specified separately and involve the extra effort of an explicit modeling step that links the gestures to the executable dialog model, after the gestures have been implemented for a specific gesture recognizer.

With GestIT Spano et al. [9] show and categorize the difficulties to a model-based design of applications with gesture interaction. They propose a declarative and compositional framework for multiplatform gesture definitions as a step towards a new model to solve the single-event granularity problem and providing a separation of concerns. But their approach targets at later stages in the development process where applications are already created by programmers. Our goal is to enable prototyping of interactive gesture applications in earlier design phases.

2.2 Rapid Prototyping of Gesture Interaction

Rapid prototypes are an effective method if design ideas shall be implemented and evaluated with stakeholders like intended users or customers already in the design phase. These are visual approaches focusing amongst other things on the look and feel (structure and behavior) of the UI, in contrast to the above-mentioned presentation models, which are abstract UI specifications. In early stages authors like van Buskirk and Moroney [10] recommend working with paper prototypes or other low fidelity prototypes to test different ideas fast with little effort. As stated by Van den Berg et al. [11], once interactive behavior is needed, more sophisticated prototypes (e.g. implemented with HTML) are typically realized with prototyping tools like Balsamiq[4], Axure[5], or Pidoco[6]. These tools allow the creation of click-through wireframes to

---

[1] http://www.esterel-technologies.com/products/scade-suite/.

[2] http://www.nutaq.com/software/model-based-design-kit/.

[3] https://www.itemis.com/en/yakindu/statechart-tools/.

[4] https://balsamiq.com/products/mockups/.

[5] https://www.axure.com/.

[6] https://pidoco.com/en.

simulate an application. Balsamiq and Pidoco support touch gestures to be used in prototypes, but not touchless 3D gestures yet. The latter is one central topic of this work, and we incorporated Pidoco as example for our approach. Rapid prototypes focus on the perceptible presentation, while the dialog is typically given solely implicit in the quite simple form of the implemented sequence of user interface changes that can be caused by user actions.

2.3   Co-simulation

In an iterative, systematic and user-centric development the different design perspectives should be supported to an equal extent by a software tool or an environment. The interim results of each axis of the design space must be checked and their consequences understood in the other axes of the design space, due to their mutual concurrence representing all the same application (cf. Barboni et al. [1]).

An early approach to that challenge forms NVIDIAs UI Composer Studio[7]. This embedded systems tool, targeted at the automotive industry, allows designers to specify dialogs for digital dashboards and to bind them to the structure of graphical user interfaces. It relies on its own XML schema to bind the transitions of the dialog model to the expected structural ("page") changes in the presentation of the prototypes. According to Kistner and Nuernberger [5] NVIDIA UI Composer Studio eases both, the prototyping and the dialog modeling for complex applications, providing a coherent development while relying on a single tool.

The approach of Martinie et al. [6] faces a similar problem of enabling a coherent design and co-simulation of different separate aspects of an application. It binds an already existing application to a task model which is based on the already implemented workflow of the application. This is achieved through java annotations inserted within the program code of the application (changing the application program code itself). These annotations make it possible to extract the interactive widgets of the application automatically. After defining a systematic correspondence (a mapping) between these widgets and the task model, both, the application and the task model, can be co-simulated, i.e. they are executed synchronously. However, this approach is intended for later stages of the design process compared to our approach and it does not focus on gestures explicitly. In addition, the code of an application to be bound to a task model must be altered as described. But, that work is another example that shows the complexity of a bidirectional combination of models and presentation.

3   Software Environment

This section introduces our approach to support the required coherent design. The proposed solution utilizes existing, established tools for dialog modeling, rapid prototyping and gesture recognition and connects them with the help of a semantic-driven binding. Its purpose is to overcome the described shortcomings of the side-by-side use

---

[7] http://uicomposer.nvidia.com/.

of such tools, to take the mutual dependencies of the three design matters gesture, presentation and dialog into account and in sum to enable a coherent development of 3D gesture interactions.

To make the different tools work together closely, a mapping is needed. Mapping means, that semantically corresponded aspects of each tool are put into relation to each other, like the execution of a specific gesture and the associated reaction in a prototype. This forms the central prerequisite for the desired co-simulation. At design time a common set of triggers (called *sync triggers* further in this paper) is shared between the involved tools to realize the mapping and co-simulation.

3.1   Internal or External Mapping

Two types of mappings are implemented between the existing design tools to cater for the different cases that exist in practice: *Internal* and *external mapping*. If programmatic access to the internals of a program code is available, that can be used to import sync triggers and bind them to the internal control flow of the software, the mapping is implemented natively in the source code of the tool. We call this option *internal mapping*. Consequently, the actual communication between the tools is made possible via an application programming interface (API), that provides access to the required, mapping functionality. All tools must import a simple text file containing a list of *sync triggers* (trigger set) and map them to the desired internal functionality. If an event occurs in one tool that is mapped to a *sync trigger*, this trigger is subsequently called in the other tool via the involved trigger APIs.

For software tools with no or too limited access to the program code of the tool itself a concept called *external mapping* is used. This approach keeps the necessary changes on the software code as minimal as possible if at all. However, in this case the respective tool must feature an API that permits access to some kind of internal event system. That event system is bound to external events that are handled in other components of our environment using a separate *mapping editor*. The mapping between two tools is arranged with this editor during the design phase. As a prerequisite, the tool in question must provide a functionality to export information regarding its relevant internal events into a text file (a list of event names). These events are mapped to the *sync triggers* inside the *mapping editor*. In addition, for the intended co-execution of all involved tools a *co-simulator* is needed. During run time it processes the defined mappings by translating events outcoming from a tool into *sync triggers* and vice versa.

3.2   Environment Overview

In this section we detail our approach by means of a case study with the following software products as exemplary tools for the different axes of the design space:

- Presentation: Pidoco (see Footnote 6) for rapid prototyping of graphical UI.
  Pidoco is a client/server software tool with web front-end using up to date web technologies. It allows quick creation of click-through wireframes and fully interactive prototypes to simulate and test the look and feel of an application concept.

- Dialog: Yakindu (see Footnote 3) for building statecharts.
  Yakindu is a set of plugins written in Java within the Eclipse RCP and IDE environment[8] consisting of four main parts: statechart editing, simulation, validation and code generation.
- Gestures: Microsoft Kinect and a gesture simulator.
  The Kinect (Version 2)[9] is a combination of soft- and hardware for building and recognizing full body gestures. Instead, or in parallel, a gesture simulator can be used, which can trigger gesture events (as if done by the Kinect).

Internal and external mappings had to be realized. The Pidoco company allowed the native extension of their software tool to support *internal mapping* between *sync triggers* and the actions of the UI prototypes built with the Pidoco tool. The *external mapping* approach was used for the dialog modeling inside Yakindu since this tool features an extension API. A direct *internal mapping* of gestures was not desired by Yakindu. Therefore, this case study featured a combination of *internal and external mapping*. Figure 1 gives an overview of the case-specific implementation of our environment.

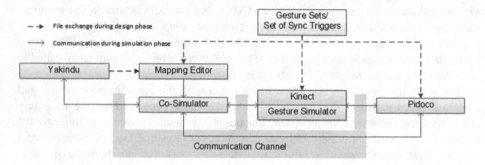

Fig. 1. Overview of implemented environment

In general, in the design phase a set of *sync triggers* must be compiled. Our *sync triggers* consist of a set of gestures, which are expected to occur, and they serve as a key data structure since all involved software tools are bound to it. For this implementation, this set of *sync triggers* (simple JSON file) was imported into the Kinect recognizer and in parallel into a *gesture simulator* software. This enabled the two tools to trigger gesture recognition events within the environment (resulting in the invocation of corresponding *sync triggers*).

Pidoco's native extension can import a *sync trigger* set (same JSON file), providing functionality to bind single *sync triggers* to reactions inside a UI prototype and, thus, to react to received triggers. Yakindu was extended with an export functionality for statechart events and variables via the extension of its existing API. When working on a

---

[8] https://www.eclipse.org/downloads/packages/eclipse-rcp-and-rap-developers/heliosr.
[9] https://developer.microsoft.com/en-us/windows/kinect.

concrete prototype, the user must import this statechart information (also a JSON file) into the *mapping editor*, where it must be bound to the *sync trigger* set by the user.

These mappings saved either inside a tool (*internal mapping*; in this case with the Pidoco tool) or externally in the mapping editor (*external mapping*; Yakindu, Kinect, gesture simulator), are subsequently used in the simulation stage for the synchronized execution of the tools. In our case study implementation, if a gesture is recognized by the Kinect gesture recognizer or is triggered manually within the *gesture simulator*, it is sent over through the shared communication channel. The Pidoco software tool listens for these events and then checks, if a prototype transition is mapped to an incoming *sync trigger*. It then reacts accordingly by carrying out the determined reaction. Each change during runtime within the UI prototype simulation caused by a user (e.g. a button click) is in turn propagated over the shared communication channel to all applications.

Based on the defined mapping between gestures and *sync triggers*, both structures are translated into one another by our *co-simulator*. A gesture, whether triggered by the Kinect recognizer (or, alternatively, the *gesture simulator*) is translated into statechart events and then sent to Yakindu. Each event occurring inside the statechart tool is sent to the network respectively. It is then translated back into gestures, respectively *sync triggers* by the *co-simulator* for the other tools to react.

In our case study the possibility to test and evaluate the interplay of prototype artefacts from two or three axes of the design space in parallel is demonstrated, using either real gestures or simulated ones. The next sections provide more details about the purpose of all parts of the environment including the implementation of required additional software components.

3.3 Gesture Processing

Gesture recognition was accomplished with a tool chain using Microsoft's Kinect (version 2). Typically, gestures are first recorded with the Kinect Studio[10] and then processed with the Visual Gesture Builder[11] resulting in a set of gestures. For our case study, these gesture sets were then extended with the required meta data including name, description of involved body parts and additional input values for the gesture recognizer. This editing task was implemented with the Kinect SDK in form of a separate component called *gesture editor*, where the *sync trigger* (JSON) file is created.

With our case study implementation, it is also possible to create gesture sets inside this *gesture editor* without recording actual gestures. These "virtual" gestures are composed of the mentioned meta data and a descriptive video demonstration. A *gesture simulator* can use both the "virtual" gesture sets, and the sets recorded with the Kinect to trigger *sync triggers*.

---

[10] https://msdn.microsoft.com/de-de/library/dn785306.aspx.

[11] https://msdn.microsoft.com/de-de/library/dn785304.aspx.

3.4 Mapping

Pidoco. As mentioned above, for the design of the presentation, i.e. a UI prototype, the mapping between gestures respectively *sync triggers* and actions within prototypes was implemented inside Pidoco (*internal mapping*). Actions like mouse clicks, touch gestures or motion of a mobile device can be configured as triggers inside Pidoco for user interface reactions without requiring any programming. These reactions range from UI page changes to playing sounds or highlighting areas. Each interaction consists of a user action and a system reaction. These interactions can be added via a context menu (see Fig. 2) to every interactive element on the screen. To support the *internal mapping* approach the Pidoco company extended this context menu, so that the array of assignable actions includes gestures as additional actions (see Fig. 2, ①).

To specify gestures as actions within a prototype a gesture set (a set of sync triggers) must be loaded via file import into Pidoco first (another functionality that was also added to the Pidoco software). The gestures are then available as actions in the aforementioned context menu. After selecting an action (see Fig. 2, ②) it can be bound to the desired reaction (see Fig. 2, ③).

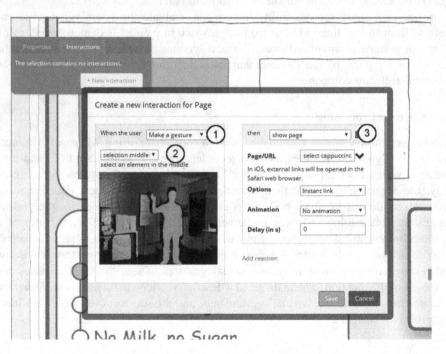

Fig. 2. Mapping in Pidoco (extract)

Yakindu. For the design of the dialog, mappings must be created in the external *mapping editor* (*external mapping*). It maps gestures onto events within model statecharts. First, events are to be assigned to state transitions inside Yakindu. They trigger the transitions, representing dialog changes, if all defined conditions are met. The basic version of the Yakindu software is open source and provides a flexible extension interface, enabling the extraction and processing of design and runtime information.

To create the *external mapping*, information about the internal events and variables of a specific statechart must be exported. This export functionality was developed as a so-called decoupled code extension using the built-in features of the Yakindu API. The extension builds a JSON file automatically. All the events of a Yakindu statechart (see Fig. 3, ①) are represented in this JSON file. To establish the binding the user must import the file into the *mapping editor* inside our environment. The *mapping editor* then extracts the trigger information. Afterwards the Yakindu events (see Fig. 3, ②) must be mapped to the *sync triggers* (see Fig. 3, ③) by the user.

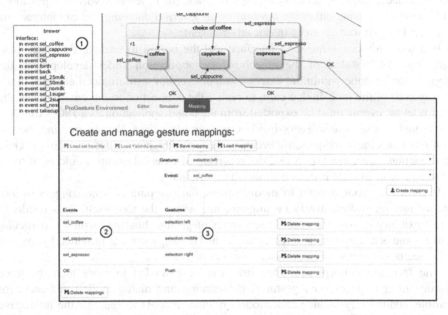

Fig. 3. External Mapping in Yakindu ① and the mapping table in the mapping editor (② and ③) (extracts)

3.5   Co-simulation

Consequentially, both *internal and external mapping* were considered during the simulation stage to synchronize events and triggers between the involved tools. All three or just two of the tools can run synchronized this way. Whatever change is occurring in one of the tools, it is transferred to the others so that these can react accordingly. Triggers are sent to the shared communication channel, which was implemented as an event bus. The Kinect gesture recognizer and the *gesture simulator* simply send the *sync triggers* that correspond to the current gesture recognition. In Pidoco each incoming trigger is checked if it is valid for the current page. This is true if a reaction is specified for the trigger. In that case, the reaction is executed in the UI prototype.

For the Yakindu tool the *co-simulator* of our environment uses the mapping table of the *mapping editor* to translate Yakindu events to *sync triggers* and vice versa. This mechanism works continuously while in simulation mode, forwarding the messages between the participating software tools. If an incoming event meets the conditions of a transition as defined in the statechart inside Yakindu the simulation of the statechart continues.

4   Generalizability of the Approach

Our environment is applicable to other combinations of tools, as well as to other interaction techniques, like touch or mouse control. As a prerequisite it must be possible to define a common set of *sync triggers*. Then, the different involved applications can be controlled using either the *internal or the external mapping* and can interact via the event bus, without changes in our environment.

If a tool provides a message interface and the option to retrieve the states (and changes to these states) of the objects of the application under development, the mapping can be done within the external *mapping editor* with minimal changes to the existing code of the tool. In that case, to realize the connection to our environment, the set of relevant events must be exported from the target application as a JSON file. It is then bound to the *sync triggers* inside our *mapping editor*. During runtime the *co-simulator* sends the corresponding events to the tool, which can react accordingly. Only both functionalities, the export and the receiving of external events would need to be added to a tool, in case it does not provide it originally.

If a software tool is open to modifications, the mapping of *sync triggers* to tool functionality may alternatively be implemented within the tool itself. This results in more flexibility to react to specific semantics of gesture bindings within a particular software and is advantageous if for example the UI design options provided by the tool shall specifically reflect the additional concept of gestures.

The mapping concept presented here can be extended to more than the three regarded design spaces (i.e., gestures, presentation and dialog model) and may, for example, additionally include task models or other models to describe the interactive behavior of software applications like the Interaction Flow Modeling Language (IFML)[12]. For that purpose, it may be necessary to extend our *mapping editor* and *co-simulator* to support new types of events.

Even an alternative gesture recognizer can be used, e.g. the Leap Motion sensor[13]. We plan to support it in the future, because of its ability to recognize hand and finger gestures. After the usual binding, as explained above, the Leap gestures would be processed by our environment in the same way as the Kinect gestures from our case study.

---

[12] http://www.ifml.org/.
[13] https://www.leapmotion.com/.

5 Discussion and Future Work

In this paper, we present our work on an environment for rapid prototyping of 3D gesture interactions. To support the early phases in the design of 3D gesture interactions we consider three design matters: gestures, dialog model and presentation. Rather than developing completely new software to cover the tremendous breadth of required functionality we decided to combine already known and established software tools that developers are familiar with. We show a case study on how to combine Microsoft Kinect gestures with Yakindu statecharts (for dialog modeling) and Pidoco rapid UI prototypes within a novel, integrated environment that serves a coherent design process. It allows detailed consideration of the mutual dependencies of these three design matters and enables designers to change perspectives by switching between them flexibly during the design and evaluation of applications with 3D gesture interactions.

We designed the functionality of the proposed environment based on a thorough user-centered requirements engineering with industrial suppliers of software tools and with partners that hold relevant use cases. An evaluation of the described resulting implementation with real users, to find out how beneficial our approach is for designers, is still under work. Parts of the environment as implemented in the described case study (with Pidoco and the *gesture simulator*) were used by computer science students of our university as part of their study projects building and evaluating gesture interaction applications. We found out, that they could work effectively with the separate tools and the combination of both even without any previous training. Only minor issues concerning the usability of the UI of the environment (e.g. naming of buttons) occurred but were considered for the further development of our environment.

The core parts of the proposed environment are, first, two kinds of mapping as ways to bind gestures to prototypes and to statecharts, and, second, a *co-simulator*. If existing software is open for extension to import sets of gestures and bind them to their control flow, mapping can be done inside the existing tool (*internal mapping*). If changes to existing software must be kept to a minimum, instead an API is required to trigger and export events to bind them to gestures in a separate mapping editor that was developed especially for this purpose (*external mapping*). Both types of mapping are used at runtime to evaluate the gestures in the context of the UI prototype and dialog model respectively. The *co-simulator* guarantees the synchronized execution of prototype and dialog model once a gesture is recognized or its respective event is triggered.

The two proposed approaches for mapping in combination with the implemented event bus for bi-directional communication provide flexibility for the integration of different types of software tools into the environment and ensure high interchangeability of implementations. Alternative tools only need to support one of the two described mappings and then can be combined with our environment.

However, using different software tools can also cause inconsistency in the semantics of the overall application design. With this work a synchronized simulation environment is proposed, but not a synchronized model. This necessitates future work that ensures consistency between presentation and dialog.

In addition, gestures are currently translated simply into sync triggers. But there is more information that could be exchanged meaningfully between applications, like values of variables and attributes from the dialog model to the presentation. For example, counter variables held in Yakindu could be reflected in a Pidoco prototype to enrich the prototyped UI with some functionality provided by the dialog model. Or gestures can consist of several events (cf. the granularity problem in Spano et al. [9]) or must be traced continuously, resulting in more complex *sync triggers*. Our environment will be expanded to support those increased *sync triggers* as well.

Acknowledgments. This research was financially supported by the German Federal Ministry of Education and Research within the framework of the program Forschung an Fachhochschulen - IngenieurNachwuchs (project no. 03FH007IX5).

References

1. Barboni, E., Ladry, J.-F., Navarre, D., Palanque, P., Winckler, M.: Beyond modelling: an integrated environment supporting co-execution of tasks and systems models. In: Proceedings of the 2nd ACM SIGCHI Symposium on Engineering Interactive Computing Systems, pp. 165–174. ACM, New York (2010)
2. Bomsdorf, B., Blum, R.: Early prototyping of 3D-gesture interaction within the presentation-gesture-dialog design space. In: Kurosu, M. (ed.) HCI 2014. LNCS, vol. 8511, pp. 12–23. Springer, Cham (2014). https://doi.org/10.1007/978-3-319-07230-2_2
3. Bomsdorf, B., Blum, R., Hesse, S., Heinz, P.: WeBewIn: Rapid Prototyping bewegungs-basierter Interaktionen. In: Boll, S., Maaß, S., Malaka, R. (eds.) Mensch & Computer 2013: Interaktive Vielfalt, pp. 251–260. Oldenbourg Verlag, München (2013)
4. Feuerstack, S., Anjo, M.D.S., Pizzolato, E.B.: Model-based design and generation of a gesture-based user interface navigation control. In: Gomes, A.S. (ed.) Proceedings of the 10th Brazilian Symposium on Human Factors in Computing Systems and the 5th Latin American Conference on Human-Computer Interaction, pp. 227–231. Brazilian Computer Society, Porto Alegre (2011)
5. Kistner, G., Nuernberger, C.: Developing user interfaces using SCXML statecharts. In: Schnelle-Walka, D., Radomski, S., Lager, T., Barnett, J., Dahl, D., Mühlhäuser, M. (eds.) Proceedings of the 1st EICS Workshop on Engineering Interactive Computer Systems with SCXML, pp. 5–11 (2014)
6. Martinie, C., Navarre, D., Palanque, P., Fayollas, C.: A generic tool-supported framework for coupling task models and interactive applications. In: Ziegler, J. (ed.) Proceedings of 7th ACM SIGCHI Symposium on Engineering Interactive Computing Systems, pp. 244–253 (2015)
7. Meixner, G., Paternó, F., Vanderdonckt, J.: Past, Present, and Future of Model-Based User Interface Development, i-com 10, 2–11 (2011)
8. Pintér, G., Micskei, Z.I., Majzik, I.: Supporting design and development of safety critical applications by model based tools. In: Annales Universitatis Scientiarum Budapestinensis de Rolando Eötvös nominatae Sectio Computatorica, pp. 61–78. ELTE (2009)
9. Spano, L.D., Cisternino, A., Paternò, F., Fenu, G.: GestIT: a declarative and compositional framework for multiplatform gesture definition. In: Forbrig, P., Dewan, P., Harrison, M., Luyten, K. (eds.) Proceedings of the 5th ACM SIGCHI Symposium on Engineering Interactive Computing Systems - EICS 13, p. 187. ACM Press, New York (2013)
10. van Buskirk, R., Moroney, B.W.: Extending prototyping. IBM Syst. J. **42**, 613–623 (2003)
11. van den Bergh, J., Sahni, D., Haesen, M., Luyten, K., Coninx, K.: GRIP. In: Paternò, F., Luyten, K., Maurer, F. (eds.) Proceedings of the 3rd ACM SIGCHI Symposium on Engineering Interactive Computing Systems - EICS 2011, p. 143. ACM Press, New York (2011)

Towards Tool-Support for Robot-Assisted Product Creation in Fab Labs

Jan Van den Bergh[1]([⊠]) [iD], Bram van Deurzen[1] [iD], Tom Veuskens[2] [iD],
Raf Ramakers[1] [iD], and Kris Luyten[1] [iD]

[1] Hasselt University - tUL - Flanders Make, Expertise Centre for Digital Media,
Wetenschapspark 2, 3590 Diepenbeek, Belgium
{jan.vandenbergh,bram.vandeurzen,raf.ramakers,kris.luyten}@uhasselt.be
[2] Hasselt University, Hasselt, Belgium
tom.veuskens@student.uhasselt.be

Abstract. Collaborative robot-assisted production has great potential for high variety low volume production lines. These type of production lines are common in both personal fabrication settings as well as in several types of flexible production lines. Moreover, many assembly tasks are in fact hard to complete by a single user or a single robot, and benefit greatly from a fluent collaboration between both. However, programming such systems is cumbersome, given the wide variation of tasks and the complexity of instructing a robot how it should move and operate in collaboration with a human user.

In this paper we explore the case of collaborative assembly for personal fabrication. Based on a CAD model of the envisioned product, our software analyzes how this can be composed from a set of standardized pieces and suggests a series of collaborative assembly steps to complete the product. The proposed tool removes the need for the end-user to perform additional programming of the robot. We use a low-cost robot setup that is accessible and usable for typical personal fabrication activities in Fab Labs and Makerspaces. Participants in a first experimental study testified that our approach leads to a fluent collaborative assembly process. Based on this preliminary evaluation, we present next steps and potential implications.

Keywords: Human-robot collaboration · Toolkit
End-user development

1 Introduction

Robots were introduced in manufacturing during a time where replicating a single design for mass-market was a dominant strategy that enabled more people to enjoy the advantages of technology. In recent years, however, focus returns to customized or even personalized products. Likewise, robotic support is evolving to support these more flexible production requirements. Collaborative robots or

© IFIP International Federation for Information Processing 2019
Published by Springer Nature Switzerland AG 2019
C. Bogdan et al. (Eds.): HCSE 2018, LNCS 11262, pp. 219–230, 2019.
https://doi.org/10.1007/978-3-030-05909-5_13

cobots are introduced as cheaper, more flexible robots than traditional industrial robots. Cobots can be reprogrammed by their operators to support customized, shorter-lived tasks. While these tools are effective, these still require separate, offline programming of the robot. This can be cost effective for customized products where there is still some repetition of the same task. It however becomes undesirable for personalized or one-off production. Such production is already happening in Fab Labs and Makerspaces.

In this paper, we explore how programming robotic support for personalized production in e.g. Fab Lab or Makerspace can be realized. To do so, we started from the tasks that creators need to perform when they want to create a new three-dimensional object. These tasks include the conceptualization of the product, trying things out digitally, specification of the different parts of the artifact, creation of all components using machines, such as laser cutters and 3D printers, and finally assembly of the artifact.

While technological support exists for most of these steps, the assembly step is still a manual process that may sometimes be cumbersome. In this paper, we start from the assumption that a robot could support this step and could assist the creator by offering a third hand. We present our envisioned integrated toolkit, as well as the current prototype that includes a design tool as well as robotic support that assists during the assembly process. We present the results of a first preliminary study with the toolkit's robotic support and offer directions for future work.

2   Related Work

Our approach partly relies on a CAD (computer-aided design) model of the product that a *maker* wants to create. There are already some approaches that use CAD data to ease programming of robots. We provide a short selection of related work on how CAD models are already used to program robots and on different approaches to end-user programming of robots.

2.1   Tools for CAD-Based Robot Programming

CAD-based programming is not a new idea; it was already investigated over 30 years ago [3]. It however is still an active research area that also benefits from advances in commercial tools, as is exemplified by some recent approaches.

Neto et al. [7,8] propose such a CAD-based system. It uses Autodesk Inventor as the CAD system and the communication is through the API. Starting from a CAD model of the robotic cell, the user generates a robot program by drawing the desired robot path. The end effector position and rotation has to be defined as well, by placing simplified tool models along the robot paths. Interpolation is implemented on the end effector path to smooth out the movement. The user defines areas of risk where the interpolation is applied. The needed information is automatically extracted, analyzed and converted into robot programs. Sensor data can be used to track the movement in real-time and make adjustments on the fly. The proposed tool is tested with two different experiments in which offline programs are created. The results of the tests show that the system is easy to use and within minutes an user can generate a robot program.

Baizid et al. [1] presented an Industrial Robotic Simulation Design Planning and Optimization platform named IRoSim. The platform is based on Solidworks and uses its API to extend the functionality. The goal of the platform is to offer an intuitive and convertible environment for designing and simulating robotized tasks. The platform includes various 3D models that are essential for developing any robotized tasks including different types of robotic arms. Besides aiding in the creation of the robotic program, the platform can be used to check the reachability of the end effector, to simulate the motion, and to validate the trajectory to avoid possible collisions. These can be used for time optimization and collision avoidance of the robotic task designed with the platform.

These approaches are aimed at professional users and want to support them in creating more complex robot programs. In contrast, our approach is aimed a end-users and targets a specific, albeit customizable toolkit.

2.2 End-User Robot Programming Approaches

End-user programming of robots is receiving much attention from the research community as it is essential to deliver on the promises of robotics in many sectors including both social and manufacturing and maintenance applications. There is significant diversity in approaches to realize this.

CoStar [10] lets users program robots using physical demonstration or graphical behavior trees that can be quickly reconfigured to deal with other, but similar situations. The system is cross platform, building on the capabilities of ROS [12].

Hammer [6] uses a block-based language, inspired by Scratch [13], as part of an integrated development environment for robot programming that runs on a tablet. It also includes the option of a teaching pendant, which allows direct control over a virtual model over the robot.

Pedersen and Krüger [11] propose an approach that links body poses to specific pre-programmed skills. These skills are higher level robot tasks that combine different robot actions and observations such as object detection. End-users can than use the gestures (in combination with a graphical user interface) to program the robot.

Orendt et al. [9] confirmed that the use of One-Shot Programming by Demonstration (programming a robot with a single demonstration) can be effective and intuitive, especially for end-user participants that successfully accomplished the tasks in the experiment. The results held regardless of the instruction modality. This type of programming by demonstration, in combination with a graphical programming environment is also used in industry to deploy collaborative robots.

Sefidgar et al. [14] propose the use of situated tangible programming; programming a robot through tangible instruction blocks within its operating environment. They found that people can comprehend and create robot programs with little or no instructions.

In contrast to these approaches that aim to make it easier to program robots, our approach is a step towards making programming the robot nearly transparent to the end user. In addition to these approaches aimed at programming robot behavior, there also several efforts to ease programming of interaction with robots. As the interaction with the robot is predefined in our proposed approach, we don't give an overview of these approaches but refer to recent work on this topic, such as that of Van den Bergh and Luyten [2].

3 Envisioned Approach

People go to a Fab Lab or Makerspace to create physical things with all kinds of machines, such as laser-cutters or 3D printers. These machines require digital models of the physical forms to be created. When considering tool support for further support of this creation process, we tapped into this aspect and used a digital model of the artifact to drive robotic support. We want to minimize the required knowledge to use the approach to 3D manipulation in a desktop tool and assembly skills.

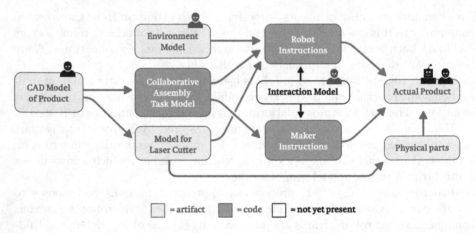

Fig. 1. Envisioned process for collaborative human-robot fabrication in Fab Lab. Input from human or robot is indicated with a symbol. Black indicates input per product, otherwise only configuration of the setup is required. Support in the current toolkit (Sect. 4) is indicated using differences in background color. (Color figure online)

Figure 1 gives an overview of our envisioned process and all artifacts that it uses or creates. All rounded rectangles represent artifacts. The background color indicates how the model is represented in our current prototype (Fig. 2). Most steps are thus completely automated, only two steps require input from the maker: CAD model creation and creation of the actual product. Two other steps (environment model and interaction model) are used to configure the environment.

The *CAD model* specifies the components that will used in the physical model and their configuration in 3D space. The order in which these components appear in the model is used to determine the order in which the components will be used to create the physical model. The creation of the CAD model, currently can thus be regarded as a virtual programming by demonstration exercise. The CAD model is thus used to create a *collaborative task model* of the assembly by allocating tasks to the robot (fetching plates and holding them in place) or the maker (fixing the plates using connection pieces), although this model is not externalized in a separate file. The plates used in a CAD model are also extracted and combined in a *model for a laser cutter*. This information is also used to determine where plates are to be picked up by the robot. To do this, the information is combined with information in the *environment model*. This latter model is also used to decide to which position the robot should bring a specific plate so that it is close enough to the product under construction to be fixed to it. The maker is guided through the whole assembly process with instructions provided by the tool. Currently a push on a small red button when the robot (or platform) should perform the next action but we plan to make this more flexible through the inclusion of an *interaction model*, which would enable implicit or explicit, perhaps even multimodal human-robot interaction. Several approaches can be considered to accomplish this [2].

4   A Flexible Toolkit for Robot-Assisted Assembly Tasks

Our system includes a physical setup, consisting of a robotic arm and movable assembly platform, and a CAD tool that computes the collaborative assembly steps using the robotic arm. A set of predefined shapes of various sizes can be used to model a 3D object in the CAD tool; these shapes represent the different plates our setup can use. During assembly of the physical object, the robotic arm will pick the appropriate plate and put in position so the user can further assemble the modeled object. Assembly steps that required "a third hand", e.g. screwing together two plates under a specific corner, can now be completed much more easily. Furthermore, the robotic hand is instructed on the order and placement of the plates by the CAD tool, and requires no further programming or intervention by the user.

Physical Setup. Our current setup is based on the Commonplace Robotics Mover6 robotic arm[1] (Fig. 2b). This robotic arm has a relatively large reach (up to 80 cm with the default end effector) and has 6 degrees of freedom. The custom end effector has a bellows suction cup to pick up and hold the plates. There are four small cushions to keep plates perpendicular to the end effector.

The position of the movable platform and the robotic arm need not be perfect. It is sufficient if these are close enough together. The movable platform and the robotic arm allow small manual adjustments. For example, slightly moving the robotic arm by hand, rotating the model or tilting the model.

---

[1] https://www.cpr-robots.com/products/mover6.html.

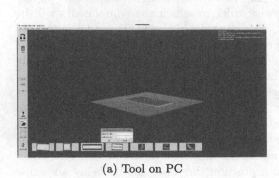

(a) Tool on PC

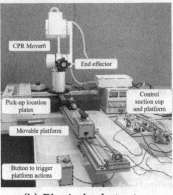

(b) Physical robot setup

Fig. 2. Two parts of the current toolkit: makers use the tool on PC (a) to create CAD models. The tool guides assembly with support from the robot setup (b).

CAD-like Toolkit. A CAD-like tool was built on top of Autodesk meshmixer (Fig. 2a). In this tool the user can build the desired model by selecting the supported primitives. It supports positioning plates at a 45, 90 or 135° angle, the ability to create custom sized plates, and automatic extraction of a plates file that can be used to laser cut the required plates of the model.

To support plates at different angles the code that automatically calculates the instructions for the robotic arm should not only take the position of the plate into consideration, but when a plate is angled also any plates beneath it. To prevent hitting that plate, the robotic arm may be required to hold the plate from the other side.

In the toolkit the user can specify the dimensions of the plate and place it into the model. These plates should be custom created using a laser cutter when the user wants to build the model. The suction cup end effector that is used with the Mover6 robotic arm, enables it to pick up plates without first having to attach metal pieces to these plates. The robotic arm can pick up plates directly from the original laser cut plate, if placed on a fixed position next to it. The 6 degrees of freedom allow the robotic arm to move freely over the plate, which isn't possible with the Arduino Braccio robotic arm.

When a user wants to build a model that uses custom size plates, he is required to laser cut the plates first. To make the toolkit usable for as many people as possible, automatic creation of a plates file is supported. This file can be used directly with a laser cutter to laser cut the plates. The plates are placed next to each other, the first plate is the base plate, the second plate the second plate in the model and so on. Around all the plates a buffer of 20 mm is created, which is used to hold all the plates in the correct position when placed next to the robotic arm.

5 Evaluation

5.1 Method

A formative study was conducted to evaluate and further refine our approach. The goal of the user study was to explore the overall usability of building a model in collaboration with a robot arm. The overall process of assembling a physical object of a model with the robot was tested. Our study started with a brief overview of the design tool, after which participants assembled a dice tower model in collaboration with the robot (see Fig. 3a). When the participant finished the object, we asked the participant to fill in a questionnaire followed by a structured interview. We selected the dice tower as the physical object to be made, because it requires assembling plates at an angle that is not perpendicular, uses various custom plate sizes, and is basically more complex than a basic tray but still feasible to assembly in a limited amount of time.

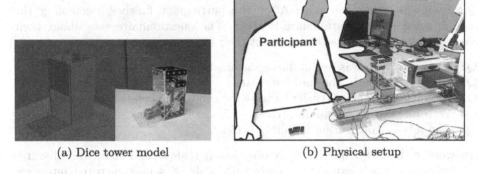

(a) Dice tower model   (b) Physical setup

Fig. 3. The dice tower model (a) that participants built with the setup (b).

Participants and Apparatus. The study was conducted with four participants (all male and between 23 and 35 years old) that have some familiarity with personal fabrication. Three participants had constructed a physical object in a Fab Lab setting at least once. Three of the participants were computer science students.

During the user study, we recorded the participants using a webcam facing the user. This webcam was connected to a second computer setup behind the participant (Fig. 3b). On this computer, the observer made notes in real time using Techsmith Morae Recorder[2].

Procedure. The user study consists of the following three parts: a study introduction, the assembly process, and a questionnaire and interview to close.

---

[2] https://www.techsmith.com/morae.html.

Study Introduction. The study starts with getting the informed consent of the participant. Next, the researcher familiarizes the participant with the design tool. They demonstrate how the tool can be used to design a 3D model of a physical object. They open the model of the dice tower (Fig. 3a) in the design tool on behalf of the participant, and inform them about the instructions that are shown during the assembly process, and how progress during the assembly process is visualized by the tool.

Assembly Process. The researcher starts the assembly process by attaching the base plate of the model on the platform. The last instruction the participant receives is to start with attaching the corner pieces to the base plate, as shown in the tool. All other instructions are given by the design tool, which the participant assembles the model without further guidance. During the assembly process, the researcher annotated the video recordings in real time to ease analysis after the experiment. The participants are allowed to ask questions during the process if they are not sure how to proceed.

Questionnaire and Interview. After the participant finishes assembling the model, a one-page questionnaire is given. The questionnaire asks about their connection to a Makerspace and about their experience during the assembly:

Q1 The robot arm was useful during assembly.
Q2 The instruction in the tool are clear.
Q3 Building a model was easier because the robot holds plates at the right spot.
Q4 Your role during assembly is clear.
Q5 The robot's role during assembly is clear.

Answers to the latter questions are on a Likert scale from 1 to 5 (fully disagree - fully agree). Each experiment ends with a short, semi-structured interview including open ended questions on their experience.

5.2   Results

Observations. Most completion times were similar (20, 21, 23 min). One participant was faster (15 min), but he had a less polished result. Time was spent between looking at instructions and doing the assembly. In case of doubt, additional time was spend reading instructions.

The robotic arm holds the plate in the required position, after which the user attaches the plate to the model. The idea is that the user attaches the plate with just enough bolts so that the plate stays in place, after which the robotic arm can move away. Moving the robotic arm out of the way gives the user more space to work. This was not clear to most of the participants, especially in the first step. Some going as far as to attach all the corner pieces on the plate before moving the robot arm away. The participant stated the instructions in the tool were clear, but they experienced two main problems during the assembly.

All participants experienced a problem when the robotic arm picks up a plate. It waits with holding the plate in the desired position until the user presses the step button again. This step allows the user to make a last check before continuing with the next plate. This was explained in the instructions:

```
The robot is picking up the next plate, it's finished when
 ↪ holding the plate.
The platform moves to the required position, it's finished
 ↪ after moving.
------------------------------------------------------------
Press the STEP-button when the previous step is completed, to
 ↪ start the next step in the build process.
```

This explanation was however not clear to any of the participants. They expected the robotic arm to pick up a plate and hold it in one action. Thus when the robotic arm stopped they were not sure what to do. Some of the participants thought they had to attach corner pieces to the plate already. Two participants asked the researcher how to proceed in this step. One of them later indicated that he did not notice the instructions immediately because he was not sure if the step was finished. The other participants read the instructions again and saw that they should press the step button again.

A second problem occurred when the participants were finishing the active step, by tightening the last-added plate and placing the required corner pieces. During this step, the user is allowed to rotate the model to a position in which he can better reach it. The user however has to return the holder to the original position, before starting a new step. The stepper motor that is used in the movable platform does not know whether the platform rotated. This means that the tool assumes to execute rotations from the original position. The instructions in the tool do not explain this to the user, which is why three of the participants expected the platform to always rotate to the correct position. One of the participants did not rotate the platform at all because he expected that the platform should stay in its original position.

Questionnaire and Interview. Participants rated the overall experience of building a model with the robot arm positively (3x 4, 1x 5 on Q1). They all experienced the robot as helpful during the assembly (same ratings as Q1). Three out of four would use the setup again to build another model. The fourth participant would prefer not using the robot, but he saw potential for people with less technical knowledge or for children. This correlates with the answers to Q3: 1x 3, 2x 4, 1x 5. Participants generally agreed that the roles were clear in Q4 and Q5; only one rating of 3 for clarity of the human role, all other ratings were 4 or 5. No one experienced the system as too slow, when asked about it. One participant read the instructions and prepared for the next step while the robot was picking up the next plate. All the participants would use the design tool to design their own 3D model. One participant indicated that it would be easier than creating a 3D design from scratch using other CAD software.

All participants indicated that they sometimes had problems inserting a bolt into a hole, because the end effector was in the way. Especially on the smaller plates. A second problem that the participants indicated was with the very small bolts and nuts, which made it hard to tighten them. The problem was the most common in combination with the corner piece at a 45° angle. These corner pieces have little room left to insert the bolt or hold the nut in the right place. Some of the positions in which a corner piece had to be placed were hard to reach with your fingers, which also made it harder to attach the plate.

Summary of Results. The study that was executed was only a small one, but it still gave some valuable information. It showed that there is potential in using such a setup to aid users in building a model, even for more technical users. The way the robot arm and the movable platform work together to show the user how the model should be built, is helpful. One of the participants even indicated in the interview that he experienced it as building with a third hand.

The results of the user study indicate that the position of the robotic arm and the platform do not have to be perfect, as long as manual adjustments are possible. During the study, an early indication of problems associated with the assembly process occurred. Most of these problems can be fixed by improving the instructions and streamlining the build process. The participants provided insights in improvements that can be made to the tool and the process.

6   Discussion

The current prototype toolkit and the preliminary evaluation indicate the proposed approach is feasible. It is possible to generate all instructions for both maker and robot in a collaborative human-robot assembly process based on a 3D CAD model and an environment description. The resulting collaborative human-robot application is appreciated by potential users in the target group.

Fig. 4. The setup of an early prototype with the Arduino Braccio robot.

The results of the experiment indicate however that further work is needed to come to an intuitive walk-up-and-use version. This may require custom interaction possibilities, which can be provided through the envisioned inclusion of an interaction model. An example of a small change could be the addition of a soft button on the end effector of the robot that allows the maker to indicate that the robot no longer needs to hold the plate near the product under construction. This kind of interaction is similar to push interactions that are explored in industrial collaborative robot (cobot) applications. Cobots, however, typically have such sensors already built-in as part of their safety system.

The empirical results also indicate that requirements for speed and precision were met by the current prototype and cobots, which support higher speeds, more accurate movement, but at a much higher cost, may not be required to deploy robots in this specific type of application. It may even be possible to reconsider even cheaper robots, such as the Arduino Braccio, which was used for the creation of the initial, more basic, versions of the toolkit (Fig. 4).

The literature available on work instructions in the professional environment to address problems with the instructions for the makers may also be useful in this non-professional environment. Haug [5] proposed a framework for work instruction quality, while several studies are available that provide more information on which modalities can be best used to provide instructions. Funk et al. [4] evaluated some alternative modalities from which projection seemed to be most promising, but the main drawback in the study of e.g. a tablet solution may be less relevant in the current setting.

7 Conclusion

We presented a toolkit that contributes a new approach to program robots. It complements existing approaches that allow programming by demonstration with direct robot manipulation or without, tangible programming, mobile programming, or use of end-user programming languages such as Scratch. The approach embeds the programming of a human-robot collaboration activity within activities that the robot users naturally perform as part of their activities.

The tool may benefit from additional refinement: improved presentation of instructions as well as integration of an interaction model. The results obtained with this minimal effort approach are promising. Definitive conclusions on the viability of such approaches are however subject to further research. While the presented approach naturally fits the use of robots in assembly applications, the overall idea may even be applied in other domains, such as social robotics.

Acknowledgements. This research was partially supported by Flanders Make, the strategic research centre for the manufacturing industry. We thank the reviewers for their constructive comments.

References

1. Baizid, K., et al.: IRoSim: Industrial Robotics Simulation Design Planning and Optimization platform based on CAD and knowledgeware technologies. Robot. Comput. Integr. Manuf. **42** (2016). https://doi.org/10.1016/j.rcim.2016.06.003
2. Van den Bergh, J., Luyten, K.: Dice-R: defining human-robot interaction with composite events. In: Proceedings of the ACM SIGCHI Symposium on Engineering Interactive Computing Systems, pp. 117–122, EICS 2017. ACM, New York (2017). https://doi.org/10.1145/3102113.3102147

3. Duelen, G., Bernhardt, R., Schreck, G.: Use of CAD-data for the off-line programming of industrial robots. Robotics **3**(3), 389–397 (1987). https://doi.org/10.1016/0167-8493(87)90055-6
4. Funk, M., Kosch, T., Schmidt, A.: Interactive worker assistance: comparing the effects of in-situ projection, head-mounted displays, tablet, and paper instructions. In: Proceedings of the 2016 ACM International Joint Conference on Pervasive and Ubiquitous Computing, pp. 934–939, UbiComp 2016. ACM, New York (2016). https://doi.org/10.1145/2971648.2971706
5. Haug, A.: Work instruction quality in industrial management. Int. J. Ind. Ergon. **50**, 170–177 (2015). https://doi.org/10.1016/j.ergon.2015.09.015
6. Mateo, C., Brunete, A., Gambao, E., Hernando, M.: Hammer: an android based application for end-user industrial robot programming. In: 2014 IEEE/ASME 10th International Conference on Mechatronic and Embedded Systems and Applications (MESA), pp. 1–6. IEEE (2014). https://doi.org/10.1109/MESA.2014.6935597
7. Neto, P., Mendes, N.: Direct off-line robot programming via a common CAD package. Robot. Auton. Syst. **61**(8), 896–910 (2013). https://doi.org/10.1016/j.robot.2013.02.005
8. Neto, P., Mendes, N., Araújo, R., Norberto Pires, J., Paulo Moreira, A.: High-level robot programming based on CAD: dealing with unpredictable environments. Ind. Robot Int. J. **39**(3), 294–303 (2012). https://doi.org/10.1108/01439911211217125
9. Orendt, E.M., Fichtner, M., Henrich, D.: Robot programming by non-experts: intuitiveness and robustness of one-shot robot programming. In: 2016 25th IEEE International Symposium on Robot and Human Interactive Communication (RO-MAN), pp. 192–199. IEEE (2016). https://doi.org/10.1109/ROMAN.2016.7745110
10. Paxton, C., Hundt, A., Jonathan, F., Guerin, K., Hager, G.D.: CoSTAR: instructing collaborative robots with behavior trees and vision. In: 2017 IEEE International Conference on Robotics and Automation (ICRA), pp. 564–571. IEEE (2017). https://doi.org/10.1109/ICRA.2017.7989070
11. Pedersen, M.R., Krüger, V.: Gesture-based extraction of robot skill parameters for intuitive robot programming. J. Intell. Robotic Syst. **80**(1), 149–163 (2015). https://doi.org/10.1007/s10846-015-0219-x
12. Quigley, M., et al.: Ros: an open-source robot operating system. In: ICRA Workshop on Open Source Software, vol. 3, p. 5 (2009)
13. Resnick, M., et al.: Scratch: programming for all. Commun. ACM **52**(11), 60–67 (2009). https://doi.org/10.1145/1592761.1592779
14. Sefidgar, Y.S., Agarwal, P., Cakmak, M.: Situated tangible robot programming. In: Proceedings of the 2017 ACM/IEEE International Conference on Human-Robot Interaction, HRI 2017, pp. 473–482. ACM, New York (2017). https://doi.org/10.1145/2909824.3020240

Usability Evaluation of Model-Driven Cross-Device Web User Interfaces

Enes Yigitbas[1(✉)], Anthony Anjorin[1], Ivan Jovanovikj[1], Thomas Kern[2],
Stefan Sauer[1], and Gregor Engels[1]

[1] Paderborn University, Zukunftsmeile 1, 33102 Paderborn, Germany
{enes.yigitbas,anthony.anjorin,ivan.jovanovikj,
stefan.sauer,gregor.engels}@upb.de
[2] Diebold Nixdorf AG, Heinz-Nixdorf-Ring 1, 33106 Paderborn, Germany
thomas.kern@dieboldnixdorf.com

Abstract. User Interface (UI) development is a challenging task as modern UIs are expected to be available across a wide range of diverse platforms while assuring high usability for heterogeneous users. Model-driven engineering principles have been applied in the context of multi-device and cross-device UI development to tackle complexity in development. While previous work related to usability evaluation of model-driven UIs primarily focused on single- and multi-device UIs, an investigation of the usability of model-driven cross-device UIs was not fully covered yet. In this paper, therefore, we present a model-driven UI development (MDUID) approach for cross-device UIs and analyze whether the applied MDUID approach has a positive impact on the usability of the generated UI. To accomplish this, we conduct a usability evaluation based on the generated UI for a cross-channel banking web application. The usability evaluation results provide detailed feedback regarding fulfillment of different usability criteria and enable improvement of involved models as well as model transformations.

Keywords: Model-driven UI development · Usability
Cross-device UIs

1 Introduction

Nowadays users are surrounded by a broad range of networked interaction devices (e.g. smartphones, smartwatches, tablets, terminals etc.) for carrying out their everyday activities. The number of such interaction devices is growing, new possible interaction techniques are emerging and modern UIs are expected to be available across a wide range of diverse platforms.

In the context of our research and development project with our industrial partner Diebold Nixdorf AG[1], we have focused on the development of cross-device user interfaces that can span across various platforms and support a cross-channel banking experience.

---

[1] https://www.dieboldnixdorf.com.

© IFIP International Federation for Information Processing 2019
Published by Springer Nature Switzerland AG 2019
C. Bogdan et al. (Eds.): HCSE 2018, LNCS 11262, pp. 231–247, 2019.
https://doi.org/10.1007/978-3-030-05909-5_14

Figure 1 shows the underlying example scenario where cross-device UIs are used in the context of a cross-channel banking web application. The idea is that banking services are accessible through different channels and depending on the situation, customers can access the service through any channel they wish to use. For example, if the customers pursue a cross-channel interaction for a payment cashout process, they can begin an interaction using one channel (*Prepare Cashout* at *Desktop-PC* at home), modify the transaction on their way on a mobile channel (*Edit Cashout* via *Smartphone*), and finalize it at the automatic teller machine (*ATM*). As the described scenario covers different devices with varying platform properties and interaction techniques, each target platform has specific needs regarding its UI. Especially the target platform *ATM* has different hardware capabilities. In the example scenario, the coupling between *Smartphone* and *ATM* can be established through *Authorization via NFC* technology or via the classical way using a banking card (*Authorization via Card*). For authentification, an eye-tracker is integrated into the ATM where the customer can enter a password by gazing at predefined password symbols (*Authentification via VisualPin*).

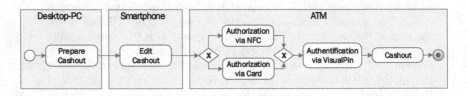

Fig. 1. Example scenario

As the motivational example scenario indicates, UI development is a challenging task due to the trade-off between efficiency and usability: creating different UIs available across various devices while assuring high usability for heterogeneous users.

In the past, model-driven user interface development (MDUID) approaches were proposed to support efficient development of UIs. Widely studied approaches are UsiXML [8], MARIA [15], and IFML [3] that support the abstract modeling of user interfaces and their transformation to final user interfaces. Although those MDUID approaches increase the efficiency and consistency in the generation of multiple UI variants, existing usability studies show that completely automated approaches are not optimal in terms of the quality regarding the usability of the UI [2].

As usability is an important criterion for user acceptance and user experience of interactive systems, usability issues have to be taken into account when developing multiple variants of a UI, especially for a cross-device usage scenario as in our case. Therefore, a proper investigation of applying MDUID for cross-device UIs and its impact on the usability of the generated UI is essential to identify usability problems and determine whether acceptance by the user is given.

While previous work in the context of usability evaluation of model-driven UIs covered single- [1] and multi-device [2] UIs, our goal is to investigate the usability of generated cross-device UIs. In this regard, our analysis focuses on the usability evaluation of model-driven cross-device UIs and the user's perception of the cross-device interaction based on our MDUID approach. By conducting a usability evaluation experiment with different users, we aim to understand current limitations of our MDUID approach for cross-device UIs and identify improvement potential.

The remaining sections of this paper are organized as follows: Sect. 2 presents our model-driven cross-device UI development approach. In Sect. 3, we describe the setup of our usability evaluation study and present the main results. Related work is presented in Sect. 4 and finally Sect. 5 concludes the paper and gives an outlook on future work.

2   Model-Driven Cross-Device UI Development Approach

In this section, we recapture our approach for model-driven cross-device UI development from previous work [17] and show its application for the motivated cross-channel banking scenario.

2.1   MDUID Approach for Cross-Device UIs

An overview of our model-driven cross-device UI development approach is depicted in Fig. 2. The model-driven development process for cross-device UIs is divided into three phases. In the first phase, *Modeling*, a *Domain Model* described as a UML class diagram and an *Abstract UI Model* based on the Interaction Flow Modeling language (IFML)[2], serve as specification of the data entities as well as structure, content and navigation needed to characterize the UI in an abstract manner.

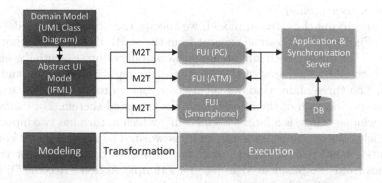

Fig. 2. Model-driven cross-device UI development approach

---

[2] http://www.ifml.org/.

The second phase, *Transformation*, deals with the automated transformation of the *Abstract UI Model* to different final UI (*FUI*) representations for the varying target platforms PC, ATM and Smartphone. For this purpose, several model-to-text transformation *(M2T)* templates were defined that transfer the *Abstract UI Model* to the *final UIs*.

The last phase, *Execution*, is dedicated to executing the heterogeneous UI views on different target platforms. For this purpose, a common UI framework can be used were data is exchanged between different platforms/channels. In order to support a seamless handover between channels and allowing task-continuity for the user, our approach includes an *Application and Synchronization Server*, which is responsible for storing and sharing of data (e.g. UI state or user preferences). The UI state, including entered input data by the users, is stored and restored, allowing users to move across channels while seamlessly continuing their tasks.

2.2   Application of the Approach

In the following, we describe how the above described model-driven approach was applied to the motivated example scenario (see Fig. 1) for generating cross-device UIs for the cross-channel web application.

Based on the existing IFML Editor Eclipse plugin[3], developers are able to specify the domain and abstract UI model.

In Fig. 3 an excerpt of the specified domain model is shown in form of a UML class diagram. The depicted domain model covers main concepts and relations to represent a banking application. In our example case, each *User* of the cross-channel banking web application has at least one account. To each account any number of a *BankCard* and *Transaction* are assigned. A transaction includes the respective attributes like date, amount of money, balance etc. Each transaction can in turn be detailed in form of a *Denomination* describing the specific banknotes that are wished to be withdrawn. The enumeration on the right side of the domain model show possible expressions for certain data types, such as bank card type or user profile.

After specifying the domain model, we specify the abstract UI model based on IFML. Figure 4 shows a small excerpt from the IFML model that is characterizing the UI for our cross-channel banking web application. Essentially, one can see the abstract UI modeling of the masks for the registration, login, and main windows. The three main windows themselves contain more elements to enable a detailed specification of the interaction objects nested therein. For example in the login window, there is a form "LoginForm", which in turn has two input fields (SimpleField) for entering username and password. The *LoginWindow* contains also events - (shown in a circle) - such as *"Register"* or *"Log in"* for triggering actions from the business logic (see for example Action *"Register"*). If you follow the event *"Register"* in the login window, the corresponding navigation

---

[3] http://ifml.github.io.

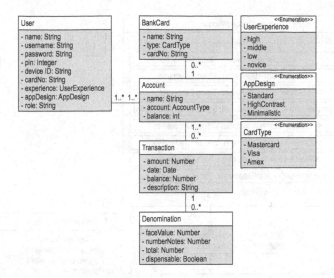

Fig. 3. Excerpt of the domain model for the cross-channel banking application

edge follows to the registration window. In a similar way, the other masks *"RegistrationWindow"* and *"MainWindow"* are modeled to specify the abstract UI model.

The specified domain model and the IFML model serve as input for our code generator to transform them to the specific final UIs for the varying platform. For transforming these models into final web UI views, we implemented an Xtend[4] plugin that maps the IFML model elements to specific HTML5 elements. The Xtend plugin includes different Xtend templates to transfer the IFML source model into web UIs supporting manifold devices. During the transformation process, the application's view is built upon basic components with a custom look & feel, like buttons, text input fields, dropdown lists, tables, etc. As a basis for these components, we implemented components based on the *HTML5 Web Components*[5] specification promoted by Google as W3C standard. Our custom components are sensitive to the application environment they are being used in (desktop, mobile, ATM) and adapt themselves accordingly. On mobile devices, for example, buttons are larger and more suitable for touch operation than on desktop devices. During the execution phase, the generated web views build up a HTML5/JavaScript single-page application running in a web browser. It exchanges JSON messages with the back-end server through HTTP/REST. The back-end server is implemented in JavaScript and uses Node.js[6] as its runtime environment. It is built upon Google's V8 JavaScript engine also used by Google Chrome and provides a high-performance runtime environment for non-blocking and event-driven programming. In order to support task continuity and

---

[4] http://www.eclipse.org/xtend.

[5] https://www.w3.org/TR/components-intro.

[6] https://nodejs.org.

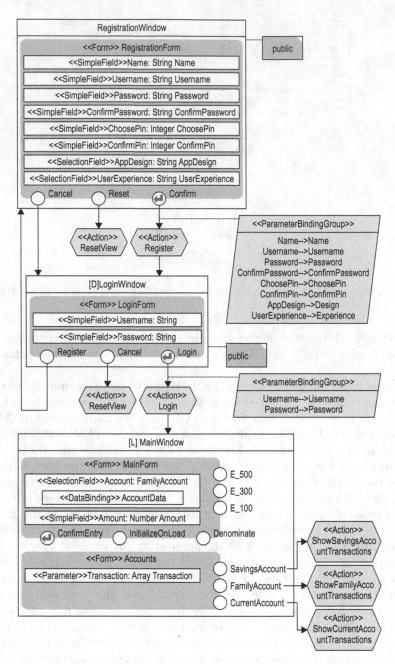

Fig. 4. Excerpt of the IFML model for cross-channel banking application

transfer application state between devices, the current state name and its associated context are saved to the Application & Synchronization Server. Inside a view controller and prior to saving a state, all context information necessary for recovery is added to a state-context object. This includes the UI's view-model, as well as any other necessary information associated with the current state. To invoke a previously saved state, the application just needs to retrieve the current state name and invoke it.

Figure 5 shows the different generated final UIs for our cross-channel banking web application. To be more specific, the *MainWindow* for the cash withdrawal process is shown for each involved device Desktop, Smartphone and ATM.

More technical details regarding the transformation and execution phases can be found in our previous work [17] where we present used technologies, languages and frameworks for the generation and execution phases in more detail.

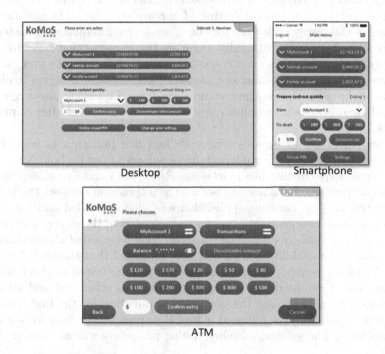

Fig. 5. Generated UIs for different device types

3   Usability Evaluation

While the previous section recapitulated our existing solution for model-driven cross-device UI development and showed its application in the context of a cross-channel banking application, the main goal of the paper is to analyze the usability of such a generated cross-device user interface.

Therefore, in the course of our industrial research project we conducted a usability test to assess the quality of model-driven cross-device web UIs. The goal was to evaluate how well or poorly the generated cross-channel banking web application called "KoMoS" and its user interface performed, and how satisfied the users were in completing two withdrawal tasks, one based on the classical way using a single access point on the ATM and one based on a cross-device usage scenario. In this section, we first describe the setting and procedure of our usability study. After that, we present the results of our usability study measured in terms of effectiveness, efficiency and satisfaction as suggested in ISO 9241-11 [7].

3.1   Setup Usability Study

We set up a usability laboratory at Diebold Nixdorf AG to conduct the usability test. Figure 6 shows the general setting of our usability lab. The usability test area contains the involved devices for the cross-device interaction: *Desktop-PC*, *Smartphone*, and *ATM*. Additionally, there are two cameras that serve to record the user interaction with the overall system. *Camera A* focuses the user, to track user behavior (facial expressions, gestures, etc.) and *Camera B* serves to observe the input of the user. Beside the test area, we have a question answering area, where participants answer an online questionnaire using a tablet after completing their task.

The test involved 15 persons where we had five participants from Paderborn Universities (mainly CS students), five employees from Diebold Nixdorf AG (from different departments like marketing, R&D, etc.) and five elderly persons where two of them lived in a nursing home. The interaction between the user and the generated KoMoS banking application was video-recorded and logged. An instructor and one independent observer participated in the study. The instructor interacted with the user while the observer took a record of observations and assisted during the usability test. Users were informed that the usability of the generated KoMoS banking application was going to be tested to check whether the system met their needs. No pretask training was scheduled and all of the participants were going to see the generated application for the first time. The design of the usability test followed a logical sequence of events for each user and across tests. The general usability testing procedure was as follows:

- Users were given information about the goals of the test and the setup of the usability laboratory. They were also informed about the video recording for analysis purposes.
- Users were given a series of clear instructions that were specific for the test. They were advised to try to accomplish the tasks without any assistance, and that they should only ask for help if they felt unable to complete the task on their own. Users should also use the think-aloud technique while accomplishing the task, so that possible usability problems could be analyzed.
- Users were asked to complete two different types of tasks. The first task was to withdraw a predetermined amount of money from the ATM - a classical

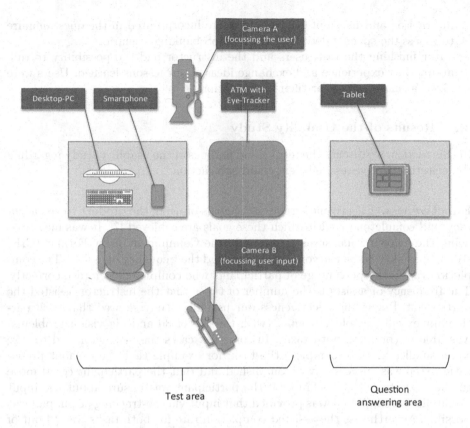

Fig. 6. Usability setting

cashout at the ATM using a bank card and PIN. For this task, the participants received a bank card with the corresponding PIN. The second task was to withdraw money based on the cross-device interaction scenario, so the users had to start preparing a cashout at the Desktop-PC, edit the cashout at the smartphone and finalize it at the ATM. For avoiding a possible ceiling effect, there was no time limit to complete the tasks.
– Users were then asked to fill in an online questionnaire after completing the last task. This questionnaire is arranged in a hierarchical format and contains: (1) a demographic questionnaire which is used to confirm their age, job description and gender. They also scored their attitude towards technology usage and especially their experience with the involved device types. (2) several measures of specific interface factors based on the IsoMetrics questionnaire [4] for the evaluation of graphical user interfaces (ISO 9241/10). Each item of this questionnaire is rated on a scale from one to seven with positive statements on the right side and negative statements on the left side. Additional space that allows the users to make comments is also included in the questionnaire. (3) Additional specialized questions regarding cross-device

interaction and usage of eye-tracking were incorporated in the questionnaire
to assess the specific details of the KoMoS banking scenario.

- After finishing the test, users and the instructor had the possibility to talk
  about their experience and exchange ideas about lessons learned. Users were
  given a small reward for their participation.

3.2   Results of the Usability Study

In this section, we discuss the results and findings of the usability study regarding
the criteria effectiveness, efficiency and satisfaction.

Effectiveness. Effectiveness relates the goals of using the product to the accuracy and completeness with which these goals are achieved [7]. It was measured
using the following measures proposed in the Common Industry Format (CIF)
[16] for usability tests: the completion rate and the frequency of assists. The completion rate is the percentage of participants who completed each task correctly.
The frequency of assists is the number of times that the instructor assisted the
participant. Regarding effectiveness our usability study showed that each participant except one older woman (with the age of 86 and big vision problems)
was able to complete both tasks. In some few cases the instructor had to give
some smaller hints to complete the task: for example that the cashout preparation step was successfully accomplished and that the participant could move
to the next step at the ATM or if the participant was unsure about the input
possibilities a small hint was provided that input via eye-tracking or pin pad was
possible. Nevertheless the assisted completion rate for both tasks was 14 out of
15 participants.

Some observed usability problems regarding effectiveness:

- Layout/Design: The denomination dialogue which supports the selection of
  specific banknotes during the withdrawal process was not intuitive for all
  users. Some of the elderly participants for example clicked directly on the
  banknote symbols (which were inactive by construction) instead of the "+"
  Symbol for selecting specific banknotes. Furthermore the structure of the
  menu was not optimal for some users. Although the most important functions
  were directly accessible, some participants needed more time to get used to
  the menu and the different button types which were used in the KoMoS
  banking application.
- System Feedback: The participants missed at some points in the system dialog
  feedback from the system which helps them to know about the next steps.
  For example, some of the users were not sure after preparing the cashout on
  the smartphone if they have finished this task. Furthermore, the users wished
  feedback on possible input techniques. As we have different input methods
  (Pin-Pad, Touchscreen and Eye-Tracker on the ATM) they were not sure
  when to use which input method.

– Difficulty with operating the application via eye-tracking: The users were not familiar with controlling an application via eye-tracking. So different questions arose: Where can one look without causing a wrong entry? How long I have to gaze at a specific UI element (symbol) to select it?

Efficiency. Efficiency relates to the resources expended in relation to the accuracy and completeness with which users achieve goals [7]. For the evaluation of the efficiency, the required time for the different two tasks was measured. Table 1 shows a comparison between the needed time for accomplishing both tasks. For accomplishing the classical cashout process using the generated KoMoS banking application only on the ATM, the participants needed approximately 64 s in average. Compared to this reference scenario the completion of the task in the cross-device scenario takes approximately 135 s in average. In this regard, we should notice that the classical cahout process is a common known activity for all participants (although the used app is new). In contrast, most of the users were not very familiar with the cross-device scenario where different devices and interaction techniques were involved. Nevertheless, in the cross-device scenario we can observe that the needed time for finalizing the withdrawal process at the ATM takes only approximately 46 s in average since the transaction has been already prepared on the smartphone. The majority of the overall time with 135 s in average was needed for preparation at the smartphone (89 s in average). Thus, the stay at the ATM is reduced by about 25% by a cross-device interaction compared to the classical ATM cashout process. If we imagine that the preparation of the transaction on the smartphone is done in an idle time, this can be seen as a time saving.

Table 1. Efficiency: Comparison between ATM reference scenario and Cross-device scenario

Scenario	ATM	Smartphone	Total
Reference (ATM-only)	64 s	-	64 s
Cross-Device	46 s	89 s	135 s

Satisfaction. Satisfaction is defined as freedom from discomfort, and positive attitudes towards the use of the product [7]. For the evaluation of the satisfaction criteria, we measured and analyzed the questionnaire answers of the participants. As depicted in Fig. 7 the evaluation of the satisfaction criteria shows a positive feedback of the participants regarding the generated UI of the KoMoS banking application. In total average, the interaction with the UI received the score 5,2 out of 7 which is quite acceptable. While, participants especially honor the criteria like ease-of task handling, learnability or liquid usage across different device types, they also point out that some aspects like system feedback, personalization and adaptability are not optimally solved through the generated UI of the KoMoS banking application.

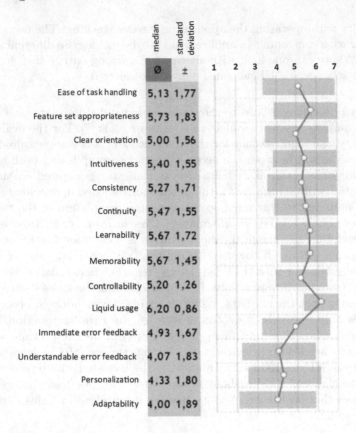

Fig. 7. General usability results regarding satisfaction criteria

The second part of the questionnaire covers specific aspects about the cross-device baking scenario. In this regard, user's satisfaction of the generated UI regarding authorization via card vs. smartphone (NFC), authentification via PIN vs. Eye-Tracking and the device switches were assessed based on questions. Figure 8 shows that there are not big differences in the authorization via card or smartphone regarding comfortability and quickness. However, the participants honor authorization via smartphone (NFC) as more hygienic. In contrast to that, classical authorization via bank card is perceived as more secure by the users. Regarding the both authentification types, the classical solution based on PIN entry is seen as more quick but rather unhygienic, while the Eye-tracking authentification takes longer but increases the satisfaction regarding hygiene as the users do not have to touch the Pin-Pad.

In summary, the usability evaluation results show that cross-device UIs automatically generated based on our model-driven approach are accepted by the majority of the users. The high rate of effectiveness for both tasks indicates that it is possible to automatically generate the UI for a cross-channel application scenario with the needed functionality. However, detailed feedback regarding

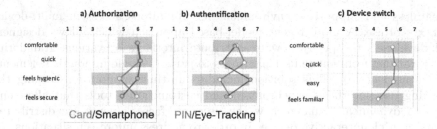

Fig. 8. Usability results regarding specific aspects

satisfaction and user comments also show that there is improvement potential. Especially the aspects layout design, system feedback, personalization and adaptability show potential for further improvements. In this connection, existing model-driven UI development approaches have to be incorporated with explicit modeling and transformation techniques for better supporting user assistance and adaptation.

4   Related Work

In recent years, a number of approaches have addressed the problem of UI development for multi-device and cross-device user interfaces. While there are several existing approaches in this direction, the number of usability evaluation studies focusing on UIs generated based on a model-driven approach is limited to a few examples. In this section, we especially review prior work that explores the development of multi-/cross-device user interfaces and usability evaluation of model-driven user interfaces.

4.1   Multi-/Cross-device UI Development Approaches

The development of multi-device UIs has been subject of extensive research [13] where different approaches were proposed to support efficient development of UIs for different target platforms. Model-based and model-driven UI development approaches were proposed to create multi-device UIs based on the transformation of abstract user interface models to final user interfaces. Widely studied approaches are UsiXML [8], MARIA [15], and IFML [3] that support the abstract modeling of user interfaces and their transformation to final user interfaces.

Previous work by the research community has also covered concepts and techniques for supporting the development of cross-device user interfaces. One of the concepts here is called UI migration, which follows the idea of transferring a UI or parts of it from a source to a target device while enabling task-continuity through carrying the UI's state across devices. In [14] for example, the authors present an agent-based solution to support migration of interactive applications among various devices, including digital TVs and mobile devices, allowing users to freely move around at home and outdoor. The aim is to provide users with a seamless and supportive environment for ubiquitous access in multi-device contexts of use. A more recent model-based approach which allows designers and developers to specify how to distribute interfaces at various granularity levels, ranging from entire user interfaces to parts of single interactive elements is presented in [10]. This solution includes run-time support for keeping the resulting user interfaces synchronized and customization tools that allow end users to dynamically change how the user interface elements are distributed across multiple interactive devices in order to address unforeseen situations.

In the case of web applications, most solutions rely on HTML proxy-based techniques to dynamically push and pull UIs [5]. An extension of this concept is presented in [12], where the authors propose XDStudio to support interactive development of cross-device UIs. In addition, there is also existing work on the specification support for cross-device applications. In [20] for example, the authors present their framework Panelrama which is a web-based framework for the construction of applications using distributed UIs. In a similar work [6], the authors present Conductor, which is a prototype framework serving as an example for the construction of cross-device applications.

4.2 Usability Evaluation Approaches

Due to the low number of usability evaluation studies existing for model-driven UIs and different scope of analysis criteria, it is very difficult to make comparisons among the existing usability evaluation approaches. In earlier work, Chesta et al. evaluated a multi-platform user interface generated by TERESA [11] according to several criteria: tool interface (intuitiveness, learnability), tool functionalities (completeness, developer satisfaction), final product obtained by employing the tool (user satisfaction, maintainability and portability), and approach cost/effectiveness (development efficiency, integrability). Their results suggest that the usage of the MDE approach improved some of these metrics compared to a manual approach where the user interface is manually produced.

Abrahao et al. [1] conducted an experimental study testing the usability of user interfaces that were automatically produced by MDE techniques. Based on their usability evaluation study the authors were able to identify main usability problems for the generated user interface. They argue that valuable feedback based on such experimental studies can be used to improve the used models and their transformation to final UIs. In this context, they also underline the concept of *usability proven by construction* as the insights from the usability study can be used for defining design guidelines or anti-patterns for developing highly usable UIs.

A further usability study for multi-device UIs generated by MDE techniques was presented by Aquino et al. [2]. The authors describe an MDE approach that generates multi-platform graphical user interfaces (e.g., desktop, web) that are subject to an exploratory controlled experiment. The usability of user interfaces generated for the two mentioned platforms and used on multiple display devices (i.e., standard size, large, and small screens) were examined in terms of satisfaction, effectiveness and efficiency. The results of the paper suggest that the tested

MDE approach should incorporate enhancements in its multi-device/platform user interface generation process in order to improve its generated usability.

While above mentioned approaches focus on the usability evaluation of generated UIs for single or multi-device platforms, our goal is to analyze usability of generated UIs across different devices. Therefore we especially take into account the perception of the users regarding the cross-device interaction. A similar usability evaluation approach to our study is presented in [9] where the authors introduce a cross-platform usability analysis model. While this approach provides a conceptual framework for analyzing usability of cross-device UIs, it does not focus on generated UIs using MDE techniques and also do not provide an experimental study in this regard.

5   Conclusion and Outlook

In this paper, we presented a usability study for cross-device user interfaces that were automatically generated based on a model-driven approach. We conducted a usability test with 15 different users based on a cross-channel banking web application to analyze strength and weaknesses in the usability of the generated cross-device UIs regarding effectiveness, efficiency and satisfaction. The usability evaluation results serve as an indicator to identify usability problems and can be used to further improve the existing model-driven UI development approach that was applied.

In ongoing work we are focusing on the usability evaluation of adaptive UIs that have been promoted as a solution for context variability due to their ability to automatically adapt to the context-of-use at runtime. Therefore, we have established a model-driven engineering approach [18] for adaptive UIs including an authoring environment [19] and design a suitable usability evaluation method for adaptive UIs.

Acknowledgement. This paper is based on some of the work within "KoMoS", a project of the "it's OWL" Leading-Edge Cluster, partially funded by the German Federal Ministry of Education and Research (BMBF). We also acknowledge the support of the project "Mittelstand 4.0" funded by the German Federal Ministry for Economic Affairs and Energy.

References

1. Abrahão, S., Iborra, E., Vanderdonckt, J.: Usability evaluation of user interfaces generated with a model-driven architecture tool. In: Law, E.L.-C., Hvannberg, E.T., Cockton, G. (eds.) Maturing Usability. HIS, pp. 3–32. Springer, London (2008). https://doi.org/10.1007/978-1-84628-941-5_1
2. Aquino, N., Vanderdonckt, J., Condori-Fernandez, N., Dieste, O., Pastor, O.: Usability evaluation of multi-device/platform user interfaces generated by model-driven engineering. In: Proceedings of the 2010 ACM-IEEE International Symposium on Empirical Software Engineering and Measurement (ESEM 2010) (2010)

3. Brambilla, M., Fraternali, P.: Interaction Flow Modeling Language - Model-Driven UI Engineering of Web and Mobile Apps with IFML. The MK/OMG Press, New York (2014)
4. Gediga, G., Hamborg, K., Duentsch, I.: The IsoMetrics usability inventory: an operationalisation of ISO 9241–10. Behav. Inf. Technol. **18**(1999), 151–164 (1999)
5. Ghiani, G., Paterno', F., Santoro, C.: Push and pull of web user interfaces in multi-device environments. In: Proceedings of the International Working Conference on Advanced Visual Interfaces (AVI 2012), pp. 10–17. ACM, New York (2012)
6. Hamilton, P., Wigdor, D.: Conductor: enabling and understanding cross-device interaction. In: Proceedings of the SIGCHI Conference on Human Factors in Computing Systems (CHI 2014), pp. 2773–2782. ACM, New York (2014)
7. International Organization for Standardization. ISO 9241–11: Ergonomic requirements for office work with visual display terminals (VDTs) - Part 9: Guidance on usability (1998)
8. Limbourg, Q., Vanderdonckt, J.: USIXML: a user interface description language supporting multiple levels of independence. In: Engineering Advanced Web Applications: Proceedings of Workshops in connection with the 4th International Conference on Web Engineering, pp. 325–338. Rinton Press (2004)
9. Majrashi, K., Hamilton, M., Uitdenbogerd, A.: Cross-platform usability and eye-tracking measurement and analysis model. In: Proceedings of the 26th Australian Computer-Human Interaction Conference on Designing Futures: The Future of Design (OzCHI 2014), pp. 418–421. ACM, New York (2014)
10. Manca, M., Paterno', F.: Customizable dynamic user interface distribution. In: Proceedings of the 8th ACM SIGCHI Symposium on Engineering Interactive Computing Systems (EICS 2016), pp. 27–37. ACM, New York (2016)
11. Mori, G., Paterno', F., Santoro, C.: Design and development of multidevice user interfaces through multiple logical descriptions. IEEE Trans. Softw. Eng. **30**(8), 507–520 (2004)
12. Nebeling, M., Mintsi, T., Husmann, M., Norrie, M.: Interactive development of cross-device user interfaces. In: Proceedings of the SIGCHI Conference on Human Factors in Computing Systems (CHI 2014) (2014)
13. Paterno', F., Santoro, C.: A logical framework for multi-device user interfaces. In: Proceedings of the 4th ACM SIGCHI Symposium on Engineering Interactive Computing Systems (EICS 2012), pp. 45–50. ACM, New York (2012)
14. Paterno', F., Santoro, C., Scorcia, A.: Ambient intelligence for supporting task continuity across multiple devices and implementation languages. Comput. J. **53**(8), 1210–1228 (2010)
15. Paterno', F., Santoro, C., Spano, L.D.: MARIA: a universal, declarative, multiple abstraction-level language for service-oriented applications in ubiquitous environments. ACM Trans. Comput. Hum. Interact. **16**(4), 19:1–19:30 (2009)
16. Scholtz, J.: Common industry format for usability test reports. CHI Extended Abstracts (2000)
17. Yigitbas, E., Kern, T., Urban, P., Sauer, S.: Multi-device UI development for task-continuous cross-channel web applications. In: Casteleyn, S., Dolog, P., Pautasso, C. (eds.) ICWE 2016. LNCS, vol. 9881, pp. 114–127. Springer, Cham (2016). https://doi.org/10.1007/978-3-319-46963-8_10
18. Yigitbas, E., Stahl, H., Sauer, S., Engels, G.: Self-adaptive UIs: integrated model-driven development of UIs and their adaptations. In: Anjorin, A., Espinoza, H. (eds.) ECMFA 2017. LNCS, vol. 10376, pp. 126–141. Springer, Cham (2017). https://doi.org/10.1007/978-3-319-61482-3_8

19. Yigitbas, E., Sauer, S., Engels, G.: Adapt-UI: an IDE supporting model-driven development of self-adaptive UIs. In: Proceedings of the ACM SIGCHI Symposium on Engineering Interactive Computing Systems (EICS 2017), pp. 99–104. ACM, New York (2017)
20. Yang, J., Wigdor, D.: Panelrama: enabling easy specification of cross-device web applications. In: Proceedings of the SIGCHI Conference on Human Factors in Computing Systems (CHI 2014), pp. 2783–2792. ACM, New York (2014)

Usability Evaluation and UI Testing

Absolute Indirect Touch Interaction: Impact of Haptic Marks and Animated Visual Feedback on Usability and User Experience

Regina Bernhaupt[1,2]([✉]), Dimitri Drouet[2], and Michael Pirker[2]

[1] Department of Industrial Design, Eindhoven University of Technology, Eindhoven, the Netherlands
r.bernhaupt@tue.nl
[2] Ruwido, Neumarkt am Wallersee, Austria
{Dimitri.Drouet,Michael.Pirker}@ruwido.com

Abstract. Goal of this paper is to investigate usability and user experience (UX) of a touch-based control of user interfaces that the user can not directly interact with. An example is a user controlling the television screen via a touch interaction on the remote control, or the driver of a car using touch to control the input on the steering wheel for the middle-console screen.

Based on a controlled within subject experiment investigating touch based interaction with and without a haptic mark we replicate findings on usability that it is significantly faster to complete a task with haptic marks on the touch area than without haptic marks. For user experience the dimensions of pragmatic quality and attractiveness were rated higher for touch input with a haptic landmark. The variation of user interface animations for target selection did not have a significant impact on user experience, showing that the tactile feedback is the most prominent factor to determine user experience.

The contribution concludes with a discussion how replication of studies must become part of user-centered design and development processes to handle the threat of outdated research due to technology change.

Keywords: User experience · Absolute touch input element · Usability Automotive · Interactive TV · Remote control

1 Introduction

Figure 1 shows an example of absolute indirect touch interaction: When changing the TV channel on the remote control, the area the user touches corresponds to the area on the user interface: if the finger is in the upper left corner, the upper left corner on the screen is selected. Once the finger is moved to the right one step, the corresponding element in the grid is selected. Using a haptic mark on the touch area allows the user to feel the position, without the need to look at the touch area. The finger position in this interaction is absolute, as moving one step to the right, moves one step to the right on the screen. The interaction itself is indirect as, evidently, the user is not touching directly the user interface, but touches the touch area of the control grid, to have an effect in the user interface.

© IFIP International Federation for Information Processing 2019
Published by Springer Nature Switzerland AG 2019
C. Bogdan et al. (Eds.): HCSE 2018, LNCS 11262, pp. 251–269, 2019.
https://doi.org/10.1007/978-3-030-05909-5_15

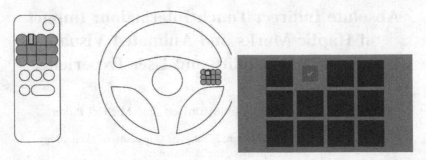

Fig. 1. The touch interaction element on a remote control (left) or on a driving wheel (middle). If the finger is positioned on the orange area, the related element on the screen (right, green arrow) is highlighted. When pushing the area, the item in the user interface is selected. (Color figure online)

The problem is that as touch technologies are changing and improving, it is important to verify if enhancements in the technology as well as the material still lead to the same impact on usability and how such novel touch concepts are perceived in terms of user experience (UX).

Main research question was to understand if usability effects like improvement of time taken for the completion of the task still holds, and what type of user experience is associated to such an interaction. In terms of UX enhancement a set of animations was investigated looking for possible improvements of UX. A controlled experiment was performed to answer these questions.

In the following, the article shows the current state of the art on touch interaction (that is indirect and/or absolute) in terms of usability. Then the method is described, followed by results and a discussion of the results. The article concludes by a more general discussion on how to change user-centered design and development processes to take into account the replication of findings based on technology change.

2   Related Work

2.1   Using Touch for Controlling User Interfaces via a Distance

Direct touch interaction on a screen is becoming a de-facto standard for interactive systems like mobile phones or tablets. While touch interaction with direct and immediate feedback on the area you touched is taken up quickly, the usage of touch to control elements on a distant screen is perceived as less usable [17]. While usability seems to be lower, industry [32] claims that using touch elements as control elements for interaction on a distant screen enhances user experience. Such elements of (technological novel) touch input for distant screens is currently considered for in-car systems for secondary driving tasks, for in-home applications like interactive TV and even for aircraft cockpits.

The traditional solution for any task including navigation, selection, or in general interaction with a visual display from a distance are buttons, knobs or sliders [32]. A recent trend is the incorporation of touch as means of interaction, ranging from using tablets to interact with large displays [1] to incorporating touch elements in cars, especially for secondary tasks while driving [34]. Touch interaction for distant screens or displays is different from the direct touch interaction known from mobile phones, tablets or touch screens, as the touch input is performed on an area dissociated from the output area, typically a distant screen.

For touch interaction on a distant screen there are in general two ways to map the user input to the movement on the distant screen: absolute and relative. Absolute mapping is defined as a homothetic correspondence between the position of a contact on the input surface and the position of an object on the output display [12]. In other words, it is a position-to-position and velocity-to-velocity mapping between the input and output device [18]. In contrast, relative mapping/pointing is the correspondence of the displacement on the input surface and the displacement of an object on the output display. It generally involves a non-linear transfer function to support fast movements over large distances and precise interactions with small objects [12]. Absolute pointing is claimed to be easier to learn [18], and to be more natural and convenient; however, absolute pointing also has disadvantages.

Absolute pointing could lead to parallax error [4], or perception error due the apparent shift of the interaction area against a background when the observer position is not aligned with the device. It could also lead to occlusion effects - when interacting, the finger, hand and/or arm can hide a part of the output device and can even totally occlude small targets [33]. Forlines et al. [11] report that absolute touch interaction is uncomfortable on large displays and/or during long use. Relative pointing is said to be less natural than absolute pointing and more difficult to learn, but on the contrary it allows speeding up the interaction as different transfer functions can support movement over longer distances [12].

Touch as interaction technique to interact with user interfaces on distant screens has been discussed controversially for different application domains, including the television [32], automotive [30] or aeronautic [15] domains.

Compared to other types of interactions, e.g. input elements like knobs, sliders or other forms with haptic feedback, a set of disadvantages is reported for touch interactions:

- Touch misses the dimension of immediate haptic feedback [37].
- Touch was reported to be less efficient [32] for selection and navigation tasks.
- Touch was reported to be less effective [32] for selection and navigation tasks.

On the other hand, touch interaction is increasing user experience, especially the overall hedonic quality and the user's need for novelty in a product or novelty of an interaction technique, compared to standard interactions like buttons [32].

2.2 Absolute Indirect Touch

Absolute indirect touch is the use of one-to-one mapping between a separated touch input device and a distant display.

Norman & Norman [25] compared the use of a Nintendo Wii Remote for a selection task in three different conditions. The first condition was absolute pointing using an infrared camera to detect the movement, the second one was stabilized absolute pointing using the camera coupled with a 6-axis accelerometer, and the last one was relative pointing using only the gyroscope. They conclude that the advantage of absolute pointing compared to relative pointing is its intuitiveness. However, in their study relative pointing showed better performance and users preferred relative pointing to absolute pointing. The intuitiveness stems from the direct mapping users learn during all their live. König et al. [18], who proposed a precision enhancing technique for absolute pointing devices, confirm the hypothesis that absolute pointing is a more natural and more convenient pointing experience, as it provides easier hand-eye coordination compared to relative pointing. However, König et al. pointed out the common problem shared by all absolute indirect pointing approaches, which is the missing precision - especially when using high resolution displays.

Gilliot et al. [12] investigated the influence of form factors on absolute indirect-touch pointing performance in two studies. In the first one, they compared two different screen sizes (196 × 147 mm, 66 × 50 mm) and two visual conditions (looking at the input device, not looking at the input device). They found that users get better performances when they can look at the input surface, and that scale does not affect user performance. In the second experiment, they compared several aspect ratios between the input and the output device, and they conclude that the same aspect ratio leads to better performance.

Pietrosek and Lank [31] investigated spatial correspondence between a smartphone screen and a projection screen to select targets. They investigated two different conditions. In the first one, the desired target was displayed on the projection screen and on the smartphone screen, while in the other condition the desired target was only displayed on the projection screen. They found out that error rate was 3.5% (of screen width) when the target was mirrored on the smartphone screen, while it doubled to around 6% when the target was only displayed on the distant screen.

Palleis and Hussmann [28] explored the effect of touch indirectness on spatial memory and navigation performance in a 2D panning task. Comparing direct absolute touch to indirect absolute touch, they found out that spatial memory performance is not decreased by a spatial separation of touch input gesture and visual display, and also that decreasing the size of the input surface increases navigation efficiency.

For the automotive domain, Sheik-Nainar et al. [34] compared three different touch interaction techniques for target selection for drivers in cars: direct absolute pointing, indirect absolute pointing and indirect relative pointing. Their study revealed comparable performance for absolute indirect touch and absolute direct touch in terms of efficiency, effectiveness, distraction, and user preferences. Compared to relative indirect input, absolute indirect input showed better performances, lower distraction and higher user ratings.

For interaction with large displays the ARC-Pad [22] is an indirect interaction technique for interacting with large displays using a mobile phone's touchscreen. It combines absolute and relative pointer positioning. Tapping with ARC-Pad roughly positions the cursor to the corresponding location on the distant screen, using an absolute mapping. Then the user can adjust the cursor location by sliding her finger on the touchscreen, using a relative mapping. This technique reduces clutching by half compared to a cursor acceleration technique.

2.3 Tactile and Visual Feedback in Touch Interaction

Bruke et al. [6] compared the effect of visual-auditory and visual-tactile feedback on user performance in a meta-analysis of 43 studies. They selected studies that reported at least one comparison between single modes and multimodal combinations, and that reported a measure of error rate, reaction time, and/or performance score outcome. They found that visual-tactile feedback provides a significant advantage over using a visual-only feedback system, and that visual-tactile feedback is particularly effective when multiple tasks are being performed, and under normal workload condition.

Another finding of this meta-analysis is that while multimodal feedback seems to enhance performance, improving performance scores and reducing reaction times, it has little or no effect on error rate.

Pasquero and Hayward [29] investigated the use of tactile feedback in the task of scrolling through a long list of items. They conducted a study with two different conditions - in the control condition, no tactile feedback was provided, while in the experimental condition, a short tactile feedback was provided when the user moves from an item to another, and a longer tactile feedback was provided every 10 items. They measured the frequency at which users needed to look at the screen. They observed an average reduction of 28% in the number of glances that the users required to complete a task with tactile feedback compared to the number of glances that the users required to complete a task without tactile feedback.

Treskunov et al. [36] investigate how haptic feedback affects the user experience of a touchpad-based television remote. They conducted two user studies with two haptic prototypes. A pilot study with eight users, employing smartphones to simulate a directional touchpad, revealed that users preferred enabled haptic feedback. Encouraged by the results, they conducted a second study. In this study they use a touch remote control coupled with a Linear Resonant Actuator on the back of the remote. They compared three haptic conditions (5 ms, 25 ms, No Haptic). They did not find significant effects on time, error, or ratings. However, at the end of the study users were asked to choose which haptic condition they preferred, and although some participant did not make any distinction between the 5 ms and the 25 ms conditions, eight of the nine participants preferred haptic feedback over no haptic feedback.

HaptiCase [9] is an interaction technique for smartphones that provides back-of-device tactile marks that users sense to estimate the position of her finger in relation to the touchscreen. By pinching the thumb to a finger at the back, the finger location is transferred to the front as the thumb touches the touch screen. The study revealed that users were more accurate for eyes-free indirect typing with HaptiCase compared to having no tactile marks. The second study investigated the impact of tactile targeting on visual targeting, when both targeting strategies are combined. Users where both faster and had a lower offset to the target when being able to look at the input device compared to when they could not look at the input device. Guerreiro et al. [13] attached tactile marks on mobile devices' touch screens to guide blind people's interactions. It showed positive effects on the acquisition of targets on screen, and it was perceived as helpful by users.

2.4   Animations

Early work by Disney [35] shows that Animations affect user experience in general. Chevalier et al. [8] revisited the pioneer work of Baecker and Small [2] about the place of animation in interfaces. They concluded that user experience is the most important aspect for using animations. Merz et al. [23] investigated how different animation principles for animated transitions in mobile application influence the perceived user experience. They conducted a pilot study in which they compared three different animation styles: slow in and slow out, exaggeration, and linear. The results of this pilot study showed a tendency that animation style could affect the perception of UX.

2.5   Research Overview

Table 1 gives an overview on current literature related to the dimensions absolute and relative mapping, direct and indirect mapping and is complemented by the categories visual feedback, tactile feedback and animation. As highlighted with checkmarks, the contribution of this article is to understand how a combination of absolute indirect touch input with visual feedback and/or haptic feedback influences usability, and especially the overall user experience, as this dimension is not explored in the current literature.

Table 1. Overview on the state of the art summarizing contribution on touch research for usability and user experience. The highlight marks the contribution area of this article

	Effectiveness	Efficiency	Satisfaction	UX	Naturalness
Absolute mapping	[9, 12, 13, 18, 22, 25, 28, 29, 31, 34, 36]	[9, 12, 13, 18, 22, 25, 28, 29, 34, 36]	[13, 18, 22, 25, 28, 29, 34, 36]	[36]	[18]
Relative mapping	[22, 25, 34]	[22, 25, 34]	[22, 25, 34]	[36]	
Direct pointing	[9, 13, 28, 29]	[9, 13, 28, 29]	[9, 13, 28, 29]		
Indirect pointing	[9, 12, 18, 22, 25, 28, 31, 34, 36]	[9, 12, 18, 22, 25, 28]	[9, 18, 22, 25, 28, 34, 36]	[28]	Missing
Visual feedback	[6, 9, 12, 31]	[6, 9, 12]		Missing	Missing
Tactile feedback	[6, 9, 13, 29, 36]	[6, 9, 13, 29, 36]	[9, 11, 36]	Missing	Missing
Animation	[19]	[19]	[8, 19]	[8, 19, 23]	[7, 19]

3   The Problem of Touch Interaction with Haptic Marks

To support absolute touch interaction in situations where the screen is out of reach for the user, we developed a touch interaction element with haptic marks that can be applied in various contexts and domains, e.g. as an interaction element in the car to control secondary tasks while driving, in a cockpit for tasks where the pilot cannot reach the screen, or for standard applications like TV to be included in a remote control. Figure 1 shows some possible usages of such an absolute touch interaction element with haptic feedback.

Contrary to absolute touch elements mapping the touch input to the user interface one to one (1:1), this touch interaction element has a number of fixed areas that can be varied depending on the constraints and necessities for the different domains, mapping the area on the touch input field absolute to the fixed area on the user interface. The number of elements on the touch input depends on the application area. For tasks with high cognitive load and risk, like in cars [34], there are only 3 × 3 fields, while for areas with less cognitive load, or more entertainment oriented applications like the TV or interactions on large screens, there are more fields (e.g., 4 × 3, 3 × 4, or larger), see also Fig. 1.

The haptic marks support the user in achieving their goals by offering the opportunity to use them without having to look at them, as the haptic marks can easily be felt with the fingertips. As opposed to a flat touch area where the user has to evaluate the position of the pointer on the distant screen constantly, the haptic marks support ease of use, efficiency, and effectiveness by providing unobtrusive haptic feedback on the touchpad and simplify target acquisition on the distant screen.

General goal of this research is to focus on touch interaction as an input for distant displays, such as television screens, car displays or aircraft displays. Put simply, we aimed to investigate whether haptic feedback ("to feel"), visual feedback ("to see"), or a combination of both are more important to the user, and how this affects usability and UX.

3.1 Research Question and Hypothesis

The research questions were the following: (1) How does the presence or the absence of haptic marks influence usability of the system and affect user experience? And (2) How does the presence or absence of animated visual feedback influence the usability and the overall user experience?

Hypothesis 1 (flat vs haptic marks): There is a significant difference in terms of usability (efficiency, effectiveness, satisfaction) and user experience (naturalness, aesthetics, hedonic and pragmatic qualities) when using the flat touch interaction input element compared to using the touch interaction element with haptic marks.

Hypothesis 2a (visual feedback/no feedback): There is a significant difference in terms of usability (efficiency, effectiveness, satisfaction and naturalness) and user experience (naturalness, aesthetics, hedonic and pragmatic qualities) when using a system with animated visual feedback compared to using a system without visual feedback.

Hypothesis 2b (visual feedback with three different curves): There are significant differences in terms of user experience (naturalness, aesthetics, hedonic and pragmatic qualities) when using a system with animated visual feedback that uses ease in combined with easy out, a linear curve or only easy out.

3.2   Method, Participants and Procedure

A within-subject design was performed with 16 participants. The experiment consisted of two parts: in the first part of the experiment, the independent variables are the remote control and the feedback condition, while in the second part of the experiment, the independent variable consists of the type of animation used (cf. Tables 2 and 3). Both parts of the experiment collected data about usability and user experience metrics using measures through observation and logging, standard questionnaires, short semi-structured interviews upon completion of conditions, as well as short interviews at the end of the experiment.

Sixteen participants (14 male and 2 female), aged from 21 to 25 years (mean = 23, SD = 1.41) took part in the study. The sample was a convenience sample recruited via Facebook, mailing lists and personal contacts. In order to avoid biases caused by a missing familiarity with touch interaction, we recruited young people, as they are more likely familiar with touch interaction. All participants use a touch device at least several times a week, and own either a smartphone or use a tablet at home. All of the participants were right handed, with normal or corrected to normal vision, and no participant indicated to be color blind. Daily TV consumption ranged from no TV usage to up to 4 h – 2 participants indicated to never watch TV (12.5%), 6 participants watch less than 30 min a day (37.5%), one participant up to an hour (6.3%), 4 participants up to two hours (25%), one participant up to 3 h (6.3%), and 2 participants up to 4 h (12.5%).

Table 2. Conditions for the first part of the experiment based on the two independent variables

Independent variables	Values	Descriptions
Type of touchpad	With haptic marks	12 distinct debossed areas
	Flat	No distinction between the areas, flat touch area
Visual feedback	With visual feedback	Highlighting of tiles on touch. Downscaling of tiles on press.
	Without visual feedback	Control Condition

Table 3. Second system's independent variables & values for the second part of the experiment

Independent variable	Values	Descriptions
Animation curve	Ease In / Ease Out	Animation is slowed down at the beginning and the end, and sped up in-between
	Linear	Speed of the animation is constant the entire time
	Ease Out	Animation will speed up at the beginning and slow down at the end

The daily smartphone usage ranged from no usage to more than 4 h a day – one participants stated to not use a smartphone (6.3%), 2 participants use it up to an hour (12.5%), 4 persons use it up to 1.5 h a day (25%), another four persons use it up to 3 h (25%), while one person uses it up to 4 h (6.3%). Finally, 4 persons indicated that they use their smartphone for more than 4 h every day (25%).

3.3 System Information

In order to evaluate the touch element with haptic marks, two remote controls where produced: one included a standard touch interaction pad, while the other included haptic marks. Figure 2 shows the two remote controls used in the experimentation. The driver software for both remote controls is identical, and both touch areas, regardless of the haptic marks, send information in a 12 byte array (for a 3 times 4 grid). Each byte indicates how close the finger of the user is to the sensor on a scale from 0 to 255 for the given area – this allows interpolating the position of the user's finger on the touch grid. The only difference between the two remote controls is that the sensors of the flat touch area are slightly more sensitive to account for the differences in the height of the touch area without the recessed haptic marks: this implies the same sensor sensitivity for both remote controls.

Fig. 2. Touch interaction element with haptic marks integrated in a remote control (left) and without haptic marks (right)

The user interface prototype consists of a page with 12 tiles (4 columns, 3 rows). During the experimentation dots appear pseudo randomized on the tiles. Users have to click on the corresponding area of the remote to select the indicated tile. Correct selections are indicated with a green checkmark, incorrect selection with a red cross on the item. Figure 3 shows the user interface for the different conditions.

Fig. 3. User Interface with correct selection (left) and incorrect selection (right)

For the second part of the experiment, the user interface (UI) consisted simply of twelve areas with a set of TV channels (see Fig. 4 below) and images simulating a TV channel displayed in the background.

Fig. 4. User interface with twelve areas showing TV channels

3.4   Material

In the first part of the experiment, two versions of the prototypical UI were tested in order to provide two different feedback types for the condition that offers visual feedback within the user interface. The condition with feedback offered two visual clues for the interaction, which were a highlight of the corresponding tile in the UI when an area of the remote control was touched, as well as a temporary downscaling of the corresponding tile in the UI when an area of the remote control was pressed. The condition without feedback did not offer this visual feedback.

The tiles in the UI have a square shape and occupy the maximum space on the screen, taking into account the gaps at the border and between two tiles (see Fig. 3).

The background of the prototype is medium gray, the tiles are black with a different opacity whether they are highlighted or not, and the dots are white. This choice of color was made to avoid any biases related any types to color blindness. The contrast between the dot and a tile is important (above 50%) even if the tile is selected.

For the second part of the study, the UI only changed in terms of animations used (see Table 3). A variation of the remote control with haptic marks was used, enhanced by two buttons (left/right) that allowed changing pages within the grid.

The experiment was conducted in a usability lab that resembles a living room. The room is equipped with a 40 inch TV with 4 k resolution, two sofas, and a coffee table. Two cameras recorded each session, one behind the user to have an 'over-the-shoulder' view of the interaction with the remote control and capture the use of the remote control, and the second one below the TV in front of the user to capture the facial expressions and posture of the user. The prototypical user interfaces used in the study were running on a small form factor computer behind the television to give the participants the impression that they are using a normal TV with a set-top box.

The experiment started with an introduction about the general goal of the study, followed by a demographic questionnaire that investigated the media consumption habits of the participants and a short pre-interview. Subsequently, participants were introduced to the user interface, and were asked to perform tasks – the selection of dots on the tiles of the UI for the four experimental conditions in the first part of the experiment, and the selection of specific channels in the UI for the three experimental conditions in the second part of the experiment. The experiment used a within-subjects design, where each participant evaluated all four conditions for remote control and feedback in the first part of the study, and the three different conditions for the animations in the second part of the study. Condition order was randomized and counterbalanced within the sample, and each evaluation sessions lasted about 45 min.

For each task in each condition, task completion rate, task completion time, and number of errors were collected. After each condition, participants were asked for ratings regarding the ease of use of the system, how comfortable it is to use the system, how natural the use of the system was perceived by the user, how accurate the remote control was perceived, how smooth the interaction with the system was, how responsive the system was, and how pertinent and suitable the animations were for the given tasks. Additionally, the participants were filling in the SUS [5] questionnaire and the AttrakDiff questionnaire [16] after having completed the tasks for each condition.

After the two parts of the experiment, participants were asked which remote controls they preferred in terms of usage and in terms of design, as well as which one they perceived as more accurate in a closing interview. Test subjects did not receive any compensation for their participation.

Tasks

The selection task in the first part of the experiment consisted of a sequence of 24 dots that were randomly appearing on one of the 12 tiles of the user interface (two dots per tile per condition) that the participants needed to select as fast and as precise as possible. The procedure was repeated for each of the four experimental conditions (without visual feedback, and without haptic feedback (1); without visual feedback, and with haptic feedback (2); with visual feedback, and without haptic feedback (3); and with visual feedback, and with haptic feedback (4)).

The selection task in the second part of the experiment consisted of a sequence of eight channels that the user needed to select one after the other, again as fast and as precise as possible. The procedure was repeated for each of the three experimental conditions of the second part of the experiment (Ease In and Ease Out animation; Linear animation; Ease Out animation only).

4 Results

The data of the two parts of the experiment was analyzed with respect to the experimental conditions and the underlying research hypotheses.

4.1 Impact of Haptic Marks and Visual Feedback on Usability

Usability: Task Completion Time

Haptic marks on the remote control have a significant influence on users' performance: when using the remote control with haptic marks, users were faster in terms of task completion (flat: mean = 00:02.29; haptic marks: mean = 00:01.30) which is statistically significant: a Mann-Whitney test indicated that task time was significantly faster for the remote control with haptic marks (Mdn = 00:01.00) than for the flat remote control (Mdn = 00:01.30; U = 194823,5 p = .000).

Providing visual feedback increases the task completion time from 00:01.55 to 00:02.03. A Mann-Whitney test indicated that task time was significantly faster for the No-Feedback condition (Mdn = 00:01.00) than for the Feedback condition (Mdn = 00:01.30; U = 206449, p = .000).

This is in line with previous findings that people tend to wait until the visual feedback is over, but feedback is important for such types of tasks in case of interruptions [6].

Usability: User Ratings of the Interaction

Haptic marks do furthermore significantly influence users' ratings and perceptions on the following dimensions: perceived speed, perceived likelihood for errors, perceived difficulty, comfort, naturalness, accuracy, smoothness and responsiveness. Table 4 gives an overview on these results.

Usability: Impact of Visual Feedback

The Feedback/No Feedback condition yielded significant results for perceived comfort (Mdn: 3 for no-feedback; Mdn: 2 for feedback), perceived naturalness (Mdn: 2 for no-feedback; Mdn: 1.5 for feedback), as well as pertinence of the animation (Mdn: 2.5 for no-feedback; Mdn: 1.0 for feedback), where the scale was ranging from 1 being best to 5 being worst. Additionally, also attractiveness scored significant results (Mdn:.71 for no-feedback; Mdn: 1.0 for feedback) on a scale from −3 (worst) to +3 (best).

The Feedback/No Feedback condition did not yield significant results for speed feeling, error rate feeling, perceived difficulty, perceived accuracy, perceived smoothness, perceived responsiveness, success percentage, and both hedonic quality identification as well as stimulation.

Interaction Effects

There was no statistically significant interaction effect between the feedback condition and the type of remote control used on the combined dependent variables, $F(14, 47) = 1.390$, $p = .196$; Wilks' $\Lambda = .707$.

Table 4. User ratings: mean value with/without haptic marks and description of the performed test. Mean on scale 1 to 5, 1 being best.

	Haptic, Mean (SD), N = 32	Non-Haptic, Mean (SD), N = 32	Mann-Whitney U, p (2-tailed)
Perceived speed	1.59 (.134)	2.69 (.176)	U = 210 p = .000
Perceived likelihood for errors	1.34 (.085)	3.06 (.185)	U = 97,5 p = .000
Perceived difficulty	1.47 (.090)	2.75 (.191)	U = 177,5 p = .000
Comfort	2.06 (.155)	2.91 (.192)	U = 292 p = .002
Naturalness	1.50 (.110)	2.69 (.187)	U = 196 p = .000
Accuracy	1.72 (.157)	3.28 (.181)	U = 132,5 p = .000
Smoothness	1.75 (.156)	1.94 (.195)	U = 477 p = .613
Responsiveness	1.47 (.142)	1.81 (.158)	U = 389 p = .065

4.2 Impact of Haptic Marks/Visual Feedback on User Experience

User Experience

A Kruskal-Wallis H test showed that there was a statistically significant difference in **pragmatic quality** as well as **attractiveness** between the different study conditions. No difference has been observed in the variables for perceived smoothness, perceived responsiveness, hedonic quality – identification, as well as hedonic quality - stimulation between the different study conditions (see Fig. 5 for AttrakDiff metrics for the different study conditions).

4.3 Impact of Animation Type

Statistical analysis compared usability and user experience metrics of the different animation conditions of the second part of the study. There were no significant differences in the scores for the usability and user experience metrics between the conditions 'Ease In /Ease Out', 'Linear', and 'Ease Out', except for error count between the 'Linear' and the 'Ease Out' condition which was significantly higher for the 'Linear' condition – Mann Whitney U = 88, N = 32, Z = -2.104, p = .035, r = .37. These results might also be biased by channel logos unfamiliar for the user, as most of the time, errors were related to confusing channel logos.

4.4 Final Interview

In the closing final interview, twelve of the sixteen participants stated they preferred the remote control with the haptic marks (75%), while four participants stated to prefer the flat remote control (25%).

Users were also asked whether they have perceived a difference between the test sessions of the second part of the experiment, where only the animation types changed between the tasks. The majority of participants (10 persons) indicated that they did not recognize differences, while 6 persons stated they perceived differences. The differences that the users observed were related to the speed (4 persons), the fluidity (1 person), and the change of the page on the UI (1 person).

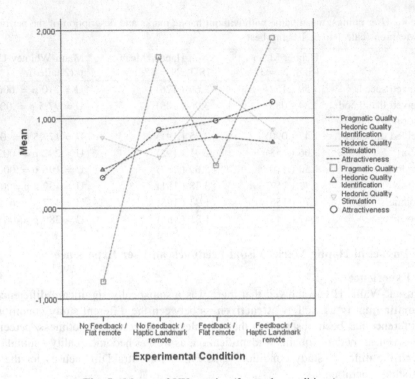

Fig. 5. Means of UX metrics (for study conditions)

Finally, participants were asked if they preferred one session over the others in the second part of the study. Seven of the 16 participants did not state any preferences four participants preferred the Ease In /Ease Out session, three persons preferred the Ease Out session, while two persons stated to prefer the Linear animation session.

5 Summary

Our study shows that using haptic marks significantly improves usability and some aspects of user experience. Usability indicators showed significantly better scores for the haptic landmark remote control (faster for task completion; higher perceived speed, lower perceived likelihood for error, lower perceived difficulty, more accurate, more responsive). These findings were supported by the ratings for pragmatic quality in the AttrakDiff questionnaire which were significantly better.

In terms of user experience the haptic marks influence the users' perceptions on comfort, naturalness and attractiveness. The sub-dimension hedonic quality of the AttrakDiff questionnaire with its sub-dimensions stimulation and identification did not yield significant results. A possible explanation is that the type of task is too narrow and the prototype user interface to limited in terms of functionality to allow the investigation of UX. In similar studies of interactive TV systems using a broader range of tasks we were able to show influences on UX by manipulation type of interaction technique [32].

Our second hypothesis regarding the influence of visual feedback on usability and user experience was limited verified. For the usability metrics, we did not observe significant differences between the feedback/no-feedback conditions except for the task time, which was significantly slower with feedback than without it, which is in line with previous findings that people tend to wait for animations to finish. Pragmatic quality in the AttrakDiff was close to being significant (.052), but not within the 95% confidence interval.

Concerning user experience, the visual feedback conditions did not yield significant differences regarding the hedonic quality dimension, which could be again explained by the fact that the type of task is too narrow and the prototype user interface to limited in terms of functionality to allow the investigation of UX, but we observed significant results for perceived comfort, perceived naturalness, as well as attractiveness. This indicates that visual feedback has a positive impact on some aspects of UX.

Variations in terms of animation speed curves during the second part of the experiment did not show significant differences in terms of usability or user experience. This could be explained by a selective perception bias. Users were asked to find channels without any information about changes in terms of animation. The majority of them were likely so focused on finding the right channels, that they did not realize the change of animation. This assumption is consistent with the final interviews, where the majority of participants stated that they did not observe differences between the three sessions, and also no clear favorite was noticeable when the participants were asked for their preferred session.

The results of our experiment suggest that touchpads enhanced with haptic marks are a possible solution to overcome current limitations of touch. It also indicates that even if visual feedback was not as significant as tactile feedback, it still has an impact on UX, and should be taken into account when it comes to absolute indirect touch interaction design.

We acknowledge that the mean age of our sample is quite young. This was chosen on purpose, as we were aiming for a high familiarity with touch devices and smartphones.

6 Discussion and Future Work

In Software engineering, processes have been tuned and adapted to take into account specific software qualities such as safety [3], reliability [21], learnability [20] or usability [26]. One issue with these contributions is that focusing on improving a specific property might damage other ones are they are usually conflicting [10]. Beyond, what is missing in all of these processes are clear indications of when and how to re-evaluate scientific findings, due to technology changes. For instance, while the process presented in [24] allows integrating evaluation results (through scenarios) into task models, the integration of a pure repetition of evaluations is not considered. This missing re-confirmation and replication of knowledge can be a threat for the scientific community. As user centered design and development (UCD) approaches require iterative design and detailed evaluation at each iteration step [14], it means that evaluators' work is not well supported as it is difficult to compare evaluation results from different UCD stages.

In this particular case it became clear that conflicting software properties like users judgment on usability and user experience were aligned, but that traditional approaches for enhancing the user experience (animations) did not impact the judgment of the users. Thus, an advancement in this field should look more on the haptic feedback, than on any type of visual feedback, which is outside of the mainstream approaches currently applied in the field.

For the indirect absolute touch interaction itself, future work will focus on the investigation of the technology with a larger set of users that includes a broader variety of tasks to better address the UX dimension. In terms of technology the haptic touch remote control will be enhanced with different elements, like a relative touch element, in order to enrich the interaction technique by combining the advantages of both mappings.

On a longer term we intent to investigate an automotive application of the haptic touch element. We will adapt our solution to this different context e.g. using less fields. And we will conduct a secondary-task experiment and investigate the effect of the haptic marks on user attention, cognitive load, and usability. Based on the current results, we expect that haptic marks will reduce distraction and provide a more eyes-free experience than other touch-based user interface that are currently on the market.

Concerning the integration of replication studies and continuous evaluation of upcoming technologies a series of investigation in industrial (design) oriented context is underway to develop enhanced user-centered design and development processes that will be able to integrated a set of software qualities, including usability, user experience, reliability, safety and security. This work will conclude efforts that are on the way for more than 10 years [27].

References

1. Avellino, I., Fleury, C., Beaudouin-Lafon, M.: Accuracy of deictic gestures to support telepresence on wall-sized displays. In: Proceedings of the 33rd Annual ACM Conference on Human Factors in Computing Systems (CHI 2015), pp. 2393–2396. ACM, New York (2015)
2. Baeker, R., Small, I.: Animation at the interface. In: The Art of Human-Computer Interface Design, pp. 251–267. Addison-Wesley Longman Publishing Co., Inc. Boston (1990)
3. Basnyat, S., Palanque, P., Schupp, B., Wright, P.: Formal socio-technical barrier modelling for safety-critical interactive systems design. Saf. Sci. 45(5), 545–565 (2007)
4. Bieber, G., Abd Al Rahman, E., Urban, B.: Screen coverage: a pen-interaction problem for PDA's and touch screen computers. In: Proceeding of the Third International Conference on Wireless and Mobile Communications (ICWMC 2007), pp. 87–87. IEEE (2007)
5. Brooke, J.: SUS: a 'quick and dirty' usability scale. In: Jordan, P.W., Thomas, B., Weerdmeester, B.A., McClelland, A.L. (eds.) Usability Evaluation in Industry. Taylor and Francis, London (1996)

6. Bruke, J.L., et al.: Comparing the effects of visual-auditory and visual-tactile feedback on user performance: a meta-analysis. In: Proceedings of the 8th International Conference on Multimodal Interfaces (ICMI 2006), pp. 108–117. ACM, New York (2006)
7. Chang, B.W., Ungar, D.: Animation: from cartoons to the user interface. In: Proceedings of the 6th Annual ACM Symposium on User Interface Software and Technology (UIST 1993), pp. 45–55. ACM, New York (1993)
8. Chevalier, F., Henry Riche, N., Plaisant, C., Chalbi, A., Hurter, C.: Animations 25 years later: new roles and opportunities. In: Proceedings of the International Working Conference on Advanced Visual Interfaces (AVI 2016), pp. 280–287. ACM, New York (2016)
9. Corsten, C., Cherek, C., Karrer, T., Borchers, J.: HaptiCase: back-of-device tactile marks for eyes-free absolute indirect touch. In: Proceedings of the 33rd Annual ACM Conference on Human Factors in Computing Systems (CHI 2015), pp. 2171–2180. ACM, New York (2015)
10. Fayollas, C., Martinie, C., Palanque, P., Ait-Ameur, Y.: QBP notation for explicit representation of properties, their refinement and their potential conflicts: application to interactive systems. In: Clemmensen, T., Rajamanickam, V., Dannenmann, P., Petrie, H., Winckler, M. (eds.) INTERACT 2017. LNCS, vol. 10774, pp. 91–105. Springer, Cham (2018). https://doi.org/10.1007/978-3-319-92081-8_9
11. Forlines, C., Vogel, D., Balakrishnan, R.: HybridPointing: fluid switching between absolute and relative pointing with a direct input device. In: Proceedings of the 19th Annual ACM Symposium on User Interface Software and Technology (UIST 2006), pp. 211–220. ACM, New York (2006)
12. Gilliot, J., Casiez, G., Roussel, N.: Impact of form factors and input conditions on absolute indirect-touch tasks. In: Proceedings of Proceedings of the 2014 CHI Conference on Human Factors in Computing Systems (CHI 2014). ACM, Toronto (2014)
13. Guerreiro, T., Jorge, J., Gonçalves, D.: Exploring the non-visual acquisition of targets on touch phones and tablets. In: 2nd Workshop on Mobile Accessibility (MobileHCI 2012). ACM, New York (2012)
14. Gulliksen, J., Göransson, B.: Usability design: integrating user centered system design in the software development process. In: IFIP TC 2013 INTERACT Conference (2003)
15. Hamon, A., Palanque, P., André, R., Barboni, E., Cronel, M., Navarre, D.: Multi-Touch interactions for control and display in interactive cockpits: issues and a proposal. In: Proceedings of the International Conference on Human-Computer Interaction in Aerospace (HCI-Aero 2014), Article 7, 10 p. ACM, New York (2014)
16. Hassenzahl, M.: The interplay of beauty, goodness, and usability in interactive products. J. HCI **19**(4), 319–349 (2004)
17. Kim, J., Koren, I.: Comparing relative and absolute touch input for remote controls. In: Proceedings of the Conference on Human Factors in Computing Systems (CHI 2015), pp. 97–108. ACM. New York (2015)
18. König, W.A., Gerken, J., Dierdorf, S., Reiterer, H.: Adaptive pointing – design and evaluation of a precision enhancing technique for absolute pointing devices. In: Gross, T., Gulliksen, J., Kotzé, P., Oestreicher, L., Palanque, P., Prates, R.O., Winckler, M. (eds.) INTERACT 2009. LNCS, vol. 5726, pp. 658–671. Springer, Heidelberg (2009). https://doi.org/10.1007/978-3-642-03655-2_73
19. Liddle, D.: Emerging guidelines for communicating with animation in mobile user interfaces. In: Proceedings of the 34th ACM International Conference on the Design of Communication (SIGDOC 20166). Article 16, 9 Pages. ACM, New York (2016)
20. Martinie, C., Palanque, P., Navarre, D., Winckler, M., Poupart, E.: Model-based training: an approach supporting operability of critical interactive systems. In: Proceedings of Engineering Interactive Computing Systems (EICS 2011), pp. 53–62 (2011)

21. Martinie, C., Palanque, P., Navarre, D., Barboni, E.: A development process for usable large scale interactive critical systems: application to satellite ground segments. In: Winckler, M., Forbrig, P., Bernhaupt, R. (eds.) HCSE 2012. LNCS, vol. 7623, pp. 72–93. Springer, Heidelberg (2012). https://doi.org/10.1007/978-3-642-34347-6_5

22. McCallum, D.C., Irani, P.: ARC-Pad: Absolute + Relative cursor positioning for large displays with a mobile touchscreen. In: Proceedings of the 22nd Annual ACM Symposium on User Interface Software and Technology (UIST 2009), pp. 153–156. ACM, New York (2009)

23. Merz, B., Opwis, K., Tuch, A.N.: Perceived user experience of animated transitions in mobile user interfaces. In: Proceedings of the 2016 CHI Conference Extended Abstracts on Human Factors in Computing Systems (CHI EA 2016), pp. 3152–3158. ACM, New York (2016)

24. Navarre, D., Palanque, P., Paternò, F., Santoro, C., Bastide, R.: A tool suite for integrating task and system models through scenarios. In: Johnson, C. (ed.) DSV-IS 2001. LNCS, vol. 2220, pp. 88–113. Springer, Heidelberg (2001). https://doi.org/10.1007/3-540-45522-1_6

25. Norman, K.L., Norman, K.D.: Comparison of relative versus absolute pointing devices. In: Human-Computer Interaction Technical Report, HCIL (2010)

26. Palanque, P., Barboni, E., Martinie C., Navarre, D., Winckler, M.: A model-based approach for supporting engineering usability evaluation of interaction techniques. In: Proceedings of Engineering Interactive Computing Systems (EICS 2011), pp. 21–30 (2011)

27. Palanque, P., Basnyat, S., Bernhaupt, R., Boring, R., Johnson, C., Johnson, P.: Beyond usability for safety critical systems: how to be sure (safe, usable, reliable, and evolvable)? In: Proceedings of the 2017 CHI Conference on Human Factors in Computing Systems (CHI 2007), pp. 2133–2136. ACM. New York (2007)

28. Palleis, H., Hussmann, H.: Indirect 2D touch panning: how does it affect spatial memory and navigation performance. In: Proceedings of the 2016 CHI Conference on Human Factors in Computing Systems (CHI 2016), pp. 1947–1951. ACM. New York (2016)

29. Pasquero, J., Hayward, V.: Tactile feedback can assist vision during mobile interactions. In: Proceedings of the SIGCHI Conference on Human Factors in Computing Systems (CHI 2011), pp. 3277–3280. ACM, New York (2011)

30. Pfeiffer, M., Kern, D., Schöning, J., Döring, T., Krüger, A., Schmidt, A.: A multi-touch enabled steering wheel: exploring the design space. In: Extended Abstracts on Human Factors in Computing Systems (CHI EA 2010), pp. 3355–3360. ACM, New York (2010)

31. Pietroszek, K., Lank, E.: Clicking blindly: using spatial correspondence to select targets in multi-device environments. In: Proceedings of MobileHCI 2012, pp. 331–334. ACM, San Francisco (2012)

32. Pirker, M., Bernhaupt, R., Mirlacher, T.: Investigating usability and user experience as possible entry barriers for touch interaction in the living room. In: Proceedings of the 8th International Interactive Conference on Interactive TV&Video (EuroITV 2010), pp. 145–154, ACM, New York (2010)

33. Roudaut, A., Huot, S., Lecolinet, E.: TapTap and MagStick: improving one-handed target acquisition on small touch-screens. In: Proceedings of the Working Conference on Advanced Visual Interfaces (AVI 2008), pp. 146–153. ACM, New York (2008)

34. Sheik-Nainar, M., Huber, J., Bose, R., Matic, N.: Force-enabled touchpad in cars: improving target selection using absolut input. In: Proceedings of the 2016 CHI Conference Extended Abstracts on Human Factors in Computing Systems (CHI EA 2016), pp. 2697–2704. ACM, New York (2016)

35. Thomas, F., Johnston, O.: Disney Animation: The Illusion of Life. Abbeville Press, New York (1981)
36. Treskunov, A., Darnell, M., Wang, R.: Active haptic feedback for touch enabled TV remote. In: Proceedings of the 2015 ACM on International Conference on Multimodal Interaction (ICMI 2015), pp. 319–322. ACM, New York (2015)
37. Zimmermann, S., Rümelin, S., Butz. A.: I feel it in my fingers: haptic guidance on touch surfaces. In: Proceedings of the 8th International Conference on Tangible, Embedded and Embodied Interaction (TEI 2014), pp. 9–12. ACM, New York (2014)

Factors Affecting the Choice of Usability Evaluation Methods for Interactive Adaptive Systems

Amira Dhouib[1(✉)], Ahlem Assila[2], Abdelwaheb Trabelsi[3],
Christophe Kolski[4], and Mahmoud Neji[1]

[1] Miracl Laboratory, Faculty of Economics and Management Sciences,
University of Sfax, B.P. 1088, 3000 Sfax, Tunisia
{amira.dhouib,mahmoud.neji}@fsegs.rnu.tn
[2] CESI, LINEACT, 7 Bis Avenue Robert Schuman, Reims, France
aassila@cesi.fr
[3] Saudi Electronic University, Dammam, Saudi Arabia
atrabelsi@seu.edu.sa
[4] LAMIH-UMR CNRS 8201, Université Polytechnique Hauts-de-France,
Valenciennes, France
Christophe.Kolski@uphf.fr

Abstract. Choosing the appropriate usability evaluation methods is a key part of the usability evaluation process of interactive adaptive systems. This step needs the consideration of different factors, leading to a multi-criteria decision analysis problem. In this paper, we present a review of the main factors reported in the literature which can affect the selection of usability evaluation methods for interactive adaptive systems. Three of the most commonly used usability evaluation methods are selected and classified according to these factors. The results of this research are used by applying a decision aid method in order to guide the choice of suitable usability evaluation methods for a given adaptive system in the field of tourism.

Keywords: Interactive adaptive system · Usability evaluation method
Decision process

1 Introduction

As for all interactive systems, usability plays an important role in the success of Interactive Adaptive Systems (IAS)[1] [1]. The usability evaluation of IAS represents an essential part of their development process. It may be conducted through the use of suitable Usability Evaluation Methods (UEMs). In the IAS literature, several UEMs are available [3, 4]. These methods aim mainly to detect the usability issues. Given this variety, non-specialists and even specialists can encounter difficulties in selecting the

---

[1] According to Jameson and Gajos [2], an interactive adaptive system represents an "Interactive system that adapts its behavior to individual users on the basis of processes of user model acquisition and application that involve some form of learning, inference, or decision making".

© IFIP International Federation for Information Processing 2019
Published by Springer Nature Switzerland AG 2019
C. Bogdan et al. (Eds.): HCSE 2018, LNCS 11262, pp. 270–282, 2019.
https://doi.org/10.1007/978-3-030-05909-5_16

most appropriate UEM(s) in particular settings [4, 5]. Choosing appropriate usability evaluation method(s) is a crucial task of the IAS evaluation process [6]. This task depends usually on different factors, such as number of stakeholders, available time, etc. [4]. Applying a Multi-Criteria Decision Analysis (MCDA) method for the suitable UEMs choice is one strategy to deal with multiple and conflicting factors. One of the main steps of the decision analysis process is to define the factors that impact the choice of alternatives. In this research, we provide a general overview of the factors affecting the choice of alternative UEMs. We also classify three common usability evaluation methods for IAS according to the considered factors. These include heuristic evaluation, cognitive walkthrough, and usability test. Lastly, we use the finding of this analysis to guide the choice of suitable methods for the usability evaluation of a target adaptive system as a whole using ELECTRE I (Elimination and Choice Translating Reality) method.

It is common to identify in the IAS literature two kinds of evaluation. The first one is named *layered evaluation*, which aims to separate the adaptation process into its layers and to assess each one individually where necessary and feasible [7]. The second one is *evaluation as a whole* (or traditional evaluation), which considers the adaptation as one block. Various UEMs can be applied in conjunction with the layered evaluation as well as the evaluation as a whole. In the IAS field, a limited number of works have been focused on the guidance of the choice of appropriate UEMs. For instance, Paramythis et al. [7] proposed a layered evaluation framework that breaks the adaptation process into five separate layers. They provided a comprehensive overview of the appropriate evaluation methods and attributes to be applied in individual layers and evaluation as a whole. Regarding the use of MCDA, it has been observed that very few studies exist, apart from the ones in our previous works [8, 9]. These studies focus on the choice of suitable evaluation methods for the layered evaluation given particular evaluation settings. While assessing adaptation layers individually allows one to answer questions which are not possible to approach in a "monolithic" entity, there are some assessment questions that require treating the adaptation process as a whole. One example of the questions that can be examined when conducting the evaluation as a whole is "does the adaptive system achieve its goals?" [7]. To the best of our knowledge, there are no attempts to date that provide a review of the common factors affecting the selection of UEMs and that explore the most potential benefits of MCDA to identify appropriate methods for the usability evaluation as a whole of IAS. For instance, the use of MCDA allows the consideration of a variety of criteria that are important for the decision analysis by considering both quantitative and qualitative aspects.

The present paper is organized as follows. First, we briefly outline the usability evaluation methods for IAS, focusing on three common ones (Sect. 2). Second, we present the proposed decision process for choosing the appropriate usability evaluation methods for IAS (Sect. 3). Then, the study investigates the main factors that can affect the choice of usability evaluation methods for IAS and analyzes the considered UEMs in relation to these factors (Sect. 4). An application of an MCDA method is provided in Sect. 5. The aim is to guide the selection of the most suitable methods for the usability evaluation of a given adaptive system as a whole. Lastly, we conclude the paper with a summary and some future directions (Sect. 6).

2   Focus on Three Usability Evaluation Methods for Interactive Adaptive Systems

2.1   Heuristic Evaluation

It describes a method in which expert evaluators examine a user interface in order to discover the usability problems [10]. In the IAS field, expert evaluators need to have expertise in heuristic evaluation and they are required to understand the meaning of the particular heuristics applied for adaptive systems [7].

2.2   Usability Test

The main purpose of this method is to give a group of real users well-defined tasks to perform and to ask them to record what happens [11]. Certain observational methods can be applied in conjunction with this method such as co-discovery, retrospective testing, etc. In the IAS field, certain modifications to observational methods are required. For instance, in contrast to interactive (non-adaptive) systems, an IAS necessitates interrupting the users in order to ask them about the adaptations that occur explicitly.

2.3   Cognitive Walkthrough

During this evaluation method, a group of expert evaluators construct typical user tasks in order to detect the difficulties encountered by novice users [12]. When evaluating adaptive systems, some modifications to this method are needed. For instance, multiple-action sequences per task have to be given to expert evaluators. For each action, the expert evaluators have to examine four main questions: "Will the user expect to be asked to do this?", "Will they notice the control (e.g., button)?", "Will they realize that the control is appropriate for this step?", and "Will progress be apparent once it has been used?" [7].

3   Usability Evaluation Methods' Choice Process

As shown in Fig. 1, the decision analysis process starts with a preparatory step, where the goal of the decision problem is defined. The aim consists in selecting the appropriate UEMs for interactive adaptive systems. This step also defines the actors involved in the decision process, including a Decision Maker (DM) and an analyst. In this research, a decision maker can be a novice evaluator; s/he can also be an expert evaluator who needs to be assured in the suitable UEMs. Finally, s/he can be a project manager who needs to be aware of the UEMs to be applied given particular evaluation settings. The next step consists in determining the set of alternative UEMs that define the aspects relevant to the decision problem. Then, the factors (or criteria) that can affect the choice of these UEMs are identified. Different criteria should be considered when selecting appropriate UEMs for interactive adaptive systems. Once relevant criteria are retained, the performance table should be established. Each alternative

UEM is classified with respect to the considered criteria after a detailed analysis of studies such as [3, 4, 7]. Next, an appropriate MCDA method needs to be selected in order to solve the considered decision problem. The decision maker has then to give information about the evaluation constraints of the target IAS. Usually, some parameters need to be set up in an MCDA method, such as the weight associated to every criterion. The weight refers to the relative importance of each criterion. It can be determined by the DM or estimated using a specific weighting method[2]. The next step consists to establish the outranking relations for the different alternative UEMs. Before proposing the final list of appropriate UEMs, it is essential first to test the robustness of the results by varying the MCDA method's parameters and observing the effect on the results. On the basis of such an analysis, it is possible to study the validity of the results. The results are said to be robust only in the case where they are not modified to any significant extent by varying the parameters [13]. After an analysis of the results, the DM has to express the satisfaction level s/he obtained from the proposed UEMs.

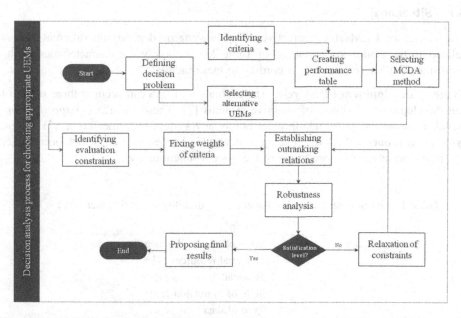

Fig. 1. A flowchart illustrating the decision analysis process for the choice of Usability Evaluation Methods (UEMs).

A score is attributed; it may adopt either (1) useful, when the list of UEM(s) satisfies the evaluation constraints, or (2) not useful, when the list of UEM(s) is not suitable due either to the non-satisfaction of the evaluation constraints (e.g., exceed the

---

[2] Different weighting methods have been proposed in the MCDA literature to assign weights to decision criteria. One example of these methods is the 'equal weights' method. It consists in distributing weights equally among all criteria and has been used in different problems [13].

available number of users, etc.) or to the lack of proposals. In this case, a relaxation of constraints has to be performed by proposing a list of actions to the DM.

4 Factors Affecting the Choice of Usability Evaluation Methods

One of the main parts of the UEMs' choice process is to define the factors that reflect the impact of each alternative on the decision problem. This step has a great influence on the decision process's success. As already stated, this research seeks to present the common factors that influence the choice of UEMs in the IAS field. As shown in Table 1, three groups of criteria are considered (e.g., situational factors, characteristics of stakeholders, and adaptivity aspects). It is essential to highlight here that this list is not exhaustive and may be completed with other factors.

4.1 Situational Factors

The choice of UEMs for interactive adaptive systems depends on different factors related to the evaluation situation. In Table 2, we classify the characteristics of the considered UEMs (cf. Sect. 2) according to these factors.

Stage of Development Life-Cycle. The evaluation of IAS can occur at three stages of the development life-cycle of adaptive systems [7]. These include (1) *specification*, which refers to the phase taking place before any system implementation, (2) *design*, which occurs during the IAS' development, and (3) *implementation*, which occurs after the implementation of a prototype of the system functionality.

Table 1. List of criteria affecting the choice of usability evaluation methods for IAS

Group of criteria	Criteria
Situational factors	Stage of the development life cycle [7]
	Temporal resources [4]
	Financial resources [4]
	Style of evaluation [15]
	Type of data [16]
Characteristics of stakeholders	Number of users [17]
	Number of evaluators [17]
	Availability of direct access to users [18]
	Level of expertise of evaluators [19]
Adaptivity aspects	Intrusiveness of adaptivity [17]
	Reusability adaptation rules [17]

Temporal Resources. The application time of a usability evaluation method represents an important factor which affects its choice [4]. The duration can be represented by an ordinal scale (i.e., low, medium, or high).

Financial Resources. Another factor distinguishing UEMs is the required budget [4]. This criterion can be assessed using a three-level scale (i.e., low, medium, or high).

Style of Evaluation. Usability evaluation methods may be performed under laboratory conditions, as well as in the work environment [15]. In order to evaluate this criterion, *yes* is used to model the evaluation conducted in laboratory conditions, and *no* otherwise.

Type of Data. Usability evaluation methods can be distinguished according to the type of data they deal with, specifically, whether these data are qualitative or quantitative [16]. In order to evaluate this criterion, *yes* is used to model that an evaluation method provides qualitative data, and 0 otherwise.

Table 2. Classification of UEMs according to the situational factors

	Heuristic evaluation	Cognitive walkthrough	Usability test
Stage of the development lifecycle	Design	Design	Implementation[a]
Temporal resources	Low	Medium	High
Financial resources	Low	Low	High
Style of evaluation	Yes	Yes	Yes
Type of data	Yes	Yes	Yes

[a]It is essential to highlight that it is possible to apply usability test using Wizard-of-Oz when a target system's functionality has not been implemented yet. In the case of this paper, the interest is on using usability test without Wizard-of-Oz technique.

4.2 Characteristics of Stakeholders

A crucial consideration when selecting UEMs is the characteristics of the stakeholders involved in the usability evaluation process. In Table 3, we present a classification of the considered UEMs according to the characteristics of stakeholders.

Number of Users. This concerns the total number of users to be involved to use a specific UEM [17].

Number of Evaluators. This refers to the total number of evaluators to be involved to apply a given UEM [17].

Availability of Direct Access to Users. The evaluation of interactive adaptive systems can be carried out in the presence of real or representative users [18].

Table 3. Classification of UEMs with respect to the characteristics of stakeholders.

	Heuristic evaluation	Cognitive walkthrough	Usability test
Number of users	0	0	15+
Number of evaluators	3+	3+	1+
Availability of direct access to users	No	No	Yes
Level of expertise of evaluators	High	High	Medium

Level of Expertise of Evaluators. This refers to the evaluator's expertise and knowledge of UEMs [19]. The level of expertise can be: *low*, *medium*, or *high*.

4.3   Adaptivity Aspects

One other important consideration when choosing UEMs is the adaptivity aspects (e.g., reusability adaptation rules, and intrusiveness of adaptivity). Table 4 presents a classification of the considered UEMs based on these aspects of adaptivity.

Reusability Adaptation Rules. The reusability adaptation rules can influence the choice of UEMs [17]. It may adopt two values either simple or complex. In order to evaluate this criterion, *yes* is used to model simple reusability adaptation rules, and *no* otherwise.

Intrusiveness of Adaptivity. This underlines the frequently-given suggestions of the interactive adaptive systems [17].

Table 4. Classification of UEMs according to the adaptivity aspects.

	Heuristic evaluation	Cognitive walkthrough	Usability test
Reusability adaptation rules	No	No	No
Intrusiveness of adaptivity	Yes	Yes	Yes

5   Illustrative Example of Using an MCDA Method for Choosing Appropriate UEMs

Let us assume that a DM, who is in this case a novice evaluator, is interested in identifying the appropriate UEMs for the usability evaluation of a given adaptive tourist guide system. The adaptive system adapts the user interface and the content according to the needs and requirements of the tourists. It helps them to easily find the most appropriate itineraries, schedules, etc., according to their requirements and preferences. Furthermore, the system can be adapted based on the device on which it is displayed (i.e., desktop, Smartphone). Many adaptive systems of this type have been studied and proposed in the literature over the last decades [20, 21].

As already presented, the interest of this study is related essentially to choosing the appropriate methods for the usability evaluation as a whole. To support the decision process of the choice of UEMs, the DM has to consider the evaluation constraints of the whole system to be evaluated without separation between its adaptation layers. This situation deals with *choosing problem* (P.α)[3], where the goal is to select one or a combination of UEM(s). For this study, one MCDA method is adopted, namely the ELECTRE I method. In the sub-sections that follow, we give a brief overview of the ELECTRE I method and details to justify the choice of this MCDA method as well as an application of the ELECTRE I method.

5.1   Brief Description of the ELECTRE I Method

ELECTRE I method is an MCDA method based on an outranking relation *(aSb)*[4] that aims to increase a set of alternatives in a reduced subset called kernel set [22]. This latter contains the best alternative(s). The ELECTRE I method is based essentially on the following steps:

Calculating the Concordance Index (C(a,b)). The aim is to test the strength of the criteria coalition in favor of the agreement to the outranking relation. In this step, the discordance index is computed as shown in (Eq. 1), where W_k represents the weight for each criterion and $f_k(a)$ is the score for alternative a under criterion j.

$$C(a, b) = \frac{1}{W} \sum\nolimits_{j: f_k(a) \leq f_k(b)} W_K$$
$$Where\ W = \sum\nolimits_{k=1}^{m} w_k, \ w_k > 0 \tag{1}$$

Calculating the Discordance Index (D(a,b)). The aim is to measure the rejection against the assertion *aSb*. In this step, the discordance index is computed as shown in (Eq. 2). More details about the ELECTRE I method can be found in [22].

$$D(a, b) = \begin{cases} 0 & \text{if } f_k(a) > f_k(b),\ \forall k \\ \frac{1}{\partial} \max[f_k(a) - f_k(b)], & Otherwise \end{cases} \tag{2}$$
$$Where\ \partial = \underset{a,b,k}{max}[f_k(a) - f_k(b)]$$

5.2   Why Adopt ELECTRE I Method?

Numerous MCDA methods exist in the literature. Each one has some advantages depending on where it is applied. According to [24], the choice of a suitable MCDA method depends mostly on the type of information available and the nature of the

---

[3] Three types of decision problems can be distinguished according to Roy [23], namely choosing problem (P.α), ranking problem (P.γ), and (3) sorting problem (P.β).

[4] Where a and b are two alternatives to compare.

decision problem to be solved. As stated earlier, the decision problem to be treated in this study corresponds to (P.α). A number of MCDA methods are appropriate to decision problems involving choice, such as the ELECTRE I method and its variant ELECTRE IS. Some differences between these methods exist. The main novelty of the ELECTRE IS method, for example, is the use of indifference and preference thresholds [22]. These discrimination thresholds aim essentially, in this case, to take into account the imperfect knowledge character of the DM with respect to the evaluation of alternatives. Such imperfect knowledge may arise when two alternatives are susceptible to be characterized with the same performance, which disables the DM to clearly express a preference relation for any pair of alternatives. For the problem analyzed in this case, it is presumed that neither indifference nor preference thresholds are necessary to model the preferences of our DM. Then, ELECTRE I method is retained since it seems to be appropriate for this decision problem. The main advantage of this MCDA method consists in using pair-wise comparisons between alternative UEMs, so that one can select the appropriate one or a combination of UEMs according to different criteria [25].

5.3   Application of the ELECTRE I Method

The use of ELECTRE I method requires the identification of a set of input data about the given decision problem. Firstly, the DM has to identify the UEMs applicable to the candidate usability attributes to be assessed. Three representative UEMs are considered in this study, namely cognitive walkthrough, heuristic evaluation, and usability test (cf. Sect. 2). After determining the set of criteria, a performance table should be established which consists of the evaluation of alternative UEMs through the retained criteria (Cf. Tables 2, 3 and 4). Then, the decision maker is asked to answer a questionnaire in order to explore the constraints about the usability evaluation of the given adaptive system. An example of these questions is: "When will the usability evaluation of the given adaptive system be done?". In this study, the evaluation as a whole occurs in laboratory conditions during the implementation stage. As already stated, ELECTRE I is retained. A set of input data has to be determined for this MCDA method such as the relative importance of criteria. In this study, the DM considers that the decision criteria at the same level have equal weights. The outranking relation of ELECTRE I method involves two calculations, including the concordance and the discordance indices (Cf. Sect. 5.1). The outranking relation is based on the concordance and discordance thresholds. Table 5 presents the concordance matrix, which aims to measure the strength of the criteria coalition in favor of the agreement to the outranking relation.

Table 5. Concordance matrix.

	Heuristic Evaluation (HE)	Cognitive Walkthrough (CW)	Usability Test (UT)
Heuristic evaluation (HE)	–	0.616	0.4
Cognitive walkthrough (CW)	0.916	–	0.45
Usability test (UT)	0.833	0.85	–

Then, the discordance matrix, which aims to measure the rejection against the assertion *(aSb)* is calculated (Table 6).

Table 6. Discordance matrix.

	Heuristic Evaluation (HE)	Cognitive Walkthrough (CW)	Usability Test (UT)
Heuristic evaluation (HE)	–	0.266	1
Cognitive walkthrough (CW)	0.333	–	1
Usability test (UT)	0.166	0.15	–

In order to interpret the information shown in the concordance and discordance matrices (Tables 5 and 6), two thresholds (*p* and *q*) should be defined. These thresholds aim to establish the outranking relations between alternatives and to define the desired concordance and tolerated discordance. The concordance threshold *p* refers to the minimum concordance index needed for outranking whereas the discordance threshold *q* reflects the maximum discordance index required for outranking. The values for both threshold parameters are fixed as follows: p = 0.67 (represents the average of the concordance matrix); q = 0.48 (represents the average of the discordance matrix). Table 7 illustrates the outranking relations between alternative UEMs.

Table 7. Outranking relations between alternative UEMs

$C_{UEMi, UEMj}$	$C_{UEMi, UEMj} \geq p$	$D_{UEMi, UEMj}$	$D_{UEMi, UEMj} \leq q$	$UEM_i => UEM_j$
$C_{HE,CW} = 0.616$	No	$D_{HE,CW} = 0.266$	Yes	–
$C_{HE,UT} = 0.4$	No	$D_{HE,UT} = 1$	No	–
$C_{CW,HE} = 0.916$	Yes	$D_{CW,HE} = 0.333$	Yes	CW => HE
$C_{CW,UT} = 0.45$	No	$D_{CW,UT} = 1$	No	–
$C_{UT,HE} = 0.833$	Yes	$D_{UT,HE} = 0.166$	Yes	UT => HE
$C_{UT,CW} = 0.85$	Yes	$D_{UT,CW} = 0.15$	Yes	UT => CW

The results obtained by the ELECTRE I method may be expressed in the form of a graph, as shown in Fig. 2. The arrows emerging from the nodes represent the outranking relations between alternatives. Each node corresponds to an alternative UEM. Once the analysis of the robustness of results is carried out, the decision maker has to express his/her satisfaction level obtained from the proposed UEMs. In this study, the Usability Test (UT) method has no incoming arrows. It outranks Heuristic evaluation (HE) and Cognitive Walkthrough (CW) method. The latter outranks heuristic evaluation method. Hence, the usability test can be stated to be the most appropriate method for the evaluation as a whole of the given adaptive system. It is essential to highlight that these results depend essentially on the given evaluation context and can change from a situation to another.

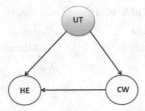

Fig. 2. Outranking graph

6   Conclusion and Future Work

During the usability evaluation of IAS, a careful selection of UEMs should be performed in order to fit better the situation of the evaluated system. As a contribution to the IAS field, this paper summarizes firstly the most common factors that affect the selection of UEMs for a particular situation. Three of the most commonly used methods for evaluation as a whole are classified then according to the identified factors. Indeed, the knowledge obtained in this research is used in order to support the choice of appropriate methods for the usability evaluation as a whole. Towards this end, the ELECTRE I method is retained. An application of this MCDA method is presented to support the UEMs choice process for a target adaptive system in the field of tourism.

Future work will investigate to apply our proposal in other areas of adaptive systems (e.g., adaptive learning system, adaptive e-commerce system, etc.). We also intend to propose a Multi-Criteria Decision Support System (MCDSS) that integrates ELECTRE I into its model base subsystem. This MCDSS will guide our DM by providing powerful capabilities in the exploration and the comparison of alternative UEMs.

References

1. Benyon, D.: Adaptive systems: a solution to usability problems. User Model. User-Adap. Inter. **3**, 65–87 (1993)
2. Jameson, A., Gajos, K.Z.: Systems that Adapt to Their Users. In: Julie, A., Jacko, J. (eds.) The Human-Computer Interaction Handbook: Fundamentals, Evolving Technologies and Emerging Applications, pp. 246–251. CRC Press, Boca Raton (2012)
3. Gena, C., Weibelzahl, S.: Usability engineering for the adaptive web. In: Brusilovsky, P., Kobsa, A., Nejdl, W. (eds.) The Adaptive Web. LNCS, vol. 4321, pp. 720–762. Springer, Heidelberg (2007). https://doi.org/10.1007/978-3-540-72079-9_24
4. Dhouib, A., Trabelsi, A., Kolski, C., Neji, M.: A classification and comparison of usability evaluation methods for interactive adaptive systems. In: 9th International Conference on Human System Interactions, Portsmouth, UK, pp. 246–251 (2016)

5. Xavier, F., Nigel, B., Tomás, A. E.: UCD method selection with usability planner. In: Proceedings of the 6th Nordic Conference on Human-Computer Interaction: Extending Boundaries (NordiCHI 2010), pp. 829–830. ACM, New York (2010)
6. Effie, L., Ebba, H., Gilbert, C. (eds.): Maturing Usability: Quality in Software. Interaction and Value. Springer, London (2007). https://doi.org/10.1007/978-1-84628-941-5
7. Paramythis, A., Weibelzahl, S., Masthoff, J.: Layered evaluation of interactive adaptive systems: framework and formative methods. User Model. User-Adap. Inter. **20**, 383–453 (2010)
8. Dhouib, A., Trablesi, A., Kolski, C., Neji, M.: EvalCHOICE: a decision support approach for the usability evaluation of interactive adaptive systems. In: Proceedings of the 21st International Conference KES, Elsevier Procedia Computer Science, Marseille, France, pp. 864–873, September 2017
9. Dhouib A., Trabelsi, A., Kolski, C., Neji, M.: Towards the layered evaluation of interactive adaptive systems using ELECTRE TRI method. In: Proceedings of the 12th International Conference on Software Technologies (ICSOFT 2017), Madrid, pp. 163–170 (2017)
10. Nielsen, J.: Heuristic evaluation. In: Nielsen, J., Mack, R.L. (eds.) Usability Inspection Methods, pp. 25–64. Wiley, New York (1994)
11. Dumas, J.S., Redish, J.C.: A Practical Guide To Usability Testing. N.J. Ablex Publishing Corp, Norwood (1999)
12. Mahatody, T., Sagar, M., Kolski, C.: State of the art on the cognitive walkthrough method, its variants and evolutions. Int. J. Hum. Comput. Interact. **26**, 741–785 (2010)
13. Zardari, K., Ahmed, S.M., Shirazi, Z., Yusop, B.: Weighting Methods and their Effects on Multi-Criteria Decision Making Model Outcomes in Water Resources Management. Springer Briefs in Water Science and Technology. Springer, Heidelberg (2015). https://doi.org/10.1007/978-3-319-12586-2
14. Wang, J.J., Jing, Y.Y., Zhang, C.F., Zhao, J.H.: Review on multi-criteria decision aid in sustainable energy decision-making. Renew. Sustain. Energy Rev. **13**, 2263–2278 (2009)
15. Dix, A.J., Finlay, J.E., Abowd, G.D., Beale, R.: Human-Computer Interaction, 2nd edn. Prentice-Hall, Staffordshire Hemel Hempstead (1998)
16. Assila, A., Oliveira, K., Ezzedine, H.: Integration of subjective and objective usability evaluation based on ISO/IEC 15939: a case study for traffic supervision systems. Int. J. Hum. Comput. Interact. **32**(12), 931–955 (2016)
17. Primož, K., Matjaž, D., Danijela, M.: Adequateness of usability evaluation methods regarding adaptivity. Simpozijum o računarskim naukama i informacionim tehnologijama (2007)
18. Wixon, D., Wilson, C.: The usability engineering framework for product design and evaluation. In: Helander, M., Landauer, T., Prabhu, P. (eds.) Handbook of Human-Computer Interaction, pp. 653–688. Elsevier Science B.V, Amsterdam (1997)
19. Karat, J.: User-centered software evaluation methodologies. In: Helander, M., Landauer, T. K., Prabhu, P. (eds.) Handbook of Human-Computer Interaction, 2nd edn, pp. 689–704. Elsevier Science B.V, Amsterdam (1997)
20. Hariri, M., Tabary, D., Lepreux, S., Kolski, C.: Context aware business adaptation toward user interface adaptation. Commun. SIWN **3**, 46–52 (2008)
21. Taktak, H., Moussa, F.: Service-oriented application creation process in ubiquitous environments travel assistant mobile application. Int. J. Pervasive Comput. Commun. **13**(3), 300–330 (2017)
22. Roy, B.: The Outranking Approach and the Foundations of ELECTRE Methods. Theory and Decision (1991)
23. Roy, B.: Méthodologie Multicritère d'Aide a la Décision, Economica, Paris (1985)

24. Guitouni, A., Martel, J-M., Vincke, P.: A Framework to Choose a Discrete Multicriterion Aggregation Procedure, Defence Research Establishment Valcatier (DREV) (1998)
25. Bouyssou, D., Duckstein, L., Goicoechea, A., Zionts, S.: On Some Properties of Outranking Relations Based on a Concordance-Discordance Principle, Multiple Criteria Decision Making, pp. 93–106. Springer, Berlin (1992)

Towards a Model to Address the Interplay Between IoT Applications and Users in Complex Heterogeneous Contexts

Carmelo Ardito[✉] , Danilo Caivano , Lucio Colizzi ,
and Loredana Verardi

Dipartimento di Informatica, Università degli Studi di Bari Aldo Moro,
Via Orabona, 4, 70125 Bari, Italy
{carmelo.ardito,danilo.caivano,lucio.colizzi,
loredana.verardi}@uniba.it

Abstract. Internet of Things (IoT) is now pervasive in most business and Public Administration processes. Along with the dizzying development of technological solutions, in recent years new methodological approaches are emerging with the objective of abstracting IoT functionalities, in order to manage them as resources in project management methodologies. A critical aspect is the representation of the knowledge grasped from the data acquired by IoT devices, since different types of users interact with such data with different goals. In order to transform them in knowledge, data have to be organized in a proper way and meaningfully provided in an IoT application specific for that type of user. In this paper, we propose the Knowledge Stratification Model that technical experts can take into account when developing an IoT application. The model, which organizes the knowledge elements in three layers, aims to identify the data produced by IoT devices and integrate them into business processes, thus making them meaningful for the user. A semantic approach, based on three subsets of ontologies specific for each model layer, is proposed to represent domain knowledge and to solve the technological and user interaction semantic issues characterizing complex and heterogeneous contexts as Smart City.

Keywords: Business processes · Knowledge model · Ontology

1 Introduction and Motivation

The Internet of Things (IoT) is the most pervasive technological trend of the last years, because it represents the contact point between the physical and the digital world through the use of Internet technology. IoT represents a global technological infrastructure, based on interoperable standards and protocols where objects, both physical and virtual, acquire attributes, identities and personalities, communicate with each other and modify their behavior according to rules, conditions and the evolution of the whole ecosystem. Thanks to the IoT, everything can take on new functions, collect and communicate information, receive commands, and support people in a multitude of old and new tasks.

© IFIP International Federation for Information Processing 2019
Published by Springer Nature Switzerland AG 2019
C. Bogdan et al. (Eds.): HCSE 2018, LNCS 11262, pp. 283–293, 2019.
https://doi.org/10.1007/978-3-030-05909-5_17

The miniaturization of electronics, the speed of data transmission, the spread of mobile devices, the growing computational capacity and Internet-based communication protocols have transformed scenarios and frameworks, since the IoT systems perform functions that are widespread across the territory and involve a multitude of actors (as in Smart Cities), allowing contextual information to be provided to users (Smart Environments). The result is a transformation of traditional business processes, in which the IoT necessarily becomes a resource and a driver: the focus is on data and their exploitation through a pervasive use of digital technologies in order to connect, innovate and manage the whole business value chain.

Smart City projects aim at making urban area more efficient in terms of mobility, environment, economy, living, people, and governance. For this purpose, technology must be easily usable by citizens, as well as businesses and public institutions; it must be distributed, shared and horizontal, in order to foster citizens' participation. The digital process of city transformation, therefore, requires a strong and drastic paradigm shift compared to the past, putting the citizen at the center and the government at its services, with particular emphasis on their simplicity and usability. It is not only an issue of publishing some information in Open Data format, but of adopting a new paradigm based on the idea of citizens' active participation, moving from passive service consumers to Smart Citizens, who are actors in the definition of services and co-creators of new ideas. The typical culture of participation of a Smart City would be perfectly translated, at a technological level in the application development process, with the adoption of the User-Centered Design approach, which considers the stakeholders and the end users as co-designers of a solution, even if they do not have programming or technological skills [1].

However, in order to adopt a User-centered perspective, we have to provide answers to questions regarding the use of the most suitable semantics for an application, both for describing the application domain and for considering the different types of users that interact with it. In other words, we have to provide tools for solving the ambiguity of many terms and for representing the information with the most suitable constructs, not only for the application domain but also for the user that interacts with it. For example, the Public Administration (PA) domain is composed of numerous subdomains representing the different operational areas of a city (Mobility and Traffic, Environment, Tourism, Health, etc.). A multitude of actors (e.g., administrative employees, politicians, citizens, companies, domain experts) are involved: they have different interests, technological skills and execute different tasks. The same IoT device could be used in several subdomains of the PA: the detected data can therefore assume a different semantic meaning according to the process in which they are used, or to the user type whether it is inside the same PA (e.g., a process manager) or outside the PA (e.g., a citizen).

The data collected through the IoT device must be appropriately enriched with attributes and semantic relations in order to be transformed into information useful and semantically comprehensible to the user, and this operation must necessarily be conducted by a domain expert, who knows the scenario and the environment in depth. However, to the best of our knowledge, the topics of semantics related to the integration of business process modeling and of IoT as a new process resource in data driven systems was investigated in [2, 3] only. Semantic issues about the interplay between IoT-based applications and different types of users in complex and heterogeneous contexts, such as Smart Cities, are still neglected.

This paper aims to describe and explore issues related to the semantic characterization of IoT-based application development in the Smart Cities domain: it proposes a user-centered approach oriented to software developers, who must evaluate semantic issues related to user's interaction. The paper describes which ontologies are needed to support the development of an IoT application using a user-centered approach. A formal classification of attributes and semantic relations is proposed, to be used according to the considered user perspective, in order to:

- use the most appropriate subset of attributes and semantic relations extracted from different ontologies involved in the development of an IoT-based application in the Smart Cities domain;
- solve conflicts or disambiguate concepts that are available in various of the considered ontologies;
- encourage and support the reuse of ontology subsets in the development of IoT-based applications.

The paper is organised as follows. Section 2 provides a brief overview of the existing studies on ontology in the IoT domain. Section 3 illustrates the proposed approach and suggests a classification for the semantic structures involved in the development of IoT-based applications. Section 4 reports conclusions and future work.

2 Related Work

While the technological issues due to the variety of involved actors have been successfully addressed through the development of methods and techniques of participatory design and facilitated visual programming - from software design patterns such as Model-View-Controller (MVC) to Web mashups (see, for example, [4, 5]) - the questions regarding the use of the most suitable semantics for an application remain open, both for describing the application domain and for considering the different types of users that interact with it.

Studies related to the integration of IoT and business processes are already available in the literature [6, 7]. In particular, they address how to extend the standard process modelling approaches, such as the Business Process Model and Notation (BPMN), in order to include IoT as a process resource [2, 7]. However, such studies have mainly focused on process modelling and on technological aspects of the IoT. Further challenges are posed from a semantic point of view, but those authors who considered this aspect also approached it from an organisational and technological perspective. For example, Bauer et al. defined a common and unified ontology to overcome the problems related to the heterogeneity and interoperability of IoT devices [8].

In literature there are various studies about semantic technologies applied to the IoT domain, in order to enable interoperability and foster machine to machine communication [9]. Various research initiatives addressed the IoT domain, by proposing reference architectures (such us the European FP7 project "The Internet of Things

Architecture" (IoT-A) [8]), and semantic models [10]; the European H2020 FIESTA-IoT project provides a simplified semantic model called IoT-Lite [11]. Bajai et al. [12] propose a survey of the existing ontologies which include ontological IoT concepts (e.g., sensor capabilities and context-awareness) and identify the core concepts required for developing an IoT application.

Instead, there is a limited number of works about the integration of Business Process (BP) modeling techniques in the IoT domain. Mayer et al. [2] propose an integrated view of IoT concepts in BP modeling. Suri et al. [3] introduce a semantic model (IoT-BPO) by re-using and extending concepts from IoT-Lite and build relationships between concepts of the BP domain (i.e., tasks) and concepts of the IoT domain (i.e. devices, service).

3   The Knowledge Stratification Model

Let we consider the use case of a municipality that is installing devices equipped with different sensors that provide data on traffic and air pollution. These raw data, that in Fig. 1 we call *Real World Data*, are:

- A (lat, long): coordinates of the location where the device is installed;
- S_1 (vehicle counter sensor): numbers of vehicles passing through A at time t;
- S_2 (CO_2 sensor): milligrams of CO_2 in A at time t.

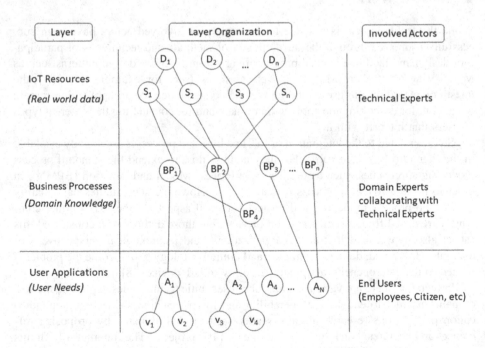

Fig. 1. The Knowledge Stratification Model (KSM).

Further data (S_3, ..., S_n) could be collected by additional sensors. S_1, ..., S_n data represent the input data for one or more Business Processes of the Municipality. For example, the S_1 raw datum is one of the input, together with A, to process P_1 "Road congestion quantification" of the Mobility Department for determining road congestion levels (calculated as the number, exceeding a pre-established threshold, of vehicles passing through A in a time interval); A and S_1 data are also the input to process P_2 "Air pollution level measurement" of the Environment Department, which processes it together with S_2 to determine the pollution level in a time interval of a specific area of the city (to which point A belongs) due to the transit of vehicles.

The connections between elements of the same layer indicate interactions and/or combinations between these elements. For example, sensors S1 and S2 are in the same device D1; process P4 uses processes P1 and P2; User application A1 offers different views, as v1 and v2.

The connections between elements of different layers indicate how raw data produced by sensors are transformed first into information (through calculation procedures and algorithms), then into knowledge (through contextualization in the domain of knowledge, e.g. Environment or Mobility, and correlation/combination with other data), called Output Knowledge. The knowledge produced by the business processes is then represented through User Applications aimed at end users who can be both internal (employees, politicians, etc.) and external (citizens, businesses, associations, etc.) to the Municipality.

The User Applications have to satisfy the needs of the different users who interact with them, through semantic and graphic constructs aimed at facilitating usability. In fact, appropriate visualization and interaction techniques support users in distilling knowledge, which becomes "awareness" of reality (or "wisdom" as defined by Ackoff in the DIKW architecture [13]) and in turn can generate further knowledge, which is the typical example of Open-data reuse (see Fig. 2).

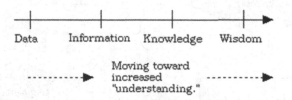

Fig. 2. Ackoff's DIKW architecture.

The model in Fig. 1 also shows the actors and their involvement in the different layers:

- Technical Experts are software developers, who define and implement procedures and constructs for interfacing the sensors with the Business Processes;
- Domain Experts are experienced and representative users of the considered domain, who collaborate with the Technical Experts to formalize the domain knowledge at the level of both processes and terminology, as well as the semantic concepts most suitable for that domain;

- End Users are all users who can interact with the User Applications, differentiating them by their role with respect to the Public Administration (employees, citizens, businesses, politicians, etc.).

In order to support designers in creating IoT applications, the KSM model has to guide them in organizing the domain concepts, in identifying the data produced by IoT devices and in integrating them into business processes, thus making them meaningful for the user.

The EER schema reported in Fig. 3 shows how the concepts of IoT Resource, Process, Output Knowledge and User are related to each other. The schema implements a recursive structure of multi-graph type.

Each process has a specific classification or taxonomy (e.g. executive process, business process, generic process of domain, specialized process of domain, etc.) and, possibly, shares some phases (sub-processes) with other processes, as modelled by the self-relation "Pr_hierarchy".

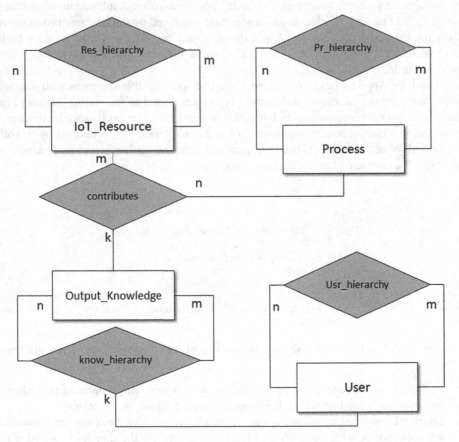

Fig. 3. A EER schema modelling the KSM.

The classification potentialities of recursive topological structures permit to semantically describe IoT resources (which can be simple sensors, devices, actuators or other complex systems) with the self-relation *"Res_hierarchy"*. The ternary relationship *"contributes"* represents the transition from information to the knowledge gained from IoT data processing performed by business processes. The Output_Knowledge can also be organized according to a tree topology structure, which is suitable for building interface templates that depend on the characteristics and needs of the specific user: it is been modelling through the ternary relationship *"know_hierarchy"*.

The EER model shows how the concepts of IoT Resource, Process, Output Knowledge and User are related to each other, but it cannot allow to infer new knowledge, because table instances generated from the EER model have values only when the process occurs. Moreover, EER does not consider some critical issues related to: (1) technology, e.g. interoperability between heterogeneous IoT resources; (2) process modelling, e.g. considering the IoT resource as a business process resource; (3) user interaction (disambiguation of terms, graphical constructs suitable to user skills, etc.). Such criticalities can be addressed by adopting a semantic approach, based on a OWA(Open World Assumption) modelling and a specific ontology for each layer of the KSM and also for the interaction among layers (see Fig. 4).

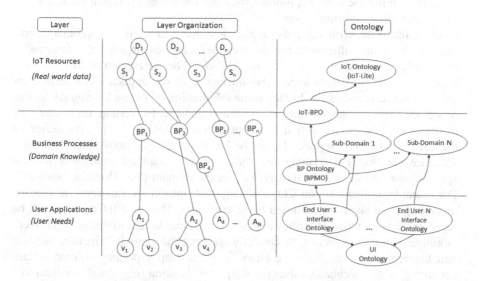

Fig. 4. Ontologies underlying the KSM model.

The ontological model is composed of the ontologies that Technical experts should use for developing IoT applications and it shows how the ontologies are connected each other: the arrows point towards the ontology to be imported. Technical experts must use a subset of these ontologies, creating or just importing the necessary ones, in order to consider all the layers of the KSM model:

- **Iot Ontology:** an ontology, for example the IoT-Lite ontology [11], is necessary due to the heterogeneous characteristics of the devices (different vendors, protocols, etc.). The IoT ontology allows Technical expert to standardize IoT Resources through semantic annotations avoiding technological issues, as interoperability. For example, the vehicle counter sensor could be associated with the geographical coordinates of the installation point and with the street name in the applications for the Mobility Department and for the Environment Department, respectively. The same "location" attribute could therefore be used in a different way, with some effects on automatic procedures based on attributes (e.g. geolocation on a map) or on the activation of internal processes within the public administration that uses them.
- **Business Process Ontology:** in order to be meaningful for the business processes, which are often represented with BPMN, IoT Resources need to be integrated into business processes and not be considered as external to them. A suitable ontology is the IoT-BPO ontology [3], which bridges IoT concepts with Business Process concepts. Moreover, it is necessary to take into consideration also an ontology to describe each subdomain of PA (Sub-Domain Ontology) to manage the semantic issues related to the domain knowledge. For this reason, the collaboration between domain experts and technical experts is fundamental, since the former can guide the latter in defining the most appropriate meaning for a concept which could also be found in multiple business processes.
- **User Application Ontology:** the applications have to adopt a vocabulary comprehensible to its different users, so that they can benefit from the knowledge produced by business process execution. This could be represented in different ways according to the different users who interact with the application, due to their different interests and skills. In fact, some information on the underlying devices or processes may not be of interest or understandable by certain users due, for example, to very specific domain concepts. Thus, according to [14], the design of the user application interfaces has to be based on specific ontologies (End User Interface Ontology) describing the most suitable graphical constructs for the specific user and on the vocabulary used in the domain (Sub Domain Ontology). For example, information on CO_2 and Pm_{10} will inform the Environment Department employee about air pollution trend over time. The same information will be represented as an index of traffic congestion over time for the Mobility Department employee. Instead, a citizen, to correctly interpret the same information, needs a suitable representation, as a geochart[1] (e.g., a map reporting colored circles according to the calculated values), a simple explanation (e.g., "high-medium-low pollution level") or a push notification service for his/her mobile device (e.g., by a Telegram channel).

The semantic approach also permits to infer knowledge not explicitly defined in the model through a semantic reasoner, thus allowing Technical Experts to develop new services and applications.

---

[1] https://developers.google.com/chart/interactive/docs/gallery/geochart.

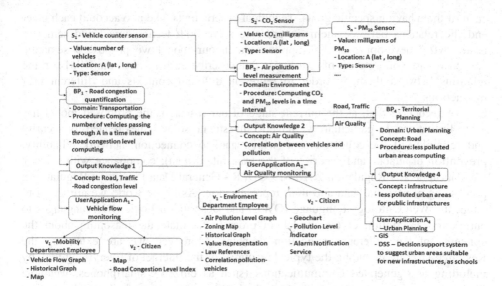

Fig. 5. Applying the KMS to the considered case study.

The schema in Fig. 5 applies the KMS model to the considered case study. In the Transportation domain, the procedures of BP_1, on the basis of the number of vehicles passing through the point A in a time interval as detected by the sensor S_1, compute the road congestion level. The output knowledge is related to the concepts "Road" and "Traffic". The User application A_1 "Vehicle flow monitoring" provides different views using user interface elements suitable to specific users, i.e., v_1 for Mobility Department employee and v_2 for citizens. In the Environment domain, the procedures of BP_2 compute the level of CO_2 and PM_{10} thanks to the data returned by the sensors S_2 and S_n located in the point A. The output knowledge is related to the concepts "Air Quality" and it is provided to users by the A_2 "Air quality monitoring", which shows a pollution level graph to the Environment Department employee (v_1) and a geochart to citizens (v_2), who can be possibly warned by an alarm notification service.

The knowledge generated by BP_1 (concepts "Traffic" and "Road") and BP_2 ("Air Quality") permits to infer new knowledge about "Infrastructure" useful in the Urban Planning domain. In BP_4 "Territorial Planning", a procedure computes the less polluted areas and also allows users to infer the best place for building a school. A User application could represent this knowledge in a GIS platform or in a Decision Support System (DSS) for the Urban Planning Department.

4 Discussion and Conclusion

In this paper, we presented a three-layer model for organizing the elements of knowledge of an IoT application in complex heterogeneous contexts, such as Smart City. In such contexts, traditional business processes have been transformed, due to the need of integrating real world data through IoT and of considering a multitude of users, each of them having specific goals. Technical experts must take into account each layer and the relations between them, in order to solve both technological and semantic issues when developing an IoT application. In our model we propose a semantic approach based on a subset of ontologies that describe each layer of the KSM and the relations between them, in order to represent different contexts and different user interactions.

We recognize that, at the current stage of our research, the proposed model has some limitations. In particular, we have to investigate some issues related to: security and reliability of the collected data (with regard to connection, network reliability, prevention of attacks and security of the transmitted data); compliance with privacy legislation (as EU Regulation 2016/679 GDPR - General Data Protection Regulation); processing of personal data and their representation. As future work, we are going to adopt the Web Ontology Language (OWL) and Description Logic (DL) languages to enrich the description of the model, in order to facilitate the reasoning about the concepts of the different application domains. Moreover, we are extending the Resource layer by including the typical resources of the Internet of Everything that, by including user-generated communications (such as citizen's smartphones, wearable devices, etc.) and interactions with networked devices, introduces further technological and semantic issues, for example new business processes must be defined to filter the collected data, to protocol citizens' alerts and include them in the administrative management. Our research group is already working on this topic, since the need of augmenting smart devices with semantic attributes emerged in our studies for proposing visual interaction paradigms to allow end users to define smart visit experience in the Cultural Heritage domain [15].

Acknowledgments. This work is funded by Italian Ministry of Education, University and Research (MIUR) through **PON Ricerca e Innovazione 2014-2020** - Asse I "Investimenti in capitale umano" - Azione I.1 "Dottorati Innovativi con caratterizzazione industriale" (CUP H92H18000210006 and H92H18000200006 approved with D.R.n.991 on 29/03/2018 of University of Bari Aldo Moro).

References

1. ISO/IEC 13407: Human-Centred Design Processes for Interactive Systems (1999)
2. Meyer, S., Ruppen, A., Magerkurth, C.: Internet of Things-aware process modeling: integrating IoT devices as business process resources. In: Salinesi, C., Norrie, Moira C., Pastor, Ó. (eds.) CAiSE 2013. LNCS, vol. 7908, pp. 84–98. Springer, Heidelberg (2013). https://doi.org/10.1007/978-3-642-38709-8_6
3. Suri, K., Gaaloul, W., Cuccuru, A., Gerard, S.: Semantic framework for internet of Things-aware business process development. In: IEEE International Conference on Enabling Technologies: Infrastructure for Collaborative Enterprises (WETICE 2017), pp. 214–219 (2017)
4. Ardito, C., Costabile, M.F., Desolda, G., Latzina, M., Matera, M.: Making mashups actionable through elastic design principles. In: Díaz, P., Pipek, V., Ardito, C., Jensen, C., Aedo, I., Boden, A. (eds.) IS-EUD 2015. LNCS, vol. 9083, pp. 236–241. Springer, Cham (2015). https://doi.org/10.1007/978-3-319-18425-8_22

5. Desolda, G., Ardito, C., Matera, M.: EFESTO: a platform for the end-user development of interactive workspaces for data exploration. In: Daniel, F., Pautasso, C. (eds.) RMC 2015. CCIS, vol. 591, pp. 63–81. Springer, Cham (2016). https://doi.org/10.1007/978-3-319-28727-0_5
6. Janiesch, C., et al.: The Internet-of-Things meets business process management: mutual benefits and challenges. Computing Research Repository (709.03628), pp. 1–9 (2017)
7. Meyer, S., Ruppen, A., Hilty, L.: The Things of the Internet of Things in BPMN. In: Persson, A., Stirna, J. (eds.) CAiSE 2015. LNBIP, vol. 215, pp. 285–297. Springer, Cham (2015). https://doi.org/10.1007/978-3-319-19243-7_27
8. Bauer, M., et al.: Internet of Things – Architecture IoT-A Deliverable D1.5 – Final architectural reference model for the IoT v3.0 (2013)
9. Szilagyi, I., Wira, P.: Ontologies and semantic web for the Internet of Things - a survey. In: Conference of the IEEE Industrial Electronics Society (IECON 2016). pp. 6949–6954 (2016)
10. De, S., Elsaleh, T., Barnaghi, P., Meissner, S.: An Internet of Things platform for real-world and digital objects. Scalable Comput. Pract. Experience 13(1), 45–57 (2012)
11. Bermudez-Edo, M., Elsaleh, T., Barnaghi, P., Taylor, K.: IoT-Lite: a lightweight semantic model for the Internet of Things. In: IEEE Conferences on Ubiquitous Intelligence and Computing, Advanced and Trusted Computing, Scalable Computing and Communications, Cloud and Big Data Computing, Internet of People, and Smart World Congress (UIC/ATC/ScalCom/CBDCom/IoP/SmartWorld). pp. 90–97 (2016)
12. Bajaj, G., Agarwal, R., Singh, P., Georgantas, N., Issarny, V.: A study of existing ontologies in the IoT-domain. CoRR abs/1707.00112 (2017)
13. Ackoff, R.L.: From data to wisdom. J. Appl. Syst. Anal. 16(1), 3–9 (1989)
14. Shahzad, S.K.: Ontology-based user interface development: user experience elements pattern. J. Univ. Comput. Sci. 17, 1078–1088 (2011)
15. Ardito, C., Buono, P., Desolda, G., Matera, M.: From smart objects to smart experiences: an end-user development approach. Int. J. Hum. Comput. Stud. 114, 51–68 (2018)

User Evaluations of Virtually Experiencing Mount Everest

Marta Larusdottir[✉], David Thue, and Hannes Högni Vilhjálmsson

Reykjavik University, Menntavegur 1, 101 Reykjavik, Iceland
{marta,davidthue,hannes}@ru.is

Abstract. In software development it is hard to know both whether the team has developed a product that fits the users' needs, and is easy to use. One way of gathering feedback from users on both these issues is to conduct formal user testing, which has been rated by IT professionals as one of the best methods for user involvement in software development. In this paper, we present a formal evaluation of a running prototype for a virtual reality experience that was scheduled to be launched 3 months later. We conducted formal user testing with five users, and recorded the problems that the users experienced while they used the VR prototype. We also collected data concerning each user's impressions of their experience immediately after it was complete. The results show that many serious problems were identified, and that the developers found several of them to be very useful. In some cases, the user testing was regarded as having been essential to discovering these problems.

Keywords: User testing · Virtual reality · Agile software development

1 Introduction

In software development it is hard to know both whether the software development team has developed a product that fits the users' needs and is easy to use for the users. A recent study shows [22] that some developers who deliver software to users only obtain a vague idea of the usage of their system, mainly because they don't contact the users, and the users do not contact the developers. The users simply find ways to bypass any problems that they have while using the product, even though it delays their work or makes them frustrated. Both formal and informal methods have been defined for gathering feedback on the user experience from users during software development.

Agile software development has been the de facto standard for project management in software development for some time. Informal methods, such as short interviews or showing low-fi prototypes to users and discussing those, are used quite extensively in agile software development [19]. Still, formal user testing, with users solving prede-fined tasks while being observed, was rated as the best method for involving users in Agile projects [14]. The results from the same study showed that such testing is performed quite rarely, due to lack of time and money.

In this paper, we study a formal evaluation of a running prototype for *Everest VR* [26], a virtual reality experience which was scheduled to be launched three months later. We conducted formal user testing with five users, as suggested in the Google

© IFIP International Federation for Information Processing 2019
Published by Springer Nature Switzerland AG 2019
C. Bogdan et al. (Eds.): HCSE 2018, LNCS 11262, pp. 294–307, 2019.
https://doi.org/10.1007/978-3-030-05909-5_18

Design sprint process [17] and by other researchers and practitioners, for example Jakob Nielsen [24]. We recorded the problems that occurred while users participated in the VR experience and we collected data about the users' impressions of the experience immediately thereafter. We focused especially on how useful the results from the formal user testing were for further development of the product. This is rarely done in the literature. Specifically, we sought to answer the following research questions:

1. How many severe problems are found during formal user testing?
2. How useful are the identified problems for the further development of the system?

The contributions of this paper are twofold: We explain how VR software can be evaluated with 5 users in formal user testing by describing the process and the data collected. But perhaps the main contribution is that we collected data on the benefits of the results of the user testing from the actual developers and describe those results in the paper.

The remainder of this paper is organized as follows. We begin by describing some of the current literature that relates to our research questions. We then present the data gathering methods that we used in the study along with the results from the study itself. Finally, we discuss the results.

2 Background

In this section, we describe some of the current literature on designing virtual reality for users and on user evaluations.

2.1 Virtual Reality

Virtual Reality devices such as the HTC Vive (www.vive.com) allow users to observe and interact with a simulated environment as though they are physically situated within that environment. Specifically, by precisely tracking the 3D position and orientation of a display device mounted on the user's head, the user's perspective of the virtual world can be controlled using the muscles in their body, identically to how they control their perspective of the real world. For example, to obtain a better view of a nearby object on the ground of a virtual world, a user could physically move their body into a crouch and thereby move their virtual perspective closer to the object. Some VR devices (including the HTC Vive) also allow the precise tracking of hand-held input devices, which are often used to represent the user's hands inside the virtual world. These devices allow users to physically move their hands to interact with the virtual world, including manipulating virtual objects and performing gestures (e.g., pointing or waving).

An important limitation of the HTC Vive is that its ability to track the headset and hand controllers is limited to a predefined tracking volume, which has a recommended maximum base area of 3.5 m × 3.5 m; this volume limits the extent to which the user can use *only* their natural body movements to explore a virtual world. To overcome this limitation, many instances of VR software also implement a way for the user to traverse the world at scales larger than 3 m × 3 m (e.g., using a hand controller to point at and teleport to a target location).

Given the speed with which the latest generation of VR technology has been developed, it has been difficult for the designers of VR software to form and maintain a good intuition for how users will use this technology to interact with virtual worlds. This magnifies the importance of running frequent user tests during the development of VR software, to both account for the current lack of intuition and to start building stronger intuition for future projects.

2.2   User-Centered Evaluations

The goal of a user-centered evaluation activity is to gather feedback on the IT professional's work from the user's perspective [11]. The type of information gathered in user-centered evaluation has been evolving through the years. About 20 years ago, the major emphasis was on gathering information on usability problems, which are flaws in the interface that cause problems for users [23]. Parallel to this, the emphasis was also on measuring usability in a quantitative way by measuring effectiveness, efficiency, and satisfaction, as defined by the ISO 9241-11 standard [12]. During the last decade, the study of user experience has gained more attention, where more subjective factors regarding the users' perspectives using the software are measured [9]. Hence, user-centered evaluation can be used to gather information on usability problems, the three factors of usability (effectiveness, efficiency, and satisfaction), and the subjective factors of user experience. When evaluating virtual reality software, one of the factors that are of interest is the effect on the body of the user. A simulator sickness questionnaire was proposed by Kennedy et al. [16] to measure the various effects that using VR software can have on the user's body.

The evaluation activity needs to be planned, conducted, and the results need to be analyzed and reported [11]. Evaluations can be conducted to gather feedback regarding the context in which the software will be used, the requirements from the user's perspective, and on the user interface design. The feedback gathered in an evaluation identifies possible flaws or problems users have while using the software. The feedback can also include the experiences users have. These are described and IT professionals must decide what action to take in each particular case to improve the usability and the user experience of the software.

Some studies have been conducted on the benefits and drawbacks of conducting user centered evaluations. The results from a survey and interview study conducted in Denmark show that some type of user centred evaluation was conducted in almost 75% of the companies involved [2]. The study did not analyse what evaluation methods were used, and whether the evaluation included users or not. A similar study was done in Italy [1] and the results on the usage were similar; some evaluation was done in 72% of the companies involved. Internal evaluations were conducted in half of the companies involved in the study, but less than 20% conducted external evaluations by external consultants.

The major obstacles for doing user centred evaluation were examined in a study conducted in Denmark [2]. The two main obstacles found were resource demands, both in terms of time and money, and an obstacle called the "developer mind-set". One example of an issue in this category, mentioned by respondents, is that developers find it hard to think like users. In relation to this, some informants described that the main focus of IT professionals was on the programming aspect - to write beautiful code - and not so much on participating in a usability evaluation. In a similar study in Italy [1] the most frequent obstacle mentioned was also resource demands. The most frequently mentioned advantage of usability evaluation was quality improvement, reported in almost half of the cases. In the study by Vredenburg et al. [28] the main benefit for doing usability evaluation was that the practitioners gain understanding in the context of use whereas the weaknesses mentioned were high cost and versatility. The benefits and weaknesses of doing informal expert reviews and formal heuristic evaluation were similar, the benefits being the low cost and speed, but the weakness being that users are not involved in the evaluation. In these three studies, the major evaluation obstacle is the client's budget resource.

Twenty years ago, it was common to study the benefits of conducting user-centered evaluations by counting how many usability problems were found by using a number of evaluation methods to evaluate the same software. Four studies comparing evaluation methods were published in the years 1990 to 1993 [7, 13, 15, 25]. In addition, a study by Cuomo and Bowen [6] is also discussed there. In these studies an aggregated list of all problems found during user observation is made and used to describe all usability problems that can be found in the software. Then the number of problems found by using another method is compared to the aggregated list. It is common to presume that problems found while observing users in user centred evaluation are true problems that users would have in real use. Problems found by using another method are compared with the list of problems found in the user observation to calculate the effectiveness of the method. These studies were focusing on that outcome of the evaluations, which is finding usability problems.

Other studies have covered how these outcomes can be described in an efficient way to help the IT professionals to decide what to do about the problems [27]. The most efficient way of describing the results of the evaluation to the IT professionals was, for example, studied by Hornbæk and Frøkjær [10]. Their results show that IT professionals assessed redesign proposals to have higher utility than usability problem lists.

One way of determining the effect of using usability evaluation methods is to look at the downstream utility, which is defined by Law [21] as: *"The extent the improved or deteriorated usability of a system can directly be attributed to fixes that are induced by the results of usability evaluations performed on the system."* Here the effect of the usability evaluation is determined by how much it improves the actual usability of the software and not by how many problems are found. There are very few studies that report the downstream utility of using a particular user-centred evaluation method. Researchers do not agree on the scope of user centred evaluation. Cockton [5] argues that assessing the downstream utility is beyond the scope of pure evaluation methods.

In this paper we assess the downstream utility of conducting user evaluation with 5 users in a VR experience and report the findings.

3 Method

In this section we will explain the VR experience whose prototype we evaluated (*Everest VR*), how we gathered the data, the demographics of our participants, and the methods that we used to analyse the results.

3.1 Everest VR

Everest VR [14] is an interactive experience in Virtual Reality that simulates some parts of the (real-world) experience of climbing Mount Everest. The experience consists of a sequence of scenes. Some scenes can only be observed (e.g., a helicopter ride with narration near the beginning of the experience; Fig. 1), while other scenes require active participation from the user before the experience will proceed (e.g., crossing a crevasse by walking along a ladder that bridges the two sides; Fig. 2).

Fig. 1. A scene from the helicopter ride.

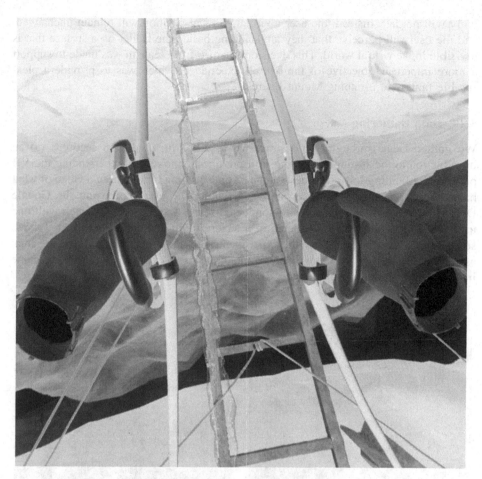

Fig. 2. A scene in which the user crosses a chasm using a ladder.

In every scene, the user can freely control their perspective in the virtual world by physically moving their head. In the scenes that require activity, the user's hands are represented by virtual mittens whose positions match the positions of the HTC Vive's hand-held controllers. Each scene that can only be observed causes an automatic transition to the next scene as soon as the former is complete. Each scene that requires interaction ends when the user performs a specific gesture in a particular context (e.g., waving in the direction of a virtual character); the next scene then begins automatically. Within an active scene, the user can use their virtual mittens to grasp various virtual objects, including ropes across a chasm and the rungs of a ladder (the user "climbs" the ladder by reaching for and grasping higher rungs to raise their virtual body; the user's feet are not tracked by the HTC Vive).

While the visuals of Everest VR are intended to be realistic (Sólfar Studios, 2016), some parts of the experience's simulation are intentionally unrealistic. For example, if the user stops grasping all of a ladder's rungs partway through a climb, their virtual body will not fall. Instead, the user's virtual, vertical position will remain unchanged, and the user will perceive that they are standing beside the ladder on a surface that is invisible in the virtual world. This decision to break from realism was made to support a more important objective of the overall experience, which was to provide a pleasurable fantasy of climbing Mount Everest.

3.2   Data Gathering

We gathered data through user testing, which was structured in 6 sections: (a) an introduction to the testing, (b) filling in a pre-questionnaire, (c) experiencing the VR prototype, (d) filling in a post-questionnaire, (e) debriefing by watching a video of what happened during the experience, and (f) thanking the user. Following the Google Design process [4], we planned and conducted 5 user testing sessions, each with one user. The user testing was conducted in a lecture room at Reykjavik University. We separated the VR play area from the experimenters by moving tables to define the area, as can be seen in Fig. 3. Figure 3 shows one of our users experiencing the video game inside the playing area while the conductor of the evaluation observes.

Fig. 3. The user testing area (Left) and a user participating in the VR experience (Right).

The execution of the user evaluations is shown in Fig. 4, by using an early version of the RAMES framework [20].

Roles	
R1. Users	Five users participated in the evaluation
R2. Evaluators	Conductor: Marta Larusdottir acted as a conductor
R3. Observers	Observers: David Thue and Kurt Van Meter acted as observers and assistants
R4. Recipients	Kurt Van Meter was the main recipient of the results
Activities	
A1. Purpose	To measure the user experience of the current prototype of *Everest VR*, to enable redesigning the system according to the results
A2. Plan	The user testing took place on Monday the 18th of April and Tuesday the 19th of April
A3. Evaluation procedure	1. Greet the participant 2. Short introduction to the procedure of the testing 3. Sign a consent form 4. Interview according to the background questions (Pre-questionnaire list) 5. Fill in the questionnaire about how the participant feels (Pre-questionnaire list) 6. Experience the VR prototype 7. Fill in the questionnaire about how the participant feels (Post questionnaire list) 8. Fill in the user experience questionnaire (AttrakDiff 2.0) 9. Discussion/debriefing about the video 10. Thank the participant
A4. Analysis of results	We used the Instant Data Analysis method described by Kellskov et al.[18]
A5. Making Decisions	Kurt was responsible for the decision making based on the results
Materials	
M1. Evaluation material	Pre-questionnaire kit including: a) introduction text for the participant, b) declaration of consent, c) pre-test questionnaire on the background, d) simulator sickness questionnaire. Post-questionnaire kit including: a) Post-test questionnaire on the overall feeling, b) simulator sickness questionnaire, c) the AttrakDiff 2.0 for measuring the user experience
M2. Support material	The VR prototype itself explained how to navigate between scenes in *Everest VR*. We also used a document containing an introduction to the procedure of the testing, and an introduction to the controls and the consent form.
M3. Data gathered	Background material, responses to questionnaires, usability problems, comments during debriefing sessions
M4. Results	Kurt presented the result to the team
M5. Decisions	Kurt kept track of which decisions were made
Environment	
E1. Evaluation environment	The evaluations were conducted at Reykjavik University, room M117
E2. Equipment. for data gathering	We used Camtasia to record what the user did during the VR experience
E3. Eq. to analyze results	Excel was used
System	
S1. Characteristics	VR game – Everest VR version 0.121
S2. Type	VR game
S3. Stage	Detailed prototype of the system
S4. Part	We evaluated the helicopter ride and a scene involving the Khumbu Icefall (part of the path up Mount Everest)
S5. Eq. for evaluation	Kurt provided all the equipment needed for the evaluation

Fig. 4. Execution of the user testing explained using RAMES

During the user testing, the participants filled in two questionnaires: one before the VR experience, and another afterwards. The pre-questionnaire covered background questions and the simulator sickness questionnaire proposed by Kennedy et al. [10]. The post-questionnaire contained one question on the overall feeling of the participant, the simulator sickness questionnaire, and the AttrakDiff 2.0 questionnaire by Hassenzahl [8]. We estimate that the entire process took approximately 60 person hours, including preparation, conducting the user testing, and analysing the data.

3.3 The Participants

We had 4 males participating in the user testing and one female. Their age was from 25 to 54 and they had all experienced virtual reality before (some only once or twice). Three said they had played a lot of video games, one said some, and one said that he/she had played none. We also asked about their experience in hiking and mountain climbing: one had extensive experience, three had some experience, and one had no experience. Four of the participants had heard about Everest VR before.

We asked if the participants ever experienced fear of heights or vertigo and some had experienced some, one said he/she had not, and one had quite serious fear of heights, but no vertigo. We also asked them to fill in a simulator sickness questionnaire to be able to see the difference in how they felt before and after experiencing the VR prototype.

3.4 The Data Analysis

To analyse both our observations of the users experiencing the *Everest VR* prototype as well as what they told us during the debriefing, the conductor and the two observers met the day after the user testing was complete and performed an instant data analysis as proposed by Kellskov et al. [13]. Some of the results of our instant data analysis session can be seen in Fig. 5. In total, we recorded 30 user problems and four positive experiences.

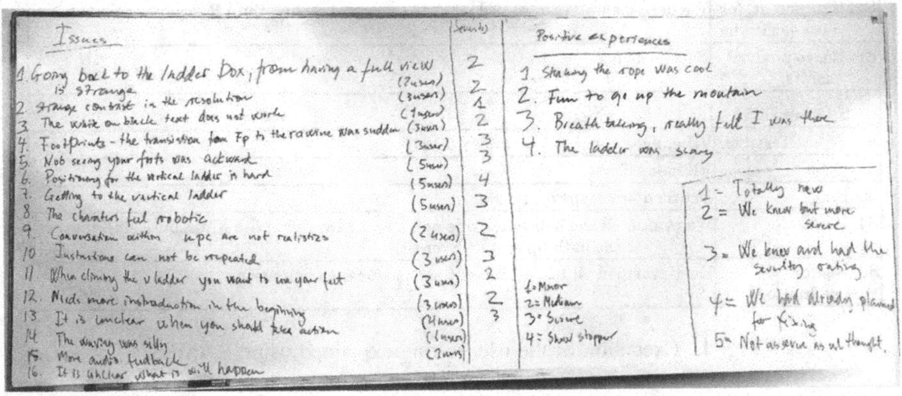

Fig. 5. The results of the instant data analysis session.

We brainstormed on the outcome of the user testing on a whiteboard by writing a list of user problems. For each problem we wrote the number of users having that problem and agreed on a severity for that problem. We categorized the severity as follows: 4 = Showstopper, 3 = Severe problem, 2 = Moderately severe problem, and 1 = Minor problem.

3.5   Analyzing the Impact of the User Problem List

Two months after we completed the user testing sessions, one of the observers of the user testing (who was also responsible for Quality Assurance (QA) at Solfar Studios) analyzed the impact of the user problems for further development of the system. He categorized each problem in these categories:

1 = Addressed
2 = No action
3 = No action, new tech needed
4 = No action, good for future design of the system
5 = Action not decided yet

He also remarked on whether any of the problems were particularly useful; these included problems that the team did not know about before the testing began, or problems whose severity they had estimated incorrectly.

4   Results

In this section, we describe the results of the user testing. First we describe the results from the questionnaires, and then we describe the results from the user problem list and the categorization of the impact of the user problems.

4.1   The User Problem List

The user problem list contained 30 problems. In Table 1, the number of problems in each severity category can be seen.

Table 1. Number of user problems in each severity category

Severity Category	Number of problems	Average number of users
Showstopper	1 problem	5 users
Very severe problem	5 problems	3,6 users
Moderately severe problem	15 problems	2 users
Minor problem	9 problems	1 user
Total:	30 problems	

As shown in Table 1, 21 of the found problems were severe (either moderately, very, or a showstopper). The showstopper had the description: "Getting to the vertical ladder by waving confused everyone, and the icon is almost invisible – this is particularly bad because you feel trapped in a corner (and are in the corner of the space)". An example of a very severe problem is: "Instructions cannot be repeated (people missed, didn't hear or were too overwhelmed by the visuals to take in verbal instructions)". Additionally, an example of a moderately severe problem is: "Want more audio feedback (immersion – environmental audio)".

4.2   The Impact from the User Problems List

The impact of the user problem list was estimated by asking one of the observers, (who was also responsible for Quality Assurance (QA) at Solfar Studios) to report what decisions had been made regarding each of the user problems, two months after the user testing. In Table 2, the results of this categorization are described.

Table 2. Number of user problems in each severity category

Severity category (number of problems)	Impact	Marked as useful
Showstopper (1)	Addressed	Very useful
Very severe problem (5)	4 addressed, 1 future design	1 very useful, 1 useful
Medium severe problem (15)	10 addressed, 2 no action 1 new tech needed, 1 not decided, 1 future design	4 useful
Minor problem (9)	4 addressed, 3 no action, 2 new tech needed	

The QA person especially marked 3 problems that were categorized as a showstopper or very severe problems right after the evaluation, as very useful or useful two months after the user testing. For the showstopper he remarked: "This testing was key in pointing out the importance of that." Additionally, for one of the very severe problems he remarked: "Huge impact on this from testing and we continue to reposition to find the best layout".

Out of the 15 problems marked as medium severe problems right after the evaluation, he marked 4 as useful two months after the evaluation. He also remarked for one of the medium severe problems: "Being addressed, and was useful to have fresh eyes to underline the importance of this".

5 Discussions

Public adoption of Virtual Reality devices has been slow [15]. As a result, a large percentage of the potential participants of software evaluations will have never experienced any environments using Virtual Reality technology. When evaluating the use of VR devices that perform positional tracking (such as the HTC Vive), some amount of initial unfamiliarity seems likely to persist even for participants who have experienced VR environments before, as the most widespread VR devices (e.g., the Gear VR and Google Cardboard) lack any positional tracking; this lack substantially limits the user's experience of a virtual world. Having participants who are unfamiliar with (aspects of) VR technology represents a serious challenge to any evaluation of a VR experience, as each user's reaction to the technology itself will likely be confounded with their reaction to the experience that one hopes to evaluate. To evaluate a VR experience independently from its supporting VR technology, one must consider only participants who have sufficient prior familiarity with that particular technology. Unfortunately, the percentage of the population that meets this criteria is likely to be very low, making it difficult to obtain a sufficient sample size to support reliable generalizations. A potential alternative could be to attempt to control for prior VR familiarity by applying statistical analysis techniques, but doing so would require a reliable, population-general model of how prior VR familiarity affects the metrics along which a target experience is to be evaluated. To the best of our knowledge, such a model does not yet exist. Until the population's familiarity with VR devices increases, it seems likely that all studies of VR experiences will suffer from the confounding effects of each user's unfamiliarity with the VR technology being used.

User involvement during agile software development in the software industry has been found to be both informal and explicit [16]. Feedback from users is gathered in an informal way, and not through formal user testing [2]. Still formal user testing has been given the highest rating of methods used by practitioners for involving users in the software industry [3]. The main reason for not conducting formal user testing is that it is time consuming in relation to the benefits the developers receive from the results of the evaluations [2]. Little has been done to try to estimate the value for software developers of gathering feedback from users through user testing. The study we have described shows that, even with just a few participants, useful information was indeed found in the formal testing of a novel VR experience.

References

1. Ardito, C., et al.: Usability evaluation: a survey of software development organizations. In: Proceedings of International Conference on Software Engineering and Knowledge Engineering (SEKE 2011), Miami, FL, USA, pp. 282–287 (2011)
2. Bak, J.O., Nguyen, K., Risgaard, P., Stage, J.: Obstacles to usability evaluation in practice: a survey of software development organizations, In: Proceedings of NordiCHI 2008 Conference, Lund, Sweden. ACM Press (2008)
3. Bradshaw, T.: VR industry faces reality check on sales growth. Financial Times (2017). https://www.ft.com/content/f7e231ee-fc84-11e6-96f8-3700c5664d30. Accessed 06 May 2018

4. Cajander, Å., Larusdottir, M., Gulliksen, J.: Existing but not explicit-the user perspective in scrum projects in practice. In: Kotzé, P., Marsden, G., Lindgaard, G., Wesson, J., Winckler, M. (eds.) INTERACT 2013. LNCS, vol. 8119, pp. 762–779. Springer, Heidelberg (2013). https://doi.org/10.1007/978-3-642-40477-1_52

5. Cockton, G.: I can't get no iteration. Interfaces 63, 4–5 (2005)

6. Cuomo, D.L., Bowen, C.D.: Understanding usability issues addressed by three user-system interface evaluation techniques. Interact. Comput. 6(1), 86–108 (1994)

7. Desurvire, H.W., Kondziela, J.M., Atwood, M.E.: What is gained and lost when using evaluation methods other than empirical testing. In: People and Computers VII, pp. 173–201. Cambridge University Press, Cambridge (1992)

8. Hassenzahl, M., Burmester, M., Koller, F.: AttrakDiff: Ein Fragebogen zur Messung wahrgenommener hedonischer und pragmatischer Qualität. In: Mensch & Computer 2003, pp. 187–196. Vieweg+Teubner Verlag (2003)

9. Hassenzahl, M., Tractinsky, N.: User experience-a research agenda. Behav. Inf. Technol. 25 (2), 91–97 (2006)

10. Hornbæk, K., Frökjær, E.: Comparing usability problems and redesign proposals as input to practical systems development. In: Proceedings of the CHI 2005 Conference, Portland, Oregon, USA. ACM Press (2005)

11. ISO 9241-210: Ergonomics of human-system interaction – Part 210: Human-centred design process for interactive systems. International Organisation for Standardization, Geneva (2010)

12. ISO 9241-11: Ergonomic requirements for office work with visual display terminals. International Organisation for Standardization, Geneva (1998)

13. Jeffries, R., Miller, J.R., Wharton, C., Uyeda, K.: User interface evaluation in the real world: a comparison of four techniques. In: Proceedings of CHI 1991 Conference, New Orleans, Louisiana, USA (1991)

14. Jia, Y., Larusdottir, M.K., Cajander, Å.: The usage of usability techniques in Scrum Projects. In: Winckler, M., Forbrig, P., Bernhaupt, R. (eds.) HCSE 2012. LNCS, vol. 7623, pp. 331–341. Springer, Heidelberg (2012). https://doi.org/10.1007/978-3-642-34347-6_25

15. Karat, C.M., Campbell, R., Fiegel, T.: Comparison of empirical testing and walkthrough methods in user interface evaluation. In: Proceedings of the CHI 1992 Conference, Monterey, CA, USA. ACM Press (1992)

16. Kennedy, R.S., Lane, N.E., Berbaum, K.S., Lilienthal, M.G.: simulator sickness questionnaire: an enhanced method for quantifying simulator sickness. Int. J. Aviat. Psychol. 3(3), 203–220 (2009). https://doi.org/10.1207/s15327108ijap0303_3

17. Knapp, J., Zeratsky, J., Kowitz, B.: Sprint: How to Solve Big Problems and Test New Ideas in Just Five Days. Simon and Schuster, New York (2016)

18. Kjeldskov, J., Skov, M.B., Stage, J.: Instant data analysis: conducting usability evaluations in a day. In: Proceedings of the Third Nordic Conference on Human-Computer Interaction, pp. 233–240 (2004)

19. Larusdottir, M.K., Cajander, Å., Gulliksen, J.: Informal feedback rather than performance measurements – user-centred evaluation in Scrum projects. Behav. Inf. Technol. 33(11), 1118–1135 (2013). https://doi.org/10.1080/0144929X.2013.857430

20. Larusdottir, M.K., Gulliksen, J, Hallberg, N.: The RAMES framework for planning and documenting user-centred evaluation. Behav. Inf. Technol. (2018)

21. Law, E.L.-C.: Evaluating the downstream utility of user tests and examining the developer effect: A case study. Int. J. Hum. Comput. Interact. 21(2), 147–172 (2006)

22. Law, E.L., Larusdottir, M.K.: Whose experience do we care about? analysis of the fitness of Scrum and Kanban to user experience. Int. J. Hum. Comput. Interact. 31(9), 584–602 (2015). https://doi.org/10.1080/10447318.2015.1065693

23. Lazar, J., Feng, J.H., Hochheiser, H.: Research Methods in Human-Computer Interaction. Wiley, New York (2009)
24. Nielsen, J.: How many test users in a usability study (2012). https://www.nngroup.com/articles/how-many-test-users/
25. Nielsen, J., Phillips, V.L.: Estimating the relative usability of two interfaces: heuristic, formal, and empirical methods compared. In: Proceedings of the INTERCHI 1993 Conference, Amsterdam, Netherlands. ACM Press (1993)
26. Sólfar Studios: Everest VR (2016). http://www.solfar.com/everest-vr/. Accessed 06 May 2018
27. Thorgeirsson, T., Larusdottir, M.K.: Case study: are CUP attributes useful to developers? In: Proceedings for the COST-294 Workshop: Downstream Utility: The good, The Bad and The Utterly Useless Usability Feedback, Toulouse, France, pp. 50–54 (2007)
28. Vredenburg, K., Mao, J.-Y., Smith, P.W., Carey, T.: A survey of user-centered design practice. In: Proceedings of the CHI 2002 Conference, Minneapolis, Minnesota, USA. ACM Press (2002)

Posters and Demos

Early Incremental User Testing Design Approach Validation for Satellite Command Center's Application

Jonathan Tolle[⊠]

Thales Alenia Space, 06156 Cannes, France
jonathan.tolle@thalesaleniaspace.com

Abstract. Thales Alenia Space has recently widely deployed user centered design process in their software product conception. This standard breaks today technology and data centric approach by integrating end-users all along the iterative design stages: context and usage understanding, end-user need specification, quick mockups and end-user validation. This paper is a return on experience. It describes and investigates a dirty UCD methodology relevance based on prototyping and user testing only (skipping user research first activities). This process is made to fit project which needs front-end requirements at day one.

Keywords: User testing · Incremental software design · User centered design Return on experience

1 Introduction

User centered design is a well-known software conception standard in ergonomics and human factors fields (ISO 9241-210) [1]. To guarantee system's utility and usability, it implies four stages where end-user is integrated within many ergonomics methods such as focus group [2], participatory design [3], interviews, job task-model based analysis [4], persona specification [5] and so on. In some constrained industrial context, deploying every practices cannot be possible. Thales Alenia Space believes that every process can be tailored and scaled to fit every project. For our new satellite command center (SCC) procedure executor named PRISM, we try a dirty UCD approach based on incremental mockups and user testing only. As user requirements were taken from our previous product version, this process enables earlier front-end development than classical ergonomics methodology.

This testimonial explains first how we integrated UCD activities within agile development process. Then we briefly present our study case PRISM and its incremental mockups. Next, we inspect our process relevance from usability metrics and user feedbacks. Does this approach lead to solution convergence? Does it bring high quality interaction and high user satisfaction? Does it allow continuous interaction improvement? From these problematic, the paper concludes on a preliminary analysis of this dirty UCD approach (ongoing work). Please note this article doesn't list any SCC user needs. It only aims to analyze the process relevance from ergonomics point of view.

C. Bogdan et al. (Eds.): HCSE 2018, LNCS 11262, pp. 311–318, 2019.
https://doi.org/10.1007/978-3-030-05909-5_19

2 Process Overview

Industry often works with subcontractors while developing products. When interaction designers are not involved in project planning phase, it may results to a development-first approach without much consideration for ergonomics activities [10]. It can be hard to break this convenient design culture as subcontractor is employing software engineers in tight timeframe. In this context, we try a new incremental process to deal with early front-end development requirements.

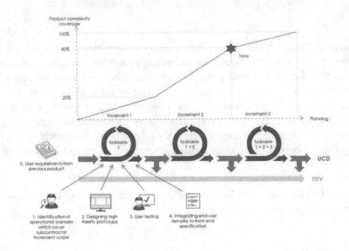

Fig. 1. 'Early incremental user testing design approach' activities

To ensure usable and useful software, we empirically plan 3 user test increments with a minimum of 5 participants per end-user test [6]. These tests are based on the walkthrough ergonomics methodology [7] by using fictive operational scenarios. Scenario's increments are built from simple and non-risky interactions (increment 1) to complex widget and data visualization interactions (increment 2 and 3). Scenario coverage (e.g. "1 + 2 + 3") between increments allows us to compare if previous front-end modifications bring better ergonomics satisfaction through usability metrics. At the end of each increment, user observations are discussed with the project manager before integrating them to subcontractor's agile development: considering usability gain over development planning, feasibility and effort.

3 Study Case: PRISM

PRISM is a web-based application inside the SCC eco-system. It basically executes procedure (list of command and automatic checks edited from SCOPE) to the real satellite or to a test platform such as avionic test bench, simulator, and other electrical ground system through the communication module (CMCS) (Fig. 2).

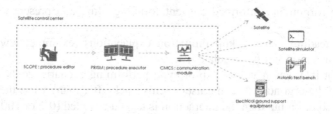

Fig. 2. PRISM simplified eco-system

Fig. 3. Increment 1: main screen which displays direct feedback of the procedure execution

Fig. 4. Increment 2: main screen which displays direct feedback of the procedure execution and provides complementary services to end-user

Thales Alenia Space has specified a graphical charter for every web applications and lot of reusable widgets have already been designed for other solutions (such as button, table, list, interactive menu, and so on). Therefore we decided to directly work with high fidelity mockups rather than having a first low fidelity prototype's iteration. Prototypes were made using AXURE software. This tool creates interactive interfaces that can simulate expected scenario's solution behavior and be used in our user testing sessions.

4   Process Inspection

4.1   User Testing Protocol

To investigate process relevance, it is important to set up a testing protocol. It allows us to compare data between increments. At the moment, two end-user test iterations have been performed (the third and last iteration will be done before product release). 10 distinct end-users participate to this analysis: 5 at first iteration and 7 at the second one (2 persons from increment 1 were involved as well in increment 2). Participants are all PRISM final end-users and come from different departments with different level of expertise. Each individual test session lasts 1 h and a half and follows the same walkthrough methodology [7]:

1. Welcome participant, Informed consent form signature and present user centered approach
2. Scenario reading and mockup limitation explanations (example: few auto scroll interactions could not be simulated)
3. Participant interaction with the prototype performing scenario goals without any help from the ergonomist. If the user seems stuck after many tries, the ergonomist gives the solution but then the interaction is tagged as failed (0% or 100% in Figs. 7 and 8).
4. System usability scale (SUS) survey to measure global software satisfaction
5. Task satisfaction scale form and user remark debriefing
6. Open questions and participant acknowledgments

4.2   User Satisfaction

System Usability Scale
At the end of each test, participants fill SUS form. SUS gives us the global satisfaction of the prototype. Rather than "Think aloud protocol", participants were not allowed to give any observation before this step. This protocol aims to avoid any ergonomist's explanation bias from participant satisfaction opinion (Figs. 5 and 6).

Fig. 5. French translated SUS result from the 5 participants of increment 1.

Fig. 6. French translated SUS result from the 7 participants of increment 2. Note that one participant results have been removed from average score due to inconsistent answers.

From increment 1 and 2, we can observe a big satisfaction deterioration: losing 17 points on SUS average score. The main empirical hypothesis raised from this drop is the higher complexity and the higher number of widgets provided between increments (see Figs. 3 and 4). For the next iteration, our SUS goal is to reach a score higher to

72/100 by moving secondary widgets out of first end-user's eye exploration (and placing them into visible/hidden panel).

Task Satisfaction Scale

SUS doesn't extract which technical task lower the satisfaction. So we decided to add a dirty homemade survey (rating from 1 to 5). This survey aims to prioritize which part of the software front-end need to be improved for the next iteration. A proper survey wasn't investigated as it would have taken too much time in the test protocol.

From increment 1 and 2, five equivalent tasks were covered (e.g. "ouverture d'une procédure") and four tasks were totally new. We can notice that modifications made between increments did bring better satisfaction for three of them (while the others stayed stable). By contrast with SUS score, it gives us a good feedback for our dirty UCD approach relevance. This chart will also be used to compare this analysis to iteration 3 and check task satisfaction progress.

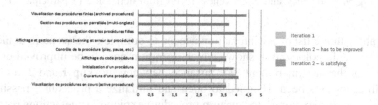

Fig. 7. Bar chart high-level functionality satisfaction result from both iterations (1 & 2). From an empiric decision, every score below 3, 4/5 is marked "has to be improved"

4.3 Interaction Quality

Interaction quality is inspected through two usability metrics:

- Effectiveness: does your participant succeeded or not to complete the interaction? (column "goal reached")
- Efficiency: does your participant make errors before completing his goal? And how long does he take to finish it? (column "error rate" and "time")

Scénario part	Interaction	Objectives	Goal reached	Error rate	Time (minute)
Ouverture et initialisation procédure A	1.01	Clic du "open procedure"	100%	0,2	
	1.02	Ouverture de la procédure A	100%	1,4	
	1.03	Configuration variables avant instanciation procédure	100%	0	
	1.04	Validation configuration et instanciation	100%	0	
Manipulation et lancement de la procédure A	1.05	Expand du step pour trouver l'instruction	80%	1,4	
	1.06	Mise en place du point d'arrêt sur l'instruction	80%	1	0,7
	1.07	Création de l'annotation	100%	2	
	1.08	Validation de l'annotation	100%	0	
	1.09	Lancement de la procédure en automatique	100%	0	
	1.10	Déroulement de la procédure "instruction par instruction"	100%	1,2	
	1.11	Relance de la procédure en automatique	100%	0	
	1.12	Visualisation de la procédure terminée	100%	0	

Fig. 8. Efficiency and effectiveness report from iteration 1 (5 participants)

Scénario part	Ref	Interaction	Result: Goal reached	Result: Error rate	Result: Time (minute)
Ouverture et initialisation manœuvre F	1.01	Clic "New procedure"	100%	1,7	11,7
	1.02	Ouverture "SAT 1"	100%	0,1	
	1.03	Ouverture "OOC Contingency"	100%	0,3	
	1.04	Selection "Manœuvre F" dans liste	100%	0,3	
	1.05	Clic sur "Select"	100%	0,7	
	1.06	Choix du mode "Interactive"	100%	0	
	1.07	Clic "Open"	100%	0	
	1.08	Initialisation "Arguments" clic sur "Submit"	100%	0	
	1.09	Initialisation "Variable externes" clic sur "Submit"	100%	0,4	
Switch et ouverture manœuvre I dans nouvel onglet	2.01	Clic sur "Active procedures"	71%	3,6	
	2.02	Clic "New procedure"	100%	0,6	
	2.03	Clic sur "Nouvel onglet"	86%	0,7	
	2.04	Ouverture "SAT 1"	100%	0	
	2.05	Ouverture "OOC Contingency"	100%	0	
	2.06	Selection "Manœuvre F" dans liste	100%	0	
	2.07	Clic sur "Select"	100%	0	
	2.08	Choix du mode "Interactive"	100%	0	
	2.09	Clic "Open"	100%	0	
	2.10	Initialisation "Arguments" clic sur "Submit"	100%	0	
	2.11	Initialisation "Variable externes" clic sur "Submit"	100%	0	
Ouverture de manœuvre F dans un nouvel onglet et lancement des deux manœuvres en parallèle	3.01	Switch onglet "PRISM"	86%	0,6	
	3.02	Clic sur droit (simulé) sur "Control" Manœuvre F	100%	2,1	
	3.03	Clic sur "Nouvel onglet"	100%	0	
	3.04	Clic sur "Play" Manœuvre F	100%	0	
	3.05	Switch onglet "Manœuvre I"	100%	0	
	3.06	Clic sur "Play" Manœuvre I	100%	0	
Gestion des warnings et des alertes. Affichage des procédures archivées	4.01	Clic sur "Warning" dans la header barre	86%	1,3	
	4.02	Clic sur "Go to"	100%	0	
	4.03	Clic sur "Continue" dans la popup de warning	100%	0	
	4.04	Switch sur la procédure Manœuvre F2 par le composant Thread	100%	1,7	
	4.05	Clic sur "Continue" dans la popup d'erreur	100%	0	
	4.06	Switch back sur la Manœuvre F dans le composant Thread	71%	1,4	
	4.07	Switch onglet "Manœuvre I"	100%	0,1	
	4.08	Clic sur "Link" de la popup d'archivage	100%	0	

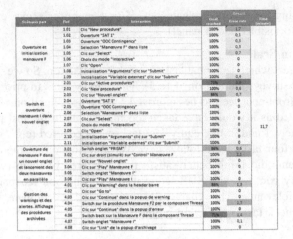

Fig. 9. Efficiency and effectiveness report from iteration 2 (7 participants)

The tables above list every interaction needed to complete the scenario at increment 1 and 2. The table colorization shows which operation need to be improved or modify in priority for the next increment. For instance, between mockup 1 and 2, a big front-end modification has been designed to open and initialize a procedure: passing from native browser "file explorer" to "custom procedure explorer" (interactions represented by #1.02 to #1.04 of Fig. 7 and #1.02 to #1.09 of Fig. 8). Surprisingly even if task satisfaction grew significantly (Fig. 9), the newer interface didn't lower interaction error rate: 1, 6 at iteration 1 and 3, 5 at iteration.

On other hand, time measures didn't bring any comparative added-value on interaction quality. Overall time evaluation must be changed to task-oriented time evaluation. For the next iteration, time should be sampled by task (column "scenario part") and task should be kept consistent on next iterations. Also by using keystroke-level ergonomics method [9], we could analyze and compare the interaction performance to what an expert would have done.

#	Vidget	Besoins / Remarques	Rapport	Besoin émis par	Quand	Gain satisfaction perçu	Complexité perçue	Status	Commentaire
98	GLOBAL	Garder une interface claire, fluide et non surchargée. Pas de fenêtre dans tout les sens. Vis-à-vis des autres SCC concurrents l'interface est très moderne	4	AIT + VCF	Test utilisateur - itération2	High	Medium	Pris en compte	
99	procedure-thread	Manque de visibilité sur le déroulement des procédures mères en parrallèle sur le satellite ainsi que leur état (mieux les mettre en valeur)	4	OPS + AIT + VCF + CCSL	Test utilisateur - itération2	High	Low	Pris en compte	
100	procedure-alerts	Les erreurs ne sont pas assez visibles. Faire clignoter le label d'erreur pour attirer le regard de l'opérateur (surtout qu'au centre de commande satellite, un opérateur est face à une multitude d'écran)	3	AIT + VCF + CCSL	Test utilisateur - itération2	High	Low	Spécification	Avec robert car partie DEV TAS
101	procedure-thread	Ajouter une arborescance / visualisation pour voir toutes les procédures en cours sur le satellite à chaque procédure ouverte (très intéressant pour les clients aussi)	5	OPS + AIT + VCF + CCSL	Test utilisateur - itération2	High	Medium	Pris en compte	Iteration 3
102	[illegible]	Ouvrir et basculer automatiquement sur les procédures qui se [illegible]	2	OPS + AIT	Test utilisateur -	High	Medium	[illegible]	Impact sur comment on [illegible]

Fig. 10. User remark list sample. Each remark is tagged with the number of people who ask for it, from which department the participant comes from, when it has been identify (increment number), what is the empirical perceived ergonomics gain if integrated and what is the perceived complexity to implement it.

4.4   Solution Convergence

Solution convergence is analyzed from the user remark number at each end of increment (see activity 4 Fig. 1).

At the first increment, we report 97 user remarks on the tested prototype. At the second iteration, we count only 51 observations (approximately −50%) for a prototype which cover more complexity and tasks. This reduction shows a first solution convergence to the final user requirements. This preliminary analysis will be corroborated with the next increment results.

4.5   Continuous Improvement

Another important point measured in our process is the continuous improvement of PRISM interactions at each increments (Figs. 11 and 12).

From remark listing (Fig. 10), every user feedback is labeled by his integration status (according to interaction designer and project manager discussion): Accepted (green) meaning "sent directly to development requirements" - To be specified (blue) meaning "related to other software system specifications" - Delayed (purple) meaning "to be investigated at next iteration" - To be discussed (orange) meaning "to be discussed with the chef architect for feasibility investigation" - Rejected (red) meaning "remark is not relevant or in contradiction with previous taken decision". From the two increment statements, we can deduce that the closer the project gets to the deadline, the fewer remarks are integrated into development (−54% accepted, +58% rejected and +80% to be discussed).

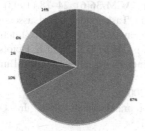

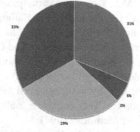

Fig. 11. Remark traceability chart iteration 1 (Color figure online)

Fig. 12. Remark traceability chart iteration 2 (Color figure online)

5   Conclusion

This paper presents the ongoing work of an early incremental user testing design approach. This dirty user centered design process allows front-end development at day one (as the first increment was prototyped and tested within 10 days). To assess this methodology relevance, we base our preliminary analysis on utility, usability and traceability metrics from two incremental user testing iterations.

As more complex features are integrated at each iteration, this approach doesn't seem relevant to keep SUS score consistently high. Also from interaction efficiency and effectiveness metrics, no significant improvements were noticed. These results are mainly due to the incremental approach where designer has to focus on next increment requirements rather than improving previous ones. From user remark traceability statement, this process doesn't as well give the opportunity to make major modifications as the development team gets closer to the release deadline.

However, homemade task satisfaction progress and user remark number analysis give a good feedback on the convergence of user needs. Furthermore, by integrating user in prototype testing loops, we identify one "game changer" idea which will be developed and test at iteration 3.

If development-first approach is requested and mandatory, this incremental user testing design approach can be applied as a dirty UCD process. Despite the lack of user research activities, our return on experience shows solution convergence and great feedback from participants but low capabilities on continuous improvement (interaction usability and remark integration) and some risks of user satisfaction drops.

References

1. Ergonomics of human-system interaction – Part 210: Human-centred design for interactive systems, ISO 9241-210 (2010). https://www.iso.org/standard/52075.html
2. Caplan, S.: Using focus group methodology for ergonomic design. Ergonomics **33**(5), 527–533 (1990)
3. Muller, M.J., Kuhn, S.: Participatory design. Commun. ACM **36**(6), 24–28 (1993)
4. Martinie, C., Palanque, P., Barboni, E., Ragosta, M.: Task-model based assessment of automation levels: application to space ground segments. In: 2011 IEEE International Conference on Systems, Man, and Cybernetics (SMC), pp. 3267–3273. IEEE, October 2011
5. Bornet, C., Brangier, E.: La méthode des personas: principes, intérêts et limites. Bulletin de psychologie (2), 115–134 (2013)
6. Nielsen, J.: Why you only need to test with 5 users (2000)
7. Wharton, C.: The cognitive walkthrough method: a practitioner's guide. In: Usability Inspection Methods (1994)
8. Van Someren, M.W., Barnard, Y.F., Sandberg, J.A.C.: The think aloud method: a practical approach to modeling cognitive (1994)
9. Card, S.K., Moran, T.P., Newell, A.: The keystroke-level model for user performance time with interactive systems. Commun. ACM **23**(7), 396–410 (1980)
10. Holtzblatt, K., Beringer, J., Baker, L.: Rapid user centered design techniques: challenges and solutions. In: CHI 2005 Extended Abstracts on Human Factors in Computing Systems, pp. 2037–2038. ACM, April 2005

Graphical User Interface Redefinition Addressing Users' Diversity

José Luís Silva[1,2]([⊠]) [iD] and J. C. Silva[3] [iD]

[1] Madeira-ITI, Funchal, Portugal
jose.l.silva@m-iti.org
[2] Instituto Universitário de Lisboa (ISCTE-IUL), ISTAR-IUL, Lisbon, Portugal
[3] Escola Superior de Tecnologia, 2Ai,
Instituto Politécnico do Cávado e do Ave, Barcelos, Portugal
jcsilva@ipca.pt

Abstract. Improvements can still be made in the development of Interactive Computing Systems (ICSs) aiming to ease their use. This is particularly true when trying to address users' diversity. Most ICSs do not adjust themselves to the user nor consider user's particularities. However, some provide solutions to address better specificities of expert and novice users. Others adjust themselves based on user's interaction history, but this does not always lead to improvements in use. An aspect that prevents to address users' diversity broadly is the fact that most of existing ICSs do not provide source code access. This means that only owners can introduce improvements on them.

This paper proposes an approach (based on both affective computing and computer vision) to broadly improve design for diversity (without source code access) for both existing and to be developed ICSs. The results are twofold: (i) example of an initial set of design guidelines; (ii) opens the way to runtime Graphical User Interface (GUI) redefinition and adjustment based on both user's features and emotions reducing therefore designers' restrictions when addressing users' diversity.

Keywords: Engineering interactive computing systems
Graphical user interface redefinition · Diversity inclusion · Design guidelines
Affective computing

1 Introduction

User interfaces (UIs) are a central aspect in any ICSs and critical for user's acceptance. According to the life cycle of a technology presented by Norman [1] there is a transition point where technology satisfies basic needs and customers are much more interested in efficiency, pleasure, and convenience. Therefore, UIs associated with a technology should be adjusted along time to meet user's expectations. Adjustment along time is also important while designing UIs because user's specificities are not always static, they change over time.

Even with the advances of user-centered approaches, design (e.g. universal design [2]) and usability (e.g. universal usability [3, 7]) issues persist [4]. According to

© IFIP International Federation for Information Processing 2019
Published by Springer Nature Switzerland AG 2019
C. Bogdan et al. (Eds.): HCSE 2018, LNCS 11262, pp. 319–326, 2019.
https://doi.org/10.1007/978-3-030-05909-5_20

Meiselwitz et al. [5] the challenges to achieve universal usability are associated to gap in users' knowledge and both technological and user diversity. Several approaches have been developed to take diversity into account when developing ICSs. Some consider that universal solutions should be considered while others ponder the use of specific designs targeted to specific user profiles as a way of embracing users' diversity. Both approaches have advantages and disadvantages. In one hand, designing for all users pose several challenges. One of the biggest challenges pointed out by Huh et al. [3] is finding the right balance between supporting all users and bringing enough profit to the designers. This is related to the fact that extreme users tend to be easily ignored due to their small number or simply because their existence is not always known. In the other hand, design for specific users or situations might deal better with extreme users but usually at the expense of compromised universality/globality.

This paper outlines a generic approach that allows the application of specific design guidelines to any individual or set of ICSs at runtime. The approach is based on the analysis of the graphical user interface (GUI) using both computer vision-based (Sikuli-based [6]) and affective computing-based approaches. Therefore, this allows the approach to be generic and without the need for ICS(s)' source code access. This enables developers and designers to improve the use of existing ICSs by empowering them to redefine existing GUIs and, consequently providing support for a wider diversity design inclusion. GUI adaptation without source code access poses several challenges as the information access and interaction should be made using computer vision-based techniques. In addition, the addressed GUI should be hidden or augmented to cope with the introduced modifications.

The article is structured as follows. Section 2 describes background concepts and presents some related research. Section 3 presents the proposed approach illustrated with an example in Sect. 4. Finally, discussion and conclusions are presented in Sects. 5 and 6.

2   Related Work

Developing ICSs that address diversity of users pose several challenges. The term "universal design" describes the concept of designing all products to be ideally usable by everyone. Universal usability [7] was introduced with the goal of facilitating the use of interfaces. From those concepts several principles, guidelines, heuristics and standards were developed [8–10]. However, those approaches are sometimes not sufficiently complete to meet usability needs of specific users [4]. They might even be contradictory [11].

Those challenges lead to the proposal of a new set of solutions to support diversity mostly based on computer vision. The ISI (Interactive Systems Integration) tool [12] enables the integration of several GUIs of different ICSs into one new GUI adapted to user's characteristics. However, features such as collecting the state of the original GUIs are still primitive. The work of Dixon et al. enables the identification of some GUI widgets [13, 14]. From this identification it is possible to build GUI pixel-based enhancements [13]. One example presented by the authors is the automatic translation of a GUI using Prefab, a tool using computer vision algorithms. The approach provides

GUI pixel-based enhancements (to a set of GUI widgets) but not its redefinition. We argue that supporting attentive real-time GUI redefinition is of major importance to foster design for diversity. Other works [15, 16] like SUPPLE [17] enable automatic GUI generation adapted to a person's specificities but it does not enable GUI redefinition of existing ones.

Several solutions from the computer vision field provide basis for GUI's widgets identification (e.g. OpenCV[1], CVIPtools[2]). For example, neural networks YOLO [18] is a real-time object detection solution that can detect over 9000 object categories from an image or video. Unfortunately, it was not applied to GUI widgets. We believe that this approach can be successfully applied to support GUI redefinition, but we are unaware of any work with this purpose or any annotated GUI widgets database essential for this purpose.

Emotion has gain importance in Human-Computer Interaction. Affective Computing [19] in particular addresses several challenges concerning with computers and emotions (e.g. ability to recognize and express emotions). The work of Tao et al. [20] and Poria et al. [21] provide an adequate review. Works in the area of affective interfaces consider emotion in the design (e.g. [22]). For example, the work of Mori et al. [23] reports results that aim to improve the understanding about what design techniques are more important to stimulate an emotion on the user. Alexander et al. [24] outlined the plan for an interface that adapt like humans to the non-verbal behavior of users. The idea has similarities with our approach however our focus is on GUI redefinition based on user's emotions but also based on other user's features (e.g. disease, experience).

3   GUI Redefinition and Design Guidelines

Prior work done by Gaganpreet et al. [25] developed an emotional state estimator that provides input for runtime GUI redefinition in the context of life critical robot tele-operation. This work is a complement to the Prefab's approach because users' emotions can be considered. However, the GUI redefinition is done manually case by case and without any guidelines.

Complementing those works enables a generic GUI redefinition for all approach fed by the user emotional state. This is beneficial because it enables designers and developers to keep existing design and source code but without preventing them to redefine the GUI to the diversity at runtime. Those advances might be further improved if user's specificities are considered. In addition, the development of a Design Guideline Provider (see Fig. 1) suggesting automatic GUI redefinitions based on both emotional user's states and specificities represent also an improvement.

Figure 1 presents the architecture of our GUI redefinition approach. It is composed by three main components that enable the proposed redefinition. They are:

---

1. Emotional State Estimator that identifies user's emotional states from their physical monitorization (e.g. via affectiva[3] and imotions[4]);
2. User's Specificities Identifier that identifies the user's profile and personality (Myers-Briggs Type Indicator[5]) from the answers provided to the questionnaire and from results of the test task performed;
3. Design Guidelines Provider that suggests design guidelines for the GUI redefinition based on the identified emotional states and user's specificities.

The output of the Design Guidelines Provider supports an automatic GUI redefinition at runtime. The old GUI is hidden running in a virtual machine and only the new GUI is presented to the user. We follow the approach made by Silva et al. [12] to enable a transparent GUI redefinition for the user. Silva et al. developed ISI, a tool that enables the creation of a new UI abstraction layer integrating different ICSs without accessing their source code. The proposed integration aims to improve end user interaction. The tool uses enriched ConcurTaskTree models and selected scenarios to generate Sikuli scripts. Each script is then associated to a widget of the new GUI. The interaction with a widget of the new GUI triggers the execution of the associated Sikuli script that will perform the task on existing ICSs.

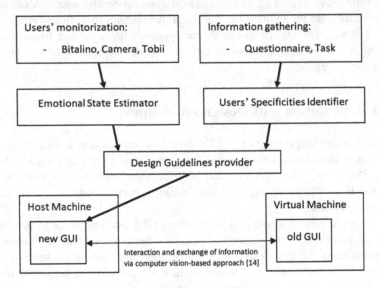

Fig. 1. GUI redefinition approach.

This work enables an innovative approach that address diversity more effectively. For this an example of an initial set of guidelines (mapping between user's

---

[3] affectiva.com (last accessed June 4, 2018).

[4] imotions.com (last accessed June 4, 2018).

[5] psycnet.apa.org/record/2013-29682-000 (last accessed June 4, 2018).

specificities/emotional state and redefinition rules) for the Design Guidelines provider are presented below.

Design Guidelines for Some Detected User's Specificities

1. Novice: step by step with tutorial;
2. Expert: automation;
3. Parkinson: selection via gaze, increase size;
4. Blind: translation rules;
5. Deaf: augmented captions.

Design Guidelines for Some Detected User's Emotional States

1. Frustrated: more effective interaction;
2. Confused: clarification, more feedback;
3. Stressed: use additional communication channels (e.g. scent, relaxing music) to appease the user;
4. Overload: split information into different communication channels (e.g. visual, audio, haptic).

This is only an example of initial set of guidelines. Machine learning algorithms will be developed to identify better guidelines based on the combination of the set of inputs detected (user's specificities and emotional states) and users' reaction. The resulting guidelines will be used as a basis for better automatic GUI redefinition.

We aim at enriching GUIs with emotional intelligence. This means that in the same way a person usually adapts to its interlocutor while interacting with him/her. Our approach enables a GUI to automatically adapt at runtime to the user that is interacting with it.

4   Example

This section as the purpose of illustrating the value of the approach with a concrete example where the opening for user diversity is made clearer.

Consider an application running on a tablet while its user is travelling by train. Due to the vibrations of the train the user becomes frustrated because he can't always hit the desired widget at the first attempt. In addition, the analysis of the interaction made revealed that the user has motor difficulties. Therefore, the input provided to our Design Guidelines provider (frustrated mental state and motor difficulties) lead to design guidelines suggestions such as:

- increase the size of icons;
- associate wrong clicks to the closer widget;
- enable gaze interaction.

Those guidelines are then automatically applied at runtime for the GUI redefinition. The GUI is updated when user emotional state changes are detected.

5 Discussion

Most contributions tend to develop models, applications or technologies to improve the design and development of new and better ICSs. This work aims to facilitate the improvement of existing ones without accessing their source code. One can argue that (old) existing ICSs tend to disappear being replaced by new versions. The fact is that several systems or old versions are still in use today. Some of them will eventually be updated in the future but the remaining ones will not. This might be explained by two reasons: (i) absence of updated versions; (ii) the user does not update it.

Several ICSs do not enable personalization nor were designed to consider diversity. Furthermore, as integration is also considered, this approach enables the application of specific or universal solutions to the set of GUIs to be integrated. Ultimately, this can lead to a new way of designing and developing ICSs where they are used, as a whole, in task and user centered design approaches. For instance, several pieces of existing software with different purposes can be merged together into a new GUI where the goal is not to expose the functionalities of the system but rather use them to empower the user to accomplish easier tasks execution.

The design of GUIs to be run on top of existing ICSs raise implementation challenges but we believe that the advantages are strong:

1. GUIs enhanced with emotional intelligence adjusting themselves to the user who is interacting with it;
2. Enable design for diversity to be automatically applied at runtime to new and existing GUIs.

Challenges of using computer vision-based techniques such as disambiguation in the identification of widgets can be reduced with anchors (UiPath[6] software follow this method). Theme variations (e.g. color, text font, size) might introduce difficulties while running the Sikuli scripts. These can be reduced by introducing transparencies in the figures provided to the scripts.

It is important to note that, although some parts are already implemented, the presented approach is an ongoing work. The solution and guidelines must be evaluated with user studies. For instance, GUI runtime modifications in one direction can be fast when detecting user confusion but should be slow when the user emotional state is going back to user "normal" state. The identification of an adequate delay to be used in this case is an example of the importance that the user studies will have.

6 Conclusions

This paper presents an approach that aims at enabling developers and designers to change any existing GUI at runtime based on both user's specificities and emotional state. This will ultimately enable designing for diversity to be broadly applied. In addition, an example of a set of design guidelines based in this innovative approach is presented.

---

[6] uipath.com (last accessed July 4, 2018).

Acknowledgments. This work was supported from Fundação para a Ciência e a Tecnologia (FCT, Portugal), through project UID/EEA/50009/2013 and by ISTAR-IUL through project UID/MULTI/0446/2013.

References

1. Norman, D.A.: The Invisible Computer: Why Good Products Can Fail, the Personal Computer Is so Complex, and Information Appliances are the Solution. MIT Press, Cambridge (1998)
2. Law, C.M., et al.: A systematic examination of universal design resources: part 1, heuristic evaluation. Univ. Access Inf. Soc. 7(1–2), 31–54 (2008)
3. Huh, J., Ackerman, M.S.: Designing for all users: including the odd users. In: Extended Abstracts on Human Factors in Computing Systems, pp. 2449–2458. ACM (2009)
4. Ruzic, L., Sanfod, J.A.: Universal Design Mobile Interface Guidelines (UDMIG) for an aging population. In: Marston, H.R., Freeman, S., Musselwhite, C. (eds.) Mobile e-Health. HIS, pp. 17–37. Springer, Cham (2017). https://doi.org/10.1007/978-3-319-60672-9_2
5. Meiselwitz, G., Wentz, B., Lazar, J.: Universal usability: past, present, and future. In: Foundations and Trends in Human-Computer Interaction. Now Publishers Inc. (2009)
6. Yeh, T., Chang, T.-H., Miller, R.C.: Sikuli: using GUI screenshots for search and automation. In: Symposium on User Interface Software and Technology, pp. 183–192. ACM (2009)
7. Shneiderman, B.: Universal usability. Commun. ACM 43(5), 84–91 (2000)
8. Shneiderman, B.: Shneiderman's eight golden rules of interface design (2009)
9. FDIS, ISO: 9241-110: 2006. Ergonomics of human system interaction-Part 110: Dialogue principles. International Organization for Standardization (ISO), Switzerland (2009)
10. ISO: Ergonomics of Human-system Interaction: Principles and requirements for physical input devices (ISO 9241–400:2007, IDT). International Organisation for Standardisation (2007)
11. Pak, R., McLaughlin, A.: Designing Displays for Older Adults. CRC Press, Boca Raton (2010)
12. Silva, J.L., Ornelas, J.D., Silva, J.C.: Make it ISI: interactive systems integration tool. In: Proceedings of the Symposium on Engineering Interactive Computing Systems, pp. 245–250. ACM (2016)
13. Dixon, M., Leventhal, D., Fogarty, J.: Content and hierarchy in pixel-based methods for reverse engineering interface structure. In: Proceedings of the SIGCHI Conference on Human Factors in Computing Systems, p. 969 (2011)
14. Morgan Dixon, A., Nied, C., Fogarty, J.: Prefab layers and prefab annotations: extensible pixel-based interpretation of graphical interfaces. In: UIST 2014, pp. 221–230 (2014)
15. Gajos, K.Z., Weld, D.S., Wobbrock, J.O.: Automatically generating personalized user interfaces with SUPPLE. Artif. Intell. 174(12–13), 910–950 (2010)
16. Gajos, K.Z., Wobbrock, J.O., Weld, D.S.: Improving the performance of motor-impaired users with automatically-generated, ability-based interfaces. In: Proceedings of Conference on Human Factors in Computing Systems, USA, pp. 1257–1266. ACM (2008)
17. Gajos, K., Weld, D.S.: SUPPLE: automatically generating user interfaces. In: Proceedings of the 9th International Conference on Intelligent User Interfaces, pp. 93–100. ACM (2004)
18. Redmon, J., Farhadi, A.: YOLO9000: better, faster, stronger. arXiv preprint arXiv:1612.08242 (2016)
19. Picard, R.W.: Affective Computing. The MIT Press, Cambridge (1995)

20. Tao, J., Tan, T.: Affective computing: a review. In: Tao, J., Tan, T., Picard, R.W. (eds.) ACII 2005. LNCS, vol. 3784, pp. 981–995. Springer, Heidelberg (2005). https://doi.org/10.1007/11573548_125

21. Poria, S., Cambria, E., Bajpai, R., Hussain, A.: A review of affective computing: from unimodal analysis to multimodal fusion. Inf. Fusion **37**, 98–125 (2017)

22. Cyr, D.: Emotion and web site design. In: Soegaard, M., Dam, R.F. (eds.) The Encyclopedia of Human Computer Interaction, 2nd edn., Chap. 40. Interaction Design Foundation

23. Mori, G., Paternò, F., Furci, F.: Design criteria for stimulating emotions in web applications. In: Abascal, J., Barbosa, S., Fetter, M., Gross, T., Palanque, P., Winckler, M. (eds.) INTERACT 2015. LNCS, vol. 9296, pp. 165–182. Springer, Cham (2015). https://doi.org/10.1007/978-3-319-22701-6_12

24. Alexander, S., Sarrafzadeh, A.: Interfaces that adapt like humans. In: Masoodian, M., Jones, S., Rogers, B. (eds.) APCHI 2004. LNCS, vol. 3101, pp. 641–645. Springer, Heidelberg (2004). https://doi.org/10.1007/978-3-540-27795-8_70

25. Singh, G., Badia, S., Ventura, R., Silva, J.L.: Physiologically attentive user interface for robot teleoperation - real time emotional state estimation and interface modification using physiology, facial expressions and eye movements. In: Proceedings of the International Joint Conference on Biomedical Engineering Systems and Technologies, pp. 294–302. ISBN 978-989-758-279-0

Integrating HCD into BizDevOps by Using the Subject-Oriented Approach

Peter Forbrig[(⊠)] and Anke Dittmar

University of Rostock, Albert-Einstein-Str. 22, 18051 Rostock, Germany
{peter.forbrig,anke.dittmar}@uni-rostock.de

Abstract. The DevOps-approach becomes more and more important because of the success of agile software development in conjunction with the continuously changing reality. It aims at unifying development and operations. A common team is responsible for both domains. Additionally, there are approaches like Continuous Software Engineering with the intention to unify business administration (Biz) and development. Even tool chains for BizDevOps are possible. The paper discusses aspects of BizDev and BizDevOps using a subject-oriented approach for supporting aspects of HCD. The focus lies on modeling user activities and business processes. Additionally, the role of domain-specific textual languages is discussed. Most important is the fact that methods from HCI like task modeling or storytelling can support BizDev and BizDevOps.

Keywords: Model-based approach · Stories · DevOps · BizDev
BizDevOps

1 Introduction

Changing requirements of interactive software systems are rather the rule than the exception. Therefore, software solutions have to be continuously updated during operation in order to respond properly to contextual changes. Classical development methods fail to address this challenge and are more and more replaced by agile approaches. Together with the increasing popularity of agile software development methods an increasing need for continuously deploying software arose. The idea of DevOps as a clipped compound of development and operations was born. It comes with automatic quality assurance and continuous delivery.

Unfortunately, agile methods such as SCRUM often lack a human-centered design perspective. Design activities such as those recommended in the ISO 9241-210 on the human-centered design process are insufficiently integrated into agile software development. For example, agile methods often do not support a systematic exploration of alternative solutions. Existing approaches to integrate HCD activities into agile process models mainly focus on the design of the user interface (UI). However, it is common ground in the fields of human-computer interaction (HCI) and interaction design that UI design needs to be informed by the analysis of the organizational context and the users' tasks and needs. It is assumed that business process models, task models, or user stories as results from such broader analysis help to derive UI models of higher quality.

Published by Springer Nature Switzerland AG 2019
C. Bogdan et al. (Eds.): HCSE 2018, LNCS 11262, pp. 327–334, 2019.
https://doi.org/10.1007/978-3-030-05909-5_21

This paper suggests a better integration of subject-oriented business modeling and task-modeling activities into agile development approaches.

2 DevOps, BizDev and BizDevOps

DevOps is currently discussed a lot in industry. It is related to development technologies and organizational aspects. "DevOps is defined as a paradigm or set of principles focuses on software delivery through enabling continuous feedback, quick response to changes and using automated delivery pipelines resulting in reduced cycle time" [13].

Very important aspects are the monitoring of the running software and the feedback for improvements in short intervals. DevOps is also discussed in the context of continuous software engineering [5]. First ideas of a disappearing boundary between development-time and run-time were published by Bares and Ghezzi [1]. In their abstract, they state: "Models need to continue to live at run-time and evolve as changes occur while the software is running." Business process models and task models seems to be candidates for such an approach. According to Humble and Farley [12], Continuous Delivery and DevOps have common goals and are often used in conjunction. However, there are subtle differences. "While continuous delivery is focused on automating the processes in software delivery, DevOps also focuses on the organization change to support great collaboration between the many functions involved" [12].

Fitzgerald and Stol [5] argue that there has to be a continuous integration of business strategy and software development. They use the term BizDev for this purpose. In the framework of Continuous Software Engineering BizDev and DevOps are separated. However, a combination of both is possible. Gruhn and Schäfer address with BizDevOps "the boundary between IT and business departments in order to allow business departments to participate hands-on in the development of parts of the system and at the same time having measures in place that allow IT to safeguard the development process" [11]. They argue that the approach makes sense for systems that reflect business innovations. It might not be appropriate for general-purpose software development.

3 Subject-Oriented Business-Process Modeling

Fleischmann et al. [6] characterize subject-oriented business-process management (BPM) as socially executable BPM. They further argue: "As organizations need to act flexible in the continuously changing landscape of the digital economy, their process work is increasingly driven by valued interactions among stakeholders [14]. Traditional … BPM does no longer fit to this changing view of processes".

It is therefore necessary to have a specification language that on the one hand is simple to learn and to use. On the other hand, the specification should be executable. The best would be if domain experts can specify their business process models by themselves. S-BPM seems to be a solution for that. Practitioners from industry report on the Metasonic[1] web page about such success stories. S-BPM specifies business processes from the perspective of subjects that communicate via messages and provides a simple notation. Subjects can be humans or software agents.

S-BPM [7] is a graphical specification language that has five language elements only. These elements are subject, message, send state, function state, and receive state. S-BPM specifications start with modeling of a communication diagram. It represents possible communications of subjects via messages. The big picture of an application is specified in this way. Details of the behavior of each subject are specified later by finite state machines. Figure 1 provides an example form [7] of a communication diagram for a vacation request of an employee. The request goes to a manager who decides about acceptance. If the request is approved human resources (HR) and the employee are informed accordingly by an approval message. If the request is turned down, only the employee gets a denial message. The subject employee is able to start the communication.

A communication diagram visualizes possible message exchanges. However, the sequence and dependences of messages are not specified. This is done in a behavioral diagram. Each subject is characterized by exactly one diagram. It consists of states and messages. Figure 2 provides in its left part a model for the dynamic behavior of an employee that consists of five states and five messages.

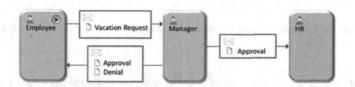

Fig. 1. Example of an S-BPM communication diagram

According to the provided specification, an employee fills a form first and sends afterwards the filled form to a manager. Having done this, the employee has to wait for an answer message from a manager. If the request is accepted, the employee can go on vacation and afterwards go to work. Otherwise, the employee has to go to work immediately. It is the intention of S-BPM to provide tool support for end-user modelling. Stakeholders should be able to edit their own behavior model.

There is the saying that "a picture is worth a thousand words". However, sometimes it is good to have a textual domain specific language as an alternative to graphical specifications.

It was our intention to have a look at a textual representation of behavioral models of S-BPM as well. We modified the grammar of the example from Fowler in such a way that behavioral specifications of S-BPM can be expressed. Right part of Fig. 2 expresses the specification of the left part of Fig. 2 in a domain-specific language.

---

[1] https://www.metasonic.de/en, last visited January 21, 2018.

Based on the textual specification java code can be generated and executed. This provides a further perspective and different experience with the domain model.

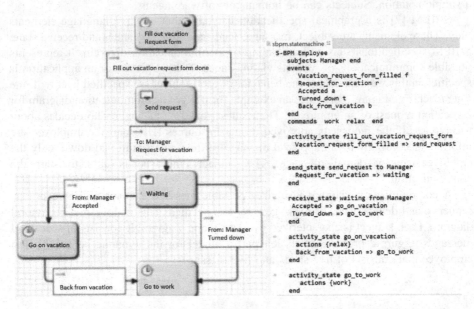

```
 sbpm.statemachine 
S-BPM Employee
  subjects Manager end
  events
    Vacation_request_form_filled f
    Request_for_vacation r
    Accepted a
    Turned_down t
    Back_from_vacation b
  end
  commands  work  relax  end

  activity_state fill_out_vacation_request_form
    Vacation_request_form_filled => send_request
  end

  send_state send_request to Manager
    Request_for_vacation => waiting
  end

  receive_state waiting from Manager
    Accepted => go_on_vacation
    Turned_down => go_to_work
  end

  activity_state go_on_vacation
    actions {relax}
    Back_from_vacation => go_to_work
  end

  activity_state go_to_work
    actions {work}
  end
```

Fig. 2. Behavioral diagram for subject employee (adapted from [7]) on the left and specification in a textual DSL on the right.

Alternatively, to the suggestion of S-BPM, activities of subjects could be specified as task models as well. The following section will discuss this aspect.

Task models are traditionally applied for designing and developing interactive systems. They describe the logical activities of users and can be the basis for user interface design. Each role of users is specified by a separate task model. The concept of roles is equivalent to the concept of subjects. Therefore, task models can specify the behavior of subjects. The DSL-CoTaL [3] was designed for such a purpose. It uses the temporal operators from CTT [4]. Additionally, preconditions can be specified in an OCL-like language. Figure 3 provides the example of the behavior of subject employee in the context of a vacation request.

```
role Employee for Vacation {
    root Asking_for_vacation = Fill_form >> Ask >> (Go_on_vacation [] Go_to_work);
        task Ask pre HR.oneInstance.Announce_holidays;
        task Go_on_vacation pre Manager.oneInstance.Accept_request;
        task Go_to_work pre Manager.oneInstance.Turn_down_request;
}
```

Fig. 3. Task model for employee.

For a vacation request, an employee has to fill a form. Afterwards ($\gg$-enabling), the employee has to ask a manager. After the employee asked, there is a choice between two tasks, going on vacation or going to work. Asking for vacation is only possible if the corresponding precondition is fulfilled. One instance of the subject human resources had to have performed the task of announcing the possibility of asking for holiday requests – in short announce holidays.

Xtext[2] can be used together with Xtend[3] for code generation. In this way, task models specified in DSL-Cotal can be visualized in different tools (see [10]).

Stories can help as well. In computer science, the term "user story" is used in different ways. They make things more interesting and improve the engagement of participants. The scenario-based approach from Rosson and Carroll [15] is based on descriptions of the use of the envisioned system.

Storytelling is used in many cultures as a means of education. However, stories are not only used for software development. They are also used in business management. Fog et al. characterize "storytelling as a Management Tool" [8]. They mention: "The stories we share with others are the building blocks of any human relationship. Stories place our shared experiences in words and images". It seems to be an excellent communication tool for BizDevOps.

4   Combining HCI Approaches with BizDevOps

S-BPM with its restricted number of language elements lets users successfully specify the behavior of their own role, their subject. Task models have been used for requirements analysis and for user-interface design. Traditionally each role is specified by a task model. This can be considered as subject-orientation. Therefore, it makes sense to use task models for business processes as well. They can replace behavioral models of S-BPM. The different models of S-BPM and task models open new perspectives that can be even further broadened by textual domain specific languages. Tool support for language engineering exists by Xtext and Xtend. It is also possible to

```
team Vacation {
    root Handling_vacation_requests =
        HR.Announce_holidays >> Process_request{*} [> HR.Finish;
    task Process_request =
        Employee.Ask >> Handle_decision >> Act_accordingly;
    task Handle_decision =
        Manager.Accept_request [] Manager.Turn_down_request;
    task Act_accordingly =
        Employee.Go_on_vacation [] Employee.Go_to_work;
}
```

Fig. 4. Team model for the holiday request example.

---

[2] https://www.itemis.com/en/xtext/, last visited January 20, 2018.
[3] http://www.eclipse.org/xtend/, last visited May 7th 2018.

specify the cooperation of subjects by task models. It is called team model in DSL-CoTaL [2, 9]. A team model is a counterpart to the communication diagram of S-BPM.

The team model consists of tasks that are executed in cooperation. A task can be preceded by a subject name. This means that the task has to be performed by an instance of this subject. Handling vacation requests is started and finished by an instance of subject HR by executing task Announce-holidays and Finish respectively.

Storytelling seems to be a good method as well for people from business administration as for developers. Textual DSLs can support the specification of task models based on stories. However, they can also be the basis for creating stories. The team model from Fig. 4 inspires the following story.

After Paula from HR sends an email to all employees to inform them that they can ask for holidays. After Fred asks for vacation, Manager Chris turns down the request from Fred and Fred goes to work. Afterwards Susan asks for vacation and Chris accepts the request from Susan and she goes immediately on vacation. Finally, Paula finishes the vacation request period.

While creating the story one might recognize that the strict order in the iterations is not reflecting the reality. Instance iteration ({#}) is a better model. It allows the start of a new iteration before the previous one was finished.

Figure 5 reflects the situation after Fred asked for vacation by animated model instances.

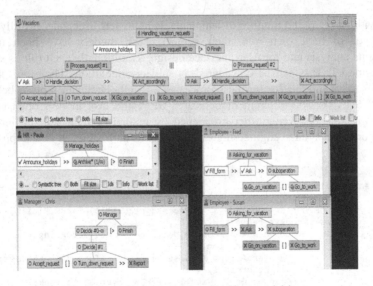

Fig. 5. Animated team model and subject model instances

On the top of Fig. 5 one can see the animated team model with instance iteration. A first iteration for a request is started. The second instance of an iteration is already prepared to be executed in parallel. One can see below, that Paula already announced holidays. Fred filled his form and asked already. Susan and Chris did not do anything yet. However, both can act while Fred has to wait for a decision.

The animation with CoTaL allows the dynamic creation of subject instances. Therefore, stories can really be well explored and improved. These stories help to validate models and the final application. The different kinds of knowledge representation (statecharts, task models, stories) should be used intertwined. Figure 6 describes the intended application of models and tools for functional requirements.

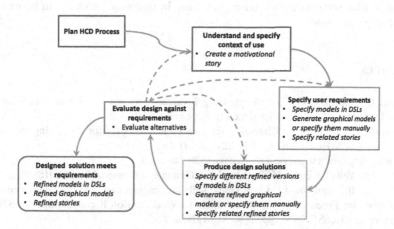

Fig. 6. Suggested human-centered-design process for functional requirements for BizDevOps

The structure of the process corresponds to the design process from ISO 9241-210. Additionally, the intended use of textual specification in DSLs, graphical specifications, and stories is added. All specifications are optional. Let us know discuss a possible tool chain for BizDevOps and the subject-oriented approach.

Gruhn and Schäfer [11] provided a software architecture for BizDevOps. The discussed tools for task modeling can be integrated as app with a corresponding plugin. For S-BPM there exists already a runtime environment that is used in several industrial companies. It can be integrated into the discussed architecture as well. In this way, the subject-oriented approach can get support by DevOps features like continuous deployment and continuous monitoring.

5 Summary and Outlook

The approaches DevOps, BizDev, and BizDevOps were discussed in the context of HCD. Communication between stakeholders is identified as the most important aspect. Therefore, social, cultural, and communication skills are necessary for all stakeholders.

Stories have been successfully used in HCI and in business administration. Therefore, they seem to be a perfect tool for BizDev and BizDevOps. They should be combined with subject-oriented notations and methods. Statecharts and task models are candidates for knowledge representation for subject behavior. Domain specific textual languages were suggested in conjunction to graphical notations. Providing different perspectives (states &tasks & stories, graphics & text) allows further insights into the domain. Tool support supports the creation of different versions of models. Therefore, alternatives can be specified without many efforts. Stories and models can be explored and the HCD process can be applied to DevOps, BizDev, and BizDevOps.

It might be possible to create even more abstract textual DSLs that fit to cognitive models of people from the business domain. A language allowing expressing stories could be a candidate for that. This language must have the option to add general information like iteration to certain expressions. In this way, models can be extracted from such specifications.

References

1. Baresi, L., Ghezzi, C.C.: The disappearing boundary between development-time and run-time. In: Future of Software Engineering Research (2010)
2. Buchholz, G., Forbrig, P.: Extended features of task models for specifying cooperative activities. PACMHCI 1(EICS), 7:1–7:21 (2017)
3. CoTaSE: https://www.cotase.de/. Accessed 20 Jan 2018
4. CTTE: http://hiis.isti.cnr.it:4500/research/CTTE/home. Accessed 15 Jan 2018
5. Fitzgerald, B., Stol, K.-J.: Continuous software engineering and beyond: trends and challenges. In: Proceedings of 1st International Workshop on Rapid Continuous Software Engineering - RcoSE 2014, pp. 1–9. ACM, New York
6. Fleischmann, A., Schmidt, W., Stary, C.: Subject-oriented BPM = socially executable BPM. In: Proceedings of the 15th IEEE Conference on Business Informatics (CBI 2013), Vienna, pp. 399–406. IEEE Computer Society (2013)
7. Fleischmann, A., Schmidt, W., Stary, C.: Open S-BPM = open innovation. In: Fischer, H., Schneeberger, J. (eds.) S-BPM ONE 2013. CCIS, vol. 360, pp. 295–320. Springer, Heidelberg (2013). https://doi.org/10.1007/978-3-642-36754-0_19
8. Fog, K., Budtz, C., Munch, P., Blanchette, S.: Storytelling as a management tool. In: Storytelling. Springer, Heidelberg (2010). https://doi.org/10.1007/978-3-540-88349-4_6
9. Forbrig, P., Buchholz, G.: Subject-Oriented specification of smart environments. In: S-BPM ONE, p. 8 (2017)
10. Forbrig, P., Dittmar, A., Kühn, M.: A textual domain specific language for task models - generating code for CoTaL, CTTE, and HAMSTERS. In: Proceedings of EICS 2018, Paris (2018). https://doi.org/10.1145/3220134.3225217
11. Gruhn, V., Schäfer, C.: BizDevOps: because DevOps is not the end of the story. In: Fujita, H., Guizzi, G. (eds.) SoMeT 2015. CCIS, vol. 532, pp. 388–398. Springer, Cham (2015). https://doi.org/10.1007/978-3-319-22689-7_30
12. Humble, J., Farley, D.: Continuous Delivery: Reliable Software Releases through Build, Test, and Deployment Automation. Pearson Education, London (2010)
13. Jabbari, R., bin Ali, N., Petersen, K., Tanveer, B.: What is DevOps?: a systematic mapping study on definitions and practices. In: Proceedings of the Scientific Workshop Proceedings of XP2016 (XP 2016 Workshops), Article 12. ACM, New York (2016)
14. Li, C., Bernoff, J.: Groundswell: Winning in a World Transformed by Social Technologies. Harvard Business Press, Boston (2008)
15. Rosson, B., Carroll, J.M.: Scenario-based design (Chap. 53). In: Jacko, J., Sears, A. (eds.) The Human-Computer Interaction Handbook Fundamentals, Evolving Technologies and Emerging Applications, pp. 1032–1050. Lawrence Erlbaum Associates, Mahwah (2002)

Intuitive User-Centered Interaction Design for ATV

Stuart Chapman[✉], Thomas Kirks, and Jana Jost

Fraunhofer Institute for Material Flow and Logistics,
Joseph-von-Fraunhofer-Str. 2-4, 44227 Dortmund, Germany
{stuart.chapman, thomas.kirks,
jana.jost}@iml.fraunhofer.de

Abstract. The communication between the human and robot in the social networked industry plays a crucial role. Autonomous robots navigate freely through the warehouses and therefore need to convey their intentions and tasks in an intuitive and understandable manner for its human counterpart. This study examines the icons on the e-Paper display of the ATV EMILI. Tasks of EMILI are the transportation of goods and collaborating with its user by adjusting its height for a safer ergonomic use. The robot communicates its status and intention via its display. The icons transfer task or error messages to its users. The icons have been evaluated in an iterative process consisting of three test phases. Based on the results of the different test phases and the technical restrictions new icons have not been developed until the requirements of the users have been matched. The error icons have been standardized and did not cause any ambiguity in their meaning, whereas the task icons had to be removed and new icons had to be developed.

Keywords: User-centered design · Human-robot-interaction
Robotic interfaces

1 Introduction

The interaction between the two main actors – the human being and the machine – harbors new challenges and problems in the sociological questions of a company. These questions arise during the implementation and integration phase of new technologies. A central concept is the sociotechnical approach, which deals with the relationship between the user and the system. As soon as a machine acts autonomously, it affects human's behavior towards this kind of machines. However, the machine is programmed to interact with its user and to intervene in cases of error. The central question arises to what extent autonomous technology must be designed so that the user feels comfortable using the technology and can carry out his or her work safe and reliable. Intuitive operation and communication between the actors are challenges that need to be met.

This paper deals with a new kind of autonomous transport vehicle (ATV) which offers intuitive interaction methods for the human. EMILI (ergonomic, mobile, interactive load carrier for intralogistics) is a combination of ATV and a small load carrier

© IFIP International Federation for Information Processing 2019
Published by Springer Nature Switzerland AG 2019
C. Bogdan et al. (Eds.): HCSE 2018, LNCS 11262, pp. 335–342, 2019.
https://doi.org/10.1007/978-3-030-05909-5_22

(SLC). It combines the compact design and standardized handling of a SLC with the capabilities of a modern ATV. EMILI can seamlessly be integrated into existing processes and systems thanks to the exact compliance with the external dimensions of a SLC (400 × 600 × 220 mm). From above you can see a load area, which has a recess for material transport and two horizontal handles, which are similar to the carrying handles of a normal SLC. There is a scissor lift under the lid, which can be extended up to 600 mm. It can adjust the height of the load-handling device as well as its storage area according to the height of the human worker. The current version of the SLC contains in front an e-Paper display. The display is 500 mm long, 137 mm high and is centered on the 400 mm wide front surface. In each case, 50 mm of the display are to both sides around the corner of the ATV and thus protrude out onto the two 600 mm long surfaces. The retractable running gear allows it for example to be stacked onto other SLC, transported using conventional conveyor technology and stored in an automated small parts warehouse. With EMILI the first ATV, which emphasizes on physical as well as psychological ergonomics, has been designed. EMILI is not restricted to certain areas in the warehouse and can be used without any external safety infrastructure. This allows real human-robot-collaboration. Further, it displays information about its state on the e-Paper display so that bidirectional interaction is possible. It can transport goods or tools to the human worker and function as a mobile picking station. Therefore, different applications like maintenance tasks as well as picking can be realized.

EMILI offers different interaction modalities. It can interact via web services with other machines and systems. Further, the human can cooperate with EMILI with smart glasses or smartphones. Natural and intuitive interaction is possible through recognizing gestures of the human worker. The physical demanding component and the exhausting procurement of goods is shifted to the robot. This new distribution of tasks increases the productivity and the user experience of the interaction. To set up a safe working environment, the icons and intentions of EMILI need to be comprehendible by everyone working in the warehouse. Therefore, EMILI has an e-Paper display that provides information about its status. This information needs to trigger intuitive action. Hence, the selection and composition of icons need to be analyzed.

2 Background

2.1 Human-Robot-Interfaces

For interfacing machines or robots, there exist different interaction modalities. Common solutions are PC-based programs or human-machine-interfaces directly at the machine control. Both are spatially limited, need special training and are therefore very inflexible. Some robots and machines offer interaction modalities via Apps on Tablets or Smartphone, which overcome the lack of spatial flexibility. Still the usage is not very intuitive since the feedback is not given directly at the robot or machine itself. In contrast, social robots e.g. Pepper [1] or Baxter [2] offer bidirectional feedback by using different colors or facial expressions to symbolize different states of the robot.

2.2   Automated Transport Vehicles

Automated Transport Vehicles are used to transport goods or people in a spatially limited space [3]. They belong to the group of discontinuous ground conveyors, are automatically controlled and move without any influence of the human [4]. According to [4] one or more ATV together with a control unit, infrastructure and components for data transmission, localization etc. build up an Automated Transport System (ATS). The usage of ATS started in the late 1950s in America [5]. From there on, they have changed regarding their flexibility and efficiency. Nowadays, there exist a variety of ATV which differ mainly in payload, navigation technology e.g. free navigation and control (centralized, decentralized or hybrid). A coming up trend in the field of ATV are low-cost ATV which enable small and middle sized companies to use ATV in their production systems or logistics facilities. Those ATV have lesser payload and drive with lower velocities so that for human-robot collaborated workspaces no external safety sensors are needed. Low-cost ATV are for example the LEO Locative of the company BITO [6] or the Weasel of the company SSI Schäfer [7].

3   Icon Description

EMILI has six different icons to display various states and in this way to provide information relevant to the user. The following sections distinguish between the warning icons and the task icons of EMILI. For the description of the warning symbols a comparison is given, as these represent a reference to already established symbols. The first three icons on the left display are for error messages and warning messages and appear in so-called "error" states. Error states are used to inform the user of error messages of any kind. The triangular symbol with an exclamation mark in the middle is similar to the street sign, immediately obvious and defined by the DIN EN ISO 7010 as a warning sign [8]. This icon lights up on the display as soon as an Error-state has occurred, for example if EMILI no longer has an internet connection, the accumulator is empty or a technical malfunction is detected.

The second icon is the battery. This makes an empty impression and contains an exclamation mark inside. This symbol appears as soon as the accumulator installed in EMILI reaches a critical battery level. In the operating systems of Android and iOS, similar icons are implemented to indicate a low battery level, usually with only an almost empty battery instead of an exclamation point. Finally, there is the icon for a missing wireless connection to the system. This consists of an exclamation point and a common symbol for a wireless internet connection, which is also widely used on mobile platforms. The three warning icons are deliberately based on already established symbols, so that EMILI users do not have to learn those icons and can immediately establish a connection between them. In addition to the three warning icons, there are three status icons indicating information about the current work task of EMILI. These icons are a square in a three-dimensional view and a circle, which in turn is divided into four quarter circles (see Fig. 1). The square represents a container. Being lit up on the display means that EMILI is currently executing a transport request.

Next to the container, a cogwheel icon has been implemented. There is an offset in the tooth position, while the gear itself remains in the same place. In this way, the illusion of a rotating gearwheel is created and the status "busy" is displayed. The rotating gear means that the robot is currently executing a task that does not necessarily require a transport request. For example, EMILI could participate in another place in a building and makes an empty run without a container. The circle with the quarters is the hint of a watch and is a qualitative statement about the theoretical duration of the task.

Fig. 1. Old task icons

4   Analysis of Icons

The information on the display of EMILI needs be comprehensive for the user and should not cause erroneous actions. Therefore, the technical as well as the human requirements have to be considered and implemented in the design of the icons. To guarantee an intuitive and safe interaction, a human-centered approach was chosen in which an online survey and interviews were conducted. These methods give straight feedback to existing icons and reveal how the icons have to be developed. By using this approach in the development stage, the costs are kept low and the users are involved.

The evaluation of the interface of EMILI took place in an iterative process. The aim of the analysis was to determine how much the icons match the expectations of the user and in cases of ambiguity and uncertain information influence the communication capability of the interface. The interface was first evaluated in an expert evaluation. An interdisciplinary team was formed, consisting of a graphic designer, computer scientists and a human factors engineer. States of EMILI consist of a composition of a facial expression, icons and text hints. In this work, we focused on the interpretation of the icons. By developing new icons, the technical compound had to be considered to ensure a smooth transition from prototyping to finally developing a new interface. The expert evaluation discovered misleading icons. In the beginning, each expert evaluated the states and the compounds of the interface on his or her own according to its meaning and how it is visualized. Afterwards, the experts came together in a meeting and problematic icons were reflected and alternative designs and compounds were developed. In particular, the time icon, the busy icon and the icon for transportation were not fully recognizable. Due to technical restrictions of the e-Paper display just a limited amount of segments was given. Therefore, the range of possible alternatives had to fit these technical requirements.

These issues were addressed in the second phase, which consisted of testing the icons with alternate icons. The used method was an online survey conducted at the Fraunhofer Institute for Material Flow and Logistics (IML). The focus lied on the ambiguous icons of the e-Paper display, discovered in the expert evaluation. Participants were given the possibility to propose other icons and give their meaning to the current and alternative designs. A total of 191 anonymous respondents took part. The interval coefficient was 95% and the error of margin was 6%. The respondents were mainly young and nearly 70% were in the range from 18–31. Continuing with the iterative process, the new icons were implemented and tested in a last test phase. Ten interviews were conducted at the Fraunhofer IML. Six participants were female and the mean age was 27. The aim of the interviews was examining if there are still issues concerning the meaning of the icons. The interview was structured and the questions were based on the results of the questionnaire and the additional comments of the participants. Participants were shown all icons without and with text hints. Afterwards participants should determine what the icons mean. The result was that all participants preferred icons with text hints. Reasons were that especially in the newly created icons, participants could better comprehend what the meaning of the icons are. The warnings signs are standardized icons, used on smartphones to illustrate the same problem statements occurring on a smartphone than on the interface of EMILI. Concerning the warning triangle, the design referred to the DIN EN ISO 7010. The idea behind using familiar icons is to mitigate confusion and to accelerate the learning stage.

The success of the combination of familiar and new icons and a new display design has been evaluated by using the User Experience Questionnaire (UEQ). The UEQ consists of six scales. Our study focused on the three scales attractiveness, perspicuity and efficiency. The three scales are of interest because our design should be easier to comprehend, more efficient and should generate an overall positive impression. The UEQ has been conducted after the interview session with ten participants. The users rated EMILI on these three factors on a 7-point Likert scale. The Likert scale consisted of semantic differential word pairs (e.g. attractive – unattractive). The benchmark analysis of the e-paper display results in a very positive outcome. The indicators for attractiveness (mean: 2.4), perspicuity (mean: 2.1) and efficiency (mean: 2.4) are located in the upper tenth of the range of values, leading to the grade: "excellent" (see Fig. 2). The results of the UEQ are presented in Table 1.

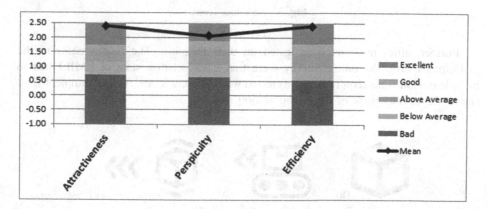

Fig. 2. Benchmark analysis of the UEQ

Table 1. Results of the UEQ

Scale	Mean	Standard deviation	N	Confidence	Confidence interval
Attractiveness	2.400	0.337	10	0.209	2.191–2.609
Perspicuity	2.067	0.306	10	0.190	1.877–2.257
Efficiency	2.400	0.516	10	0.320	2.080–2.720

The warning signs remained due to their universal meaning and were understood by all participants. On the other hand, the task icons were exchanged. Figure 3 illustrates that the cogwheel and the time icon were replaced with the three arrow icon and the avatar icon. These changes were necessary due to ambiguous understanding of the old icons and more important states to cover. The box icon is the only remaining icon in the new interface and has been adjusted due to its additional functions. The reasons for these changes are a result of the qualitative results of the questionnaire and interviews. Participants were reminded of the settings button on a smartphone when confronted with the cogwheel rather than seeing EMILI "in progress". Besides the cogwheel, the time icon became redundant. The time icon is not standardized and its period of time may vary depending on the length of the task. This leads to the conclusion that users cannot be sure of how long EMILI has been executing a command or how long the task will take. The implementation of the "Follow – Me" function led to the design of the avatar icon in combination with the arrow icon, indicating that EMILI is following its user. The arrows above and beneath the box icon illustrate that EMILI is adjusting its height and were added. Further, the three icons can interact with each other to give more reliable and precise information of the state of EMILI.

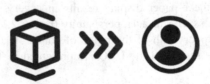

Fig. 3. New task icons.

Further, different icons were tested on their meaning. The requirements of the participants from the online survey were that transportation state of EMILI had to include motion. This requirement was tested with different icons. As an example, Fig. 4 shows the development of the transportation icon.

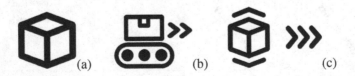

Fig. 4. Development of the transportation task icon (from a to c).

The first transportation icon (see Fig. 4a) consisted of a box. Participants stated that the box is loaded on EMILI, but did not mention that the box is moving. This led to the new designs (see Fig. 4b), which focused on adding dynamic elements or focusing on material flow, indicated by the box on the assembly line. This icon has then been evaluated as a tank or other misleading concepts. As a final icon (see Fig. 4c), we created an icon based on the box and additional implemented arrows as an icon, which in interaction with the box resembled a moving box. Due to the ergonomic height adjustment, one arrow above and beneath the box were added to simulate an upward or downward movement. Focusing on the interaction of the icons, the avatar icon in combination with the arrows display the "Follow – Me" function, whereas the box icon in combination with the aforementioned icons imply a transportation task towards the user.

5   Conclusion

The design of the new e-Paper display is based on the iOS mobile platform architectural structures. Whereas in the initial display, icons and text hints were strictly divided and the icons were placed on the left side and text hints on the right side, the icons are now placed above the artificial face in a horizontal bar (see Fig. 5). Further, the text hints and icons were divided due to their function. On the left side of the interface, warning signs and referring text hints were placed. On the right side, task signs and their referring text hints were implemented. The overall design reminds the user of a toolbar similar to a smartphone toolbar. Referring to the icons, the task icons were completely new designed and implemented. The new task icons are adapted to the needs of the user. In contrast, the warning icons were standardized and the results of the online survey and interview reveal no misleading or wrongly implemented icons.

Fig. 5. Redesigned e-Paper display of EMILI

6   Outlook

The Future work will include an analysis of the display in a real working environment with actual workers. We plan to implement a virtual 3D avatar being projected on top of the ATV indicating the status and other interaction functionality by the use of augmented reality glasses. This approach will also be evaluated with appropriate analysis methods. The ATV already has inbuilt RGB LED stripes around the bottom outline intended for status feedback. We will also research on adequate color and light sequencing functionality.

Acknowledgements. We want to thank the Innovation lab Hybrid Services in Logistics, funded by the Federal Ministry of Education and Research (BMBF) and in the Center of Excellence for Logistics and IT funded by Ministry for innovation science and research of NRW, Germany.

References

1. SoftBank Robotics: Who is Pepper? https://www.ald.softbankrobotics.com/en/robots/pepper. Accessed 4 May 2018
2. CobotsGuid: Rethink Robotics Baxter. https://cobotsguide.com/2016/06/rethink-robotics-baxter/. Accessed 4 May 2018
3. Ten Hompel, M., Schmidt, T., Nagel, L.: Materialflusssysteme Förder- und Lagertechnik, vol. 3. Springer, Heidelberg (2007). https://doi.org/10.1007/978-3-540-73236-5
4. Verein Deutscher Ingenieure VDI: VDI Norm 2510: Fahrerlose Transportsysteme (1992)
5. Ulrich, G.: Fahrerlose Transportsysteme. Vieweg + Teubner Verlag (2011)
6. BITO-Lagertechnik Bittmann GmbH. LEO Locative Das Fahrerlose Transportsystem für Behälter und Kartonagen. http://www.leo-locative.de. Accessed 26 Sept 2017
7. SSI SCHÄFER FRITZ SCHÄFER GMBH. FTS Weasel®. https://www.ssi-schaefer.com/de-de/produkte/foerdern-transportieren/fahrerlose-transportsysteme
8. DIN EN ISO 7010: Graphische Symbole–Sicherheitsfarben und Sicherheitszeichen (2013)

Trade-Off Between System Effectiveness and Context Constraints in the Design of an IoT System Giving Access to Health Care in African Rural Villages

Joseph Aneke[1] , Carmelo Ardito[2(✉)] , Danilo Caivano[2] ,
Lucio Colizzi[2] , and Loredana Verardi[2]

[1] ICT/Innovation Department, University of Nigeria,
Nsukka, Enugu State 410001, Nigeria
joseph.aneke@unn.edu.ng
[2] Dipartimento di Informatica, Università degli Studi di Bari Aldo Moro,
Via Orabona, 4, 70125 Bari, Italy
{carmelo.ardito,danilo.caivano,lucio.colizzi,
loredana.verardi}@uniba.it

Abstract. Aging population is a global concern, but the situation is even worst in developing countries where the migration of the active population from rural areas to major cities makes the elderly left in their home in the village, usually assisted by close relatives who take care of them. Far distance to accessing good health facilities provided in the city hospital usually results to the untimely death of people suffering from treatable and manageable diseases like diabetes, malaria, high blood pressure and waterborne diseases. In this paper, we present the design concept of a system for preventing and controlling people's health conditions; it exploits the possibilities of the Internet of Things technology, still trying to find a convenient balance between effectiveness, reliability and context limitations that require a cheap, affordable and easily configurable system.

Keywords: Ambient Assisted Living · Ubiquitous healthcare · Smart devices Tailoring by end user

1 Introduction

Supporting elderly or disabled people in their everyday lives has been a longstanding research area. Many researchers have addressed smart aging services, which can help people age comfortably and independently while staying in their current residence as long as possible. Aging population has been a global concern which makes a large impact on government spending and economic policy in healthcare, pension, and social benefits program more critical especially in developing countries. In Africa, a significant percentage of elderly people face distinctive challenges such as chronic diseases including heart disease, physical disabilities, diabetes, and depression [1]. Many of them live in rural village, where it is common for parents to expect their children to be around when they are aged or retired from active service. Due to migration and changes

© IFIP International Federation for Information Processing 2019
Published by Springer Nature Switzerland AG 2019
C. Bogdan et al. (Eds.): HCSE 2018, LNCS 11262, pp. 343–351, 2019.
https://doi.org/10.1007/978-3-030-05909-5_23

in family values, such a culture is becoming unpopular. The elderly are then transferred to nursing homes or remain independent in their home in the village, where they are usually left with close relatives (informal caregivers) who take care of them. Such informal caregivers are often young and technical savvy people.

Unfortunately, assessing good health facilities remains a major concern in rural villages. Very often functional health centers are concentrated in the cities, which are many kilometers far from the villages where professional health givers (doctors) are not available. All of this further worsens the plight of those having health challenges and living in the village, especially the elderly.

A multidimensional approach to integrate diverse healthcare systems are needed to prevent and control health problems of elderly people [2]. Most developed systems focus on the quality of functional aspects of life assistance services that emphasized convenience and effectiveness based on the concepts of hospitalization [1]. These services are usually not affordable, timely and sometimes complex for developing countries like Nigeria, where the annual income per capita is about $2.100, with low growth in terms of technological and infrastructure development.

We are currently working on designing a system aiming at improving health of elderly living in rural villages. We are exploiting the Internet of Things (IoT) technology, which offers plenty of possibilities for addressing the issues highlighted above. Because of the limitations of the particular context, the ultimate challenge is the identification of a cheap, affordable and easily configurable system that can be successfully applied and definitely adopted in the considered scenario. The system consists of a heterogeneous combination of apps and Arduino-based devices that connect patients and healthcare service providers remotely located. An important feature from the interaction point of view is that the system is easily configurable by non-technical people, e.g., caregivers.

In this paper that reports on our ongoing work, after a short survey of the related literature (Sect. 2), we describe the requirements emerged (Sect. 3) and the solutions proposed in the design-concept (Sect. 4). Conclusions are finally provided.

2   Related Work

Advances in sensing and network technologies allow physical objects in everyday lives to be connected with each other and thus data could be shared and work together in a collaborative way. This technological trend, has been influencing applications in many domains, including smart industry [3], smart home [4, 5], smart office [6], smart farm [7], smart grid [8], smart city [9], but also Cultural Heritage [10, 11]. Also, it would have a great impact on wellness systems and health-related services deployed in aging-in-place solutions. Embedded systems and wireless sensor networks enable a variety of sensors to be incorporated into office buildings, or wearable devices to be attached to occupants and biological signals to be directly collected from their body [12]. Data sets collected from sensors could be utilized to infer situations and help family members or caregivers monitor or perform emergency activities for the elderly and disabled. Dishman highlighted four promising areas (focused on by Intel's Proactive health research group) where technologies for adaptive aging could help older adults live healthier and more productive lives: promoting healthy behaviors, early disease detection, improved treatment compliance, support for informal caregiving using embedded systems [13].

Allowing the elderly to live at home with a reasonable level of assistance, called aging in place, is an active research area, and in particular many developed countries have drawn much interest to the related research projects. Ubiquitous healthcare (u-Health) systems are a key to handle the challenges of aging population and growing healthcare cost around the world. Such systems contribute to the revolution in medical history by providing an instant overlook into the diseases and by giving patients an emergency alert in case of any chronic problem [14]. They also enable the service providers/practitioners to remotely monitor the patient's physiological data in real-time and provide feedback [15]. In a u-Health system, sensors (either on-body or implantable) like ECG, EEG, EMG, motions/positioning, and body temperature forward their data via wireless interface to a base station or access point. This data is then streamed to the hospital via a wide coverage network such as 3G, WLAN, LAN or GPRS/SMS to a medical doctor for remote monitoring, or to hospital database for records or telemedicine or to ambulatory service in case of emergency [16]. An off-the-shelf u-Health system is, for example, the "MySignals SW BLE Complete Kit" (see Fig. 1), a development platform for medical devices and eHealth applications to develop personalised eHealth web services[1]. The kit includes 17 sensors which can be used to monitor more than 20 biometric parameters. Further sensors, possibly provided by the user himself, can be added to build new medical devices. All the data gathered by MySignals is encrypted and sent to the user's private account at Libelium Cloud through WiFi or Bluetooth. The data can be visualized in a tablet or smart phone with Android or iPhone Apps. Unfortunately, even if the proposed solution is worthwhile, the cost is as much as $2000, which makes it not affordable for the context we are considering.

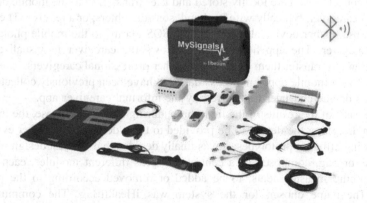

Fig. 1. The MySignals SW BLE Complete Kit (image courtesy of www.cooking-hacks.com).

---

[1] http://www.my-signals.com/.

3 Context and System Requirements

The primary challenge of a system that has to support the elderly's healthcare in rural villages is that it has to be cheap and easy to use by caregivers who have limited knowledge of technology.

We set-up a design team that included electronic engineers, as well as software engineers and interaction designers. They are the authors of this paper. Most of them are expert with IoT technologies. Moreover, the first author is a PhD student at a Nigerian University, graduated in Electronic Engineering, and currently in our Department for a 5-month visit. He is the reference person for illustrating the different facets of the Nigerian reality and providing more insights about the context requirements. Other team members have previous experience in designing technology for Ambient Assisted Living (AAL). See, for example, [17, 18].

The system design consisted of three main phases, as described in the following. In order to get more ideas on the system to be envisioned, we also took into account the projects developed as assignment to the PhD students attending a course on "IoT Technologies and Tools for Configuring Smart Environments". The assignment consisted of designing an AAL system for elderly people in destitute areas.

During the first phase, the team identified the context elements that influence the design of the proposed solution. First, the infrastructure limitations were considered and then the stakeholders and their relationships, skills and roles were identified. It emerged that the solution should be cheap and affordable, easy and simple to use with very minimal setup procedures required. It should not rely on highly sophisticated mobile devices since it is intended for rural villages where Internet services may not be available. It must be flexible so that to be adapted to a variety of diseases, stakeholders, devices and infrastructures available.

As depicted in Fig. 2, the elderly person is provided with a device able to detect different parameters (e.g., heart rate, temperature, ECG, blood pressure, glucose, pulse); the collected data are locally stored and later transferred to the mobile device of an informal caregiver, typically wife/husband, sons/daughters, or a relative. The elderly person can use his/her device also for sending SOS alarms to the mobile phone of the informal caregiver. The app here installed allows the caregiver to visualize health parameters and to transfer them to doctors or other professional caregivers. The doctor, using a Web or a mobile app, can access data that have been previously collected from the patient's device and later transferred by the informal caregiver app.

On the basis of the results of the first phase, during the second phase, the team was engaged in designing the device to be provided to the elderly people. After evaluating and discussing different prototypes, it was finally decided that the best design would be a briefcase, or bag, composed of a central unit plus different modules, each able to perform specific measurements, to be added or removed according to the patient's diseases. The name chosen for the system was iHealthBag. The communication modalities among the system components were defined.

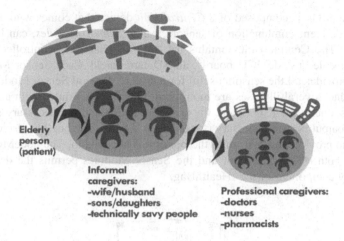

Fig. 2. Stakeholders involved in the African rural village scenario and communications among them.

Finally, inspired by [17], the design team focused on designing the pill dispenser, a further component of the patient's device that manages drug therapy administration. The pill dispenser is characterized by the following features:

- modularity, since there are the therapy may change over time;
- accurate reporting of drug intake, so that the caregivers can check that the patient is taking the pills correctly;
- remote therapy modification: if the professional caregiver decides to change the therapy, he/she can remotely program the behavior of the pill dispenser by using the visual interface available on the app installed in his/her computer or mobile phone. It is responsibility of the informal caregiver (usually a close relative of the patient) to change the pills in the dispenser accordingly.

4   The iHealthBag

Because of the limitations of the particular application context, the ultimate challenge has been the identification of a cheap, affordable and easily configurable system that can be successfully applied and definitely adopted. The iHealthBag solution is proposed as a heterogeneous combination of apps and affordable Arduino-based devices that connect patients (elderly) and healthcare service providers remotely. The system deploys a wide variety of sensors and actuator to monitor and observe the patient's vital health signs and interactively connects him/her with the informal caregiver or doctor on 24 h and 7 days a week basis.

The iHealthBag is composed of a *Central Unit* device that comes with expandable slots where different combination of sensors, called *Sensor Modules*, can be inserted (see Fig. 3). The Central Unit contains an Arduino Uno microcontroller board[2], a Bluetooth module, a nodeMCU board[3], an SD card shield. Each Sensor Module is a box which provides all the sensors useful for a disease. Several Sensor Modules can be connected, thus several illnesses are monitored. Each box is printed with a 3D printer and contains: one nodeMCU board, the specific sensors and the necessary shields for them, input/output ports if necessary (for example, a jack). The box has also connectors to take and to provide power from/to the boxes it is attached to. The nodeMCU boards available in both the Central Unit and the Sensor Modules permits the data transfer among every component of the iHealthBag.

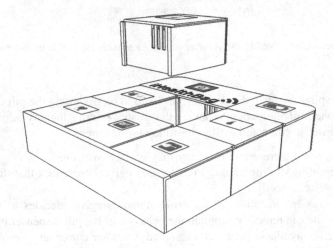

Fig. 3. The iHealthBag patient's device.

The *Pill Dispenser Module* has the same dimensions of the Central Unit Module. It contains a nodeMCU microcontroller and a number of small boxes that contain pills of different types. Each pill box has a LED light, which is automatically switched on when that pill has to be taken. To confirm that he took the pill, the patient pushes a button on the pill box and the light is switched off.

Data collected by sensors can be stored and retrieved on the SD card available in the Central Unit device and then automatically transferred to Bluetooth recipient, i.e., the informal caregiver's smartphone. Optionally, the iHealthBag can be provided with a GSM module: in this case, as a Sensor Module receives input of an anomaly with the system, the iHealthBag immediately sends message alerts to the caregiver by SMS. The caregiver, using the app installed in his smartphone, analyses the message, does some preliminary pre-defined first aid and sends outcomes to a professional caregiver

---

[2] https://www.arduino.cc/.

[3] http://nodemcu.com/.

(doctor) for professional advice. The informal caregiver app also serves to further transmit, immediately or periodically, collected data to a central server through the Internet.

In Fig. 4, which shows the interconnection platform and services management, the communication is mediated by ThingSpeak[4], an open source IoT application and API to store and retrieve data from things using the HTTP protocol over the Internet or via a Local Area Network. ThingSpeak enables the creation of sensor logging applications, location tracking applications, and a social network of things with status updates. The doctor, using a Web or a mobile app, can access the patient's data that have been previously collected from the iHealthBag device and later transferred by the informal caregiver app on ThingSpeak.

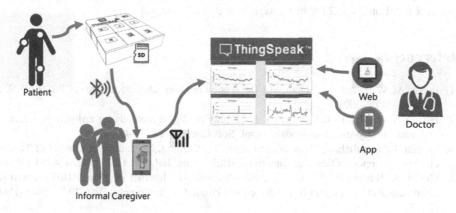

Fig. 4. Diagram representing the different components and users of the iHealthBag overall system.

5   Discussion and Conclusion

In this paper we have discussed the design concept of an IoT system aiming at giving access to good health care in rural villages. Many possibilities are offered by IoT technology for addressing such an issue, but we had to take in consideration the many constraints and limitations of the specific context. Thus, in order to propose a system that can be actually adopted in the considered context, we had to manage a trade-off between effectiveness and efficiency of the designed solution and the specific context requirements. We are aware that further issues are very significant in the AAL domain, for example, sensor reliability and data security. Still we think that our project can represent a first valid product to satisfy the requirements that would make it accessible in the considered context, namely rural villages.

The next step we are going to perform is to validate our design concept by involving a larger number of stakeholders, including patients, informal caregivers and

---

[4] https://thingspeak.com/.

doctors. Then, we want to implement a fully operational prototype of the overall system to be tested in a longitudinal study, by distributing the iHealthBag device to a sample of end users. By exploiting our experience on approaches that allow people that are not expert of technology to easily manage mobile devices [19] and smart objects [10, 20], and to configure their own applications (e.g., see [21, 22]), we are now working at the implementation of the app for the informal caregiver's mobile device as well as both the web app and the mobile app to be provided to the professional caregivers.

Acknowledgments. This work is partially funded by the Apulia Region through the project GLOBALDOC (CUP H96J17000160002, approved with A.D. n. 9 on 18/01/2017) and by the Italian Ministry of Education, University and Research (MIUR) through PON Ricerca e Innovazione 2014–2020 - Asse I "Investimenti in capitale umano" - Azione I.1 "Dottorati Innovativi con caratterizzazione industriale" (CUP H92H18000210006 and H92H18000200006 approved with D.R.n.991 on 29/03/2018 of University of Bari Aldo Moro).

References

1. Fiske, A., Wetherell, J.L., Gatz, M.: Depression in older adults. Ann. Rev. Clin. Psychol. **5** (1), 363–389 (2009)
2. Huang, Y.-P., Huang, C.-Y., Liu, S.-I.: Hybrid intelligent methods for arrhythmia detection and geriatric depression diagnosis. Appl. Soft Comput. **14**, 38–46 (2014)
3. Sisinni, E., Saifullah, A., Han, S., Jennehag, U., Gidlund, M.: Industrial Internet of Things: challenges, opportunities, and directions. IEEE Trans. Ind. Inf. **14**(11), 4724–4734 (2018)
4. Gubbi, J., Buyya, R., Marusic, S., Palaniswami, M.: Internet of Things (IoT): a vision, architectural elements, and future directions. Future Gener. Comput. Syst. **29**(7), 1645–1660 (2013)
5. Risteska Stojkoska, B.L., Trivodaliev, K.V.: A review of Internet of Things for smart home: challenges and solutions. J. Clean. Prod. **140**, 1454–1464 (2017)
6. Ryu, M., Kim, J., Yun, J.: Integrated semantics service platform for the Internet of Things: a case study of a smart office. Sensors **15**(1), 2137–2160 (2015)
7. Bhattacharjee, A., et al.: Smart farming using IOT. In: IEEE Annual Information Technology, Electronics and Mobile Communication Conference (IEMCON 2017), pp. 278–280 (2017)
8. Kaluvala, N.S., Forman, A.: Smart Grid. Int. J. E-Polit. **4**(2), 39–47 (2013)
9. Gascó-Hernandez, M.: Building a smart city: lessons from Barcelona. Commun. ACM **61**(4), 50–57 (2018)
10. Ardito, C., Buono, P., Desolda, G., Matera, M.: From smart objects to smart experiences: an end-user development approach. Int. J. Hum Comput Stud. **114**, 51–68 (2018)
11. Zancanaro, M., et al.: Recipes for tangible and embodied visit experiences. In: Museums and the Web conference (MW 2015) (2015)
12. Varshney, U.: Pervasive healthcare and wireless health monitoring. Mob. Netw. Appl. **12**(2), 113–127 (2007)
13. Dishman, E.: Inventing wellness systems for aging in place. Comput. **37**(5), 34–41 (2004)
14. Park, K., Pak, J.: Implementation of a handheld compute engine for personal health devices. Int. J. Smart Home **6**(2), 59–64 (2012)
15. Ranjan, R., Varma, S.: Object-oriented design for wireless sensor network assisted global patient care monitoring system. Int. J. Comput. Appl. **45**(2), 8–15 (2012)

16. Wu, M.Y., Huang, W.Y.: Health care platform with safety monitoring for long-term care institutions. In: International Conference on Networked Computing and Advanced Information Management (NCM 2011), pp. 313–317 (2011)
17. Buono, P., Cassano, F., Legretto, A., Piccinno, A.: A modular pill dispenser supporting therapies at home. In: International Workshop on Engineering the Web of Things (EnWoT 2018) (2018)
18. Ardito, C., et al.: Enabling end users to define the behaviour of smart objects in AAL scenarios. In: Forum Italiano Ambient Assisted Living (ForITAAL 2018) (2018)
19. Desolda, G., Ardito, C., Jetter, H.-C., Lanzilotti, R.: Exploring spatially-aware cross-device interaction techniques for mobile collaborative sensemaking. Int. J. Hum Comput Stud. **122**, 1–20 (2019)
20. Desolda, G., Ardito, C., Matera, M.: empowering end users to customize their smart environments: model, composition paradigms, and domain-specific tools. ACM Trans. Comput. Hum. Interact. **24**(2), 12 (2017)
21. Ardito, C., Costabile, M.F., Desolda, G., Latzina, M., Matera, M.: Making mashups actionable through elastic design principles. In: Díaz, P., Pipek, V., Ardito, C., Jensen, C., Aedo, I., Boden, A. (eds.) IS-EUD 2015. LNCS, vol. 9083, pp. 236–241. Springer, Cham (2015). https://doi.org/10.1007/978-3-319-18425-8_22
22. Desolda, G., Ardito, C., Matera, M.: EFESTO: a platform for the end-user development of interactive workspaces for data exploration. In: Daniel, F., Pautasso, C. (eds.) RMC 2015. CCIS, vol. 591, pp. 63–81. Springer, Cham (2016). https://doi.org/10.1007/978-3-319-28727-0_5

Author Index

Printed in the United States
By Bookmasters